POLITICAL LANDSCAPES

POLITICAL
LANDSCAPES

*Forests, Conservation, and
Community in Mexico*

CHRISTOPHER R. BOYER

DUKE UNIVERSITY PRESS

Durham & London

2015

Typeset in Chaparral Pro by Graphic
Composition, Inc., Bogart, Georgia

Library of Congress Cataloging-in-Publication Data
Boyer, Christopher R. (Christopher Robert)
Political landscapes : forests, conservation, and
community in Mexico / Christopher R. Boyer.
pages cm
Includes bibliographical references and index.
ISBN 978-0-8223-5818-3 (hardcover : alk. paper)
ISBN 978-0-8223-5832-9 (pbk. : alk. paper)
ISBN 978-0-8223-7587-6 (e-book)
1. Community forests—Mexico. 2. Forest
management—Mexico. 3. Forest policy—
Mexico. 4. Forest ecology—Mexico. 5. Forest
conservation—Mexico. 6. Forests and forestry—
Mexico. I. Title.
SD569.B694 2015
333.750972—dc23   2014041990

Cover art: *Greener*, 2014. © Miguel Plata. Image
courtesy of the artist.

To my mother,
who loves the forests

A ke kanaia este gringo.
Iasï k'oru inchakuati
chartarhuechani.
isïku undasti trenini korokani
isïku undasti ixujku jarhani.

Oh, what a scoundrel that gringo is.
Now the people of Pichátaro
will have his train in their town.
He began by laying the rails
and it looks like he plans to stay.

Juata k'eritu jikimi t'uyini
lastima usïya sami.
Xani sesi jaxeka
Juata asula jimbokimi ia
Santiago Islei sami kuadraritia

My poor little blue hill,
I feel so sorry for you.
I guess it's too bad
Santiago Slade
liked you so much.

—"A ke kanaia este gringo," a Purépecha folk song (*pirekua*)
from the late nineteenth century

CONTENTS

ILLUSTRATIONS

Political Landscapes is, in one sense, a tale of redemption, or rather of two redemptions separated from each other by half a century or so. Each of its two parts follows a similar narrative trajectory, beginning at a moment when rural people effectively lost possession of their woodlands, leading them to make tentative alliances with sympathetic outsiders such as populist politicians, forestry officials, and others. Each story culminates with an attempt to implement a system of what is now called "community forestry," in which those who live and work in the woodlands recover some of their former lands and become stakeholders in its management and sustainable use. The first of these historical cycles began in the 1880s, when the commodification of forests and nineteenth-century liberalism led to massive dispossession of village lands, followed by a revolution and land reform that crescendoed in the 1930s with the socially progressive administration of President Lázaro Cárdenas. The second round began in 1940, when the Second World War and changes in Mexico's political priorities vastly limited rural people's ability to use their own woods, prompting a new set of popular movements to recover peasant productive autonomy, and, from the 1980s to the present, the slow and incomplete return to a modernized version of community forestry in the context of neoliberalism.

These repeating patterns capture the essential dimensions of Mexican environmental history, yet I believe they obscure as much as they reveal. In the first place, the familiar cycle of dispossession, disempowerment, and redemption disregards significant changes in the way that professional foresters understood the relationship of rural Mexicans to their environment. Whereas the first generation of conservationists tended to regard rural people as backward and inherently destructive, the generation of experts who came of age in the 1940s and 1950s began to understand peasant behavior in economic rather than cultural terms. They shifted forest policy from a combination of sanctions-based regulations and didactic campaigns, to a more supple program that sought to ensure rural people a livelihood in the woods. In the second place, indigenous people and others who dwelt in the woodlands also modified their understanding of "nature" over time. They never stopped defending their property from outside threats, such as timber companies and meddlesome foresters, but they did adopt new relationships with the forestlands. Many rural people grew increasingly interested in marketing their timber and came to see the landscape as—among other things—a natural resource that professional foresters could help them to use sustainably.

It is important to understand this history in all its complexity. While historians cannot in good conscience profess to search the past as a means of uncovering "universal truths" or "historical laws" that might serve as the guiding lights for those of us who live in the present time, we can investigate the web of relationships that link historical actors to each other and to the environment in order to reflect upon the contingencies and structures that we are presented with today. Environmental history has shucked off much of the activist veneer that led an earlier generation of scholars to portray the landscape as something that was only acted upon by humans, rather than as an anthropogenic space that both structures and is structured by human behavior. Likewise, social history has moved beyond simplistic renderings of rural folk as monolithic "communities" that selflessly defend their land and culture against implacable outsiders. I do not propose to return to these historical caricatures by depicting forests as nothing more than organic sites of social contention acted upon by greedy business interests locked in contention with virtuous peasants. Instead, I suggest that state intervention into the complex and mutable rural panorama transformed the forests into political landscapes in ways that damaged the ecosystem and accentuated social injustice. I confess, in this sense, to attempting to tell this story as a cautionary tale about the disastrous policies and venality of late-nineteenth century and mid-twentieth-century "development" policy in the forestlands, in part because I worry that something similar is happening in some parts of Mexico today.

More than dissecting past missteps, I seek in *Political Landscapes* to excavate the historical conditions that allowed some communities to acquire their own forests and manage them, if not precisely sustainably, then at least responsibly. The 1910–1917 revolution became the ideological crucible for Mexican community forestry by making it possible to imagine rural people's use of their own woodlands as an expression of social justice. Operationalizing this vision proved difficult and politically inconvenient, but it found one early expression during the 1930s, when Mexican leaders established what, at the time, was arguably the world's most extensive program of locally managed timber production. The pull of what I call "revolutionary forestry" has remained strong ever since, although more often as an aspirational goal than as an actually existing practice. The history of people's efforts to actualize (or in some instances, to undermine) this paradigm reminds us that forests are more than just natural resources, and more even than a complex of living ecosystems. Rather, they are landscapes whose very appearance reflects a history of social conflict and cooperation stretching back for generations.

I hope that reading the landscape this way will encourage historians to take seriously the idea that particular forms of historical knowledge and human behavior are both inscribed on and structured by "the environment." I also hope it might remind experts in forestry and community development that the past remains very much alive for many of the people who live in the Mexican countryside today. People who dwell within the countryside inhabit a natural space shaped by the conflicts and accommodations inherited from previous generations, and they have long memories.

I need to make a few brief comments on the terminology used in this book, beginning with the institution(s) charged with managing the forest ecosystem. Mexico established a national forest service in 1908, although its formal name and administrative status have followed a twisting institutional path. Initially called the Department of Forests as a unit within the Secretary of Agriculture and Development (whose name also changed over time), it was rechristened the Office (*Dirección*) of Forests in 1912. Its duties were expanded in 1920, and it was renamed the Office of Forests, Game, and Fisheries. Forest management briefly emerged as a national priority during the presidency of Lázaro Cárdenas (1934–1940), who created the Autonomous Department of Forestry, Game, and Fisheries, but in 1940 it once again became a unit within the Department of Agriculture, called the General Office of Forestry and Game. It was renamed the Sub-secretariat of Forests and Game in 1951 and Forests and Wildlife nine years later. In 1982 the Secretariat of Agriculture and Hydrological Resources (SARH) was established, and two years later it established the General Office of Forestry. In 1994 the federal government created a new cabinet-level department to oversee environmental stewardship and resource use—including forests— initially known as the Secretaría del Medio Ambiente Recursos Naturales y Pesca (Secretariat of the Environment, Natural Resources, and Fisheries), now known as the Secretaría de Medio Ambiente y Recursos Naturales

(SEMARNAT). Since 2001, the organization charged with forest management has been called the National Commission on Forests (CONAFOR). In light of this complicated organizational history, I will refer to the federal institution charged with forest management simply as the "forest service."

Most rural villages (whether indigenous or mestizo) received agricultural lands or forests or both through the land reform in the form of land-grant plots known as *ejidos* that, while technically federal property, were and are functionally owned and administered by those members of rural villages formally enrolled as land-reform beneficiaries. I use the term *ejido* or *ejidal forest* to refer to these properties, and *ejidatario* or *land-reform beneficiary* to refer to people enrolled as members of an ejido. I use the term *land-reform village* or *ejidal village* when describing the small townships in possession of an ejido land grant. Note, however, that some indigenous communities possessed both colonial-era common lands as well as an ejido; in most of these cases (but not all), the same committee of local authorities managed both communal and ejidal land.

Finally, local authority in Mexico is almost everywhere vested in the *municipio*, a form of government that has no direct counterpart in the United States but is sometimes confusingly rendered into English as "municipality." In fact, most municipios combine the attributes of what North Americans call municipal government (in terms of administrative and police functions, for example) as well as county government (insofar as most municipios encompass several population centers within their territories). Further adding to the confusion for some North American readers, municipios are named after their "county" seat. Hence, the place-name Tanhuato could refer either to the town of Tanhuato proper or to the county (municipio) of the same name. To avoid this confusion, I will use the term *district* or *municipal district* whenever I refer to an entire municipio, although for the sake of readability I will succumb to the siren song of false cognates and refer to the officials who govern municipios as "municipal authorities."

ACKNOWLEDGMENTS

I began to work on this book a decade ago, and it has become the most fulfilling research project I have ever undertaken. In this book I tell what I consider an important story about the interrelationship between native people, resource managers, and the land. I am fortunate that colleagues, family members, and others have helped me to study this topic. They are not liable for this book's errors and omissions, but they are collectively responsible for the fact that it exists at all.

Two colleagues in particular have lent encouragement and advice since I first began to contemplate writing a social history of Mexico's forests. The first person I told about my intention to write a social history of Mexican forests is the forestry expert and scholar David Bray. Within a week of that conversation, a thick package containing dozens of articles, book chapters, and news reports arrived in the mail. It was a daunting but welcome introduction to the field. His frequent admonitions to frame this project in interdisciplinary terms have, I hope, made this a more capacious book. Cynthia Radding, one of the foremost historians of Mexico, was teaching at my sister institution in Urbana-Champaign when I first arrived at the University of Illinois at Chicago (UIC). She welcomed me into the fold of environmental history and has offered valuable and generous support ever since, all while encouraging me to foreground indigenous voices whenever possible. It is a pleasure to thank them both.

Eric Van Young and Gil Joseph invited me to present my work early on and encouraged me to pursue the project. Emilio Kourí and members of the Latin American History workshop at the University of Chicago have twice commented on draft sections of the book. My colleagues in Mexico have been particularly generous with their time and attention. Martín Sánchez, a longtime friend and colleague who is currently the president of El Colegio de Michoacán, has provided encouragement and expertise again and again. Others at the Colegio have also provided helpful advice, including Álvaro Ochoa and Paul Liffman. My colleagues at the Universidad Michoacana de San Nicolás de Hidalgo (UMSNH) have also invited me to give several workshops and presentations over the years. Gerardo Sánchez Díaz and Eduardo Mijangos, in particular, have liberally shared their thoughts and ideas for improving my analysis. Jonathan Daly, Lorena Ojeda, and Carol Curran read the manuscript in its later stages and offered suggestions as well. Adam Shannon gave me a hand toward the end. The anonymous readers for Duke University Press offered comprehensive and sometimes pointed suggestions for which I am truly grateful.

My approach to environmental history has been influenced by conversations with several colleagues whose work I have found inspirational, including Luis Aboites, Ray Craib, John D'Emilio, Antonio Escobar Ohmstede, Sterling Evans, Mark Healey, Brian Hosmer, Rick López, Stuart McCook, John McNeill, Heather McCrea, Myrna Santiago, John Soluri, Alejandro Tortolero, John Tutino, Matt Vitz, Bob Wilcox, Mikael Wolfe, Angus Wright, and Eddie Wright Rios. Emily Wakild has unselfishly shared her thoughts and suggestions for nearly a decade now. My colleagues at UIC have likewise given their attention and thought to this project, among them Javier Villa Fuentes and Joel Palka. Ted Beatty, Jeff Pilcher, and Juan Luis Sariego lent their expertise at critical junctures, for which I am particularly appreciative. Marco Aurelio Almazán, Juan Manuel Mendoza, and Arcelia Amaranta Moreno shared their research findings with me. I would also like to express my heartfelt thanks to Valerie Millholland and Miriam Angress at Duke University Press for their faith in this project and efforts to shepherd it into print. Thanks as well to Patricia Mickelberry and Danielle Szulczewski.

My research was funded by a fellowship from the National Endowment for the Humanities that allowed me to spend the 2005–2006 academic year in Mexico. Additional support came from UIC's College of Liberal Arts and Sciences, Department of History, and Office of the Vice Chancellor for Research. Much of the writing was completed during a fellowship at UIC's Institute for the Humanities. I would like to acknowledge the important work carried out by all of these institutions and those who make them run. I could not have completed this book without their support.

The pirekua (Purépecha ballad) that appears in the epigraph was performed by Catalina Román Figueroa at the Instituto de Investigaciones Históricas of the Universidad Nacional Autónoma de México in February of 2010. She and Rocío Próspero Maldonado transcribed it, and it was translated into Spanish by Ireneo Rojas H.

I am indebted to the stewards of the documents and images that constitute the basis of this book. The staff of the Archivo General de la Nación (AGN), and Joel Zúñiga in particular, were immensely helpful in making the SARH archives usable for me; thanks to the AGN as well for permission to reproduce several photographs. Juan Luis Sariego kindly opened the doors of the Escuela Nacional de Antropología (Chihuahua) archives, both literally and figuratively. Photographs were made available by Amelia Aguilar Zínzer, Gerardo Sánchez, and the Instituto de Investigaciones Históricas at UMSNH, as well as Claudia Jacobsen and the Milwaukee Public Museum, Claudia Rivers, Yvette Delgado, and Bobbi Sago at the Special Collections Department of the University of Texas, El Paso Library, and by the National Anthropology Archives of the Smithsonian Institution. Thanks as well to Jonathan Wyss of Beehive Mapping for the carefully researched maps that appear in the introduction and chapter 1.

My family has shown incredible graciousness and forbearance during the too many years it has taken to research and write *Political Landscapes*. Isaac Boyer, my son, and Amy Shannon, my wife of twenty-five years, traveled to Mexico with me several times, including the 2005–2006 research trip to Mexico City. I have fond memories of those times, but I nonetheless owe them a debt of gratitude for accompanying me, in every sense of the term, through this project. I am also grateful to Jannene, Bob, Beth, Adam, Lucinda, and Wade for their good-natured acceptance of my seemingly endless distractions. Finally, I would like to thank my mother, Carol Curran, to whom this book is dedicated, for taking me hiking in the Colorado forests when I was a child and for believing in this book so many years later.

INTRODUCTION

In 1937 an official from the Mexican forest service visited the rugged Sierra Tarahumara mountains in southern Chihuahua, which even today remain one of the nation's most isolated places. The landscape that greeted Antonio H. Sosa was unlike anything he had seen in central Mexico. He admired the "immensity, beauty, and potential" of the untouched Ponderosa and Montezuma pines that soared skyward everywhere he looked.[1] The area was also home to approximately 33,000 indigenous people known to outsiders as the Tarahumara but who called themselves Rarámuri, or "those who run on foot." Sosa regarded them as the single greatest threat to the region's ecological integrity. In his estimation, the Rarámuri hated trees with a nearly innate passion. He reported that they indiscriminately cleared the best stands of timber to make way for their cornfields or perhaps in the misguided belief that it would help to summon the rains. Since the natives could not be trusted to care for the woods, he recommended opening the region to logging by modern timber companies operating under the watchful eye of forestry experts. "If these woods were subject to a proper management regime," he wrote, "they would never disappear; on the contrary, they would produce immense benefits. However, they cannot endure much longer if they remain abandoned to their present fate, bereft of any oversight and completely at the mercy of the Tarahumara Indians."[2]

Sosa was hardly an impartial observer. He believed that the central Sierra Tarahumara was ripe for commercial logging and that timber companies, which had appeared in northwest Chihuahua four decades earlier, would jump at the opportunity to extend the logging frontier southward. It also seems clear that he misjudged the Rarámuris' ecological impact. Forests in the arid north did not grow as densely as the ones in central Mexico with which he was more familiar, and native people typically made only small clearings around their dispersed family settlements. In other words, Sosa was observing a healthy ecosystem rather than a threatened one.[3] His words reflected a rationalist ideology, typical of his day, in which

Figure I.1. The Sosa expedition, 1937. Note the Rarámuri guide in the center. *Boletín del Departamento Forestal y de Caza y Pesca* 3.9 (December 1937–February 1938), 204.

the primacy of scientific knowledge and the desirability of "modern" production appeared self-evidently superior to the "primitive" forms of local knowledge and behavior they displaced.

In time, Sosa came to question some of these beliefs. He returned to the central Sierra Tarahumara in 1965, by which point logging companies had started to extract timber on a commercial scale. He did not like what he saw. To his dismay, the forester witnessed "veritable caravans of trucks heavily laden with timber [that had been] relentlessly extracted from the forests, in a hemorrhage that seemed to have no end."[4] Far from the carefully managed logging regime he had once envisioned, the timber companies ignored the limits on extraction and indiscriminately cut the best stands of trees. Lumberjacks had also invaded an area designated for an indigenous community through Mexico's agrarian reform program, where they cut the most valuable timber and left behind erosion-prone rangeland known as *agostadero*.[5] Sosa could scarcely conceal his dismay at the local officials, who not only turned a blind eye to these events but covered them up by filing "ephemeral management plans" with the national forest service. But he did not lose faith in the basic premise of scientific forestry and continued to assert that "a well cared-for forest will never die" as long as conscientious experts could somehow govern the behavior of timber companies and rural populations.[6]

The Rarámuri had a different understanding of these events. Like most native people in Mexico, they did not value the woods in the same way as timber companies, forestry experts, and other outsiders did. Most Rarámuri regarded the woods as the organic foundation of their individual well-being and collective survival. Forests provided construction material, cooking fuel, game and food, and fodder for goats. They constituted a topography of significance by mobilizing collective memories of community, work, and ritual. In other words, forests had particular *meanings* for most native people, although not necessarily an identical one for each individual. Indeed, native people sometimes disagreed about how their forests should be used and by whom. They struggled among themselves (and with their neighbors) for control of certain stands of trees or entire woodlots. In some instances, they over-harvested their commons or remained indifferent to forest fires, invasive species, and other purported threats to the ecosystem. But Rarámuri communities did tend to close ranks when it came to defending their woods from intrusive regulations and unwanted supervision. They ignored or passively resisted the management plans devised by foresters like Sosa and, as one exasperated warden put it, evaded regulations "in an infinite number of ways."[7] But as with Sosa, their attitudes were subject to change over time. In some cases, native people agreed to work with experts to undertake carefully planned logging projects; in such instances, the Rarámuri began to appear a bit like the modern entrepreneurs that Sosa had championed as the solution to the problem of mismanaged forests.

The Rarámuri had an equally complicated relationship with timber companies. Like most rural people in the early twentieth century, native people in the Sierra Tarahumara realized that their land was—among other things—a commodity that could be bought, rented, or sold, sometimes without their permission. Indeed, some indigenous people regarded commercial forestry as a potentially attractive strategy of collective subsistence. Hundreds of native communities signed rental agreements (often on highly unfavorable terms) that allowed timber companies to log village commons in exchange for cash payments known as stumpage fees. Young men left home to take jobs in timber company work gangs, while older people cut wood on village land and sold handmade railroad ties. Yet many native people resented the politically connected timber companies that appeared unexpectedly, claiming that some new law gave them the right to log wherever they pleased. As one village spokesman wrote on learning that communal woods would thenceforth be managed by a commercial logging firm, "Even though the land no longer belongs to us, don't we belong to it? We are children of this Land, and as children we have a greater right than some Big Shot who can remove its timber just because he has money."[8] This declaration may have been intended to play on bureaucrats' preconceived ideas about the relationship between indigenous people and the natural world, but it also reflected a willingness to challenge a moral system that valued nature merely in economic terms. It suggested, in other words, that native people and timber companies may have seen the same trees, but they perceived quite different forests.

For most of the twentieth century, native people, professional foresters, and timber companies were enmeshed in a complicated network of mutual dependence. This interrelationship originated with the 1910–1917 revolution, which gave rise to a rhetoric of social justice that depicted peasant campesinos in general and indigenous people in particular as the rightful heirs to the land. The revolution also spawned a far-reaching land reform between 1917 and 1992 that transferred slightly over 60 percent of the nation's woodlands to rural communities and made Mexico one of the few nations where the woods belong to the people who live within them. Agrarian reform did not grant rural people the right to manage their woods, however. That task fell to the federal forest service. As a result, Mexico's woodlands became ecological sites of encounter and social contestation for most of the twentieth century. Villagers argued that possession conferred control of the forests, regardless of what the law said, and often reminded officials up to and including the nation's president of the government's obligation to ensure their access to the woodlands. They routinely wrote the authorities to condemn unfair contracts with logging companies, to request that something be done about potentially troublesome outsiders who settled in their midst, and above all to request exemptions from conservationist regulations that barred their access to the forests.[9] Forestry officials often ended up in the middle of these disputes, and they had strong incentives to show at least token respect for rural people's concerns, in part because foresters grew increasingly aware that they could never manage the nation's ecosystems without the compliance of those who dwelt within them.[10]

Mexican forests were shaped less by market forces, management policies, or population pressures than by the effects of political negotiation among the people and institutions that vied to determine how, and in whose benefit, they would be used. Just about everyone who staked a claim to the woodland used an idiom that combined ideas of conservation, of rights and ownership, and of social justice and the national interest. Some acts of claim-making succeeded better than others, however, and Mexican forests became what I will call "political landscapes" whose blessings were rarely shared evenly. Only in the final years of the twentieth century did forests finally begin to lose their political charge, as rural people and forestry experts built on their shared experiences to forge new and, in many senses, healthier relationships within the ecosystem.

THE LAY OF THE LAND

Mexico's borders reflect political rather than ecological frontiers. The nation encompasses no fewer than five major bioregions (biomes) ranging from the neotropical rainforests in the south to the megadiverse cloud forests of south-central Oaxaca to the Sonoran Desert. Much of the nation's topography is dominated by the parallel mountain ranges known as the Sierra Madre Occidental and Oriental, which rise in the far north, then course southward until they meld together in the densely populated volcanic belt of central Mexico. The sierras traverse the semi-arid climate of the north as well as the tropical subhumid climate of central Mexico and encompass some of the most extensive coniferous forests in the Americas. Pine-oak ecosystems predominate, but several others can be found as well, such as the Oaxacan cloud forests and the world's greatest expanses of tropical coniferous woodlands in the center-west.

Pines are a species of conifer that evolved 300 million years ago and spread into Mesoamerica during the Cretaceous era. Mexico's coniferous forests did not reach their current dimensions until the most recent ice age came to an end about 13,000 years ago, around the same time as humans arrived in the New World and many species of large mammals became extinct. The warming climate allowed pines, oaks, firs, and other organisms to occupy ecological niches formerly inaccessible to them. At the same time, Paleolithic hunters and gatherers altered the woods by culling certain species of plants and animals and favoring the spread of others. When ancient Americans discovered agriculture around 8,000 B.C.E., they further shaped forest ecosystems by clearing land for planting, harvesting wood for fuel, and burning fields (and the edges of forests) in preparation for planting.[11]

Since Mexican forests and human societies have co-evolved over several millennia, nearly all the wooded landscapes that became an object of

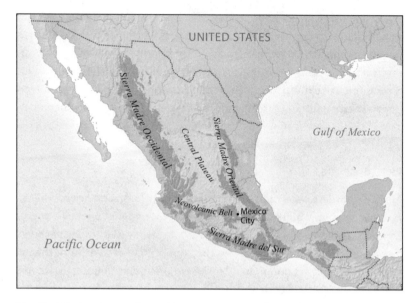

Map I.1. Mexico: Geography and Temperate Forests (shaded)

dispute in the twentieth century were anthropogenic spaces rather than pristine ecosystems or "virgin" woodlands. Ancient Americans did not necessarily live in harmony with "nature": they overcut trees, inadvertently promoted erosion, and probably overhunted and overfished during the hard times.[12] For the most part, however, indigenous peoples studied the natural world and carefully modified their surroundings in order to take what they needed without irreparably harming the land. That can be a tricky proposition in the case of forests, which are ecosystems characterized by relatively tall and abundant groups of trees—often referred to as "communities" in the scientific literature—that interact with each other and other species in intricate ways. Forests can usually withstand slow ecological change, but they are susceptible to rapid degradation when certain "keystone" species disappear overnight due to natural disaster or human intervention. They can regenerate, of course, but second-growth forests usually lack their predecessors' biodiversity, and they can disappear altogether in the face of permanent conversion to agriculture, severe erosion, or rapid climate change.

Native societies shaped forests to meet their needs, but they were likewise shaped by their natural surroundings. Geography influenced the types of settlements that native people built, the food they ate, and in some cases the social structures they devised. During the colonial era, forests afforded indigenous people with a means of subsistence and a measure of security from outsiders. These advantages grew more important in the nineteenth century, when some native people shielded themselves from unwanted intrusions by retreating deeper into the mountains. Others chose (or were forced) to use the woods for subsistence by renting or selling it. Still others began to take jobs in the timber sector and as loggers, wood haulers, charcoal makers, or sawmill workers. By the mid-twentieth century, community-based forestry enterprises offered the rural poor a route to economic security, particularly in villages that received land reform parcels, known as ejidos, through the land reform program. The economic lure of forestry also drew a small but influential group of non-native migrants to settle in the woodlands, including some who staked their own, often illegitimate claims on the land. Just as forests created opportunities for rural people, their disappearance spelled trouble. As forests were privatized or fell to the axes and, eventually, chainsaws of lumberjacks, the range subsistence options narrowed for people accustomed to using the woods for their own needs.

It is no accident that so many indigenous groups had withdrawn to remote woodlands by the nineteenth century. The Spanish colonists who ruled Mexico until 1821 had claimed the best agricultural lands for themselves and spread throughout the central plateau, the flatlands of the center-west Bajío, and other desirable areas. Most of them considered forests a wasteland, albeit one that provided the wood and charcoal necessary for the operation of colonial silver mines and urban kitchens. Apart from mission friars and the occasional adventurer, few Europeans or mixed-race mestizos settled in the wooded sierras, meaning that native people in the highlands had relatively little contact with outsiders. As the anthropologist Gonzalo Aguirre Beltrán put it, woodlands (along with tropical forests and deserts) became "regions of refuge" where indigenous societies found a degree of autonomy from the dominant culture.[13] That began to change during the late nineteenth century, when logging companies, timber contractors, settlers, and ambitious villagers claimed gigantic tracts of woodland. These interlopers made use of business-friendly legislation, such as the 1856 disentailment law that forced native communities to divide the commons and title them as individually owned fee-simple private property. Nevertheless, the woods could still provide some cover. The "abandonment" (to use the preferred term of postrevolutionary leaders) and relative remoteness of forestlands have helped the nation's largest remaining indigenous groups—such as the Maya and the Zapotec, among others—to maintain their language and customs up to the present day.

The co-evolutionary process that had characterized rural people's relationship with the forest became increasingly one-sided during the industrial era, which in Mexico's case began in earnest during the 1876–1911 dictatorship of Porfirio Díaz (a period known as the Porfiriato). Growing demand for natural resources spawned a commercial timber industry in the late nineteenth century. Initially, family-owned companies had the market to themselves, but railroads and other corporations with access to foreign capital vastly expanded the scale of production around 1900. Few observers at the time paused to wonder how the commodification of forests might affect native people, but they did sense that industrialization posed a threat to the environment. Mexican scientists were already familiar with the tenets of scientific forestry, which had established itself in Europe by the 1870s. One of its key goals was to develop techniques for "maximum sustained yield" logging, or, in other words, cutting trees at the exact rate that forests could regenerate. European foresters also experimented with ways of "improving" natural forests by managing them like plantations. They proposed to simplify the natural admixture of species, ages, and placement of trees by selectively harvesting them—or clear-cutting them altogether—and then replanting with commercially desirable species in even-aged stands that loggers could harvest more easily. Mexican experts had no illusions about cultivating such "even-aged forests" in their vast and untamed country, but they did aspire to halt the unsustainable extraction of timber and, in due course, to institute sustainable-use management plans. The problem lay in the execution. Not only would politically connected logging companies have to submit to federal oversight, but the locals would somehow need to be taught to stop using the woods "irrationally" and respect conservationist regulations instead. Scientific forestry ignored the subsistence strategies of villagers and in this sense "emptied the forests, symbolically, of its human residents."[14]

Forest conservation therefore has a checkered history of engagement with rural peoples. The second industrial revolution of the late nineteenth century generated unprecedented demands for wood used in mines, railroads, and construction. Governments (particularly European ones) scrambled to regulate logging and hired cadres of professional foresters who almost invariably ended up in state agencies dedicated to the paradigm of sustained-yield logging. Foresters typically tried to clamp down on villagers' ungoverned use of forests and gave preference to modern timber companies that had the capital and expertise to exploit resources efficiently and—at least theoretically—in accordance with the law. This pattern repeated itself in places such as the Himalayas, Cuba, Java, and the southwestern United States, where professional foresters brushed aside the locals' ownership claims and branded rural people as backward or intrinsically criminal. Bureaucracies sprouted up that combined the enforcement of often inflexible regulations with educational campaigns that touted the virtues of conservation and rational management.

Villagers typically met scientific forestry with resistance. They flaunted regulations and harvested wood illegally, either for their own use or to sell on the gray market. When caught, they pled ignorance or bribed the wardens to let them off the hook. They mocked professional foresters' pretention to understand the woods better than they did and, in extreme instances, killed wardens, intimidated local authorities, or rebelled.[15] In time, some of them accommodated to the new order. Rural people accepted the principles of scientific conservation they found most compelling, such as the idea that forest removal might harm the aquifer. Some sought to learn how to log their lands sustainably, and the savviest experts tried to strike tentative alliances with these amenable locals.[16]

Mexico was not alone in attempting to transform ecological consciousness in the countryside. For example, administrators in colonial India met popular resistance to scientific management by establishing communities of local authorities who understood the rudiments of scientific forestry and preached the gospel of conservation. Arun Agrawal has suggested that allowing local leaders to manage the woods put them in a position to advocate for practices of sustainable forest management within their villages. In Agrawal's estimation, this transformed rural people into "environmental subjects," that is, people for whom conservation constitutes a "conceptual category that organizes some of their thinking."[17]

Mexican forestry experts never seriously contemplated recruiting local leaders to promote conservation in the nineteenth century, and in any case the tiny cadre of Porfirian foresters emphasized reforestation projects rather than broader social initiatives. That hands-off approach began to change in the early twentieth century. Villagers' demand for the return of communal "land, water, and forests" (as Emiliano Zapata's 1912 revolutionary manifesto put it) was only one trigger of the revolution that broke out in 1910, but the scale of rural mobilization over the course of the next five years ensured that land reform became a signature initiative of the postrevolutionary regime. The constitution of 1917 guaranteed pueblos (villages) enough land to subsist, setting the stage for a massive transfer of property from private landowners to rural communities over the following six decades. The revolution also left an imprint on the science of Mexican forestry, which acquired a distinctly nationalist hue in the 1920s and 1930s as experts criticized the Porfirian practice of granting concessions to foreign companies that allowed for virtually unrestricted access to the nation's natural patrimony. While professional foresters never ceased lamenting what they regarded as peasant backwardness, they nonetheless learned to conform to a postrevolutionary system that extolled campesinos (rural folk) as the "favored children" of the revolutionary nation.[18] For the rest of the century, forests remained at the center of competition and negotiation between land reform beneficiaries, forestry experts, and others who ultimately determined which woodlands endured and which were converted into money, political capital, or ash.

POLITICAL LANDSCAPES

The forests we see in Mexico today are the embodiments not only of natural processes, but of political ones as well. In the unsettled years following the Mexican Revolution, a combination of social mobilization, economic reconstruction, and mutable policies invested woodlands with new, oftentimes contested, significance. The forests became what I will call political landscapes: geographies made meaningful through the interaction of private interests, collective action, and the often discriminatory application of state power in ways that one social group or more interprets as illegitimate. Political landscapes are places where contention over resources has provoked official intervention and forced historical actors to negotiate with the bureaucrats who ultimately determine which social groups will gain access to the land and its fruits.

As the historian Cynthia Radding has suggested, the meanings affixed to a particular landscape derive from its inhabitants' shared history and understanding of territory.[19] In the case of postrevolutionary Mexico, this territoriality—and even people's understanding of their shared history—were very much in flux. Land reform redeemed the poor and remade the nation's social terrain, even as postrevolutionary social contention encouraged rural people to consider themselves a campesino "class."[20] New development projects and conservationist legislation set limits on who could use the woods and under what conditions. The state—understood as bureaucrats working at the local and national levels, though not always in harmony with each other—was deeply implicated in all of these processes.

Two distinct but interrelated processes politicized Mexican landscapes during the twentieth century. One pattern began when local conflicts over land and resources provoked government intervention. Authorities routinely arbitrated disputes within villages, between neighboring communities, or among rural people and "outsiders" such as logging companies and unwelcome regulators such as forest wardens. The people on the losing side of these contests typically rejected official dispositions as exercises in political favoritism (which they often were) and either ignored them or continued to press their case through alternate bureaucratic channels. In the second pattern, the government technocrats politicized the landscape by enacting unpopular and oftentimes unenforceable regulations or by destabilizing the regulatory environment with repeated or unexpected changes to the law, both of which introduced tremendous uncertainty into questions of land tenure and access to resources. In either case, the corrupt and interventionist bureaucracies of twentieth-century Mexico increasingly politicized forest landscape because their attempts to regulate the use of resources frequently ended up aggravating local tensions rather than resolving them.

A central argument of this book is that the politicization of forest landscapes represents one of the greatest threats to their ecological integrity. People and institutions have a strong incentive to pilfer an ecosystem that has become subject to a dispute whose outcome resides in the uncertain territory of cronyism, incompetence, or unfathomable decisions by distant administrators. Villagers who believed that officials intended to "illegitimately" place their forests off-limits for logging, for example, sometimes felt compelled to cut as many trees as possible before the regulations could be enforced. In other cases, they set fire to forestlands claimed by neighbors. Likewise, logging companies such as the one Antonio Sosa denounced often tried to clear-cut timber in areas slated for ejidal land grants or inclusion in a national park. In all these instances, the combination of social contestation, shifting regulations, and uncertainty contributed to the politicization of the landscape, and hence to ecological degradation.[21]

The origins of Mexico's political landscape can be traced to the nation's first comprehensive forestry code, which took effect in 1926 and underpinned management policies for the next six decades. The law attempted to reconcile rural development with expert management, all in the context of land reform. The historical conjuncture of agrarian populism and scientific management first articulated in the 1926 code was a particularly progressive instance of what I call *revolutionary forestry*, which embedded resource use within the context of social justice *and* scientific management practices. The new law required land reform beneficiaries to obtain management plans from the forest service and establish village-level producers cooperatives, which became the only legal means of logging collectively held property.[22] The cooperatives became an important new source of employment and gave some rural people the means to earn a living by logging their own land. Trained professionals inspected each ejidal logging project and formulated detailed management plans intended to guarantee sustained-yield production. Some villagers embraced the cooperatives and developed close working relationships with federal foresters. Others resented the new policies and cut wood without a management plan, a clandestine strategy that netted only a sliver of the wood's true value.

Revolutionary forestry never had a chance to take root, however. A new generation of political leaders came of age during the Second World War and moved the nation in the direction of industrialization, a managed economy, and political centralization bordering on authoritarianism. New forestry codes passed in 1943 and 1948 suppressed the cooperatives in a bid to make private corporations the engines of economic progress. Federal authorities sweetened the pot by granting forest concessions called Industrialized Forestry Units (UIEFs in their Spanish acronym) to paper mills and timber companies. These privileged firms received exclusive access to timberlands—including woods held by ejidos, native communities, and private smallholders—in exchange for their pledges to improve the transportation infrastructure, to manage resources sustainably, and to expand the social services available to people within their jurisdictions. Few of these concession-holders did any such thing. They rarely employed local populations in appreciable numbers, and nearly all of them became the targets of intense popular resentment.

Programs to encourage rural development did not vanish, however. Cadres of anthropologists, populist foresters, and progressive politicians continued to forge links with rural people in a bid to find "appropriate" forms of local production. Even these projects politicized the forests. Both antidemocratic and populist management regimes treated the landscape in practical terms and construed the woods primarily as a potential source of income, patronage, and employment that might one day pull rural society out of poverty and backwardness. Seemingly democratic strategies were created *for* but not in collaboration *with* the populations they proposed to uplift, and officials at all levels continued to regard rural people as threats to the environment rather than as its denizens. Most of these developmentalist initiatives converted forests into denaturalized "things" subject to convoluted and often unenforceable laws.[23] The landscape acquired yet another political valence in the middle decades of the twentieth century, when the forest service devised regional management programs that favored private interests and paragovernmental corporations over ejidos and indigenous communities, administratively stripping rural people of access to their own land. Toward the end of the twentieth century, these centralized initiatives collapsed under the weight of neoliberal restructuring and foresters' increasing awareness that overregulation had done more to encourage deforestation than to constrain it. Even so, many rural people still regarded the woods as places to defend not only from commercial loggers but from "conquest" by bureaucrats as well.[24]

Rural people came to learn the language and logic of forest management, if for no other reason than to avoid missteps when dealing with the officials who wielded so much power over their woods. Village leaders signed contracts with lumber companies, appraised the regulations that distinguished legal from illegal use of the woods, and met the foresters and other experts who surveyed their property. Extension agents working for the Banco Ejidal (a development bank for the land reform sector) and other entities modeled new techniques of tapping trees, making charcoal, and managing village woodlots. Officials recruited rural folk to participate in didactic public rituals such as Arbor Day celebrations and reforestation campaigns. Before long, villagers learned to deploy the language of conservation and rationality, and of economic development and equity. Some of this linguistic innovation can be ascribed to mimicry, since petitioners often chose words and concepts they thought that bureaucrats wanted to hear. In other instances, it suggests that rural people had begun to engage with new ecological understandings of their landscape. The anthropologist Andrew Matthews has shown, for example, that contact with foresters taught native people in Ixtlán, Oaxaca, "a language of environmental degradation."[25] Many of them internalized the early twentieth-century idea that the loss of forest cover would reduce overall rainfall (a notion that professional foresters ironically had come to reject) and took pains to protect woods near sources of water or anywhere they felt it might help the local climate. In other contexts, exposure to the logic of sustainability took root as (some) villagers grudgingly accepted the need for management plans, or learned to use new and less damaging techniques of tapping pine trees, or took pains to fight the forest fires, insect infestations, or overeager loggers that threatened their woods.

It fell to the foresters employed by the federal government (and less frequently by timber companies or state-level bureaucracies) to bridge the abstract policies set down in the distant capital with the complex social landscape of rural Mexico. These middling professionals crafted management plans for small-scale local producers such as ejidos, native communities, and the modest private-property owners often called *rancheros* or *pequeños propietarios* (smallholders). Foresters were supposed to inspect each work site annually to ensure that villagers (or the timber companies that had leased logging rights from a community or ejido) had followed their management plan and, if so, to issue the necessary licenses (*guías*) for transporting timber. Foresters sometimes shirked their duties and ginned up management plans and annual reviews without ever visiting worksites. Some colluded with timber companies to allow illegal logging or accepted bribes to overlook transgressions great or small. On the other hand, these rural experts could sometimes make effective advocates for rural people. While the earliest generation of foresters generally disdained peasants and portrayed them as inherent threats to nature, a handful willingly met with local leaders and became effective advocates for local production, particularly in low-tech activities such as tree-tapping and the collection of deadwood. By the 1970s, a new generation of forestry experts, extension agents, and development anthropologists had come to regard their work as a form of social service and strove to help rural people find the means to log their own land and manage village-owned timber companies.

THE ARCHIVED FOREST

Forestry officials produced reams of documents. They wrote management studies, annual evaluations, forest-product shipment permits (guías), volumetric reports of standing timber, and correspondence with local leaders. These papers made forests legible to officials in Mexico City and linked the forest service to the individuals, ejidos, and corporations subject to regulation.[26] Sooner or later, these documents ended up at the archives located on the south end of the federal tree nursery (now called the Viveros de Coyoacán) in Mexico City, where the forest service had its headquarters until the 1990s.[27] The archive includes snippets of information about the organizational structure of the forest service as well as registers of its prop-

Figure I.2. The federal forest service offices and archive in Coyoacán, 1937. (Forest service chief Miguel Ángel de Quevedo, with beard, stands in the center.) Private collection of Luz Emilia Aguilar Zinzer.

erty, but the bulk of its documentation comprises management studies and inspection reports prepared by federal foresters between 1926 and 1994. Occasional correspondence between villagers and forest service officials punctuates the otherwise formulaic paperwork.

Like all archives, the repository functioned as a technology of governance that allowed the top tier of administrators in Mexico City to distinguish licit from illicit behavior and to glean the "facts on the ground." Theoretically at least, bureaucrats could easily determine which villages had received permission to use their lands for logging, tree-tapping, and other forestry projects, right down to one man's felling a handful of pines to make student desks for the local schoolhouse. This apparent precision masks the archives' distorted rendering of what actually went on in the countryside. Even by conservative estimates, around half of the logging in Mexico lacked official authorization and hence escaped any documentation other than the occasional citation. Even the archival descriptions of officially approved logging projects are often misleading. Villagers or company foremen routinely bribed wardens to use the same logging permit repeatedly, shipment authorizations were lent out or stolen, and overworked foresters combatting huge backlogs occasionally copied management plans nearly verbatim from one village to the next.

The archive is hopelessly compromised as a faithful record of events, but it nevertheless constitutes the record of the political landscape in which corporations gained increasingly widespread access to the woods while timber-dependent populations negotiated the shifting regulatory terrain. It describes conflicts over boundary lines and traces the often strained relations between villagers and timber companies. It shows how natural disasters like insect plagues and volcano eruptions shaped the woodlands and the lives of those who inhabited them. Exceptional documents give voice to how an individual, or a group of people, or in some cases an entire community experienced work, scientific regulation, or everyday life in the woods. The archive even hints at the limits of bureaucratic knowledge and official power in the countryside. Its holdings testify to the ways in which historical actors such as forest wardens, pirate sawmill owners, and political bosses mediated between state forestry policies and rural people. In other words, they demonstrate how conflict and accommodation transformed the landscape into an object of contention that linked officials in Mexico City with the people who lived and worked in the woods.

TOWARD A HISTORY OF MEXICAN COMMUNITY FORESTRY

Around half of all Mexican forests disappeared during the twentieth century. By the early 1990s, the country was losing between 0.75 percent and 1.3 percent of forest cover annually, a pace that threatened to eradicate a third of the remaining forest cover within two decades.[28] Ecosystem destruction on such a scale imposed staggering environmental and social costs. As one of only seventeen nations with "megadiverse" ecosystems, Mexico has an uncommonly high concentration of endemic species, many of which live in microclimates that depend on forest cover. Deforestation also deals a double blow to the global climate. Burning woods to open new land for agriculture releases carbon dioxide into the atmosphere and compromises one of the main ecosystems that transpire oxygen back into the atmosphere. The effects of forest loss are most acutely felt at the local level, however. Many of the world's most vulnerable peoples rely on forests for their cultural and material survival. The mushrooms, nuts, and small game that still complement many rural people's diets disappear when forests are destroyed, and dwindling stocks of easily accessible wood can make it difficult to meet basic needs for construction or cooking fuel. Deforestation can also cause erosion, lower water tables, and undermine the livelihoods of those who make their living in the timber industry. Some specialists worry that it will contribute to local, regional, and international instability as displaced rural people abandon their homelands and join the surging number of climate refugees worldwide.[29]

Deforestation is not inevitable, however, and it has slowed considerably in Mexico since the mid-1990s. Several factors explain this reversal, including the effects of migration out of the countryside and (one suspects) rural people's increasing reticence to venture into the backwoods increasingly controlled by drug cartels.[30] Most important, rural people working with professional foresters in several parts of the country have put into place a collaborative form of resource management known as "community forestry," which has allowed them to take responsibility for sustainably harvesting wood pursuant to management plans tailored to fit local conditions. Placing villagers in control of their own forests has several advantages over more restrictive policies. Impeding villagers' access to the woods or prohibiting logging altogether has not succeeded in Mexico, in part because rural people often ignore disagreeable regulations as unjust and turn to the black market. The forests are too big and the nights too dark for wardens to police every tree or inspect every load of timber, even if they felt inclined to do so. It makes more sense to enlist the help of local populations by giving them greater authority in forest management and turning them into allies in conservation, not least because they own most of the nation's woodlands.[31] The expansion of community forestry projects in the final decades of the twentieth century helped to curtail deforestation, particularly in the ejidos and common lands where people participate in sustainable logging and have come to regard the forests as valuable collective resources.[32]

Most scholarship traces the origins of community forestry in Mexico to changes in federal policies in the final decades of the twentieth century. According to this interpretation, the regulatory shift from a highly centralized regime of federal management to a more supple variant that responded to local needs began to take form during the presidency of Luis Echeverría (1970–1976), whose rural populism responded to growing peasant demands for productive autonomy and a viable means to make a living on the land. Researchers point above all to the collapse of sprawling state bureaucracies in the mid-1980s, when neoliberal reformers dismantled onerous regulatory structures in order to unleash the efficiencies of the open market. In the forestlands, this neoliberal revolution perhaps unintentionally opened a space for community timber enterprises and eventually reduced the legal, bureaucratic, and normative barriers to local management. The dismantling of the existing regime of state forestry that alienated rural people from their own environment opened the way for a new generation of experts to collaborate with forestland communities by ensuring that they received both the capital and technical assistance to put their woods into production.[33]

This interpretation can only partially account for the development of community management and a growing sense of stewardship. In the first place, it discounts efforts to promote local management that date back to the 1930s, when a handful of federal officials, professional foresters, and other experts encouraged rural people to take control of their ejidal woods. The producers cooperatives of the 1930s represent the clearest example of Mexico's precocious efforts to promote what we now call "community forestry." They established a clear precedent for the idea that carefully managed village logging operations could both provide rural people with a livelihood and create a viable mechanism for sustainable logging practices. Even after the populist heyday had faded, some lonely officials continued to experiment with community management by organizing unions of ejidos with their own logging company or by encouraging alternative uses of the woods, such as pine resin extraction. Later, the National Indigenist Institute (the INI, Mexico's Bureau of Indian Affairs) promoted similar initiatives in Chihuahuan native communities, while federal authorities demanded that the companies with forest concessions put at least some local people on the payroll. Although federal policies between the 1940s and the 1980s certainly did restrict rural people's ability to use their own land, closer inspection reveals that the community forestry of the 1980s can trace its origins to a legacy of local development initiatives, many of which grew out of postrevolutionary social-justice projects.

In the second place, most interpretations discount the long history of indigenous and campesino efforts to reclaim the land. Scholars who focus on federal policy tend to underestimate the historical significance of rural people's struggle to regain control of their forest patrimony, which in many instances laid the groundwork for subsequent experiences of community forestry. Villagers resisted dispossession long before the revolution and ensuing land reform, of course. But ever since 1917, rural people have routinely petitioned for ejido land reform parcels, denounced outsiders' misuse of the woodlands, and tried a variety of strategies, both legal and illegal, to use the woods as they saw fit. Village leaders learned how to navigate (and evade) shifting legal contexts and the myriad institutions that governed (or prohibited) logging. Land reform beneficiaries policed their property and politicked among each other. Not all of these experiences involved conflict: villagers sometimes learned from and tentatively engaged the foresters and other experts who alighted in their midst. Over the decades, they developed a storehouse of knowledge about bureaucratic routines, forest management, best practices in logging and tapping trees, and the finer points of community organizing.

In this book I explore the entwined history of rural society and of Mexico's state forestry apparatus during the twentieth century. I focus primarily on temperate forests, rather than on the southern tropical ecosystems that began to disappear at an alarming rate around 1970. Scientists and regulators paid little heed to tropical forests until the final decades of the twentieth century because they regarded the more thickly settled pine-oak forests of the nation's central and northern climes as the fulcrums of the nation's environmental balance and as emblems of "natural beauty . . . [and] sites that [were] picturesque, valuable, and healthy."[34] Political leaders placed those areas into national parks, where increasingly urbanized masses could reconnect with nature.[35] Temperate forests captured the imagination of Mexico's scientific elite not only because they resembled the woods in the more "advanced" and "civilized" nations of Europe and North America, but also because their relatively fast-growing conifers held the best prospects for scientifically managed, commercial exploitation.

For most of the twentieth century, professional foresters regarded swamplands and tropical species as commercially undesirable (except for a few precious hardwoods like mahogany) and as unworthy of either scientific investigation or much legal protection. They associated the tropics with economic backwardness, disease, and a discomforting profusion of exotic species. In the late 1950s, for example, one of Mexico's most prominent foresters described tropical forests as inherently sickly spaces comprised of "trees in a state of decrepitude, or mature trees that are plagued or misshapen, or trees too young to harvest."[36] Unsurprisingly, these experts rarely ventured to the tropics and usually confined themselves to the central and northerly woods that they found more intelligible, healthy, and above all profitable to manage.

The villages and temperate forests at the core of this study are located in the western state of Michoacán and in the far northern state of Chihuahua, which lies on the border with the United States. Although separated by over 1,200 kilometers, they nonetheless share key attributes. Commercial logging appeared in both states during the 1880s and remains a significant component of their economies today. Land reform movements crested in both places in the 1930s and again in 1970s, ultimately delivering valuable forests to rural communities in the form of ejido land grants, many of which benefited native people such as the Rarámuri of Chihuahua and the Purépecha (sometimes called "Tarascans" by outsiders) of Michoacán. Both states had substantially similar experiences with muscular development projects, such as the construction of hydroelectric dams, large-scale irrigation networks, and generous concessions of forestland to private companies and paragovernmental organizations. And each state experienced a significant midcentury effort to develop villagers' capacity to manage their own forests.

The two states also present striking contrasts. Chihuahua is Mexico's largest state and stretches over a quarter-million square kilometers of desert and savannah at the foothills of the Sierra Madre Oriental, a mountain range so high that snowfall is a common sight in wintertime. Chihuahua's proximity to the United States made it a favored target for foreign investment in mining, ranching, railroads, banking, and forestry during the early twentieth century. These trappings of modernity only grazed the Rarámuri and the sierras, where the majority continued to dwell in scattered family settlements and follow a semi-nomadic subsistence strategy based on shepherding goats and sheep. Mixed-race (mestizo) outsiders moved into native communities throughout the twentieth century and often staked a claim to the woods—a problem accentuated in the late twentieth century as the region fell prey to drug traffickers. The majority of the region's inhabitants spoke Rarámuri and observed the Catholic religious calendar, while heeding ancestral structures of authority. In Michoacán, native people acculturated more completely to the dominant mestizo culture over the course of the twentieth century. Like other states of central Mexico, such as Oaxaca, they nonetheless succeeded in asserting a degree of control over their woods that their northern counterparts never achieved. With a larger population but a quarter of the area of Chihuahua, Michoacán had forests that were both less extensive and more susceptible to conversion to agriculture, as epitomized by the avocado boom of the late twentieth century. With less timber to exploit, however, fewer timber companies appeared, and they had less political clout than did their northern counterparts. Rural people also had greater access to potentially sympathetic political allies thanks to the state's history of peasant mobilizations and a relatively progressive political environment dating back to the 1920s.

Mexico City lay at the epicenter of these political landscapes. As the nation's intellectual hub, it was home to the scientific and technocratic elite, whose members theorized about how to maximize forest production without harming the ecosystem or dangerously provoking the rural masses. As the masters of national politics, Mexico City's power elite not only attended to these shifting scientific debates, but also laid the ground rules that governed the use of resources. Presidents had the authority to order logging bans, to approve forest concessions, and to decide which commercial interests would gain the inside track in the bitter competitions over resources. Indeed, the use of political connections as a business strategy had a heritage dating back to the late nineteenth century, an age when foreigners had the technology and the capital to transform forest ecosystems into commodities.

In this book I divide the social history of Mexican forests into two broad periods. The first covers the era from the 1890s to the early 1940s, or roughly from the moment during the Porfiriato in which commercial logging began its meteoric growth. Although logging slowed during the revolution, it reappeared during the era of populism that culminated with the 1934–1940 Cárdenas administration. In chapter 1 I show how the commodification of forestlands led to widespread dispossession of indigenous villages and set the stage for the appearance of "revolutionary forestry," which promised rural people a chance to log their own lands under the supervision of expert foresters. The Porfirian authorities encouraged commercial logging (associated in many cases with the construction of railroads) on a scale that troubled the scientific community and brought significant social changes to the native peoples of Chihuahua and Michoacán. In chapter 2 I follow the revolutionary upheavals of 1910–1917 and describe how people who dwelt in the two states' forests came to terms with the ongoing violence. The revolution was in part a backlash to North American economic intervention in the Mexican economy, including the timber sector. Revolutionary nationalism not only animated unrest in the countryside, but also colored scientific forestry's development in the years immediately following the upheaval. In chapter 3 I suggest that foreign domination of the forestry sector and the revolutionary mobilization of the 1910s forced the nation's political and scientific elite to integrate rural people and their forestlands into their plans for the nation's ecological future.

In the second half of this volume I examine the period between the mid-1940s and the early 1980s, when forests became increasingly subject to what I call the "development imperative," wherein political leaders concluded that forest resources were too valuable to remain under the control of rural people. The presidents of the 1940s and 1950s favored national development over rural autonomy, which meant finding a way to subsume rural people's expectations to the broader project of economic modernization. In chapter 4 I trace the origins of this "development imperative" to the Second World War, when new institutional forms gave logging corporations first crack at the woodlands—including those that had already been granted to rural people as land reform ejidos. Nevertheless, villagers pushed back in many places and sometimes succeeded in solidifying their hold on the woods. In chapter 5 I explore two holistic development projects that promised to integrate local production with industrial forestry, both of which had mixed results at best. In chapter 6 I investigate the point at which the regime of state forestry slowly gave way to community control of the woodlands.

I conclude by examining some of the lessons we can draw from the social history of Mexican forests. Villagers' experience of land reform, the defense of their woods, and contact with forestry experts over the previous decades helped them assume management of forests in the 1990s, the moment at which neoliberalism and the collapse of state forestry began to depoliticize the forest landscape. By the 2000s, community forestry and the expansion of environmental movements placed people in a position to manage their own woods for the first time since the 1930s, albeit under dramatically different circumstances.

PART I

THE MAKING OF
REVOLUTIONARY
FORESTRY

CHAPTER 1

The Commodification of Nature, 1880–1910

————

When General Porfirio Díaz seized the presidency from his weakened and unpopular predecessor in 1876, it seemed as if Mexico might fall back into the cycle of instability that had characterized its first decades as an independent nation. Instead, Díaz remained in power for thirty-five years (punctuated by only one hiatus, from 1880 to 1884), until revolutionaries forced him from office, in 1911. His autocratic regime brought fractious regional leaders to heel and cracked down on bandits who thrived on political turmoil. Hacienda owners enjoyed strengthening markets and a political atmosphere that encouraged the expansion of their domains, while foreign investors attracted by unprecedented stability and business-friendly policies rushed to build railroads, mines, oil fields, and other industries great and small. By 1900, American and Canadian companies started to turn their attention to timber as well.[1] The economic development and intellectual ferment of the Díaz years, which are known as the Porfiriato, brought some parts of the nation more closely in step with the developed world in the span of a single generation. Yet the wrenching advent of Porfirian order and progress had ominous implications for a rural society that still retained many of its colonial traits. Laws ostensibly intended to modernize the market in rural property forced most indigenous communities (including acculturated ones) to privatize their collectively owned lands, or at least to incorporate themselves into holding companies. In either case, most communal property slipped into the hands of outsiders or wealthy villagers, leaving increasing numbers of rural people destitute. Some joined the ranks wage labor. At the same time, the land, water, and forests owned by the federal government or formerly held as village commons were fashioned into commodities that could be bought by investors or savvy residents who understood how to manipulate the expanding state bureaucracy.

The Porfirian order adhered to a peculiarly nineteenth-century variant of political liberalism, whose core tenets included secularism, equal rights for all, the capability of trade to grow the wealth of nations, and the virtues of individual choice. Liberalism had at least nominally become the law of the land ever since the so-called reform era of 1855–1857. When Díaz came to power two decades later, his inner circle of advisors known as *científicos* (scientists) hoped that a reinvigorated liberal agenda would finally allow the nation to overcome a colonial heritage marked by caste privileges, weak markets, and clerical prerogatives. They intended to lead Mexico down the same economic path as Europe and the United States yet despaired of their countrymen's fitness for the journey. The Church continued to wield immense authority and had little use for secularism and the sort of modernization the *científicos* envisioned. Geography made it difficult for one region to trade with another, and bandits roamed the land. Indigenous communities posed a particularly thorny problem, because many still owned common lands granted by the crown during the colonial era, but few native people could read, and they appeared hopelessly backward to the upper classes.[2] By the time Díaz became president, liberal politicians had all but given up on the liberal touchstones of political equality and individual choice; instead, they turned their attention to stimulating trade on a national and international scale. State and federal governments attracted foreign investment by granting concessions—that is, contracts that provided tax exemptions, access to public lands, and other perks—to corporations willing to invest in railroads and extractive industries. Most concessions went to foreign interests that had the requisite expertise, capital, and political connections to undertake such projects, though Mexican businesses received a modest number as well.

The científicos hoped to expand domestic commerce, and the market for rural property in particular. Liberal leaders during Benito Juárez's era (1858–1872) had forced the Church to sell off most of its properties, but their Porfirian heirs worried that too much land still languished beyond the reach of markets in village commons that could not be bought or sold. The administration dusted off the 1856 Lerdo Law, which obliged the owners of communally owned property (*comuneros*) to divide it among themselves and title it as individuals—a process known as "disentailment." The partition of village commons facilitated a massive transfer of property from rural communities to hacienda owners, wealthy villagers, and in some instances a rising class of independent family farmers known as rancheros. Many peasant communities had lost track (or simply been robbed) of the colonial documents that constituted the most direct means to establish a clear title to the commons. The absence of these "primordial titles" opened the way for unscrupulous landowners or village elites to encroach on communal property. Landowners were known to redraw their boundary lines (sometimes by moving the ubiquitous stone markers known as *mojoneras*) or to take a more direct route and fraudulently title village lands with the collusion of local officials. Even if villagers successfully managed to avoid dispossession, divide the commons, and title it with the authorities, they still faced threats to their property. Some sold it for a pittance to some local profiteer. Others fell into arrears on their tax bills, either because they lacked the money to pay, or more likely because they failed to negotiate the opaque and sometimes hostile process of making a payment at the tax assessor's office. Tax sales became a commonplace in central Mexico during the late nineteenth century and helped create a mass of land-poor villagers, whom haciendas used as a reserve labor pool during planting and harvest seasons.

Another problem was that village lands got swept up in the tidal wave of public land sales during the 1880s. The officials who made public lands available to investors needed a clear picture of the extent and location of national landholdings; however, few such maps existed. A law passed in 1883 remedied this problem by promising survey companies a third of any unoccupied public land (known as *terrenos baldíos*) they mapped. This enticing offer was meant both to compensate surveyors for their work and to encourage them not to leave any corner of the nation uncharted. According to the best available estimate, the survey companies received 21.2 million hectares of putatively public lands during the Porfiriato, and the government sold or granted another 22.5 million to private landowners. In all, 20 percent of the national territory, or an area around the size of modern-day Germany, passed into private hands, most of it between 1883 and 1893 in the frontier states and territories of Baja California, Chihuahua, Sinaloa, Sonora, and Tepic in the north, and Campeche, Chiapas, and Tabasco in the south.[3] Many of these supposedly vacant public lands actually belonged to rural people—many of them Indians—who either lacked a proper title or had failed to navigate the disentailment process successfully. Privatization on this scale was controversial even in its own day, and nowhere more than in Chihuahua. In the Sierra Tarahumara, for example, the mere presence of engineers bearing transits and plumb bobs set Rarámuri communities on edge, and rumors of indigenous uprisings dogged survey teams in the highlands throughout 1883 and 1884.[4]

Threats to village commons also came from within. Villagers who had a bit of wealth or guile were in an ideal position to buy or swindle land from their neighbors. A new class of wealthy peasants appeared in many communities, as a handful of locals gained control of what had once been the commons but had now become private property. These sorts of imbalances occurred everywhere, but particularly in communities that tried to skirt privatization orders by titling the commons in the name of a respected local figure who would figure in the cadastral roles as a private landholder. This strategy rarely succeeded in the long run. Local authorities usually spotted the ruse, and even if it worked, the new village-approved "landowner" sometimes seized the commons for himself. In other cases, peasant communities found clever ways to create a collective corporation (usually known as a *condueñazgo*) that could legally own the land as a single entity without resorting to individual ownership, but this tactic also posed threats of malfeasance, loss to tax sale, or increasing economic differentiation.[5]

Despite these pressures, most villages retained at least some of their former commons. The privatization law made allowances for villages to retain their central townsite (the *fundo legal*), the extent of which villagers usually tried to keep deliberately vague. Some communities employed the "weapons of the weak" and complied with the privatization order slowly or incompletely. Others—particularly those in remote areas—succeeded in ignoring it altogether.

The conversion of village commons into private property was only the most obvious instance of a broader trend that gripped Mexico in the late nineteenth century in which a vast array of natural resources underwent a process of commodification. Foreign-owned mines extracted silver and copper in northern Mexico, converting subterranean ore into profits. British and North American interests arrived to the rainforests of northern Veracruz and converted what local people thought of as troublesome puddles of percolating oil into one of the world's premier petroleum industries. Along the way, the oilmen oversaw "the wholesale alienation of indigenous land and conversion of the lush forest into a revenue stream," in the words of the historian Myrna Santiago.[6] Water also became a source of discord. The Italian-born owners of Michoacán's most modern hacienda not only chipped away at the common lands of neighboring villages, they opened new agricultural land by draining the marsh that villagers had used for generations as a source of fish and reeds for weaving. The stakes were even higher in the state of Morelos, southwest of Mexico City, where burgeoning sugar haciendas needed a reliable source of water to irrigate their thirsty cane fields during the dry season. According to the historian Alejandro Tortolero, landowners sought and received concessions of river water, regardless of its implications for people who lived downstream; some expropriated village lands (or other haciendas) because they had reliable springs or wells. The resulting water crisis helped touch off Emiliano Zapata's revolutionary uprising in 1910.[7] By the first decade of the twentieth century, much of Mexico's "nature" had a price tag attached.

FORESTS AND PORFIRIAN PROGRESS

Forests were the most extensive ecosystems swept up by Porfirian development. People had always used the woods as a source of fuel and construction materials. Some had been subject to intensive logging for cooking fuel and construction materials even before the Spanish conquest in 1521. But logging on an industrial scale did not appear until the 1880s, when the Lenz family acquired the venerable Loreto y Peña Pobre mill and made it into the nation's primary producer of high-quality papers. San Rafael y Anexas, based in Mexico State, entered the newsprint business a few years later. Its two primary mills had their own electric generators and rail lines tended by a workforce of 2,000. By the turn of the century the company had cornered the newsprint market.[8] More than paper mills, however, it was railroads that drove industrialization in the woodlands. Porfirian progress relied on railroads to transport industrial ores, workers, and timber to distant markets, and the steel lines expanded to nearly every state in north-central Mexico. The nation had a mere 640 kilometers of railway when Díaz took power in 1876; by the time that revolutionaries pushed him from office, in 1911, there were 24,720 kilometers of track.[9] Railroad construction created immense demand for forest products in the form of ties, construction material for trestles, and fuel for engines. The transportation revolution also made it feasible to ship and sell timber on an increasingly broad scale. Landowners and a few enterprising foreigners formed the first logging companies around the turn of the century. By 1905, major international trusts moved into the untouched pine forests of Chihuahua and developed an industry capable of exporting wood to Mexican mining centers and markets in the United States; timbermen in heavily wooded states like Michoacán, Puebla, and Oaxaca contemplated jumping into the international trade as well.[10] At the opposite end of the country, the Yucatán henequen planters razed scrubby woodlands for their agave plants, while small-time timber magnates expanded from their longtime base in the rainforests of Tabasco into the great Lacandón jungle in search of mahogany for export to the United States and Europe.[11]

The emerging timber regime held some allure for rural people. Small numbers of Rarámuri headed down into the foothills to cut wood for railroad ties in Chihuahua, for example, and scores of villages in central Mexico made a few extra pesos by renting their commons to logging companies. Some even dabbled in the business on their own. For example, the villagers of Cuanajo, Michoacán, offered to pay part of their tax arrears by cutting trees suitable for use as telegraph poles from the village woodlot.[12] For the most part, however, commodification posed a threat to indigenous commons, as forests once considered communal property filtered into the hands of private interests. Conflicts broke out in villages throughout the country over ownership and the limits of customary use. The trees themselves became monetized and hence subject to laws and complex transactions, including long-term rental agreements that many village leaders willingly or unwillingly signed with timber contractors. For the first time ever, commercial logging denuded entire hillsides and jeopardized the economic and ecological foundations of some unlucky populations.

The scale of commercial logging eventually caught the attention of Mexico's intellectual elite. Scientists and civil engineers worried that deforestation might damage the nation's climate by reducing rainfall and possibly converting some regions into desert wastelands. Even if the rains continued to fall, some observers concluded that deforestation aggravated the severity of seasonal flooding. Without vegetation, soils eroded and precipitation could not soak into the ground as efficiently. Rainwater coursed across the barren ground and swelled rivers beyond their capacity. Led by the visionary civil engineer and forestry expert Miguel Ángel de Quevedo, a collection of polymath intellectuals called on the government to regulate the industry and protect the forests. They succeeded in creating the nation's first forest service and professional school, and they organized a reforestation campaign on the outskirts of Mexico City. Despite experts' growing sense of apprehension about logging, they rarely paused to consider its impact on the people who lived and worked in the forests. When they did take rural society into account, it was usually to excoriate peasants' misuse of the woods. They had already come to imagine the woods as spaces best suited for a regime of scientific management.

COMMODIFYING THE COMMONS IN MICHOACÁN

Michoacán did not experience the breakneck industrialization that overtook the border states and the Mexico City hinterlands, nor did the privatization of village commons permit landowners to subjugate indigenous peasants to the same extent as in other parts of the country, such as the

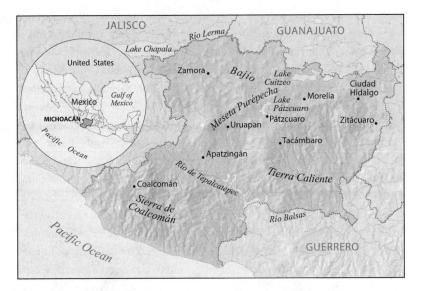

Map 1.1. Michoacán: Major Cities and Geographic Features

Yucatán. The disentailment of village commons and the halting pace of economic development nevertheless led to dispossession and to commercialization of land throughout the state. The woods were no exception. The commodification of Michoacán's forests began slowly and took place in relatively limited areas, most notably in the emerging timber heartlands around Ciudad Hidalgo and Uruapan, and then expanded alongside the railways. Most of the land caught up in this process belonged to poor rural people, although loggers also worked haciendas and federal land as well. For the rural poor, the commodification represented something of a puzzle. Most villagers preferred farmland and pastures to seemingly worthless timberland. Early conservationists lamented that peasants despised the woods and only wanted to clear the land for planting. Indeed, many villagers applauded the arrival of logging crews, particularly if they could hire on and earn a bit of money hauling logs or cutting trees. Since the most desirable agricultural land had been opened long before the nineteenth century, Porfirian deforestation did little to expand Michoacán's agriculture, and villagers soon realized that railroaders and timbermen paid little or nothing for the wood they harvested. It did not take long for most rural people to conclude that the commodification of forests represented more of a threat than an opportunity.

This was particularly true for native communities. By most estimates,

Michoacán was home to no fewer than 41,000 Purépecha at the turn of the twentieth century.[13] (Such seemingly precise numbers need to be taken with a grain of salt, however, because the category of "Indian" is notoriously mutable.) The Purépecha had peopled most of Michoacán and southern Jalisco in ancient times but had long since retreated to the pine-oak forests of Michoacán's northwestern highlands, known as the Meseta Purépecha (formerly called the Meseta Tarasca). They also settled in the warmer (and more deciduous) climes of the southern foothills centered on the town of Uruapan, as well as in some parts of the drier plains further north, around the town of Zamora. In addition, several thousand Nahua-speakers lived in the rolling Sierra de Coalcomán along the Pacific coast, where a large subhumid deciduous forest remained intact except where farmers had opened the land for planting. A larger number of Otomí had settled at the opposite end of the state during the colonial period. Driven westward by colonization, they had migrated to the rugged northeastern uplands around the Sierras of Chincua and Angangueo, where a rich diversity of oyamel fir (*Abies religiosa*), pines, and other conifers grew thickly despite the resurgence of mining in the area in the late nineteenth century.

Colonial authorities and most other outsiders had shown little interest in forests unless they flanked population centers or mines, so native people such as the Purépecha often tried to preserve their autonomy by retreating deeper into the woods. The strategy worked to some extent. Despite centuries of accommodation to European and Mexican rule, the Purépecha language continued to be widely spoken in the nineteenth century, and a substantial proportion of villagers (including most women) spoke no Spanish at all. Many native people preferred it that way. According to the Norwegian explorer Carl Lumholtz, who visited the Meseta Purépecha in the 1890s, the locals were "suspicious of all strangers and strenuously resist the intrusion of the Mexicans."[14] Yet native communities were not monolithic, unchanging cultural oases, and indigenous people had generations of experience with nonnative priests, politicians, merchants, muleteers, and others in their dealings with the outside world. Some had firsthand knowledge of the world outside their homes, which they had acquired on trips to the Pacific coast or interior cities, where they traded, worked, or visited out of curiosity. Others received formal education from the parish priest or, on rare occasions, from urban schools. Mestizos also settled in many of the native communities during the mid-nineteenth century, where they acquired land (legally or otherwise) or perhaps founded a modest enterprise such as a corn mill. Many of them married into one of the more prominent local families, and several communities ended up with minority populations of mixed-blood children. Some of these biracial people primarily identified with their indigenous peers, but most had at least one foot in the mestizo world beyond.

Forests figured prominently in Purépecha material culture and oral tradition. Folktales collected in the late nineteenth century associate the natural world with the goddess-mother Naná Cuerápperi, whose temple was located in the midst of a dense wood. In secular terms, however, the forest was a male space that Purépecha kings regarded as their own property. Young nobles proved themselves by hunting deer and jaguar in the deep forest, or in some instances by wooing their lovers there. The hero-king Sicuir-Achá hunted days on end before he learned that a treacherous band of upstarts sought to make the forest their own. He tracked them down and defeated them with the help of his father, proving his masculinity and fitness to rule.[15] On a more prosaic level, the Purépecha knew how to bleed certain species of trees to make medicines and other useful products. They put wood to a variety of uses, including handicrafts, which by the late colonial period included the famous guitars built in Paracho. They also used it for fuel and for building cabins known as *trojes* that are still visible in some places today. These homes had wooden floors and walls, a single door, and high-pitched roofs shingled with thin pine planks known as *tejamanil*. The forest remained a gendered space into the nineteenth century. Men typically left their wives at home and ventured into the woods to cut wood that they sold to complement the family income. Lumholtz reported that men from Parangaricutiro hiked into the forests at the base of Tancítaro and camped there "for weeks while making wooden troughs and spoons, and especially the shingles with which their houses are roofed."[16]

That is not to say that Purépecha or any other native people possessed some sort of innate ecological awareness. Even before the Spanish arrived, Purépecha kings found it necessary to appoint guards to keep villagers from decimating forests for firewood and construction materials. In the nineteenth century, communities tenaciously defended their woods from outsiders, yet some customary practices became ecologically harmful as the land available to them diminished. For example, swidden agriculture (opening a field by slash-and-burn, sowing it for a few seasons, then shifting to a new location and leaving the old field fallow for five years or so), while not as inherently destructive as most nineteenth-century observers believed, could nonetheless degrade the land if not executed properly. Some observers pointed out that the fires villagers set to "boil" the land in preparation for planting sometimes burned too intensely and harmed the rich layer of humus necessary for plants to grow; in other cases, population pressure or the loss of common land encouraged farmers to return to old clearings before the soil had fully recovered.[17] Likewise, woodcutters making tejamanil often cut deeply into the heartwood of several different trees before settling on one with the right timber to make shingles. The process left behind scores of wounded trees that usually died within a year.[18] And while some Purépecha people managed their woods carefully, it is clear that others took a short-term view. For example, many of the men in Capácuaro made a living by selling wood to their neighbors, but they cut trees in such vast quantities that villagers in that region worried the woods might disappear altogether. To make matters worse, Capácuaro's headman signed a rental agreement with a timber company in the 1880s without telling anyone.[19] In this case, and perhaps many others, the commodification of forests exposed the incipient social divisions among native people and drove a wedge between neighboring communities.

Commodification also created tensions between native and nonnative people. In 1873, Michoacán's most prominent agronomist reported that the value of forests had begun to rise as a result of industrial development. So rapidly did forests yield to woodsmen's axes that he worried they might vanish altogether if legislators did not pass "a wise policy of conservation."[20] Economic development was only one cause of forest commodification (and overexploitation), however. Disentailment—the official mandate to divide common land and title it as individual, privately owned parcels—also paved the way for the emerging market in forestlands by giving outsiders unprecedented access to terrain that had previously been off-limits. Most native people had little experience with fee simple land ownership, and they found it difficult to resist the economic and legal maneuverings of loggers who set their sights on native woods. Loggers used several strategies to acquire woods in the turbulent era of Porfirian privatization. In the case of Carapan, one logger arrived soon after villagers had privatized the commons and offered to buy or lease logging rights from the new landowners, but he offered only a fraction of its real value. In another case, that of Parangaricutiro, well-off mestizo setters managed to claim possession of some or all the commons and rent it out to sawmills.[21] Even though the fixing of precise boundary lines between adjacent villages had been a problem for generations, the conversion of woods into a commodity that could be bought, sold, and rented added a new element of competition and uncertainty to rural life. Conflicts between neighboring communities—or "ex-communities" as they were often labeled once they had subdivided their common lands—was often the first sign that agents from timber companies had arrived in the area and begun offering cash for the right to cut timber.[22]

Like other parts of the nation, nineteenth-century urbanization in Michoacán created a demand for construction materials, while new technologies demanded forest products for use as electrical poles and turpentine for streetlights.[23] Cities had always generated a market for charcoal and firewood for domestic use, but the increasing rate of urbanization in the late nineteenth century accentuated the demand as never before. The agronomist Gabriel Hinojosa calculated that Morelia alone used about 30,000 kilograms of charcoal per day in 1873, which translated into an annual consumption of 2.4 million *arrobas* (2.8 million metric tons) of wood per year.[24] Within a few decades, charcoal makers began delivering their wares to railheads, where they were transported to regional cities and growing metropolises like Mexico City and Guadalajara. Even people in the remote hamlet of Acachuén, a quarter-day's walk from the modest township of Chilchota, began to cut trees to make charcoal for sale in the markets of Zamora.[25] Forests in the hinterlands had always suffered from overuse, but the appearance of railroads meant that more distant ones also began to feel the effects as charcoal makers began to selectively cut hardwoods, such as oak, that urban consumers demanded.

A LANDSCAPE OF RAIL AND TIMBER

Railroads may have been the linchpin of Mexican industrialism, but they initially bypassed Michoacán. The state produced valuable commodities such as sugar from the *tierra caliente* lowlands in the Tepalcatepec Valley and silver in the Angangueo-Tlalpujahua region, yet these did not have enough economic magnetism to attract the steel rails without the use of uncommonly generous concessions. That practice began in 1877, when the newly installed Díaz administration elected to placate local business interests and granted the Palmer and Sullivan Company a contract to build a branch line connecting Morelia to the national corridor. Much to the dismay of Morelia's business class, another five years passed before construction made any headway. The line arrived to the grain-producing town of Maravatío in 1883, thanks in part to its location near the main line in Guanajuato. Two years later, engines finally puffed into Morelia. Over the next fifteen years, rails linked every major city and economic region of Michoacán, including as many as three lines moving to the sparsely populated Pacific coast.[26]

Railroad companies preferred to acquire the wood for ties, trestles, and fuel as close to the line as possible, and concession contracts were written to accommodate them. An agreement penned in 1893 with the Michoacán y Pacífico was typical. In exchange for building and operating a railway between the eastern towns of Yurécuaro and Los Reyes, the federal government granted the company permission "to take from the public lands and rivers the materials of every kind which may be necessary for the construction, operation, and repair of the road" without making any payment. The railroad could also take whatever resources it needed from private landowners as long as it paid an indemnity "in conformity with the respective laws and regulations."[27] Yet the distinction between public and private lands was not always clear, particularly when villages were in the process of privatizing their commons, nor did everyone agree on the definition of appropriate indemnification for landowners. The Yurécuaro-Los Reyes administrators turned these murky legal conditions to their advantage. They identified the forests of La Cañada (a heavily indigenous collection of eleven pueblos east of Zamora) as the best source of wood, but the native communities had never privatized their woodlots. So railroad crews simply cut wood as they pleased and made token payments to village headmen. By 1900, logging crews had harvested all of the large trees in La Cañada and villagers had little to show for it.[28]

Railroad contractors' usual practice was to rent or buy a convenient parcel of land, build a small sawmill, then acquire logging rights to the adjacent properties. Lumberjacks set up temporary camps where they planned to cut, while contractors rode into nearby communities to deal with private landowners or village headmen. If a contractor determined (with or without due diligence) that the logging camp had set up on federal property, he might not even make such a gesture. Lumberjacks typically cut all the wood within a convenient radius of the mill, leaving few trees standing. The results could be ruinous for village forests. When workers laying a section of track for the Pátzcuaro-Uruapan line arrived in the Purépecha community of San Lorenzo in 1899, for example, they handed some coins to the village headman and proceeded to clearcut all the woods they could reach. They finished off the communal lands within a year, then disassembled the sawmill and moved on. San Lorenzo's woods took six decades to recover.[29]

The railroads also made fortunes for a handful of Michoacán timber

Figure 1.1. Ajuno-Ario de Rosales Railway, ca. 1910. The firewood stacked in the foreground is fuel, as the tender filled with firewood suggests. Universidad Michoacana San Nicolás de Hidalgo, Instituto de Investigaciones Históricas, Sánchez Díaz Collection.

families, beginning with the Solís clan of Ciudad Hidalgo. In 1886, family patriarch Pomposo Solís and his associate Aquiles de la Peña installed what was probably the first modern sawmill in Michoacán, which they used to cut ties for the original spur line into Morelia. Once that project was complete, they supplied most of the wood for a new line that snaked up to the gold and silver mines in the Sierra de Angangueo and into the mountain town of Zitácuaro. Solís eventually decided to test the Mexico City market, which needed wood for fuel and construction material. Foresters later estimated that his loggers removed about twenty million cubic meters of wood from the woods around Ciudad Hidalgo during the Porfiriato.[30] Solís and his partners used the profits from logging to buy the sprawling Chaporro hacienda, which held some of the region's best stands of timber. Once they had logged it out, they leased timber rights from smallholders and villages with common lands, often for a pittance. Many of these people eventually sold their property to the Solís family or became their clients. A substantial minority of them ended up working as woodcutters, muleteers, or charcoal makers. They became Michoacán's first real timber proletariat as the Solís family business grew into a regional economic mainstay in the early twentieth century.[31]

Timbermen from the United States and Great Britain arrived in Michoacán during the final years of the nineteenth century with money in hand to build larger sawmills and sign long-term lease agreements with native communities. The most visible of the new generation of adventurers was Santiago Slade, a civil engineer from the U.S. state of Georgia who married into a wealthy Uruapan family and built a timber empire that endured for a quarter century. In 1899 he founded the first of four well-capitalized timber companies that he owned over the course of his career. Two years later, he and two North American partners formed the Compañía Nacional de Maderas and bought the Las Palomas sawmill in nearby Capácuaro for the impressive sum of 54,700 pesos, enough to buy a modest hacienda at the time. The new company acquired not only the machinery and livestock for hauling timber, but the logging rights to four communities in the municipal district.[32] The following year, Slade successfully lobbied in Mexico City for a concession to build a branch rail line to connect the Las Palomas sawmill to the Mexican National mainline to the east.[33]

The Sierra de Coalcomán in the state's northwest also attracted the interest of foreign companies. In 1908 investors from Philadelphia incorporated the Pacific Timber Company just outside of the town of Coalcomán. The company's U.S. manager began snapping up property and assembled 40,000 acres of timberland in a matter of months.[34] These woods had once formed the town commons of Coalcomán and that of its satellite villages, but had since been privatized in accordance with the disentailment law. Some villagers willingly sold to the company, but at least one landowner refused to let go of his parcel until the court ordered him to hand his title over to Pacific Timber. Villagers from the Nahua community Pómaro viewed the company's offers with less enthusiasm than the others, leading regional political authorities to demand their compliance.[35] Since the region lacked rail lines, or even roads, the company hired workers to build a canal from its sawmill in the Sierra de Coalcomán to the Guagua River, which allowed it to float the logs to a railhead downstream. The company paid far better wages than did any other employer in the region, and at least some villagers abandoned agriculture to take jobs cutting and hauling timber. The foreigners never won the sympathy of the local population, however, and the entire project ground to a halt in 1911, after a worker killed the canal works' "despotic" American manager.[36]

Logging rights appear to have been these companies' most valuable asset. Santiago Slade, for one, did not shy away from pulling strings or strong-arming the locals to lock up access to timberlands. He arranged for Governor Aristeo Mercado to help the company acquire logging rights upland from Uruapan, in the area around Cherán. The company also tried to wrest control of the rich communal woodlands from the Purépecha community of San Juan Parangaricutiro as well. When village leaders refused to grant sign a lease agreement, Slade got around the problem with fraudulent contracts, penned in 1907, with two prominent families who lived in town (one a mestizo family, the other a Hispanized indigenous one). Villagers quickly got wind of the ploy and barred the loggers from entering their woods. Community leaders refused to accept the "rental" payments that company agents tried to foist on them or just about anyone else willing to take the money, even after municipal authorities threatened to jail anyone who refused to accept the disbursements. The standoff continued for two years, until Slade opted for more direct measures. His men attacked Parangaricutiro and burned half the houses to the ground in 1909, the year that locals called the "año del quemazón," or the year of the inferno. Even thereafter, they obstinately refused to allow the loggers onto their woods, and eventually the revolution focused Slade's attention elsewhere.[37] The entire event became so embedded in local lore that community authorities could still recall the details of the incident seventy years later.[38]

Slade competed fiercely against rivals like the García family of Nurio and Vicente Bravo of Cheranhuátzicuirin for logging rights in northwestern Michoacán. As early as 1902, he began using shady means to obtain rental agreements for forests in the indigenous villages around Uruapan. Most often, he either paid off village leaders or treated them to a stint in jail if they refused to sign. If that did not work, the loggers could always arrange for the local prefect to designate a more pliant community representative.[39] Once the paperwork was in order, logging companies such as Slade's made modest payments of "a few coins" to the village coffers in order to create the appearance of legitimacy. Native people needed the silver more than ever, since the logging contracts prohibited them from such traditional cash-generating activities as charcoal making and selling tejamanil shingles (presumably because these practices used the wood that the company wanted for itself). Villagers could not easily seek relief from the courts because the company had most judges and municipal authorities in its pocket. By the final years of the Porfiriato, the competition over logging rights in the Meseta Purépecha had reached a frenzied pace. Discontent with fraudulent rental agreements had spread everywhere, but those who protested when loggers moved into their lands were routinely threatened, beaten, jailed, or impressed into the federal army.[40] Not only had the woods become commodities; they had become contested spaces.

NEOCOLONIALISM AND NATURE IN CHIHUAHUA

The process of industrialization and commodification overtook Michoacán slowly, but it washed over Chihuahua like a flash flood. Proximity to the United States made Chihuahua's mines and forests an attractive target for North American investors, particularly once the Chiricahua Apache leader Geronimo surrendered in 1886 and brought an end to six decades of investment-inhibiting Native American resistance. Like other border states, Chihuahua's economy boomed thanks to mining, railroads, and commercial agriculture. Cattle barons like Luis Terrazas and the U.S. newspaper magnate William Randolph Hearst snapped up vast expanses of grassland, and silver mines prospered in the Bocoyna region for the first time since independence.[41] Unlike other border states, Chihuahua also possessed immense and virtually untouched forest resources that appealed to railroad and mining companies hungry for fuel, ties, and telegraph poles. The growth of cities in the Mexican north and as far away as Texas grew the market for lumber and other construction material. The cattlemen, bankers, and politicos who held levers of power in Porfirian Chihuahua typically had family and business ties on both sides of the border, and they rushed to test the potential of international trade in forest products.

Unlike the mines in the nearby states of Sonora and Arizona, which extracted industrial ores, Chihuahuan mines mostly produced precious metals. Silver had attracted Spanish settlers northward during the colonial era, but easily worked veins grew scarce in the eighteenth century. Mining virtually ground to a halt during the wars of independence in the 1810s and remained in the doldrums until American colonist-miners reversed the trend during the Porfiriato. The primary authors of the turnaround were John Robinson and his successor Alexander "Boss" Shepherd, who successively acquired the rights to a legendary silver vein in the southwestern town of Batopilas. Shepherd was a shady developer whose fortunes took a dive after accusations that he had accepted kickbacks for construction projects in Washington during the Grant administration. He and his family arrived in the sierras in 1880 and took up residence in the Hacienda San Miguel, which served as headquarters for the Batopilas Mining Company and as a sumptuous but fortress-like family compound. He imported

Map 1.2. Chihuahua: Major Cities and Geographic Features

modern machines and demanded both discipline and allegiance from his workers. For a while, Batopilas became a typical borderlands mining town, where American foremen supervised mestizo and indigenous workers who arrived at the mine to make a living or maybe just to break away from village life.[42]

The excavation of ore and dirt had a predictably harmful impact on the environment. Tailings frequently washed into the river that served as the town's main water supply, for example, and the townspeople in Batopilas complained in 1901 that they had turned the river "as white as milk and as thick as *atole* [cornmeal porridge]." Residents considered the river poisonous, infectious, and fetid, especially when it slowed to a trickle during the dry season. Shepherd's own doctor allegedly told townsfolk not to drink from it, though Boss Shepherd confidently maintained that the cloudy water was actually healthier now that it had been fortified with minerals.[43] The company started using cyanide in the refining process in the 1880s, apparently because nearby gold mines had successfully mastered the MacArthur-Forrest cyanide amalgamation technique. The presence of the deadly poison so close to the town's primary water supply helps to explain the repeated health scares during the early 1900s.[44] Moreover, mines swallowed huge amounts of wood for mineshaft beams and ties for ore-cart lines (both of which required periodic replacement), as well as fuel for machinery and the refining process. Woodcutters had already stripped nearby forests in the mid-nineteenth century, so they needed to venture further afield to find stands of viable timber by the time Shepherd came on the scene.[45] The shortages had grown so desperate by 1900 that the company hired a professional forester from the United States whose job was to select the best woods to use for construction and as fuel for steam engines. As it turned out, he had only a rudimentary understanding of the northern Mexican ecosystem and thus had trouble identifying certain species of trees in the sierras and seemed unsure of the biological charac-teristics of the ones that he did recognize.[46]

Like the mining company, foreign-owned railroads initially bought timber for construction. There were tracks and trestles to build, and steam engines that needed fuel. As in Michoacán, many of these companies received concessions to log "public" lands, particularly in Indian country. Unlike the case in Michoacán, some railroad companies planned entire rail lines with the explicit goal of creating a binational timber industry.

Three railroads launched between 1896 and 1899 made the mineral, cattle, and above all timber resources of the Sierra Tarahumara available to markets in Mexico and the United States. The first to lay track was Chihuahua and Pacific, a company launched by a consortium of New York investors to make the great timberlands of the sierras accessible from Chi-huahua City.[47] Its owners gushed about the "immense tracts of pine and oak timber" that awaited cutting, which would also open the prairies and the broad mesas to cattle ranching.[48] The business plan did have one hitch, however: although the railroad company would be able to harvest enough wood for its own construction needs, no major timber companies existed in Chihuahua that could market the rest. In response, the manager of the Chihuahua and Pacific invited Governor Enrique Creel (whose family was not coincidentally one of the major stockholders in the railroad) to a din-ner in New York City, where he introduced him to Frank Morrill Murphy, the Arizona-based director of a mining and railroad syndicate known as the Development Company of America. Having grown up in sawmill towns of the Midwest, Morrill knew good timber when he saw it.[49] With Creel's help, his company paid half a million dollars for 300,000 hectares on the eastern slope of the Sierra Tarahumara rumored to hold some of Mexico's most valuable forests. The crew that had scouted the land, known as the García tract, described finding yellow pines that measured four feet in diameter at the trunk and towered up to seventy feet "without a limb to mar their symmetry."[50] The lower altitudes also held commercially valuable species, including oak, maple, ash, walnut, cedar, juniper, and sycamore. White pine, fir, and spruce could be found at the highest elevations. In all, the timbermen arrived at the unlikely estimate that the García Tract held three billion board feet—more than enough to build a railway from Chihuahua to Saint Louis—which the Development Company of America intended to log off completely within a quarter of a century.[51]

Murphy planned to ship the timber to Arizona and use it in his railroad and mining interests there, but the high cost of transport made the venture untenable. Within a few years, he transferred most of his land to the adventurer-capitalist William C. Greene, who needed a reliable source of wood for his famous Cananea copper mine in the neighboring state of Sonora. Greene founded the Sierra Madre Land and Lumber Company with capital borrowed from Terrazas-owned banks and began logging in late 1904. Within a year, the company had nine small sawmills up and running. Although most of Greene's empire collapsed soon thereafter, the Land and Lumber Company soldiered on and built the first industrial sawmill in the sierras, sited in a newly built town appropriately named Madera (Spanish for "wood"). A modest installation capable of sawing a mere 10,000 board feet per day, it performed well enough that investors approved the construction of a new mill with fifty times the capacity.[52] Other foreign interests moved in as well. In 1906 the Minnesota-based Cargill Lumber Company bought 182,000 hectares of land that Minister of the Economy (Hacienda) José Yves Limantour and his brother Julio had acquired in the Guerrero and Absolo districts a decade earlier. The company president, W. W. Cargill, approved the deal for 642,772 pesos (around $8 million in 2010 terms) after touring the area in person. The company began cutting trees in Bocoyna soon afterward, despite the local population's sometimes violent resistance. Cargill idled his mills when the U.S. economy soured the following year, however, and they never reopened.[53]

Meanwhile, the railroads continued to consume wood at a faster-than-expected pace. One problem was fire. Few Chihuahuan railways fitted their rolling stock with spark arrestors, the iconic bowl-like extension that topped most steam engines' smokestacks and kept embers from shooting into the air. Most U.S. states required railroads to install spark arrestors by the 1880s, but Mexico did not enforce their use south of the border. As late as 1912, the administrator of William Randolph Hearst's Babícora hacienda complained that improperly equipped trains spewed embers and caused fires that destroyed large swaths of woodland every year.[54] Moreover, railroads continued to use wood for fuel even when coal became available. Reeling from the market crash known as the Bankers' Panic of 1907, the Chihuahua and Pacific deliberately chose not to convert its rolling stock to coal because it wanted to maintain the demand for fuelwood. The railroad was entirely dependent on the timber industry because the anticipated boom in ranching never materialized in southern Chihuahua. Managers of the under-used railway even offered to haul timber at cost through 1908.[55]

The following year, a new consortium of investors consolidated most of these rail and timber companies into a single, vertically integrated trust, which had been assembled by the entrepreneur Fred Stark Pearson and his Canadian partner James H. Dunn. Backed by many of the same patrons as the old Chihuahua and Pacific, the new syndicate took control of nearly all the track along the Sierra Tarahumara foothills and christened them the Mexico North Western Railway. The consortium acquired Greene's forest properties (and what remained of Murphy's, as well as some smaller tracts) and the partially completed sawmill, all of which became assets of a newly chartered corporation called the Madera Lumber Company. By 1910, it had assembled over 600,000 hectares of its own land and acquired the rights to 90,000 more. All told, this gave the new company access to over 2,600 square miles of virtually untouched timber.[56] The state legislature declared that the company performed a "public service" (*utilidad pública*) and granted it a thirty-year tax exemption, in exchange for which company owners agreed to redouble their investments in the firm. In 1910 the company built a sawmill in the newly settled town of Pearson (now Mata Ortiz) and invested four million dollars in the existing Madera plant, which employed a workforce of over fifteen hundred Mexicans, Chinese, and North Americans. The company turned a healthy profit that year, though foresters later observed that it did so via uncontrolled logging along the most easily accessible railroad trunk lines.[57] By that point, the company's trains were hauling sawlogs out of the mountains as fast as lumberjacks could cut them. The wood was dried, sawed, and sent north to El Paso. From there, it supplied markets as far away as the U.S. East Coast. By the eve of the revolution, the timber industry was Chihuahua's largest employer, and speculators from both sides of the border rushed to buy whatever timberland they could find in anticipation of the boom times to come.[58]

Figure 1.2. Madera Lumber Company sawmill, ca. 1910. Photograph by Gertrude Fitzgerald. University of Texas at El Paso Library, Special Collections Department, Gertrude Fitzgerald Photographs, PH025.

Local observers felt less sanguine about the trade in forest products. An editorial published in a Chihuahua City newspaper in November 1910—only a few days before the date that Francisco I. Madero had set for an uprising against the Díaz regime—pointed out that logging had become one of the state's most important industries virtually overnight and employed thousands of North American and Mexican workers. Yet the foreign interests logged forests ruthlessly. The paper complained about the "savage" way the foreigners used the land, "seeking to make a quick profit, heedless that today's greed might be the root of tomorrow's misery."[59] The newspaper did not object to the commercialization of the forests per se, but gave voice to a growing sense of misgiving about its social and environmental costs.

THE ECOLOGY OF COMMODIFICATION

When he first arrived in Batopilas, Boss Shepherd sent logging crews to cut wood on the hillsides that surrounded his mines, just as his predecessors had done. In the early years, he followed the existing custom of allowing locals to follow the logging crews and collect the debris that the lumberjacks left behind. This arrangement was the linchpin of a modest local economy in which wood gatherers, usually coaxing along a half-lame donkey or two, made a very modest living collecting the debris and excavating trunks of larger trees, which they either sold to charcoal makers or cured themselves and sold in town. By late 1880, however, the scarcity of wood and increasingly inflexible enforcement of property rights began to jeopardize this marginal industry. In 1887 Batopilas woodcutters learned that times had changed when company logging crews began to collect the debris (known as slash) after cutting. Soon, firewood became scarce in the mining town, and property owners everywhere began charging a fee to gather firewood in the hills.[60] This turn of events came as a shock to the wood gatherers the mining company charged with trespassing on its woodlots outside of town, none of whom understood property rights the same way as Boss Shepherd did. Refugio Hernández told the court that he made a living by salvaging wood from the slash heaps in the mountains and that "no one had ever prohibited the public from using the woodlands." Although he had "never hesitated to cut firewood" before the trespassing charge, he reluctantly agreed to ask permission before gathering wood again. Another woodcutter said, "Everyone knows that anyone can use the wood up there." Since he owned only one mule that could not move much wood, he had no idea that he wasn't supposed to fell a few trees or pick up slash on company lands. A final wood thief, seventy-year-old José María Meza, said that he spent much of the week helping out the company "as a neighbor," in exchange for which he expected to cut wood on the company's land. He seemed bewildered that the company would break what he understood as its customary reciprocity with country people and begrudge him access to the timber debris, which were his only source of income.[61] The mining company's lawyers easily dispatched such arguments by pointing out that it had the sole legal authority to decide who could use its land. Within a few years, the company declared timber off-limits even to its own renters. After 1900, only the company's own lumberjacks (and the independent woodcutters they hired) were allowed onto the mountainside.[62]

The company's sudden interest in asserting control over the timber coincided with its owners' expanded claims over natural resources in general, including not only ore and timber, but river water as well. One reason for this shift had to do with simple economics: as wood grew scarce and railroads pushed into the sierras, good timber acquired an unprecedented monetary value. It made good business sense to cut potential rivals out of

Figure 1.3. Gathering wood to make charcoal, ca. 1896.
Photograph by C. B. Waite. Smithsonian Institution,
National Anthropological Archives, item 00846200.

the fuelwood business. But perhaps Shepherd had other motives as well. Could he have intentionally elected to stake a stronger symbolic claim over natural resources? It seems likely that Shepherd meant to use his status as landowner to impose a new kind of moral economy in Batopilas, one in which the mining company—and the Porfirian order it represented—had the sole prerogative to arbitrate between the woodsmen and the forest. If so, his gesture reflected a determination to shift from a social order based on a symbolic relationship of neighborliness and the collective use of common lands, to a more impersonal regime of property rights, markets, and individual ownership associated with political liberalism.

Such an interpretation would help explain why the commodification of forests occurred not only in the commercial world of railroads and mining centers, but also in more out-of-the way places. For example, indigenous woodsmen from the community of Huáchara, in what is now the district of Urique, found themselves in a similar situation to their counterparts in Batopilas. They had lost their commons to a survey company early in the twentieth century, though the land eventually reverted to the federal government. In 1909 the independent silver miner (*gambusino*) and future revolutionary Rafael Becerra, who had a license to work the federal property, asked the authorities to punish some Rarámuri men who still treated the territory as if they owned it. Municipal officials responded by ordering one of Becerra's own employees to investigate the situation. Predictably, the authorities sided with the miner and ordered the indigenous men out of the area.[63]

The commodification of Chihuahua's forests posed the most serious threat to Rarámuri autonomy in generations. Thick woods and harsh terrain had sheltered most Rarámuri against colonialism precisely because it discouraged outsiders from venturing into the sierras, especially after a series of seventeenth-century rebellions sent silver miners and Jesuit missionaries scurrying away. The chastened Jesuits returned in the 1670s and once again began to baptize converts, some of whom settled on missions that gave Christianized natives a measure of protection from forced work in the silver mines to the south. Other Rarámuri rebuffed Hispanic society altogether and withdrew deeper and northward into the forest, where their main contact with outsiders came through trade.[64] No matter which strategy the Rarámuri followed, the forests also helped them to avoid Jesuits' admonitions to settle in compact, European-style townships; then, as now, most native people in the Chihuahua highlands lived in widely scattered and semiautonomous family compounds known as *rancherías* spaced half a kilometer or more from each other. The tendency to disperse took such deep root that the mestizos who arrived in the area in the eighteenth and nineteenth centuries followed suit, and few actual towns appeared in the Sierra Tarahumara until the 1950s.[65] That is not to say that the Rarámuri did not interact with each other. Native people gathered to contribute collective labor on each other's land, and they traveled to the nearest churchyard on Sundays to hear mass, particularly during Holy Week. After the service, men assembled to debate issues confronting their pueblo; three or more of them might also hold court to adjudicate any conflicts and stand in judgment of petty thieves, adulterers, and others who had transgressed the law or local customs. Corn beer (*tesgüino*) invariably flowed liberally at these gatherings. The men served themselves first, while women stood at the margins until they, too, received their share of the drink. These semi-ritual festivals, known as *tesgüinadas*, usually stretched through the afternoon and into the evening. Guitars and violins marked time as couples danced. Acquaintances floated into conversation or revived an old argument. As alcohol broke down social barriers, men sometimes fell into vicious fights, while couples sneaked away for illicit sex.[66]

Most of the 40,000 Rarámuri who dwelled in the Sierra Tarahumara in 1900 followed the same subsistence strategy that their ancestors had adopted in the colonial era based on a managed ecology of goats and maize.[67] Corn was the staple food, but it fares poorly in the high, cold sierras without fertilizers of some sort. The Rarámuri solved this problem by collecting manure from their herds of goats and spreading it on the fields with the first spring rains. The goats (and a smaller population of sheep) also produced wool, which women loomed inside their houses. The animals represented most families' primary source of capital, and young boys tended the animals as they foraged on the scrubby grasses that grew in clearings or browsed on tender shoots of young pine trees. In the winter, highlands families reunited and herded their goats to the warmer valley floors. They spent the coldest months in caves outfitted with ingenious venting systems that allowed fires to burn continually. These caves seemed so accommodating that outsiders sometimes mistook them for permanent dwellings. Once the weather improved, the families gathered their few possessions, along with their hunting dogs and goats, and returned to the higher elevation where the annual cycle began once again.[68]

The Rarámuri had a reputation as expert woodsmen. They gave specific names to each of the six species of oak that grew in the sierras, for example, and devised uses for pines ranging from construction to torches for nighttime travel. They wove grass collected in the forest understory into high-crowned hats, although later generations abandoned this tradition and adopted bandannas as their preferred headwear. Pine pitch was used to treat rattlesnake bites or foot injuries incurred during the epic footraces for which they were (and are) famous. The American anthropologists Wendell Bennett and Robert Zingg visited the sierras in the early 1930s and reported that the natives wielded steel axes more quickly and efficiently than lumberjacks could use modern saws. Native men carefully appraised trees before felling them, then split them into roofing poles and boards for wooden houses known as *galíki*, which they could build communally in the course of a single day and then consecrate with a tesgüinada that night. They also used wood for fences as well as for storehouses, which were notched together with so much precision that they kept rats and squirrels away from the prized stockpile of maize. Many also tended small orchards of apple trees, which bore fruit for the Rarámuri to eat or sell.[69] When they needed to open new land for planting, indigenous men usually girdled trees with axes, waited for them to die, and then burned them, a process that returned some of their nutrients to the soil. Most people believed that the smoke rising from the flames helped to form rainclouds and promised a year of abundant rains.[70]

The Rarámuri were not trapped in cultural amber while the world changed around them. They had traveled to the mines during the colonial period, and most of them tentatively accepted Jesuits and their messages about Christianity. A few had encountered President Benito Juárez, who had fled to Chihuahua during the French intervention of 1861–1867; decades later, their descendants often reminded authorities that Juárez had pledged to protect their land from outsiders. None of these experiences brought as much change to the sierras as did the advent of Porfirian progress, however. The renaissance of mining encouraged new patterns of migration as hundreds of Rarámuri traveled alone or as families southward to the Batopilas area, where they took bottom-rung jobs hauling rock or crushing stones. Others traveled to the logging camps around Madera looking for work.[71] Mestizos and acculturated Indians, whom the Rarámuri called *chabochi*, began to settle in the woods, bringing a new round of cultural change. A barely literate schoolteacher who was posted to Cusárare in 1895, for example, reported that his anti-alcoholism campaign had angered many locals, who accused him of dishonoring the tesgüinada. He nonetheless reported that he won over some people.[72] Other settlers in Rarámuri country had less humanitarian motives. Most mestizos regarded native land as unclaimed property and the local people as indolent barbarians best suited for hard labor, ideally of the unpaid variety. They had the reputation of expecting the Rarámuri to behave as servants who could run errands, provide alcohol, or perhaps offer sexual diversion. Some settlers arrived with cattle that they let roam freely and graze on the native people's carefully tended crops.[73]

The most serious threat to native commons no doubt came from the railroad and mining trusts, particularly the Madera Lumber Company whose landholdings included the northern reaches of Rarámuri territory. It is unlikely most communities could have survived had loggers cleared woods and replaced them with cattle ranches. Once the loggers had finished off the more northerly forests, they would doubtless have cast their sights southward to the Rarámuri heartland. But the loggers never had the chance. Even before the revolution put a temporary halt to commercial logging in the 1910s, Mexico City's scientific elite sounded the alarm about the environmental consequences of unregulated logging.

CONSERVATION AND THE BIRTH OF SCIENTIFIC FORESTRY

For most of the nineteenth century, the management and conservation of forests fell under the competency of city governments (*ayuntamientos* and *municipios*). Spanish precedent had explicitly charged local authorities with managing woods and waters in their respective jurisdictions, and Mexico's first governments saw no reason to change these regulations after independence. As late as 1855, Antonio López de Santa Anna reiterated that local officials should manage Mexico's "woods, forests, and groves," and he charged them with protecting and conserving forestlands as "the ancient laws" demanded.[74] In subsequent decades, the federal government reversed course and began to exert control over the woods (as well as rivers and other sources of water), culminating with the Porfirian state's "federalization" of resource management in the final years of the nineteenth century.[75]

The assertion of federal authority owed its success in no small part to Díaz's broader consolidation of administrative power. Post-independence turmoil culminated with a brutal civil war known as the War of the Reform (1857–1861), followed by the French neocolonial adventure that briefly transformed the nation into an empire ruled by a Hapsburg prince, between 1864 and 1867. In these circumstances, President Benito Juárez had a few opportunities to confront the trade in mahogany and tropical cedar extracted from rainforests in the southeastern state of Tabasco. The federal government had placed a tax on the export of precious timber in 1854, but it was rarely collected. In 1861 the Juárez administration passed comprehensive regulations governing forests on federal land, with a particular eye to reining in the lucrative hardwood trade. The new regulations demanded that logging companies register their claims to public land with the regional delegate of the Ministry of Development (Fomento), pay the requisite taxes, and replant ten seedlings for every mahogany or tropical cedar tree they cut. The ministry's regional delegates were charged with making an annual inspection of logging camps to prevent "harm to national property" and with staffing every municipal district with forestry personnel, including sub-inspectors and forest wardens, the latter of whom "preferably would be natives [*naturales*] of that place who have both the integrity and the knowledge of the land necessary for their post, and who would be required to arm themselves with a rifle or long knife."[76] The few wardens hired at this point found themselves hopelessly overextended and did little if anything to curb the Tabasco mahogany bosses' legendary abuses of their workers and the environment.[77]

The Díaz administration reiterated these regulations in 1881, but tacitly acknowledged that they lacked traction. The following year it sent a circular to the nation's governors reminding them of the law and ordering them to crack down on charcoal manufacturers who cut live trees to make their wares. In 1888 the Ministry of Development made yet another stab at gaining control of the forest trade, this time by requiring the masters of ships that traded in precious woods to create escrow accounts subject to forfeiture if contraband were discovered onboard. They were dead letters all.[78]

Trade in commercially harvested timber more than tripled between 1890 and 1900 thanks to the advent of huge railroad concessions in the north and the ongoing mahogany trade in the far south.[79] Logging expanded so rapidly—and remained so firmly in foreign hands—that legislators and conservationists agreed that the time had come to establish clearer limits. The Díaz administration published a law in 1892 that restricted access to the forests surrounding Mexico City, although these regulations, too, were roundly ignored. Two years later, the government created new guidelines for logging on federal land, including terrenos baldíos (the ostensibly vacant public lands that, in many cases, were home to native peoples). The legislation created a new category of "agents" charged with managing these "vacant" lands, and it reaffirmed the duties of forest wardens and sub-inspectors, who were now tasked as well with identifying species that could be used for afforestation, combating forest fires, and keeping livestock from damaging regrowth. The law detailed the responsibilities of companies working on federal land and instructed them to cut only those trees that sub-inspectors had marked both above and below the cut-line with a special hammer, and to use mature trees only after removing any branches that could damage others as they fell. Despite this elegant legislation, very few wardens actually inspected logging sites. Few logging companies, if any, filed management plans with the Ministry of Development, although at least some railroads and mining companies put professional foresters on staff.[80]

Scientists and intellectuals contemplated these largely ineffectual policies with a growing sense of alarm. The idea that forests protected the land against erosion, aridity, and ultimately desertification had circulated in Europe since ancient times. It gained a scientific imprimatur in the eighteenth century, as intellectuals and colonial administrators became convinced that trees' vascular respiration helped to maintain humidity in woodlands.[81] In the Americas, these theories received a major boost from Alexander von Humboldt's influential research in the Valley of Aragua, Venezuela, which convinced him that the disappearance of forests exposed the soil to "the direct action of the sun," increasing average temperatures and reducing precipitation, and hence threatening natural springs. Humboldt suggested that tree roots helped to fix the soil and capture runoff. Deforestation promoted erosion by making the ground less porous, meaning that rainfall coursed directly into rivers instead of soaking into the ground and increased the potential for torrential flooding during the wet season.[82] He reiterated these findings in Mexico, where he concluded that the "want of trees" was responsible for the aridity of the densely populated central highlands.[83]

By the late nineteenth century, the belief that deforestation interfered with precipitation had become well established in the imaginations of experts and the popular classes alike.[84] Mexico's intellectual elite considered the Humboldtian desiccation thesis a settled question, and scientific associations in the nation's capital published several studies underscoring the idea that forests moderated the climate by capturing humidity in their soils, tree leaves, and tree needles, thereby recharging aquifers and regulating rainfall. The loss of forest cover, in contrast, portended erosion, torrential flooding, and the progressive desiccation of the national territory—a process that some writers believed had occurred in Egypt and Syria.[85] Mexican scientific consensus also construed temperate forests (implicitly associated with Europe and the United States) as inherently hygienic places populated by trees that functioned as "veritable machines of health."[86] Their soil was believed to keep dangerous microbes at bay, while transpiration replaced "carbonic acid" (i.e., carbon dioxide) with life-giving oxygen and warded off insalubrious miasmas produced, it was thought, by swamps, mangroves, and stagnant waters.[87] Some of these ideas moved beyond the salons of urban intellectuals. Most rural people appear to have believed that the rains no longer fell as abundantly as they once had and that the disappearance of forests had something to do with it. They blamed railroads for declining precipitation, not only because the belching steam engines swallowed vast quantities of wood, but because their huge plumes of sooty steam were suspected of driving away the rainclouds.[88]

Some experts disagreed with Humboldtian desiccation theory. A commission empaneled by the Mexican Geographical and Statistical society in 1870 and headed by the renowned intellectual Ignacio Ramírez concluded that forests depended on rain but did not necessarily attract precipitation. Its final report suggested that any vegetation (including agricultural crops) could perform the same climatic services that forests did.[89] The agronomist Rómulo Escobar came to a similarly iconoclastic conclusion three decades later. By 1900, landowners and rural people throughout the nation were convinced that the rains had diminished as forests gave way to agriculture and railroads. Reasoning that the loss of forest cover would correlate with changes in annual rainfall, Escobar tested von Humboldt's ideas by looking for trends in twenty-five years' worth of precipitation data collected from meteorological stations in several Mexican cities. He concluded that annual rainfall had indeed declined on a national scale from 1878 to 1898, but had rebounded thereafter despite the ongoing trend of deforestation. In any case, precipitation fluctuated widely throughout the entire period. More damning still, the regions with the greatest declines were not the ones with the highest rates of deforestation. Escobar concluded that there was no direct correlation between the disappearance of forests and rainfall patterns, and attributed people's perception of climate change to other causes, such as landowners' increasingly heavy use of rivers for irrigation, which left less water for rural people to use.[90]

SCIENCE INTO PRACTICE

Although the Humboldtians and their adversaries disagreed about the particularities of forests' influence on rainfall, the Mexican scientific community agreed that the disappearance of woodlands would spell disaster for nation's climate. Yet no one seriously proposed to prohibit logging altogether. Most experts suggested that the legislators should promote conservation by limiting the extent of commercial logging and prohibiting such "primitive" practices as slash-and-burn agriculture. State governments were among the first to respond. For example, the Veracruz state legislature prohibited logging around the capital city in a bid to sustain a forest greenbelt that might impede unhealthy miasmas from reaching the populace. In Michoacán, Governor Prudenciano Dorantes ordered local officials to keep statistics on forests under their jurisdiction and created a registry intended to enumerate everyone "engaged in the cutting of woods in large or small scale."[91] The following year, state authorities in Durango made the unprecedented move of fining timbermen accused of felling half a million trees without the requisite permits.[92] These policies did not add up to a national policy, however, and regulatory actions such as Durango's probably had more to do with fiscal concerns than ecological ones.

As commercial logging expanded into the densely populated parts around central Mexico, experts demanded a more systematic response. Leading the charge was Miguel Ángel de Quevedo, the scion of a wealthy family from Jalisco who spent much of his childhood in France after the death of his parents. Quevedo graduated from the renowned École Polytechnique in 1887 with a degree in hydrological engineering—an apt course of study insofar as French experts attributed an uptick in torrential floods in the mid-nineteenth century to peasants clearing the land for agriculture. Quevedo returned to Mexico the following year and launched a successful career as a civil engineer. He briefly directed the massive project to drain Lake Texcoco adjacent to Mexico City, before an accident at the worksite forced him to resign. His experiences convinced him that the disappearance of forests in Mexico followed the French pattern. The loss of forest cover, he concluded, had shifted the pattern of precipitation and made flooding an ever-present threat.[93] In 1900 he attended an international conference on urban hygiene in Paris, where the world's leading experts presented evidence that forests and parks helped to regulate the climate around cities; forests also produced fresh air and hence a healthier atmosphere than in urban areas surrounded by denuded land or swamps. Alarmed by what he had learned, Quevedo put his career on hold and accepted a position as Mexico City's director of public works.[94]

From his perch in municipal government, Quevedo lobbied President Díaz to lay down national regulations on forest use, which earned Quevedo the nickname that followed him for the rest of his life: the Apostle of the Tree. When Díaz made only token gestures, Quevedo created his own organization, the Junta Central de Bosques y Arbolados (Central Committee on Forests and Woods), which became a branch of Mexico City's municipal government in 1904. Within a matter of years, the junta doubled the number of parks in the capital and replaced an earlier generation of European trees with native species better suited for its high altitude and dry climate, and it assumed responsibility for Mexico City's Arbor Day festivities, which had become an annual festival in many parts of the country pursuant to an 1893 decree from the secretary of development (*fomento*). Quevedo also converted a family estate south of the capital into a tree nursery, which provided saplings for the parks and for a modest reforestation project south of the city. He later donated the nursery, known as the Viveros de

Coyoacán, to the federal government, and it served as the nation's primary seed farm and headquarters of the forest service for most of the twentieth century. Quevedo's bureau was reassigned to the federal government's Ministry of Fomento in 1908, and Mexico's national forest service was born.[95]

The following year, Quevedo accepted an invitation from Gifford Pinchot, his counterpart in the newly created U.S. Forest Service, to attend the North American Conference on Conservation of Natural Resources. Theodore Roosevelt presided over the conference, which was soon hailed as the crucible of international conservation. Like the other delegates, Quevedo pledged to develop a regime to limit exploitation of temperate forests (while ignoring the ongoing pillage in tropical areas) and launched a renewed effort to reforest the El Ajusco mountain outside of Mexico City—an area that he argued had been devastated by peasants seeking wood for fuel.[96]

Quevedo set an ambitious agenda for the newly federalized forest service. In addition to planting trees that beautified cities and made them more hygienic, he hoped to build an institution capable of managing the nation's forests, researching their extent and composition, and disseminating this knowledge in scientific and popular venues. Within a year, the fledgling organization had begun to study possible locations for forest reserves that would "safeguard our climatology and conserve rivers and springs."[97] Quevedo used his European contacts to invite five professors from the French National School of Forestry, at Nancy, to found a forestry school in Mexico. The new institution was located in Santa Fe (in the Federal District) and reproduced Nancy's curriculum, with core courses in precipitation hydrology, natural science, logging methods, and dasonometrics (the science of calculating tree volume, growth rate, and valuation). The school echoed the French institution's utilitarian goals and trained its students to devise sustained-use management plans based on a biological and economic calculus that disregarded the needs of people who already lived in the forestlands. (Ironically, this perspective discounted the influential theories of Frédéric Le Play, a preeminent French sociologist of the time, who argued that peasants who used the forests for income were the people most likely to protect them.)[98] The instructors also gave practical instruction. On a trip to the Desierto de los Leones, west of Mexico City, the French experts completed the first dasonometric study of a Mexican forest and showed students how to investigate the prior use of a stand of trees, to gauge its current volume of timber, and ultimately to set the right pace of logging to achieve a sustainable harvest. Later surveys addressed the forests in Quintana Roo and the Islas Marías, off the coast of Nayarit.[99]

Graduates from the school formed the core of the professional forest service. They fanned out and began projects to restore the woods in some of the nation's most visible ecosystems, such as the spectacular mountains around El Chico, Hidalgo, and the greenbelt around the city of Veracruz. Others were posted to the tropical forests along the Gulf of Mexico, where they monitored the hardwood logging in the states of Campeche, Tabasco, and Veracruz, though they apparently ignored logging companies' notorious impressment of lumberjacks, who often ended up virtually enslaved in remote rainforest logging camps.[100] In a portent of things to come, the forest service conformed to what one historian has described as the scientific elites' "urban environmental imagination."[101] The corps was overwhelmingly based in Mexico City and focused virtually all of its attentions on nearby forests. Half of its twenty-six permanent inspectors were posted in the Federal District and usually denied poor people's requests to use the woods while favoring petitions for federal land filed by paper companies and the largest logging interests. Most of the reforestation projects also targeted the Valley of Mexico, as did the only substantive attempt to "improve" an ecosystem: in the late 1900s, foresters introduced hardier species of pine from the desert north to the hillsides surrounding the capital. They also tried to confront dust storms blowing out of the desiccated Lake Texcoco by planting rows of eucalyptus, the fast-growing but notoriously thirsty Australian species originally imported to Veracruz in the 1870s and promoted soon thereafter by urban-hygiene advocates as a means of improving air quality in Mexico City.[102]

COMMODIFICATION AND COALITION

The Porfirian timber economy vastly outstripped the regulatory capacity of the Porfirian forest service. Commercial logging in states such as Michoacán and Chihuahua would have been difficult to control under the best of circumstances, but Quevedo chose not to station inspectors in either state (despite warnings from his own staff) and concentrated his limited institutional resources to Mexico City and its environs.[103] Administrative centralization made sense from an institutional perspective insofar as the forest service had originated in Mexico City and formed part of a larger federal bureaucracy based in the nation's capital. Yet this centripetal bias had the troubling effect of privileging urban social concerns over rural ones. Like their French mentors, Mexican forestry officials emphasized the benefits that forests offered to cities, such as their supposed capacity to purify the air and improve hygiene, and paid little attention to the complex relationship between rural people and the woods. Moreover, Mexico City afforded a distorted perspective on the national panorama. While it is true that the surrounding mountainsides had undergone some commercial logging (mostly by paper companies and charcoal vendors) that had partially denuded the El Ajusco and the Iztaccíhuatl foothills, most deforestation in the Valley of Mexico was the result of centuries of habitation. Rural people cleared the land for agriculture and cut wood for fuel and building material. As a result, forestry experts who contemplated the landscape from Coyoacán consistently overestimated the threat that the lower classes posed to the ecosystem while downplaying the effects of commercial logging. Finally, administrative centralization may also help explain why forestry officials billeted in Mexico City tended to propose national resource policies that privileged temperate pine-oak forests and made few allowances for the nation's other—typically more ecologically diverse—forest ecosystems.

Urban intellectuals had few points of contact with rural people during the Porfiriato, and the forest service's orientation effectively foreclosed any chance of finding common ground in the woods. Although commodification put peasant subsistence strategies into jeopardy in many places, experts such as Quevedo never seriously considered recruiting rural people as allies in the nascent conservationist movement. If anything, they considered them more of a threat than virtually unregulated logging in the north or the unceasing extraction of tropical hardwoods in the south. Conversely, few if any villagers reached out to the forest service. Rural people had a long tradition of seeking out powerful outsiders who might help them resolve local problems, but it seems that peasants never considered the possibility that the forest service might have assistance to offer.

Villagers' estrangement from expert foresters was a symptom of the broader social cleavages that beset Mexico during the waning years of the Porfiriato, when skilled workers, some peasant groups, and segments of the middle class began to complain about Díaz's autocratic rule. Violent strikes erupted at William Greene's Cananea copper mine in Sonora (1906) and at the Río Blanco textile complex in Oaxaca and Veracruz (1906–1907), while peasant unrest percolated in Chihuahua, Morelos, Veracruz, and beyond. Especially in the north, economic development and internal migration had weakened small-town social bonds within families and parishes, and even between landowners and their dependents. The commodification of the landscape added new stresses to several parts of the woodlands as American and Canadian corporations gained access to the nation's best timber. North Americans also dominated the railroads; according to one estimate, American investors owned 80 percent of the stocks and bonds in Mexican railways by 1910.[104] Meanwhile, a younger generation of intellectuals and professionals worried that they would be unable to find a place in an economy organized around crony capitalism. Grinding droughts in 1908 and 1909 made matters worse. Although few would have predicted that the nation lay on the brink of revolution, no one could doubt that discontent was running high in some quarters. The massive social upheaval that wracked Mexico during the 1910s thrust popular demands at least temporarily into the political arena and created some surprising political alliances, including a short-lived attempt during the 1930s to create linkages between rural people and a newly re-founded and far more populist forest service under the unlikely guidance of Quevedo. That halting endeavor still lay decades away, however. In the meantime, the political vacuum of the revolution gave rural people a taste of what it meant to manage their own woods.

CHAPTER 2

Revolution and Regulation, 1910–1928

———

The epic revolution of 1910–1917 swept away the Díaz regime and along with it the conviction that whatever was good for the oligarchy was good for Mexico. Conflicts between villagers and landowners accentuated revolutionary violence in some areas, though access to forests rarely figured as a major source of the hostilities. Revolutionary warfare devastated thousands of families and hundreds of townships. By most estimates, a million people lost their lives or were displaced.[1] The revolution brought extreme hardship to some regional economies, while the business environment in others survived nearly unscathed, as the heaviest fighting occurred primarily on the central plateaus and unforested plains. After the guns had gone (mostly) silent, the nation's new leaders used the scale of destruction and violence as one justification to rebalance the relationship between the government and the governed. Historians have long recognized that postrevolutionary governments promised land reform, state support for labor unions, the expansion of education, anticlericalism, and the nationalization of key industries, but they have paid less attention to another fundamental aspect of this project. The postrevolutionary state staked its authority to dispose of the nation's natural resources (including water, soil, forests, and eventually minerals and hydrocarbons) on the basis of its capacity to manage them rationally.[2] Political leaders of the 1920s intended not only to assert sovereignty over Mexico's natural resources, but also to control their use through the application of scientific and ultimately conservationist concepts.

Armed with the revolutionary imperative of rational management, a newly empowered cadre of experts argued that the conservationist project should begin with the forest products that could help reconstruct the nation's economy after nearly a decade of warfare. As Miguel Ángel de Quevedo observed, "High levels of development would result from the use of scientific knowledge and ever more perfected techniques for the exploitation of natural resources."[3] Nevertheless, experts like Quevedo continued to worry that uncontrolled logging and deforestation would harm society by changing the hydrological regime.[4] The revolution had also caused a spike in rural-to-urban migration, making forests more critical than ever in public-health initiatives because, as Quevedo argued, woods had the capacity to act as "veritable filters of the unhealthy atmosphere."[5]

The revolution had changed the political calculus in other ways as well. Conflicts over forestlands may have played only a tiny role in the war, but the instability of the revolutionary years accentuated existing tensions in the woodlands and sparked some new ones. In Michoacán, the relative anarchy of the 1910s allowed some villagers to occupy lands they claimed as their own, but it also allowed timber companies to intensify existing operations and expand into new areas. These sorts of agrarian conflicts surfaced less frequently in northern states like Chihuahua, where unrest exacerbated tensions between foreign-owned logging companies and their largely Mexican workforce. Scientists could do little more than watch these encounters unfold, since the revolution battered and eventually destroyed the tiny forest service they had pieced together in the early 1900s.

Once the violence subsided, in 1917, it became clear that the rationalizing logic of natural-resource management conflicted with postrevolutionary initiatives such as agrarian reform. How could forests be used conservatively in the national interest when land reform delivered them to villagers who neither understood nor necessarily benefited from the precepts of scientific management? Resolving this dilemma lay at the heart of postrevolutionary forestry. Scientists initially suggested that agrarian reform should not include the woodlands at all. When that proved politically untenable, they proposed a series of measures, ultimately compiled in the 1926 forestry code, that required land reform beneficiaries (indeed all peasant producers) to form producers cooperatives governed by scientific principles. The law strove to achieve a Solomonic compromise that allowed rural people access to forest resources provided that they adopted modern practices subject to expert scrutiny. As in the case of India explored by the historian Ramachandra Guha, Mexican scientific management not only aimed to preserve ecosystems but also to allow scientific conservationism "to reorder both nature and customary use in its own image."[6]

The law had little initial impact. Forestry officials struggled to implement the new regulations, and few rural people even knew that they existed. For the rural poor, agrarian reform and the chance to acquire their own lands mattered far more than learning the finer points about forestry regulations. But the legislation provided a glimpse of bigger things to come. It envisioned the means for land reform beneficiaries to work their own woods and even contemplated making them the central actors in the development process, but it also included paternalist oversight measures that gave forestry experts significant new authority. It represented a first step in a process that ultimately created bureaucratic forms that poor rural people neither welcomed nor fully comprehended until it was too late to preserve a major element of their revolutionary patrimony.[7]

REVOLUTIONARY LANDSCAPES

The successive waves of warfare that overtook Mexico between 1911 and 1915 did not originate with a cataclysmic popular uprising or middle-class revolt against the injustices of the Díaz dictatorship, much less against the export-oriented economic strategy that gave foreigners such a visible role in Mexico's most lucrative industries. The revolution began as a relatively narrow political competition between the aging dictator and a younger generation of ambitious politicians who drew much of their support from downwardly mobile sectors of the middle class. The proximate cause of the political crisis was the contested presidential election of 1910, which allowed the landowner Francisco I. Madero to threaten Díaz's political supremacy for the first time in a generation. Faced with electoral fraud and his own brief imprisonment, Madero called for an armed revolt that eventually inspired brief rebellions led by Pascual Orozco in Chihuahua and Emiliano Zapata in the south-central state of Morelos. The northern uprising succeeded almost before it began. A trio of highly visible military setbacks culminating with the siege of Ciudad Juárez in May 1911 convinced Díaz to turn power over to a caretaker administration and head into exile.

Up to this point, the revolution did not substantively differ from the sort of minor uprisings (also called "revolutions") that had removed dozens of unpopular presidents from office in the preceding century. Following that well-worn script, Madero took office in November 1911 and began making some modest political reforms. Yet his own presidential campaign in 1910 had awakened expectations for more thoroughgoing change among urban and rural workers, the educated but poor professional classes, and some members of the elite. Unable to mediate among these demands, Madero soon proved to be a giant with lead feet. He failed to win the allegiance of most landowners and military officers, and he alienated his former allies, Orozco and Zapata. In early 1913 the army chief of staff Victoriano

Huerta capitalized on Madero's growing unpopularity to carry out a military coup, during which the president and vice president were summarily executed. The assassination converted Madero into a martyr despite his travails as president. Three governors from Mexico's far north, along with the Zapatistas in Morelos, refused to recognize Huerta's administration. Invoking both the memory of Madero and moral principle (agrarian justice in the case of Zapata; the rule of law for the northerners), a new round of revolutionary violence gradually took on a life of its own. Northerners such as Pancho Villa joined together as the so-called constitutionalist faction of revolutionaries led by the landowner Venustiano Carranza. Aided by Zapata's peasant army in Morelos, the constitutionalist forces overran the federal army and forced Huerta into exile in July 1914. At that point, the fissures that had always existed within the revolutionary coalition grew wider, and the lack of a common enemy drove the former constitutionalist allies into outright warfare against each other. For the next year, the victors squared off in the final and most deadly stage of the war. The end came with startling suddenness in the summer of 1915, as Carranza and his allies managed to subdue (though not completely obliterate) the armies of Zapata and Villa. Carranza had effectively won the war by that fall.

Military commanders struggled to channel popular discontent into useable military manpower, and most revolutionary factions (apart from the Zapatistas) sought to place limits on spontaneous uprisings. Nevertheless, the revolution clearly drew much of its strength from the discontent of workers and peasants. Most villagers resented the dispossession of their lands during the Porfiriato, and they expected revolutionaries to do something about it.[8] Both urban and rural workers suffered from Díaz's anti-unionism, which they blamed for making their livelihoods more precarious during the economic downturn in the final years of the Porfiriato.[9] In some instances, workers resented how the foreign corporations treated them, occasionally lending a nationalist element to the litany of popular-class complaints against the prerevolutionary order.[10]

Social tension also rippled through the woodlands. Foreign companies had secured the most lucrative concessions in the southern mahogany zones and the commercial forests of the central and northern states, and they reaped impressive profits while some Mexican entrepreneurs languished. While mahogany lumberjacks endured a form of debt peonage that approached slavery, workers in the pine-oak forests of the center and north teetered between gratitude for having jobs and resentment at doing backbreaking work at the behest of Gringos. The booming market for wood products also led timber companies to encroach on village woodlots and dispossess communal property, forcing the rural people into more precarious forms of subsistence agriculture or into the labor market. The loss of woodlands was a common theme in agrarian revolts such as the one in Morelos. The Plan of Ayala, which served as the Zapatista manifesto, traced villagers' anger to hacienda landowners' usurpation of "lands, woods, and waters" [los terrenos, montes y aguas]. The Zapatistas succeeded in redistributing land while they controlled Morelos, albeit temporarily, but it is not clear what they did about forests.[11] In San Luis Potosí, where the Cedillo family declared their affinity with Zapatismo and mobilized peasants to fight in the revolution, a small ad hoc land reform did return the communal woodlands that villagers had lost during the Porfiriato.[12]

In Mexico's southernmost state of Chiapas, revolutionary unrest broke the hegemony of logging companies that extracted mahogany by forcing lumberjacks into debt and sending them into prison-like logging camps known as monterías. Constitutionalist troops in the "Usumacinta Brigade" marched into the Lacandón forest in 1913 and traveled from settlement to settlement confiscating cattle and other goods, and leaving the sawmills in ashes. They organized unions in at least a few camps, but most workers just slipped away once the soldiers canceled their contracts. As one woodcutter later told the historian Jan de Vos, "I left that hell because the revolution freed me. General Luis Felipe Domínguez arrived in 1913, and we all left with him. The revolutionaries carried our tormenters [verdugos] away in chains."[13] The soldiers did not reach every lumber camp, and the mighty mahogany interests tried to reconstitute the system of debt peonage as soon as the army was gone. But the incursion cost the timber interests most of their capital and their aura of omnipotence, and the companies never really recovered.[14]

The revolution also brought some short-lived changes to the forest itself. Warfare created demand for fuel, shelter, and matériel that only the forest could offer. For example, the woods south of Mexico City changed hands from federal forces to the constitutionalists to Zapatistas, and back again, and soldiers often used them to take cover. The army tried to flush out the rebels by setting fires that succeeded in doing little more than destroying a few stands of timber and driving the revolutionaries deeper into the mountains.[15] The constitutionalist army, including the female soldaderas who accompanied it, felled trees to build temporary shelter and gathered branches and debris to use for firewood. Quevedo witnessed one makeshift logging operation as Carranza's army built fortifications outside of Vera-cruz in 1914. He complained that troops "finished off" the trees the French foresters had planted to stabilize the artificial dune (built as a windbreak) on the outskirts of town. Without trees to fix the soil, the dune began to erode and had to be rebuilt and replanted after the revolution.[16] Moreover, all revolutionary factions needed wood for the railroads. Not only were ties needed to rebuild rail lines destroyed by retreating armies, but many military units (including Villa's entire army) lacked access to coal and needed wood to fuel the locomotives on which they so heavily depended.[17]

The revolution also ravaged the incipient forest bureaucracy. The Porfirian forest service continued to function as normally as possible until early 1913, when Quevedo responded to Huerta's military coup by arming students at the forestry school and the wardens posted in six states and the Federal District. When Quevedo complained that Huerta's federal troops had illegally cleared the trees around the schoolhouse in a failed attempt to deprive Maderista loyalists of cover, the army responded by arresting him and destroying the schoolhouse. Soon afterward, the French foresters left Mexico to avoid the unrest and because their own nation was girding for war in Europe. Their departure left only a handful of Mexican forestry experts in the country.[18] Huerta's antagonism drove many of the remaining foresters to join the constitutionalists. They never saw action against the federal army, but two wardens did scout for the constitutionalist forces in Xochimilco as they battled Emiliano Zapata's army for control of Mexico City.[19]

It is difficult to estimate the overall toll that the revolution took on the forest ecosystem, though it probably was not that great. While the logistics of warfare meant the destruction of isolated stands of timber, the broader atmosphere of violence and insecurity produced what one observer called "obligatory production bans" (*vedas obligadas*) on a much larger scale. Logging operations and the expansion of the cattle frontier came to a halt in the most intensely timbered regions, as companies mothballed their operations and workers abandoned their saws. Nearly all logging stopped in Morelos, the Federal District, Veracruz, and parts of Chihuahua between 1915 and 1918 or later, allowing the forest a moment of recovery.[20] In Oaxaca the revolution interrupted plans to found a major logging corporation. The North American H. S. Beattie had applied for an immense forest concession in 1910 and was raising capital for a major new enterprise until the unrest scared investors away.[21] As in so many other aspects, the revolution had an uneven implication for forests and those who lived in them. In the timbering heartlands of Chihuahua and Michoacán, for example, the revolution reverberated in strikingly different ways.

DISCONTENT IN THE WOODS

No fewer than two thousand men earned wages as lumberjacks and sawyers at the eve of the revolution in Chihuahua, compared to a few hundred in Michoacán. As a result, the revolution accentuated labor issues in Chihuahua rather than agrarian tensions as in Michoacán. Even so, conflicts over the woodlands did underlay many broader tensions. Some agrarian conflicts in Michoacán had roots in commercial forestry, for example. As one military leader explained, logging companies had convinced so many indigenous communities to lease their common lands that it deprived people "of the one resource they possessed in order to subsist."[22] Similarly, the growth of the great landed estates in Chihuahua meant that timber workers who lost their jobs in the 1905 economic downturn could not reasonably expect to buy their own land on which to make a living. As with salaried workers elsewhere in the country, the loss of employment often forced former timber workers to take marginal jobs and made them more willing to join the relatively well-paid ranks of revolutionary armies.

Revolutionaries found it difficult to recruit followers in Michoacán.[23] Although columns of several hundred men did take up arms during the conflict, pitched battles and social dislocation occurred less frequently there than in other parts of the country. Social contention in the woodlands usually took the form of sporadic confrontations between villagers and landowners over access to village woodlots. The indigenous residents of San Ángel Zurumucapio, near Uruapan, for example, had complained as early as 1907 that the neighboring hacienda of Jucutácato had illegally occupied its lands with the connivance of the local prefect. The absentee hacienda owners responded the following year by having the local leader Agapito Motuto conscripted into the army. Once the revolution loosened local authorities' grip on the area, the villagers turned the tables. They torched the hacienda's blacksmith shop in retribution for collecting wood for charcoal from Zurumucapio's former commons. A few years later, they invaded the hacienda's own woodlots, ran off the field hands, and began cutting trees to make their own charcoal.[24]

Similar events elsewhere in the state suggests that rural folk saw in Madero's "revolutionary" movement the opportunity to roll back the worst effects of forest commodification. The villagers around Lake Pátzcuaro, for example, seethed at the dispossession of communal woodlands during the Porfiriato. As Madero's revolution flared in the north, they seized the hated timber merchants Rafael and Antonio Ibarrola and considered lynching them before their resolve flagged. A few months later, a fiesta in nearby Pichátaro turned ugly when indigenous villagers confronted the manager of the town's foreign-owned timber company. At first the locals demanded money, then an altercation broke out and they shot the manager with the only shotgun in town. A similar act of insubordination occurred nearby, when villagers who heard a false rumor that Madero planned to divide up the land decided to take matters into their own hands. They invaded the Hacienda de la Orilla, a property owned by the French Mirabeau-Rothschild consortium that had dispossessed several villages along the coast, and began cutting woods and grazing their livestock as if the company had never been there—or perhaps to ensure that it would not return.[25] On the other side of the state as well, rural people invaded or repossessed lands they had lost to encroaching timber interests. The rising value of timber sent the villagers of Senguío into their communal woods in 1915, much to the displeasure of the administrators of the neighboring Chincua hacienda that claimed to own the property. Hacienda administrators jailed seven indigenous loggers (all from the same family, it seems) and sent their own work gangs into the woods.[26]

Most timber companies continued to operate in Michoacán for the duration of the revolutionary decade, and a few even took advantage of the growing anarchy to increase the scope of their logging.[27] The state inspector of forests reported in 1911, for example, that logging crews had made "excessive cuts" on indigenous lands, far above legal limits and in violation of their rental agreements.[28] Though not mentioned by name, one of these companies was no doubt the Compañía Industrial Maderera, owned by the North American Santiago Slade, which continued to produce lumber and railroad ties in the Meseta Purépecha during the early 1910s.[29] As Slade moved crews onto new lands further to the north, lumberjacks repeatedly tangled with the locals. Slade's employees had already earned a reputation as thugs, but some villagers nonetheless tried to mount an armed resistance during the Huerta dictatorship of 1912–1914. They harassed logging crews and pelted their camps with stones. Slade responded by organizing a militia that won Huerta's formal blessing to help keep "order" in the countryside. Company guards ranged widely in the Meseta Purépecha and threatened to kill anyone who stood against the dictatorship or Slade's company. According to one report, they burned the village of Copándaro to the ground. But as Huerta's government slowly lost its grip on the nation, Slade found that his own position also became increasingly precarious. He abandoned the countryside altogether in 1913, when a local revolutionary rallied villagers in Cherán and launched a frontal assault on the timber company's installations.[30]

After the major revolutionary battles had come to an end, in 1915, banditry posed a new challenge to logging operations in Michoacán. The first attack came in 1914, when outlaws ransacked the "timber hacienda" of San Joaquín Jaripeo, in the district of Zinapécuaro, not far from the state capital. They overran the hacienda again three years later, destroying the sawmill and selling off or slaughtering the estate's cattle. Even after the armed bandits disappeared, in 1920, the owner found that the combination of high taxes and unrepaired railways made it impossible to commence work again. He also had to contend with villagers, some of whom had probably ridden with the bandits, who filed a petition for a land reform parcel. Local agrarians threatened to occupy the hacienda and log its wood on their own accord. In a 1921 letter to the Ministry of Government, a lawyer for the landowners desperately resorted to the discourse of conservation in a bid to head off impending land invasion. If "ill-intentioned or merely foolish people" take possession of the hacienda, he wrote, "they could irreparably damage these woods, which have always been worked in a prudent manner subject to the rules governing the best forestry practices."[31]

The link between "banditry," timber operations, and popular mobilization was hazy in Jaripeo and indeed in most of the state, but there can be little question that both landowners and rural people tried to use the turmoil to gain some sort of advantage in the woodlands. Lumbermen such as Santiago Slade quickened the pace of logging, while villagers in the Meseta Purépecha invaded lands they considered their own. Yet Michoacán's relative quietude during the revolutionary decade ensured that only a handful of such episodes took place. The revolution burned far more brightly in Chihuahua, where first Pascual Orozco and later Pancho Villa formed huge popular armies. Rather than lead to massive land invasions, the revolution accentuated labor conflicts in Chihuahua's forest sector and ultimately dealt an irreparable blow to the state's largest timber conglomerate.

The Madera Lumber Company, owned by Fred Stark Pearson, had invested heavily in its Chihuahua operations beginning in 1908, and continued to plow funds into the two big sawmills until the revolution encroached on Madera, in 1912.[32] The owners tried desperately to keep the saws spinning because the price of wood climbed briskly in these years, rising 63 percent between 1912 and 1914 at the point of embarkation in Manzanillo. The company also received a substantial order for packing crates from the Armour Corporation in late 1913 and the first half of 1914, on top of the never-ending demand for railroad ties and mining timbers.[33] The owners also had their investments to protect. The Madera Lumber Company sunk around 30 million dollars into real estate, railroads, and the two huge sawmills between 1909 and 1918, and the foreman wanted to avoid making layoffs that might ignite protests in these costly plants.[34] He felt that out-of-work sawyers would most likely join the revolutionaries and "create serious depredations," such as cannibalizing equipment or torching the mills. Even so, the company briefly closed two times in 1911, then for a longer period in 1912–13, and once again in late 1914.[35]

The owners believed that the best way to keep the operation afloat was to ensure that the North American workers, numbering a thousand before 1911 and five hundred thereafter, were as content and compliant as possible. The company cultivated a paternalist bond with its North American and Mexican skilled workers, by building schools, churches, medical and recreational facilities (including a bullring and cock pit), and quality housing inside the city limits.[36] Foremen preferred to hire married North American workers willing to settle their families in the company town, because they believe it ensured a stable workforce. When revolutionaries appeared in the region in 1912, administrators gave up on that idea and paid to move workers' families to El Paso and out of harm's way, although they expected the men to remain behind and tend the machinery. When all else failed, managers could resort to paying for military protection. Once the revolutionaries established control of Chihuahua, the manager asked the rebel commanders Pascual Orozco and José Inés Salazar to maintain order in the mill, though he would have preferred for a detachment of U.S. troops to do the job. Conditions changed again in 1913, and the manager had no qualms about asking Victoriano Huerta, the newly installed dictator, to post federal soldiers at the mill. A few months later, he asked revolutionary troops aligned with Pancho Villa to provide protection against local bandits.[37]

The fact that company managers fretted so much about security arrangements suggests not only a fear of banditry and looting—though local children did like to shoot out the mill's windows with slingshots—but also a deep mistrust of their own Mexican workers. Some of these misgivings must have derived from the preferential treatment that North Americans

Figure 2.1. Company housing in "American Town," ca. 1910. Photograph by Gertrude Fitzgerald. Special Collections Department, University of Texas at El Paso Library, Gertrude Fitzgerald Photographs, PH025.

received in comparison to their Mexican counterparts. While the company built modern housing for all skilled employees in Madera and Pearson, it segregated workers into two settlements, one called American Town, which was home to a clubhouse as well as most of the schools and medical facilities, and the other called Mexican Town, which had few amenities and housing the company referred to as "cottages." Only the most skilled Mexicans had access to even this diminished level of company housing; the rest had to fend for themselves.[38] Such corporate chauvinism cropped up repeatedly. When Villistas began to force Madera Lumber Company to accept revolutionary scrip in 1912, for example, managers apparently demanded that their Mexican workers accept it for their wages even though North American workers continued to receive their pay in gold.[39] Mexicans' resentment of such double standards helped to prompt a walkout at the Madera plant in 1912, though the workers' primary complaint was that the company allowed Chinese merchants to hold a monopoly of food and dry goods stores in town.[40]

Reports in 1911 and 1913 routinely mentioned that unskilled workers at the Madera mill felt "ill sentiment" toward foreign managers. As the *El Paso Times-Democrat* quipped, the company's Mexican workforce harbored "a constitutional hate for all Americans."[41] Whether workers in fact resented North Americans in general or the Madera Lumber Company in particular

Figure 2.2. Housing in "Mexican Town," ca. 1910. Photograph by Gertrude Fitzgerald. University of Texas at El Paso Library Special Collections Department, Gertrude Fitzgerald Photographs, PH025.

is an open question. American administrators at the mills believed that the primary source of Mexican workers' bitterness was the recurring *closure* of the sawmills, which threw the sawyers out of work and left them with no alternative but to enlist in one army or another. On the other hand, Pablo Orozco's revolutionary faction recruited many of the Mexican workers at the Madera plant in February 1912, though the mill continued to operate with a skeleton crew of North Americans.[42] Some Mexicans continued to sympathize with Orozco and his "red flaggers" even after he rebelled against the Madero government the following year. Whatever the case, some workers at the mill apparently believed that Orozco sympathized with their grievances against the Americans.[43]

A striking incident in 1913 revealed the extent of some workers' discontent. The company suspended operations when revolutionaries arrived in town in July, and the foreman invited a small group of Villistas to move into the newly vacated houses in Mexican Town. Apparently, he thought the Villistas could protect the plant against the depredations of Orozco's men. Perhaps the fact that the mayor (*presidente municipal*) of Madera was a Villista also played into his decision. On 15 August, a detachment of eighty federal soldiers who opposed the Villistas occupied the town and killed the mayor, prompting the revolutionaries encamped near the mill to slip into the woods during an unexpected downpour that afternoon.

Figure 2.3. Villistas arrive in Pearson (now Mata Ortiz) in 1913, under a banner that reads "Welcome Back, Brave Boys." Photograph by Gertrude Fitzgerald. University of Texas at El Paso Library Special Collections Department, Gertrude Fitzgerald Photographs, PH025.

At that point, the *federales* turned ugly. Though nominally under the command of Col. Federico Córdova, their real leader was a close ally of Orozco, Marcelo Caraveo. The soldiers—some of whom appear to have been former mill workers—rode through Mexican Town and murdered an "old, hardworking" black employee named John Henry Thomas. Some of Caraveo's federal soldiers knew the mill well enough to recognize the paymaster, Edward Hayes, whom they cornered and ordered to declare his political allegiances. We do not know what Hayes said, but Caraveo shot him on the spot and rifled his pockets for money. Afterward, the soldiers sought out the manager and lectured him about American meddling in Mexico and his company's ill-conceived dalliance with Villa.[44]

As soon as the federals left, bearing 2,000 dollars in pilfered cash and merchandise, the foreman loaded the remaining employees onto a train and headed for Ciudad Juárez, on the U.S. border. The passengers included 75 North Americans and a similar number of Chinese, as well as 150 "loyal" Mexican employees who preferred to leave the area.[45] The owners did try to reopen the plant one last time, in 1915, but they quickly shuttered it and left it idle until it burned to the ground, in 1919. Not until 1922 did the company rebuild, this time a substantially smaller plant, and begin work again. The huge plant in Pearson did remain open in the interim and briefly flourished in 1917 and 1918, when three shifts of workers produced four million board feet of lumber per month, mostly in the form of railroad ties for Mexican railroads and the U.S. market. At its peak, the Pearson plant had a total of 3,500 employees working in the sawmill and nearby lumber camps. The town boasted a market, supermarket, post office, ice-making plant, butcher shop, hotel, hospital, school, 72 houses for salaried employees, and 85 houses for workers. But in late 1918 it, too, succumbed to economic pressures and closed for good.[46]

The events in Madera were minor episodes in the revolution, and those in Michoacán barely registered at the national level. Nevertheless, they epitomized the sorts of social stresses that the revolution brought into sharp relief. Clashes between foreign employers and workers in Chihuahua or between timbermen and indigenous communities in Michoacán mirrored the simmering conflicts that burst into the open in factories and rural landscapes throughout the nation. By the time that Carranza's armies returned in triumph from the decisive battles against Villa in 1915, issues such as foreign economic influence, agrarian disputes, and workers' rights had become fully part of "the Revolution." Now the nation's new paladins had no alternative but to address them.

THE POLITICAL ECOLOGY OF LAND REFORM

In the fall of 1916, Venustiano Carranza—the staunchly nationalist but politically moderate leader of the constitutionalist faction that won the revolution—convened a constitutional convention packed with his allies and charged it with formulating a document that reflected the nation's changed political circumstances. Ever the believer in incremental change, Carranza proposed a draft constitution that made no dramatic additions to the nation's existing laws nor did it promise significant new rights to citizens. To many of the idealistic delegates who attended the convention, Carranza's draft was a half measure that did not fulfill the "promises of the revolution." Few could agree on precisely what these promises entailed, but they recognized that something needed to be done about labor tensions and disquiet over land tenure. Carranza's own generals—including his right-hand man Alvaro Obregón—had forged an alliance with unionized workers during the revolution, and Carranza himself had signed a largely symbolic decree in 1915 that promised to restore land to dispossessed villages. Many delegates had a heightened sense of nationalism, not only because they believed that Díaz had offered too many sweetheart deals to foreign investors, but because the U.S. army had once again entered Mexican soil in pursuit of Villa for his raid on Columbus, New Mexico, in March 1916.

The delegates' accentuated sense of sovereignty and revolutionary obligation to the popular classes encouraged them to pass a series of measures that radically curbed the privileges of groups construed as antirevolutionary, such as foreigners and the clergy, while bestowing a host of new rights on all citizens, and on the popular classes in particular. In its final form, the constitution of 1917 guaranteed free and secular education, national healthcare, and the right of workers to unionize. Its signature provision was Article 27, which rejected the idea that individuals had an inalienable right to property and declared that land and natural resources "ultimately pertain to the Nation," which had the right to dispose of them in the public interest. It also placed limits on foreign ownership of minerals, petroleum, and property near the seashore. Perhaps most notably, Article 27 established the legal foundation for the land reform that became the defining characteristic of Mexican rural politics until 1992. As much a declaration of principles as one of legislative intent, Article 27 articulated a revolutionary vision of social redemption.

The delegates did not dwell on the plight of Indians, because they preferred to use ethnically neutral terms that addressed the landless poor as a class. Nevertheless, they understood that native people faced particular challenges. The national and international press routinely described Zapatistas and other agrarian revolutionaries as "Indians," thereby associating indigeneity with the question of land reform. One of the nation's foremost public intellectuals, Manuel Gamio, had added his voice to the discussion in a series of newspaper editorials and in a book, *Forjando Patria* (Forging the Nation, 1916), that challenged the stereotype of indigenous people as violent savages. He contended that the nation could only progress by embracing its indigenous heritage and bringing native people into the social mainstream. Gamio rejected the essentialist orthodoxy that Indians' inherent inferiority or biological deficiency were to blame for their economic marginalization and pointed instead to centuries of racism and official neglect. In his view, anthropologists had a patriotic duty to bring about "the redemption of the indigenous class" through an "ethnic fusion" with dominant, mestizo culture.[47] Gamio modeled his vision during a six-year archeological project in the Valley of Teotihuacan. In addition to investigating the spectacular pre-Hispanic ruins, he carried out ethnographic research on the living Nahua people who farmed in the shadows of the great pyramids; he even provided the Nahua with irrigation technology and showed them how their ancestors had used the land. Gamio's advocacy helped to kindle the *indigenista* movement of the 1920s, which placed native culture on the national agenda. Intellectuals revived traditional handicrafts that had languished for generations, and they reframed archaeology as a study in the nation's cultural heritage. Eventually, political leaders established a government bureau to deliver social services to indigenous people.[48] Although land reform was not an explicit part of the indigenista program, it bolstered the position of native leaders and progressive schoolteachers, many of whom seized the opportunity to file petitions for ejido land grants in the nation's most socially marginalized regions.

Article 27 also articulated another postrevolutionary aspiration: the nationalist push to wrest natural resources from foreign hands and rationalize their use. The law gave the federal government the authority to adjudicate disputed boundary lines and vested it with broad authority to regulate the use of minerals, petroleum, water, and forests. Its guiding spirit was that the state should impinge on private property "in the public interest" in order to administer "the utilization of natural resources . . . to conserve them and ensure a more equitable distribution of public wealth." In essence, it directed the government to sustainably manage resource use on behalf of the commonweal.

It was no coincidence that Article 27 married the revolutionary principle of social justice with the state management of resources. Miguel Ángel de Quevedo had insisted for years that the federal government needed to take charge of resource extraction, and he later claimed to have played a role in injecting these ideals into the constitution. According to his memoirs, Quevedo managed to bend Carranza's ear while the president was his guest in his country house soon after the convention had begun its deliberations in Aguascalientes. Quevedo claimed that he convinced Carranza to ask his two most loyal supporters to include the goal of conservation in Article 27.[49] No other sources attest to Quevedo's behind-the-scenes intervention, though it appears that one of President Carranza's staunchest allies did give a boost to the conservationist plank while the article was being reviewed for final ratification.[50]

Article 27 is probably best known as the constitutional basis for the 1917–1991 agrarian reform. During the revolution, several military leaders had pledged to help villagers recover the property illegally taken from them during the Porfiriato. The constitutionalists had even made some symbolic land grants in revolutionary hotspots such as Chihuahua and Morelos (the homeland of Zapatismo). With the promulgation of the constitution in February 1917, a steady trickle of requests began to appear from elsewhere as well, particularly from villages that competed against haciendas for agricultural land in central Mexico.[51] Most agrarian organizing had to be done at the local or, at best, state level because President Carranza covertly discouraged land reform, and his successor Alvaro Obregón (1920–1924) viewed it as a stopgap measure to defuse social tension until he could "modernize" the countryside by creating a class of smallholders tied to regional and national markets.[52]

Requests for land grants kept coming nonetheless. In 1922 the federal legislature promulgated a uniform land reform code that established two pathways of agrarian reform. In the first instance, indigenous communities could request the *restauración* (restitution) of their commons if they could fully document that an outside party had illegally appropriated their commons. Most indigenous people preferred this route because it vindicated their claims of landowner malfeasance and awarded them direct possession of the land. Very few petitions for restitution succeeded, however, because villagers could rarely produce unimpeachable evidence of illegal dispossession, and in any case land reform bureaucrats preferred to follow the second route—the more administratively streamlined process of *dotación*, through which the state granted a parcel of land known as an ejido to villagers. Several technical aspects of the dotación process made it less appealing to rural people, however. In the first place, villagers did not technically own ejidal land; instead, the state granted them permanent usufruct rights of land that technically belonged to the nation. That meant that land reform beneficiaries (ejidatarios) could neither sell nor use the land as collateral for credit. Villagers also disliked the fact that ejidos were created by nationalizing hacienda property and turning it over to villagers without any public declaration of hacienda owners' wrongdoing. On the contrary, it created the appearance that the state alone had the moral authority to bequeath landed wealth to rural people.[53]

In principle, the dotación process began with a formal petition signed by every male head of household who wished to be enrolled as a potential beneficiary. In practice, the final list of ejido beneficiaries sometimes included outsiders or people who had only recently settled in the area, and it might exclude longtime residents who had run afoul of local power brokers. The petition might refer to a specific plot of land, though in later years most villagers left the selection of an appropriate parcel up to the land reform bureaucracy. Wherever possible, the government formed ejidos on existing federal property, but that was rarely the case, and most land reform parcels were cobbled together by expropriating portions of one or more private properties, whose owners received indemnities ranging from undesirable government bonds to generous cash settlements. Most landowners regarded the land reform as confiscatory, and a significant minority tried to head off the process by dividing their properties into parcels too small to be subject to expropriation. Others sent gunmen to persuade neighboring villagers that it would be unwise to file a land reform petition.[54] If the proper documents arrived on the governor's desk (or after 1936, at the Land Reform Administration in Mexico City), and the authorities determined they had merit, they would order a preliminary land survey and grant beneficiaries provisional possession—another point at which landowners sometimes put up a fight. The paperwork ultimately came before the president, who made the final determination about whether to establish a permanent ejido. By then, months or years might have passed since the villagers filed the original petition. The final step involved making a definitive map of the ejido and walking the boundary lines in the presence of the men officially enrolled as ejido beneficiaries. Assuming they concurred with the survey (they sometimes didn't), the villagers received definitive possession of the land and elected an administrative team to handle finances, the apportionment of plots, and other such administrative tasks.

Mexican scientists contemplated the land reform program with a deepening sense of dread. Quevedo and his followers believed that rural people lacked the education and comprehension (or as they typically put it, the "*cultura*") to properly manage the nation's precious forest resources. Scientific consensus in the 1920s attributed a full 80 percent of deforestation to rural people's misguided use of the woodlands, and experts despaired of rural people's "primitive" and "criminal" use of the forests.[55] They regarded it as unwise and in a sense perverse to allow peasants to request forestlands through the land reform. As Quevedo complained in a speech in 1924, the agrarian movement "completely ignored the healthy principles of forest economy, and rather than encourage conservation and the well-being of rural pueblos and their forest resources, [had] promoted their destruction."[56] Scientists had no faith in the agrarian reform bureaucracy, which they accused of a "lack of oversight" for having turned over great stands of timber to "ill-prepared communities."[57] Without the guidance of experts, these scientists concluded, land reform beneficiaries would finish off their woods within a matter of years.

In contrast to the disordered world of peasant production on ejidos, most experts pinned their hopes on the predictable world of highly capitalized logging operations. As Salvador Guerrero, the head of the forest service, wrote in 1922, land reform officials should refrain from breaking up the largest timber holdings because "great stands or stretches [of forest] under the dominion of a single proprietor" were the only ones that could be "submitted to a standardized plan of exploitation." He recognized that logging companies had ravaged the timberlands in the past, and that the foreign-owned companies in the north had performed particularly badly by making substantial clear-cuts and leaving behind nothing but bare ground, which threatened to cripple the region's climate. Nevertheless, he believed that large-scale property owners could be compelled to adopt a "strict conservationist regimen" through the judicious application of legal sanctions and economic enticements.[58] Other scientists saw a similar potential in railroad companies, which had "powerful means to put our forest resources to work" if only they began to manage the resources more carefully. While railroad companies had certainly contributed to the "ruin" of many forests in the past, proper legislation would ensure that they, like the great timber companies, would make efficient and easily supervised stewards of the woodlands.[59]

Yet land reform marched forward regardless of such sentiments, and scientists concluded that the most viable approach was to reform peasant practices. As a first line of action, Mexican forestry officials began to lay down the precepts for what would eventually become known as community forestry, by teaching rural people to respect and care for the land that the state had put under their care. As the distinguished naturalist Ángel Roldán argued in 1929, foresters needed to "raise the consciousness" of rural people—particularly indigenous ones—and teach them to conserve the forest "in a measured and sober" way. At that point, it would be easy to convince rural folk that well-managed woods represented "the fruit of their own abnegation and care," on which their well-being depended.[60] In the words of another forestry expert, teaching rural people to make a living through the rational use of their forest wealth would fulfill the "basic ideal" of the Mexican Revolution by ensuring the "social and economic improvement of the peasant class."[61] A key problem, however, was the lack of a means to get this conservationist message across to the public.

In 1921 Quevedo, along with Julio Riquilme and other members of the nation's intellectual elite, founded the Sociedad Forestal Mexicana. By 1923 the society had 130 members. It functioned both as a professional association and as an advocacy group even though most of its funds derived from a modest government subsidy.[62] Its first order of business was to propose a regulatory framework. Writing in the inaugural issue of the society's journal, *México Forestal*, Quevedo argued that "reasonable people [*personas sensatas*] and all manner of cultivated institutions are preoccupied by the grave dangers posed by deforestation and therefore energetically solicit that the government enact measures to put an end to the disorganized and ruinous exploitation of forest resources."[63] Quevedo had once mused about the virtues of extreme sanctions such as colonial-era laws that punished unauthorized logging with death, but in 1922 he made the more measured proposal that all watersheds and public lands unsuited for agriculture should be designated as forest preserves and that logging on private-property village commons should be closely regulated.[64]

Officials at various levels had made piecemeal conservationist decrees since the end of the revolution. Agriculture officials sent state governors a circular in 1922 warning that "logging great extensions of forest" threatened to exhaust natural resources, kill off natural springs and result in the "degradation of the land, which will become wastelands [*eriales*] or even deserts." Later that year, Obregón established two modest forest reserves. In 1923 the Department of Agriculture invoked Article 27 to demand that timber companies file environmental impact studies of the land they intended to log. Few did so.[65]

The legislative outline that Quevedo and his associates originally proposed in the pages of *México Forestal* eventually became the Forest Code of 1926, whose goal was "to regularize the conservation, restoration, propagation, and utilization of forest vegetation."[66] The law (and its enabling legislation, or *reglamentación*, which passed the following year) authorized the creation of a national forest service and regulated nearly every aspect of logging. It also made provisions to protect forests in important watersheds and granted the forest service oversight of logging on public, private, communal, or ejidal land. The heart of the legislation called for a radical change in the way that villagers harvested and sold their timber by requiring people who belonged to ejidos and native communities to form producers cooperatives and obtain a scientific management plan from the forest service. The cooperatives would negotiate timber sales directly with sawmills, bypassing the speculators known as *contratistas*, whom most experts considered little better than con men. As one official wrote in 1930, the contratistas used the "ignorance" of rural people as a "rich vein" to tap; he accused the middlemen of making a fortune by paying next to nothing for the wood and labor they extracted from villagers.[67]

Private landholders received far greater latitude than did ejidos and indigenous communities. They faced none of the requirements to form special organizations for producers, nor were they subject to the same degree of scrutiny by the authorities. Nevertheless, the law did place far greater restrictions on private property than did most other laws in the Americas at the time. It required landowners to file a complete management plan with the forest service before putting their woods into production and stipulated that the largest commercial operations should hire a full-time forester charged with developing a ten-year management plan.[68] Private owners, like villagers, needed to obtain a complete set of logging permits, known as guías forestales, attesting to the legal provenance of logs, sawn lumber, and other forest products transported on roads and railways.

The guías were a singularly efficient means to oversee compliance with forestry regulations. Rather than attempting to police logging operations at the point of production, it was far easier to inspect wood as mule trains (and later, trucks) crawled along the roads or as workers loaded logs onto railroad cars. The 1926 law therefore included a series of measures allowing for thorough inspections of forest products shipments. No timber, lumber, or pine resin could be moved without a complete set of logging licenses, transshipment permits, and purchase orders from the logging concern, all of which had to be filled out in sextuplet and handed over to the proper authorities at various points in the production process. These documents could only be granted by senior officials (initially, the local representatives of the secretary of agriculture, and by the 1940s, the federal authorities in Mexico City).[69] Without necessarily meaning to, the 1926 law and its successors elevated the forest guides into nearly totemic documents with the power to imbue any shipment of timber with at least the appearance of legality.

Although the 1926 law had a number of provisions intended to increase the efficiency of commercial logging and thus to aid in the overall conservation of resources, it unintentionally created barriers to villagers' entry into the timber market. To take one seemingly prosaic example, the law prohibited the use of hatchets for cutting commercial timber because hand tools left more debris and hence wasted more wood than saws. (Villagers could use hatchets to collect wood for domestic use, however).[70] This modernizing and seemingly commonsense requirement aimed to maximize the usable wood from each tree. Yet most villagers owned hatchets and felt comfortable using them; saws were expensive and more specialized tools, and few rural people could justify the expense of buying a second implement to cut wood.[71] Even though forest wardens only sporadically enforced this provision, its main effect was to criminalize the most common peasant logging practice and to lower the value of ejidal timber by effectively making it contraband.

Despite its complexity and lack of grounding in the social realities of rural society, the 1926 Forestry Code made it possible for land reform beneficiaries to use their woods and sell the products of their labor on the open market. It set down the principle that the good of the nation demanded the protection of forest ecosystems, including those on private property. It even required commercial interests to abide by scientific norms in the woodlands. Yet in codifying a distinction between peasant and commercial production, the law's authors created an unbridgeable distinction between community forestry and industrial production. Policy makers tacitly assumed that peasant production would always remain artisanal and small-scale, whereas commercial production would drive the economy in a scientific and rationally sensibly way. Commercial producers had mere paperwork to contend with, while the rural people, who for the most part worked on lands they received through the agrarian reform, needed to establish cooperatives that would ultimately determine who had the right to work collectively owned forests.[72]

LAND REFORM IN THE SIERRA TARAHUMARA

The revolution lingered in Chihuahua longer than in other parts of the country. Pancho Villa finally surrendered in 1920, the same year that the first postrevolutionary elections brought Ignacio C. Enríquez into office as governor. He inherited a state beset by economic chaos and political uncertainty, and he responded by establishing over two hundred ejidos and a handful of homestead-like "colonies" divided out of huge Porfirian estates such as the Terrazas hacienda.[73] Enríquez and his immediate successors took a pragmatic approach to agrarian reform, which they regarded as a means to build political clienteles in the countryside. Yet the redistribution of land did meet the demands of villagers, many of whom were revolutionary veterans who formed agrarian leagues between 1919 and 1923 to request ejidos in the prime agricultural zones of central Chihuahua.[74] Nineteenth-century military colonies (*presidios*) such as Namiquipa and

Cuchillo Parado also demanded the restitution of territory they had lost to the swelling cattle haciendas of the Porfiriato.[75] Enríquez's openness to agrarian demands combined with officials' fear that a revived Villismo might invigorate the military rebellions led by Adolfo de la Huerta in 1923 or Gonzalo Escobar in 1929 to make Chihuahua one of the primary sites of land reform before Lázaro Cárdenas's 1934–1940 presidency.

Agrarian reform had a very different face in the Sierra Tarahumara, where few indigenous communities in the highlands requested ejidos. In some cases, mestizo settlers (chabochis) filed the paperwork and used the land reform process to appropriate resources and labor from native people. Most of the mestizos who settled in Rarámuri rancherías had arrived either as lumberjacks or miners, so they had at least some knowledge of the booming demand for wood products in the late 1910s and 1920s. Railroads continued to consume the majority of national timber production in the mid-1920s. Not only did trains use wood as fuel throughout much of Chihuahua, but rebuilding track created a yawning demand for wood. According to one forester, railroads required 8 million–10 million ties per year in the 1920s, accounting for around 1 million cubic meters of wood, enough to build a line from Denver to Chicago.[76] The Pearson-owned North Western Railroad line used 50,000 ties to rebuild after the revolution, plus an unknown additional amount of wood to restore 45 bridges destroyed in the fighting.[77] Even the big Madera Lumber Company sawmills could not satisfy this market, opening the door once again to the Rarámuri woodcutters who had made railroad ties by hand ever since the early 1900s.

Land reform provided one opportunity to gain a toehold in the buoyant timber industry. Mestizos requested ejidos on behalf of Rarámuri communities in at least a dozen cases, without telling of the locals what they were doing. The anthropologist Françoise Vatant points out that mestizo families living near the dispersed Rarámuri rancherías filed land reform petitions and elected themselves into ejidal offices specifically so they could lease "their" ejido's timber rights to logging companies.[78] Indeed, most of the thirty petitions that the state land reform commission received between 1917 and 1924 from indigenous communities in the Sierra Tarahumara appear suspicious. It cannot be a coincidence that ten Rarámuri rancherías in the heart of the forestlands requested ejidos over a two-month period in 1922, including four petitions filed on the same day.[79] Some villagers only learned about the existence of such petitions when they learned that they had been granted an ejido! That is what happened in the hamlet of Rocheáchi, whose leaders refused in 1927 to take possession of a huge property that its members had supposedly requested seven years previously. The village elders told the officials that they "didn't have an agrarian problem" [*no tenían el problema de tierras*] and wanted nothing to do with the federal authorities who suddenly appeared bearing documents and maps.[80] Yet the fraudulent land reform processes succeeded often enough to bring a score of indigenous communities—and their resources—more fully into the orbit of mestizo timber dealers and the federal land reform and forest bureaucracies.

The timber trade had bridged indigenous and mestizo populations for over a generation, but the advent of land reform tended to favor the mestizo side more. One example of this dynamic can be seen in the growing influence of San Juanito, a predominantly mestizo town nestled among Rarámuri rancherías fifteen kilometers outside the district seat of Bocoyna. The first settlers arrived to this town in the gently sloping sierras of southwestern Chihuahua in 1884, looking for work at the new, steam-powered sawmill that produced wood for local railroads and mines. The town grew along with the northern economy and had reached perhaps a thousand inhabitants by 1920. The town had two mills by that time, one belonging to Casimiro Almeida Fierro's Compañía Industrial Mercantil, and the other to the future timber magnate Juan González Ugarte. While both of these timber conglomerates had access to concession lands north of Bocoyna and apparently sent (mestizo) lumberjacks to fell trees and transport them back via the railroad, the sawmills themselves were small and undercapitalized operations compared to the huge plant in Madera. Most of the men who worked in San Juanito were mestizos who continually shifted between work in the lumberyards, railroads, and sawmills.[81]

In the early 1920s, the Compañía Industrial Mercantil bought a 30,000 acre tract of land outside San Juanito from the Chihuahua Timberland Company. The new corporation immediately started to ramp up the production of lumber but stumbled when it tried to enter the far larger market for railroad ties. Even though the company ignored timber regulations and made a series of clearcuts of what a pliant forester characterized as "decrepit" larger trees on its property, the Compañía Mercantil could not compete with the cheaper ties from nearby indigenous communities. As they had done for decades, work gangs of ten or twenty Rarámuri men logged trees on communal lands and sculpted them into ties using hatchets. They carried their wares to San Juanito, where lumber companies bought them for twenty centavos each, a seventh the price of the going rate. Despite the absurdly low prices, some Rarámuri men hauled ties thirty or forty kilometers to the San Juanito railhead—a trade that remained a viable business for Rarámuri men as late as the 1960s.[82]

In 1921 a number of villagers living on the outskirts of San Juanito petitioned for an ejido land grant, and five years later the government approved a relatively modest parcel of 5,100 hectares. Although subsequent observers referred to the new ejido as a "Tarahumara settlement," mestizos figured among its members and ran it as their own fiefdom. They also maintained a tolerably good relationship with the Compañía Industrial Mercantil, where some of them almost certainly had worked at one time or another. Indeed, the company did not bother to protest the loss of 1,000 hectares of timberland to the new ejido—a far cry from its usual resistance to any loss of territory to the land reform. Perhaps the fact that the ejido accounted for a tiny, semi-deforested fraction of the company's land made it easier to swallow the loss. Whatever the case, the company seems to have cared less about the actual ownership of the land than about keeping up with railroads' appetite for construction material, and its administrators soon purchased as many handmade ties as San Juanito could provide. They also bought rough-hewn ties from the approximately 2,500 Rarámuri people who lived on the company's own land. One local forester marveled at the indigenous men's skill in making between six and ten ties per day using nothing more than a hatchet, though he grumbled that they lost too many days of work to their "feckless" custom of gathering together for the ritual drinking of tesgüino.[83] In this, he completely misunderstood indigenous men's motivations. It seems clear that the natives traded in railroad ties precisely in order to preserve enough economic and cultural autonomy to celebrate tesgüinadas and other customs, without which they would probably not have engaged with the timber economy at all.

Soon after San Juanito received its ejido, the residents received permission to make intensive cuts on their new property. Native people did most of the logging (as well as the hauling and other menial tasks), while the mestizos typically worked for wages in the sawmills.[84] The scramble to produce railroad ties destroyed the remaining forests on San Juanito's ejidal lands between 1928 and the mid-1940s, even though it received a supplemental grant of more woodland in 1936. Clear-cutting did much of the damage, and the woodcutters' selection of trees only made matters worse. Railroad ties needed to be made from the heartwood (core) of a tree, so native loggers preferred to fell relatively small, younger trees that had yet to reproduce and left older and less reproductive trees standing. As a result, the forest virtually ceased to regenerate.[85] Ironically, that did not put an end to the timber business. Neighboring Rarámuri communities soon started to complain that people from San Juanito invaded their territory, illegally chopped down trees, then hauled them off to the sawmill. Foresters must have known something about this trade because they continued to issue logging and transportation permits to the San Juanito ejido for decades to come, even though the community had just "a few meager stands" of timber remaining on its own land. Forestry officials justified the fraudulent traffic in sawlogs because, as they said, most members of the ejido were Indians and "there are no agricultural lands or alternative sources of employment in this region."[86]

The land reform was not the only way for outsiders to acquire indigenous land. The forest service bureaucracy offered unscrupulous officials another avenue into Rarámuri territory. One particularly notorious official was Santiago Brooks, a North American who arrived in Chihuahua sometime after the revolution, probably to take a job in the timber industry. By the mid-1920s, he was working as a federal forest warden in Chihuahua and Sinaloa. His job acquainted him with the landscape of the Sierra Tarahumara, as well as with the regulatory routines of the forest bureaucracy. In 1927 he made a formal request for the rights to federal lands (a former concession that had expired) in Urique, some four days by horse from Creel, where he was stationed. He proposed to fell only "defective woods and decrepit trees" and agreed to pay a fee of one peso per cord for logs and fifty cents for branches and debris (*desperdicios*, known in forestry parlance as "slash"), for a total of one hundred cords per month. He concluded his petition by appealing to authorities' conservationist sensibilities, reasoning that his "culling" (*aseo*) of the forest would end "the continual forest fires that occur in those distant lands." His petition arrived at the desk of his supervisor in Chihuahua City, who quickly passed it along to his superior in Mexico City with a favorable recommendation. The entire approval process took less than a week.[87]

Within a month after Brooks began work, the mayor of Urique wrote the Ministry of Agriculture complaining that Brooks had fined the "La Fortuna" mining company 3,000 pesos for unauthorized logging on his claim. Brooks still held his position as a forest warden at the time, and he used his authority to confiscate 150 cords of wood that the company's woodsmen had felled on his property for shipment to the mine. His actions left the workers with nothing to show for their labor and forced the mine to suspend operations until it could find an alternative source of wood. The

Urique authorities implied that Brooks had taken advantage of the situation to hire the mine's woodcutters on the spot; if so, he would have been in an ideal position to negotiate with them, since they had just lost a few days' labor. The mayor pitched his own complaint in terms of conservation and nationalism. He accused Brooks of "making a considerable clear-cut [*destrozo*] of precious woods," including sabino, fir, and acacia. He drove his point home, stating, "It is a shame that our Forestry officials authorize or encourage individuals from foreign countries like the aforementioned Mr. Broks [*sic*] to kill off [*matar*] our Forest wealth without any rational or human, much less patriotic, consideration."[88]

Brooks's transparent effort to corner the labor and timber markets near Urique forced the secretary of agriculture to fire him as a warden. His allies in the government did not revoke his logging permit, however, and dismissed the municipal authorities' complaint by suggesting that they harbored "an indirect interest" in the federal lands he had leased. In fact, the federal authorities continued to renew Brooks's logging permits even after Mexico City officials started grumbling about "excessive extraction" on his land. Brooks continued to run a logging operation in the sierras that exported wood to El Paso, Texas, until the early 1930s, when he sold his rights to the ubiquitous, Mexican-owned Compañía Industrial Mercantil.[89]

The early stages of land reform in the Sierra Tarahumara and the concomitant expansion of the forest bureaucracy diminished the Rarámuri people's ability to control their own resources, in part because it blurred the line between insiders and outsiders and between forestry officials and opportunists. Nowhere was this clearer than in Cusárare, one of the largest Rarámuri communities in the sierras and one destined to become a significant timber producer in the decades to come. Village leaders requested an ejido in 1922, probably at the behest of agents from a local timber company. The authorities took quick action and approved a substantial 30,777-hectare grant, yet the residents found it impossible to work their own lands. The timber companies sent their own crews to fell the trees and only hired indigenous people to build logging roads. Daniel Galicia, the forester assigned by the secretary of agriculture to conduct management studies (*estudios dasonómicos*), issue logging permits, and manage forests in the region, soon established himself as the intermediary between indigenous land reform beneficiaries and the timber magnate Juan González Ugarte. The forester convinced the company to withdraw its lumberjacks so he could set up a "model" forestry operation in Cusárare, in a bid to demonstrate that native men would make good lumberjacks. His detractors accused him of pocketing all the profits from the new operation, however. Galicia also opened the town's only general store and sometimes paid the Rarámuri sawmill workers in scrip that could only be redeemed there.[90] In Cusárare, as in most of the Sierra Tarahumara, these sorts of irregularities dogged the land reform from its earliest days, calling into question whether it would ever fulfill the "promises of the revolution."

AGRARIAN CONTENTION IN MICHOACÁN

Politically astute indigenous men numbered among the earliest and most tenacious leaders of Michoacán's agrarian movement. Individuals such as Primo Tapia and Ernesto Prado in the northwest and Jesús Aguilar on the opposite end of the state encouraged people in scores of indigenous communities to petition for ejidos. They spearheaded the often conflictive struggle to occupy parcels of land carved from the very haciendas that had once dominated the social and agricultural landscape. Even in the politically conservative Uruapan area, Purépecha villagers filed petitions for ejidos, although they rarely got involved in the agrarian conflicts that roiled most of the state in the 1920s. Mestizo communities soon joined the agrarian movement as well, some of them led by politically committed schoolteachers and local intellectuals who regarded land reform as an instrument of class struggle.[91] The social breadth and ideologically driven character of Michoacán's agrarian movement made it difficult for outsiders to follow the Chihuahuan pattern and use land reform to capture indigenous forestlands. On the contrary, most timber interests in Michoacán tried to derail the land reform process by any means possible, from murdering agrarian leaders to suborning the surveyors sent to plot the boundaries of ejido land grants. They also relied on their control of the market. All the major companies maintained networks of agents (contratistas) who arranged long-term timber leases with ejidos and indigenous communities or established themselves as the sole buyers of wood that a given village produced.

Even so, the agrarian reform raised unprecedented questions about who would ultimately control the forests in Michoacán. In the northeastern highlands around Zitácuaro, for example, the American-owned ASARCO mining concern required substantial amounts of wood for mineshafts and fuel, and indigenous men from the surrounding communities often took jobs as woodcutters on lands that ASARCO owned or rented. When villagers in the township of El Rosario learned that they would soon be granted some of the company's prime forest reserves, they began to demand payment for the logs cut on their soon-to-be property. The company balked at what its manager called "the theft of wood from our lots in Rosario by the Indians who live there" and apparently increased the pace of wood cutting on the parcel in question. Villagers responded with a brief takeover of the company's sawmill.[92] Elsewhere, would-be ejidatarios brought lawsuits or petitioned authorities to keep landowners from logging on territory they hoped would one day be granted to them as ejidos.[93] Failing that, they sometimes took more direct action and drove company lumberjacks out of the woods.[94]

Villagers complained that landowners and logging companies preemptively clear-cut any land that they suspected the government had slated for redistribution. The representatives of one indigenous community denounced the loggers (whom they called "Spanish brigands") who suddenly appeared in nearby woods that would "quite probably" be included in their ejido grant.[95] Another set of villagers explained that the owner of a parcel targeted for redistribution had sent woodcutters into the sierras to cut everything in sight, leaving the beneficiaries with nothing but "completely denuded fields."[96] In the uncertain context of shifting occupancy and preemptive logging, Michoacán's forests became a weapon in the social struggle that gripped the highlands for decades to come.

When forest communities did succeed in taking possession of their ejido parcels, sawmill owners turned to a technique that had served them well during the Porfiriato: *rentismo*, or the use of unconscionable rental contracts with a thirty-year duration that paid villagers a pittance for the logs and railroad ties extracted from their property. Lawyers working for family-owned lumber companies in Uruapan were particularly successful in wheedling rental agreements from indigenous people in Meseta Purépecha. Forest officials understood what was happening, but they hesitated to rescind the contracts because it might choke off the communities' only secure source of income.[97] Lázaro Cárdenas tried to resolve the problem during his term as governor (1928–1932), when he ordered the Michoacán secretary of the interior to abrogate the contracts and mandated the creation of the Liga de Comunidades Indígenas de Bosques (League of Indigenous Communities of the Woodlands). Little progress was made, however, because the league never materialized and the government nullified only a handful of contracts. Cárdenas's government passed a law in 1931 that ordered the restitution of 220,000 hectares of forests to twenty communities and charged villagers with forming producers cooperatives, but contratistas somehow managed to sign new lease arrangements that once again kept villagers out of the timber trade.[98]

The growth of Mexico City and other cities in the aftermath of revolution further aggravated agrarian tensions in Michoacán. Even in the nation's capital, most people cooked with charcoal made from oak, or sometimes from mesquite or needle bush (*Acacia farnesiana*). Mexico City consumed around 700 metric tons of charcoal per day in the mid-1930s, as well as 260 railroad cars' worth of firewood every month. About a third of these products came from Michoacán, though the majority still came from the small army of independent woodsmen who hiked firewood and handmade charcoal down from the hillsides outside of Mexico City. The easiest-to-reach stands of timber disappeared quickly as forests in the Federal District fell from 22,000 hectares in 1913 to 6,000 two decades later. The foreign-owned Suchi Lumber Company of Mexico State stepped in to meet some of this demand. It supplied around two-thirds of the city's fuel wood by the mid-1930s thanks to a workforce of 800 woodcutters who received "miserable wages" for their labor.[99] By that point, the eastern Sierra de Tlalpujahua of Michoacán had already come into the orbit of the capital's thirst for wood and charcoal. The developing markets opened new avenues for peasant subsistence and deepened existing conflicts between villagers and timber interests.

One indication of these new stresses was that formerly worthless slash left over from commercial logging around Ciudad Hidalgo suddenly became the object of contention between charcoal makers and the most powerful timber family of the region—much the same as what had transpired in Chihuahua two decades earlier. The "Pomposo Solís e Hijos" company had made a fortune selling ties during the Porfirian railroad boom, and after the revolution, it continued to employ scores of lumberjacks, who felled trees with hatchets, hauled them to the logging roads and railheads, from whence they were transported to the family's Ciudad Hidalgo sawmill. Workers received their salaries biweekly in scrip, which they were encouraged to use in a company store that added a 15–20 percent markup for its merchandise.[100] The Solís family's wealth translated into expanding political power as well. Its members controlled key municipal offices in the 1920s, and one son won an influential position in the state government in 1926. At that point, the family took steps to corner the charcoal market. Until then, the independent contractors had managed the trade by organizing crews of *carboneros* (charcoal men)—casual laborers and peasants typically considered the most marginal group of forest workers—who collected the debris left behind by commercial loggers and fired it in earthen mounds. They delivered the finished product to the contractors, who sold it at the railheads around Ciudad Hidalgo. The Solís family broke the contractors' grip in one stroke by colluding with the railroads to refuse delivery from contractors. With these pesky middlemen out of the way, carboneros had no alternative but to sell their product directly to Solís e Hijos, who soon became one of the primary suppliers of the Mexico City market.[101]

The rising value of charcoal also prompted landowners to follow the familiar practice of preemptively clear-cutting disputed woodlands. For example, when the owner of the Chincua hacienda in the district of Senguío learned that the neighboring community of San Francisco de los Reyes had requested an ejido on his property, he contacted the local forester and received provisional license of dubious legality that authorized him to cut wood on the parcel in question. According to the soon-to-be ejidatarios, the hacienda owner had ordered his men to carry out the "irrational exploitation" of timber before they could occupy the land.[102] The landowner countered that his logging crews never strayed onto the territory slated for redistribution. No matter where the truth lay, the episode demonstrated that the charcoal trade had led each side to value the oak trees they had once considered a nuisance species.

Yet another case involved Aputzio de Juárez, a predominantly Otomí community nestled in the hills that ripple along the outskirts of Zitácuaro. The village's impoverished land produced few crops, and most residents worked as day laborers on nearby haciendas. Writing to President Calles in 1927, a committee comprising mestizos and indigenous people explained that they had dutifully formed a cooperative the previous year, making them one of the first in the nation to do so. They began to work "most harmoniously to sell [their] products at a very good price and succeeding in that way to greatly improve [their] situation," but a few months later the British manager of the Toluca-Zitácuaro Railroad unexpectedly refused to accept their logs and forced them to abandon the business.[103] The railroad manager had always accepted their charcoal and handmade ties before, but his attitude changed after they formed the cooperative. The villagers speculated that he had intended to hire them as lumberjacks and set himself up as a timber magnate. It turned out that the village's anger was misdirected, however. As the secretary of agriculture explained to the president's office (though apparently not to the community itself), the real problem was that the community's permission to cut wood had expired. If they wanted to keep selling charcoal at the railhead, they only needed to solicit a new one.[104] There is no indication that they ever did so, and the producers cooperative that had once seemed so promising fell victim to the forest service bureaucracy.

THE LIMITS OF AUTHORITY

The experiences of ejidos and indigenous communities in Michoacán and Chihuahua suggested that a number of systematic problems vitiated the effectiveness of the postrevolutionary state's capacity to manage the forests. The ease with which outsiders twisted the land reform in Rarámuri territories to meet their own interests and the incipient corruption of ejidal authorities in both states accompanied the land reform at every turn. Ejidos in forestlands proved particularly susceptible to the intrigues of individuals who understood how bureaucracies worked or who had strong contacts with timber companies. The revolution had not dispensed with the contratista wood buyers for sawmills, many of whom actually found it easier to work with ejidos than with indigenous commonholders with questionable colonial-era titles. The corruption of some forestry officials merely exacerbated this situation. Forest wardens and local representatives of the federal agriculture bureaucracy had privileged knowledge, not only of the rapidly evolving legal landscape imposed by state formation, but of the real, forested landscape that postrevolutionary reconstruction and urbanization rendered increasingly valuable. Some, such as Chihuahua's Santiago Brooks, acted both as government officials and as contratistas at the same time.

The 1926 forestry code provided a modicum of shelter from these ills, particularly by making producers cooperatives the sole legal vendor of forest products produced on ejidos and common lands. In theory, such a measure should have ensured that villagers received the fair market value of their products and kept middlemen at bay. Yet the forestry bureaucracy lacked the personnel and expertise to implement these regulations, even if local officials had not developed a vocation for graft and corruption. Moreover, the law construed rural people as a threat to the forest whose behavior merited close scrutiny and, if possible, modification. It criminalized some peasant practices in the woodlands and, in so doing, created an incentive for rural people to ignore or subvert conservationist regulations. This situation did not present too much of a problem in the 1920s, when few local leaders understood the law and fewer still had any regular contact with government foresters. But the officious treatment that the community of Aputzio received at the hands of forestry officials hinted at the way that these principles would function in the years to come. The red tape that kept the Aputzio charcoal makers from legally transporting their goods left them with three alternatives: they could give up on their bid to sell charcoal; or they could wait until they had completed the necessary paperwork (a lengthy process that ultimately required approval by a forestry bureaucracy already stretched thin); or they could follow the path of least resistance and sell their wares on the black market.

An increasing number of villagers chose the third route, which forestry officials coded as "clandestinity" (*clandestinaje*) or, more colorfully, as "piracy." Only a few years after scientists had succeeded in translating their vision for the forestlands into law, it was clear that legislation alone could not govern Mexico's increasingly politicized landscape. Political leaders initially shrugged off the problem. When Lázaro Cárdenas became president in 1934, however, he convinced Miguel Ángel de Quevedo, who had sketched out the legislation in the first place, to take control of the forest service. Together, the two men tried to resurrect the idea of village-based logging operations, as long as they took place under the watchful eye of professional foresters.

CHAPTER 3

Revolutionary Forestry, 1928–1942

In December 1929 the forest warden Andrés Orozco made an inspection tour of several Purépecha townships in the gently rolling hills of Michoacán's Meseta Purépecha. Orozco set out on horseback and soon reached the small village of Cocucho, where he discovered fresh stumps and other signs of recent logging activity. He knew that something was amiss because the community had never formed a producers cooperative or filed the required forestry study, much less received the appropriate permissions from his office. Orozco spent several days trying to learn who had made the unauthorized cut, but he never succeeded in identifying a culprit or learning what had become of the wood. He had to settle for giving the local authorities a tongue lashing and ordering them to put an end to the illegal cutting. From Orozco's perspective, the whole incident revealed the villagers as cunning and oblivious to the law. He wrote dispiritedly to his superiors acknowledging that he knew "the residents of that place [would] return to their fraudulent use of the forest" the moment he left town, "owing to their deprived habits and remoteness from our offices." The only hope of turning the situation around, he believed, was for the governor to demand that the municipal authorities crack down on the villagers.[1]

Orozco had stepped into a terrain that would become familiar to regulators and rural people in subsequent years—one in which each side deployed particular forms of knowledge and authority to vie against the other. The locals used their familiarity with the landscape and relative isolation to anticipate the arrival of inspectors and, if possible, to dispose of any incriminating evidence. Notwithstanding the political, social, and personal cleavages that characterized daily life in many highland communities, rural people often showed remarkable solidarity when confronted by meddlesome outsiders such as Orozco. Whether because they habitually protected each other from "the government" or because village bosses (*ca-*

ciques) had cowed their followers into silence, the members of communities typically presented a united front to forestry officials and pled ignorance when asked about those responsible for unauthorized logging. Then they resumed work as soon as the inspector moved on.[2]

Orozco found evidence of unauthorized cuts in each of the six communities he visited. At one point, he went so far as to request an armed escort from Governor Lázaro Cárdenas in order "to make [himself] respected by the Indians who carry out these actions." The governor suggested that Orozco should instead give tact and goodwill a try; persuasion rather than force might convince villagers to organize cooperatives and request the proper permissions. The forest warden took Cárdenas's proposition to heart. He discarded the idea of surrounding himself with soldiers, and resolved "to convince [the villagers] by means of advice and instruction [*consejos e instrucciones*] to request their permits as quickly as the Forest Code allows, offering them any help they need[ed] to complete the paperwork while making them see that their previous behavior was a grave violation of the law that could have a range of possible consequences."[3]

Orozco's epiphany anticipated a broad reconfiguration of the relationship between forestry experts and villagers in the 1930s. Leading intellectuals came to believe that education and technical assistance could build an environmental consciousness among rural people, converting villagers from passive objects of environmental regulation into modernized and self-disciplined environmental subjects who understood how their actions affected the natural world.[4] They recognized that a social metamorphosis on this scale would not come easily, but the stakes were high. On the one hand, conservationists such as Miguel Ángel de Quevedo continued to insist that deforestation posed a potentially catastrophic threat to Mexico's climate by reducing rainfall, increasing the potential for flooding, and rendering cities unlivable. On the other hand, scientists and political leaders regarded forests as a linchpin to economic development whose value rivaled that of the nation's storied petroleum deposits. Yet the forests' vast potential could disappear virtually overnight if it were not managed properly.[5] To meet these challenges, professional foresters proposed a series of measures ranging from Arbor Day celebrations to policy interventions intended to refashion peasants' relationship with nature.

The incipient move to educate rural people and regulate the use of forests leapt forward when Cárdenas became president, in 1934, and strove to make good on the "promises of the revolution" as he understood them. His administration rejuvenated the land reform process, assailed foreign land-owners and corporations, and coaxed the popular classes to join officially sanctioned associations meant both to empower and discipline them. He elevated the forest service to a cabinet-level ministry called the Autonomous Department of Forests, Game, and Fisheries and charged Quevedo with making it work. The newly energized organization redoubled its oversight of logging operations—and particularly of peasants' use of forests received through land reform—and launched ambitious educational and research programs that both deepened scientific understandings of Mexican ecosystems and burnished experts' claims to have privileged knowledge of proper forest management. Foresters renewed their efforts to organize villagers into producers cooperatives that functioned as community-owned enterprises while making peasant production more visible and easily controlled by local authorities. Taken together, these Cardenista initiatives reflected a broad vision of environmental governance best characterized as *revolutionary forestry*: a socioenvironmental ideology that sought to grant rural people wide latitude to work their own forestlands, subject to the often paternalistic supervision of forestry experts, and provided that they organize themselves into formally constituted organizations. At its core, revolutionary forestry proposed to modernize campesino production in order to achieve the rational, sustained use of forests. Income from logging would allow villages to bootstrap themselves into the economic mainstream while furnishing a growing proportion of the raw materials needed for national development.

Revolutionary forestry was one of many official intrusions into rural life during the period of postrevolutionary reconstruction, and rural people greeted it with a characteristic mixture of skeptical enthusiasm, indifference, and passive resistance.[6] Over time, however, an important contingent of rural society came to accept elements of its conservationist message. People in many places came to identify with village cooperatives, for example, because they regarded them as a viable means of managing their own woods and distributing the earnings from community production. In a few cases, rural people clung to their cooperatives even after a 1948 law formally abolished them. The cooperatives faced myriad challenges, however. One of the most serious derived from the paternalist attitudes of the technocratic elites who tended to conceive of rural people as a dangerously backward impediment to modernization on a par with countries that they considered more technically and "culturally" advanced.

Professional foresters in postrevolutionary Mexico worried that their nation did not measure up to the developed world's institutional capacity to manage forests and train a professional cadre of experts. In future decades, such transnational comparisons led Mexican intellectuals to conclude that their nation's ecology and social structures differed in fundamental respects from the richer and more temperate nations of the global north and therefore needed to be understood in their own terms—an intellectual development that the historian Stuart McCook has labeled "creole science."[7] In the 1930s, however, the scientists' musings led them to conclude that their compatriots' understanding of nature lagged dangerously behind those of the so-called advanced nations. These experts reckoned that their country had the ability to catch up in practical terms, such as in the drafting and enforcement of management policies, the modernization of manufacturing techniques, and the application of scientific research. What troubled them was the "backwardness" of rural society. Most intellectuals felt that Mexico came up short in terms of people's attitudes toward nature, and they knew that changing their countrymen's proclivities would not be easy. At a minimum, it would require a nationwide educational campaign built, in the first instance, around didactic civic rituals such as Arbor Day celebrations.

In the 1920s and 1930s, Mexican forestry experts published a steady stream of articles in *México Forestal* and the national press suggesting ways of bringing their country in line with more developed parts of the world. Their foremost goal was to pass conservationist legislation on a par with that of other nations (ultimately condensed in the 1926 Forestry Code), but they also suggested that Mexico follow the lead of foreign countries on issues ranging from the use of creosote to preserve railroad ties to the creation of forest reserves.[8] Quevedo, who was widely recognized as the dean of Mexican forestry, singled out the United States as a particularly worthy role model. He described it as a "Saxon, preservationist, disciplined and highly progressive" nation whose leaders intended to preserve and restore its forests thanks to the "magnificent" administration of natural resources. He also praised Japan, Switzerland, and, above all, France as examples of nations with well-developed educational and regulatory systems worthy of Mexican emulation.[9]

Quevedo placed part of the blame on a lack of effective political leadership. He complained, for example, that the authorities did nothing to stop peasants from burning their fields in the early spring to stimulate the growth of new grass and cut down on weeds, even though these fires often spread into the woods. Mexico's beautiful forests, he wrote, were being sacrificed to "pyromaniac campesinos, whom equally ignorant and perverse municipal authorities . . . abet and even encourage" to make their annual burns.[10] Other scientists agreed that Mexico's political leaders were at least partially responsible for the nation's environmental troubles. The distinguished public works engineer Roberto Gayol y Soto bitterly denounced politicians for selling out to logging interests and evading their moral obligation to protect the forests for future generations. He recognized that laws were in place to do just that, but lamented that "in practice, everything is subordinate to political considerations, and it is an illness that is killing our country."[11]

Though scientists lacked faith in political leaders' commitment to conservation, they explained Mexico's "backwardness" primarily as a consequence of its large class of impoverished and, to their eyes, atavistic rural people. Foresters often articulated the essentially tautological argument that Mexico's conservationist efforts fell short of the standards of the "advanced" world because peasants exploited forest resources in primitive and heedlessly destructive ways. More than a mere description of rural people's behavior, such arguments construed rural people's observable actions—which certainly could include the conscious or unconscious misuse of forest ecosystems—as evidence that they shared a uniform and deeply problematic orientation toward nature. Such ideas not only disregarded potentially sustainable campesino practices, but also suggested the existence of a peasant *culture* that stood as a stumbling block to forest conservation.

The language that foresters employed to discuss the nation's forests underscored their assumption that rural people represented the primary threat to the nation's ecosystems. Forestry experts routinely described the unnecessarily deep cuts that peasants used in the early twentieth century to draw the resin from pine trees as "barbarous" or "primitive."[12] Quevedo had argued as early as 1923 that native people should be prohibited from using slash-and-burn techniques to clear new lands because "such methods are repudiated as savage and condemned in advanced nations."[13] Local forest wardens echoed Quevedo's concerns about "primitive" tapping techniques and the use of fire to clear fields at the beginning of the growing season. As one warden from the state of Mexico noted, these behaviors came as no surprise "since we are not dealing here with well educated people but rather with rural folk [*gente campesina*], who for the most part lack understanding, study, and so on." He recommended putting teachers in charge of reforestation projects who could encourage people everywhere to recognize that the conservation and repopulation of forests represented a "sacred duty to our Homeland."[14]

In the 1920s, however, the forest service had no ability to carry out such a project.

The Forestry Code of 1926 was little more than a dead letter, and federal officials had few resources to command, so the Mexican Forest Society decided to make Arbor Day, known in the 1920s and 1930s as the Fiesta del Arbol, its primary means of outreach. Quevedo and his Junta Central de Bosques had organized various celebrations to plant trees and raise consciousness about urban forestry in Mexico City as early as 1893, and the Junta Central organized a revolutionary Arbor Day celebration in 1912, but Victoriano Huerta's military coup later that year put an end to the nascent educational initiative.[15] In 1922 Quevedo convinced the Forest Society to resume the tradition and expand the celebration into other parts of the republic (though educators in Michoacán had organized their own celebrations at least two years previously). He gave a speech that year in a working-class neighborhood of Mexico City in which he observed that the rising population density posed a threat to public hygiene not only because the growth of industry polluted the air but because the very process of human respiration entailed the exhalation of "highly noxious carbonic gases, meaning that man, like all animals in the urban agglomeration, constitutes a diminutive yet deleterious chimney."[16] What Quevedo's audience made of his rarified vocabulary is an open question, but his words did serve to reiterate most scientists' belief that urban life was inherently unhealthy, and that the best hope of improving conditions was to raise public appreciation of the ecological services offered by forests.

Arbor Day acquired a more overtly patriotic hue in the mid-1920s. Quevedo announced at the 1924 celebrations, for example, that reforestation projects formed an integral part of national reconstruction and helped to ensure national progress.[17] The Forestry Society reported the following year that it had organized an Arbor Day event in every major city, though by that point the majority of these events were aimed specifically at schoolchildren.[18] The federal Secretariat of Public Education (SEP), headed by José Vasconcelos, directed schools to turn their students out for the celebrations in which forestry officials and, on some occasions, notable politicians planted saplings in ceremonies captured by the flashing cam-

Figure 3.1. Elementary school students preparing to plant saplings during Arbor Day celebrations in the Colonia Campestre of San Ángel (Mexico City), 1924. *México Forestal* (March–April, 1924), 102.

eras of reporters.[19] In what may have been a typical celebration, the school inspector Evangelina Rodríguez Carvajal held an Arbor Day celebration in a land reform community outside Túxpan, Michoacán, attended by the local authorities, two schoolteachers, students, and local residents. She gave a simple speech, "appropriate for the audience," then led the enthusiastic group outside to plant forty-four saplings.[20] Arbor Day was only one of many civic rituals established in the 1920s to honor everything from motherhood to the Constitution and intended to instill a sense of patriotism and revolutionary citizenship among citizens. Nonetheless, it represented the first national initiative to disseminate a broad message of environmental conservation.

As the political atmosphere heated up in the 1930s, politicians and popular leaders took an increasingly combative stance toward wealthy landowners and others identified as exploiters of the people, and Arbor Day celebrations also acquired a harder edge. In 1934 the radical politician Francisco J. Múgica defined forest conservation as a form of class struggle, declaring in one Arbor Day speech that the popular classes should "clamor" against the despoilers (*devastadores*) of the forest. After enumerating the usual climatic and agricultural benefits of healthy forests, Múgica concluded that "society in general [*la colectividad*] and government officials will plant trees for the well-being of everyone, for the good of the nation, not for the benefit of the few."[21] In 1938 the Forestry Society claimed that every secondary school in the nation observed Arbor Day in some fashion and that "all the nation's institutions and its inhabitants in general" supported the government's "crusade" in favor of forests and against anyone who would do them harm.[22] The following year, radio transmissions, sporting events, and military parades were added to the festivities. According to the Forestry Society, students planted saplings and heard lessons about the value of trees even in the "smallest and most distant pueblos."[23]

Rural schools also promoted the ideals of nationalist conservationism in the 1930s. The forest service established eighteen small tree nurseries in public schools in 1936 and used at least some of them as "propaganda centers."[24] The following year, it announced plans to create nurseries in over a thousand more and claimed to have begun a campaign in public schools against forest fires. Officials took special aim at rural people's practice of burning underbrush and dead grass to encourage the growth of new vegetation. Schoolteachers were told to lecture their students and local fire brigades about "the grave problem caused by fire, which actually ruins pastures because it impedes reseeding and impoverishes soils by making them more alkaline and sterile and has a similar effect on the forest under-story."[25] By this point, Arbor Day celebrations were only one component of a much wider initiative to modernize not only the way that rural people used the forests, but the way they understood them. Forestry experts recognized that Arbor Day celebrations aimed at schoolchildren would not go very far toward realizing the sorts of broad changes they had in mind for the countryside. By that point, however, they had a more direct means to at their disposal.

SCIENCE, COOPERATIVES, AND PEASANT VISIBILITY

Despite the Forestry Society's lobbying and consciousness-raising efforts, there was little that Mexico City intellectuals could do to regulate the use of forests in the 1920s and early 1930s. The forest service had little administrative capacity, and its leadership had a reputation for incompetence and corruption. One of the capital's most prominent newspapers even labeled it a notorious "blight" on the Secretariat of Agriculture.[26] Only a handful of particularly well-organized ejidos (as well as most timber companies) complied with the requirement to file forest management studies and detailed logging plans. Few rural people understood forestry regulations, and those who did often ignored them. Clandestine cutting happened everywhere, from the hills outside Mexico City to the mahogany forests of Tabasco. Even when foresters such as Orozco (the warden who traveled to the Meseta Purépecha in 1929) learned about illegal logging, they rarely issued sanctions for fear of antagonizing agrarian leaders or politically connected logging companies. In any case, many people refused to comply with legal restrictions placed on their use of the land. The warden stationed in eastern Michoacán warned peasants year in and year out not to burn fields or plant near young regrowth, until finally the leaders of one Otomí community wrote authorities in exasperation to ask how they were supposed to plant corn without making these so-called *rosas*, as they had done "since very distant times."[27] Jurisdictional disputes also added to villagers' confusion. While only the Division of Forests, Fish, and Game (itself a unit of the much larger Secretariat of Agriculture and Development) had the authority to issue multiyear logging permits, the law contained a loophole that allowed federal employees and mayors (presidentes municipales) to grant short-term "provisional" authorization to log. Local officials, and in some cases army officers, routinely approved such requests, often with no more than a verbal assent. As a result, most logging operations could legally put their lands into production without informing the forest service at all.[28]

The situation changed radically when Cárdenas became president in 1934. His emphasis on resource management in general, and the forest service in particular, translated into a massive expansion of personnel. The young institution soon had 22 full-time administrators, with duties ranging from overseeing ejidal and communal land to the publication of informational pamphlets about the virtues of conservation. By the end of Cárdenas's administration the forest bureaucracy had delegations in 29 states and 224 wardens charged with overseeing 42 relatively small national parks, 9 national forest reserves, and 37 "forest protection zones" meant to preserve forests in watersheds and ecologically damaged areas where the woods needed to recuperate. Together, these protective areas accounted for over 800,000 hectares (or nearly two million acres, an area about half the size of Mexico's smallest state). Foresters also launched an ambitious reforestation project outside Mexico City, planting over a million saplings in an arc from the Desierto de Los Leones to the foothills of El Ajusco. Fearing that excessive logging elsewhere in the nation could permanently degrade certain forest ecosystems, Cárdenas also declared temporary logging bans in no fewer than 23 municipal districts.[29] The forest service began to build up a corps of professional wardens by opening a vocational school in Tlalpan (later relocated to Los Molinos, Veracruz) that recruited young men from rural areas for a three-month course of study on the basics of law enforcement, forest management, and truck driving. The Porfirian-era National Museum of National Flora and Fauna was reopened, and visitors once again browsed through exhibits on the nation's animal and plant life, along with dioramas of the national parks and murals depicting the diversity of national ecological zones.[30]

The initiative nearest to Quevedo's heart was the organization of a research center to train professional foresters and carry out studies of the nation's forest resources. President Pascual Ortiz Rubio had authorized such an entity in 1932, but a lack of funding kept it on the drawing board until 1936. The Institute of Forest Research (Instituto de Investigaciones Forestales) began to admit students the following year, and Quevedo personally taught one of its required classes. He directed the staff to begin compiling a complete geography and classification of the nation's forests—technically known as a forest inventory—that would catalogue the distribution of tree species throughout the nation. He began a second line of research into the physical qualities of commercially valuable flora in order to understand the influence of climate and soil on their growth.[31] In addition to its intrinsic scientific value, the institute's agenda had an unambiguously economic logic. From the point of view of foresters, the information it compiled was a necessary prerequisite to commercial logging, since any long-term plan required baseline knowledge about the current extent, condition, and botanical characteristics of the nation's forests.

These incipient studies codified a particular understanding of the forest ecosystem. The forest service's official journal not only announced relevant legislation and administrative orders, it featured scientific articles on such topics as the growth rates of conifer species in the experimental nurseries in Mexico City and Veracruz, complete with graphs, tables, and formulas. It published technical discussions explaining how to estimate the total volume of wood in a stand of timber expressed in cubic meters, a measure that both conservationists and loggers would find useful. Forest service researchers took a stab at enumerating the total number of pines in Mexico and arrived at the improbably precise (and likely underestimated) sum of 285,769,555 trees.[32] These sorts of studies unquestionably moved the science of forestry forward and began the long process of liberating Mexican specialists from adapting North American data to their own country's conditions. But the production, publication, and consumption of such studies also elevated the scientists and foresters who read them to the status of incontrovertible experts with specialized knowledge that distinguished them from laymen. This scientific authority conferred a unique capacity to decide how forests should be used.[33] No one believed in the rule of experts more firmly than did Quevedo himself.

In his memoirs, Quevedo traced his stint in the government to a discussion he had with Lázaro Cárdenas in 1934, when the future president took a moment away from the campaign trail to invite Quevedo into his administration. Cárdenas mentioned how much he regretted his inability to stem the pace of deforestation during his four-year term as governor of Michoacán, and Quevedo responded that the constitution permitted the federal government immense latitude in the regulation of woods and other natural resources. All that remained, he said, was for the government to establish the proper institutions.[34] Quevedo's reminiscence has a ring of truth. Cárdenas had not only taken steps to break indigenous communities' long-term contracts with lumber mills when he was governor, but he clearly believed that the federal government should have the final say on the use of the nation's resources—a viewpoint that eventually led to a standoff with foreign oil companies and his watershed decision to nationalize the petroleum industry in 1938.

Yet Cárdenas had other agendas, too, both as governor and president. Most of all, he intended to realize a grand political vision of organizing the popular classes and channeling their energies behind his regime. The producers cooperatives mandated by the 1926 Forestry Code fit this bill nicely. In theory, they could function as vehicles for organizing rural people into small-scale institutions that worked with foresters and federal administrators, while at the same time giving rural people greater authority over their own resources—just the sort of "regimented empowerment" that was the hallmark of Cardenismo.[35] The problem was that only six ejidos (all of them in Mexico state or the Federal District) had completed the paperwork to incorporate producers cooperatives by 1935, although several dozen other communities had begun the process. Spurred along by Cárdenas and Quevedo, the forest service wasted no time in moving to address the problem. Within a year, it had identified over a thousand ejidos that possessed timber and needed a forest warden to visit and organize a producers cooperative.[36] After three years, foresters had organized 498 cooperatives on ejidos and indigenous communities with common lands, primarily in the states of Mexico, Michoacán, and Guerrero. By 1940, 866 forestry cooperatives had formally registered with the Department of Agriculture, accounting for 64 percent of the nation's 1,350 forest ejidos at the time.[37]

The Cardenista vision fit squarely within the dominant current of thought among professional foresters, which regarded cooperatives as consonant with the principles of scientific management and revolutionary social justice. As early as 1930, one expert had argued that cooperatives could "achieve the basic ideal of the Revolution" by giving campesinos the means to improve their economic status, while providing administrators the means to ensure the "rational usufruct of our forested wealth."[38] Officials often used a self-consciously revolutionary language to reiterate this point. A forest service spokesman explained in 1934, for example, that cooperatives would benefit both "capitalists" and "workers" because they ensured that the fruits of peasant labor would build the national economy. Other experts predicted that they would vitiate rural people's crass profit motive and lead them to appreciate forests from an aesthetic standpoint as well.[39] A few years later, forestry officials took this reasoning a bit further and suggested that cooperatives solved one of the central contradictions of capitalism: their members functioned both as workers and the owners of the means of production, all the while displacing the intermediaries and "speculators" who took advantage of rural folk by underpaying them for their wood and then selling it to Mexican consumers at unconscionably high prices.[40]

Cardenista initiatives to use small-scale forestry as a tool of local development went beyond mere revolutionary rhetoric. In addition to vastly increasing the overall pace of land reform, the president issued a series of edicts meant to help the poorest rural people to earn a living in the woodlands. He exempted producers cooperatives from half of the fees normally required for logging permits, making it significantly easier to comply with the law. In 1938 he ordered forest wardens to exempt charcoal makers from forestry regulations even if they did not have the proper permits, because they represented the poorest of the poor.[41] Even the escalating numbers of forest wardens could be considered something of a populist initiative, since they helped to organize cooperatives and prepared the ground for professional foresters' silvicultural studies and logging plans without which ejidatarios could not legally log their land.

In addition to opening the way for rural people to make a living on the land, the increasing number of cooperatives, laws, and wardens functioned to make villagers visible to the forestry bureaucracy and hence susceptible to regulation. Cooperatives had unambiguous leaders and established membership rolls registered both with the forest service and with the secretary of the economy. Foresters extended licenses to log trees or collect wood, not to individuals, but rather to the cooperatives themselves, meaning that the members of cooperatives had the sole legal right to work on communally held lands. This situation not only opened the door to internal conflicts about just who could belong to the cooperative, but made all villagers particularly dependent on foresters, who had the authority to cancel logging permits and hence put producers cooperatives out of work.

Making peasant actions visible to the state was precisely the point. Foresters argued that the organization and regulation of cooperatives would allow them to control the use of forest resources and hence serve as a linchpin of the overall project of using resources "in an organized way and in accordance with the laws of forest conservation."[42] Above all, they predicted that cooperatives would allow them "to establish the technical norms that must guide the use of forests." In theory, the advent of cooperatives and a strengthened regulatory apparatus gave professional foresters the means to end damaging peasant practices such as cutting trees before they had reached their maximum size, building houses with commercially valuable woods rather than dead standing timber, cutting railroad ties using hatch-ets rather than saws, using commercially viable wood such as oak for tinder or charcoal, and fabricating tejamanil shingles from the heartwood of pine trees.[43] In sum, cooperatives established a means for communicating the ideals of scientific forestry to "the people" and, if necessary, for sanctioning illegal behavior.

Perhaps for this very reason, villagers sometimes refused to establish a cooperative. Quevedo commented in 1937 that forest wardens struggled to convince peasants to create the new organizations and to get existing cooperatives to obey their management plans. He attributed the problems not to peasants' conscious decision to stonewall foresters, but rather to their backwardness. The problem, he wrote, "no doubt" could be traced to the rural people who were "not accustomed to earning a living through the well-ordered use [explotación ordenada] of the forests themselves."[44] The anonymous writers of an article in the forest service's technical journal offered a more nuanced reading of the situation, noting that cooperatives took root more easily in indigenous communities, where native people had a "tradition of caring for their own forests." In contrast to this favorable stereotype of indigenous people, the foresters suggested that mestizo ejidatarios were less willing to organize because they regarded their lands as a "gift of the Revolution," to be logged off and permanently converted into agricultural land. The writers suggested that top administrators should order wardens to redouble their outreach work on ejidos, though one suspects that their presence served as a not-so-subtle reminder that campesinos needed to play by the rules established by the postrevolution-ary state.[45]

COOPERATIVES IN MICHOACÁN

A substantial number of ejidos incorporated forestry cooperatives in Mi-choacán during the Cárdenas administration, particularly between 1937 and 1940. By that point a total of ninety-one cooperatives had formally registered with the Departamento Agrario, the majority organized by local forest wardens. Cooperatives could be found in most forest ejidos in the Meseta Purépecha and the eastern sierras around Ciudad Hidalgo.[46] They no doubt helped the bureaucracy to gain a tighter grip on local pro-duction, in part because foresters could indicate which stands of trees the cooperative should cut during the following year; this assessment indirectly established how much the cooperative would earn. Despite this intrusion on their economic and ecological autonomy, many villagers eventually warmed to the cooperatives because they promised a secure source of income. In the words of one local leader who attempted unsuccessfully to incorporate the buzzwords favored by politicians, the people in his area were "extremely in economic circumstances [*sic*]," by which he meant dire poverty, and needed a cooperative to put their communal woods into production.[47] Other rural leaders had less noble intentions and regarded cooperatives as instruments to make money from the labor of others. Whatever the case, ejidos that possessed forestlands had strong institutional and economic inducements to play by the rules, and Cárdenas sweetened the pot in 1937 by lowering their taxes and by signing legislation that encouraged villagers to experiment with a new way to use the woods: tapping pine trees for the oleoresin needed to make turpentine.[48]

In these circumstances, cooperatives became one of the primary sources of (licit) income in the Michoacán forestlands, and several communities insisted on forming one. For example, delegates from the Purépecha community of Charapan who attended the Tarascan Regional Indigenous Conference in December 1937 demanded the expulsion of the Compañía Resinera de Uruapan, which had "invaded" their communal land and begun to tap pine trees for resin. Rather than letting the company do the job, they sought permission to do the same work "by the Community in a Cooperative."[49] Representatives of the Indigenous Conference investigated these events and learned that the "invasion" consisted of the company's decision to hire some of Charapan's residents to tap trees in the village commons after signing a fraudulent contract with illegitimate local leaders. A federal forester canceled the existing contracts, which contained terms unfavorable to the village, and taught residents a more efficient technique for tapping trees without harming them. He then turned production over to the villagers, who, in an ironic twist, agreed to sell the resin they collected to the Compañía Resinera—the very company they had once accused of invading their property.[50]

Producers cooperatives had the potential to help villagers overcome internal divisions and could rebuff outsiders' efforts to intimidate or trick them into selling their wares at below-market prices. Unlike most cooperatives, the one in Uruapan's indigenous "neighborhood" (barrio) of San Juan Evangelista required its forty-six members to pay a one-peso membership fee, in exchange for which they would be able to extract wood from community lands.[51] Like their counterparts in Charapan, the comuneros of San Juan Evangelista had filed the proper paperwork and received official permission to tap trees for resin. When they arrived in the communal woodlot, however, they were met by what one member characterized as a "group of people who don't need any special advantages to earn a living and have only banded together to keep us from working." Goaded by a local power broker (cacique), these interlopers chased the cooperative members out of the woods and began collecting sap themselves. The villagers hastily drafted a plea to a sympathetic political ally that succeeded in keeping these (alleged) interlopers from working the stands that the cooperative intended to use itself.[52]

It is difficult to arrive at the truth (or truths) in such cases. Did the cooperative members really have a valid claim to the contested area? Or had they just taken advantage of the law and created an organization that excluded their village rivals, who may have had an equally legitimate right to the land? These may be challenging questions to answer, but perhaps they miss the point. What matters most about these cases is that one side of the conflict predicated their claims to legitimacy on membership in the producers cooperative, while the other lacked any official standing. Rural people had learned that, insofar as the agrarian bureaucracy was concerned, the cooperative was uniquely positioned to open legal access to village commons and provide an income for its members.

Unsurprisingly, then, cooperatives sometimes aggravated local conflicts and deepened the bossism (*caciquismo*) that characterized so much of post-revolutionary agrarian politics. It appears, for example, that the producers organizations in the low valley and rolling hills of La Cañada de los Once Pueblos functioned as agents of power for the Prado family, who had ensconced themselves as the caciques of the region nearly two decades earlier. The cooperative in the Prado stronghold of Tanaquillo had a total of ninety-four members, no fewer than fifteen of whom belonged to the Prado family. Forestry officials began to complain almost immediately that the cooperative's members cut far more than its approved quota allowed and ignored the statewide ban on cutting live trees.[53] In 1941 the mayor of a nearby town, Chilchota, reported, "The residents of Tanaquillo appear to have formed a cooperative that doesn't really exist; instead, it's only a few individuals who are taking advantage of the communal woods to profit from trade" with timber companies.[54]

The mayor's complaint against the Prados went beyond economics. He also blamed the corrupt Tanaquillo cooperative for a "harmful change to the environment" of the region. In the mayor's estimation, the unusually light rainfall in La Cañada could be traced to a massive expansion of illegal

logging, which changed the hydrology of the region and had dire consequences for "public health and agriculture."[55] He repeated his charge four
months later, explaining to the regional office of the Secretariat of Agriculture that the Prados' "immoderate use of the woods" was to blame for
"harmful climate change, since it barely rains now."[56] Like many educated
people of his time, the mayor drew a tight connection between forests and
the rains they were said to attract, and he assumed that overly intense cuts
would lead to diminished rainfall. In his version of events, the misuse of
forest resources mirrored the Prados' abuse of authority. The landscape
literally reflected social ills, and society as a whole paid the price in terms
of environmental degradation and drought.

More than just making villagers' practices visible to officials and amenable to regulation, the cooperatives defined the boundaries of a privileged
productive community. In several cases, the members of a single community created rival cooperatives and vied to receive logging permits. Since
the law stipulated that each ejido could only have one cooperative, administrators had to distinguish "legitimate" groups from spurious ones. That
is what happened in the Purépecha community of Cherán when a group of
villagers who claimed to have their own duly formed cooperative wrote the
authorities to say that mestizos who had settled in the area (but had not
been formally accepted into the community) had already formed a co-op
and received permission to work the forests.[57] An official dispatched to sort
out the matter ruled against the indigenous group on the basis that they
had never filed their cooperatives articles of incorporation with the proper
authorities, whereas the mestizo "outsider" group had done so in 1939.[58]

The losers in this bureaucratic gambit understood all too clearly what
had transpired. They formulated a letter to the Secretariat of Agriculture
explaining that that their "ignorance" of the law left them unsure of where
to direct their questions or how to address their problem. The petitioners,
who claimed to speak on behalf of the vast majority of residents, said they
now recognized that they had merely been "toiling in the void" (*obrando en
basio* [sic]) when they expected that the government would recognize their
cooperative rather than the rival mestizo organization.[59] They could hardly
have expressed their condition more aptly. They knew that they lacked a
juridical presence and would not receive just remuneration for their labors
until they overcame the objections of the village bosses or won recognition
of the forestry bureaucracy. Nevertheless, they pressed their case and won
official recognition for their cooperative three years later. By then, however, the federal government had all but given up on its commitment to

cooperatives and community production, as it turned to a new regime of large-scale, industrial forestry.

THE MODERNIZATION OF PEASANT PRODUCTION

Cooperatives were the most obvious attempt to make peasant production visible to forestry experts, but they constituted only one element in the broader push to organize and rationalize peasant production in central Mexico and, above all, in Michoacán, the homeland of Cardenismo. The agrarian reform grew in geographic scope and administrative complexity during the first four years of Cárdenas's 1934–1940 presidency. The pace of land redistribution slowed considerably in 1938, at which time the number and variety of political organizers and technical advisors increased dramatically in the countryside. The arrival of technical experts, bankers, and putative advocates for the popular classes represented not so much the federalization of the agrarian movement as what might be called the "technification" of the land reform sector. Michoacán's agrarian movement had begun as a patchwork of highly localized, village-level movements under the guidance of schoolteachers, local intellectuals, and caciques, but Cárdenas moved to institutionalize it when he became governor, in 1928, by establishing a broad-based union intended to stir up and manage popular radicalism.[60] The advisors he sent to the countryside a few years later did not supplant the agrarian leagues and village revolutionaries that had made the agrarian movement into a potent political force. Instead, they worked to rationalize peasant production and advise villagers how to invest the income from ejidal logging.

Perhaps the most influential cadre of experts were extension agents employed by the federally funded rural development bank, the Banco Nacional de Crédito Agrícola (BNCA), which governed access to ejidal credit and savings. Most ejidos owed debts to the federal government for fees and professional services (some of which they did not want and had never requested). Communities that received land reform parcels in the 1920s were expected to help pay off the value of the property they received, and some of these obligations remained on the books even after the government eliminated such bootstrapping regulations in 1928. Other ejidos were expected to reimburse federal agencies, including the forest service, for the production costs of technical studies (estudios dasonómicos) needed for the approval of multiyear logging permits. On rare occasions, village residents borrowed a modest sum to complete a public works project. Representatives of the Secretariat of the Economy (like agents of the BNCA) could authorize withdrawals from ejidal and communal bank accounts, which were used either to make cash disbursements to the members of cooperatives or for public works projects like a new schoolhouse, improved roadways, or a sewage system. This financial red tape constituted yet another bid to regulate villagers' use of their collectively earned money, but it rarely worked as intended. The leaders of cooperatives usually just distributed profits however they saw fit, and many of them balked at the overall complexity and logistical difficulties of working with banks located in distant towns and meddlesome extension agents with their ledgers and calculations.

Bank representatives ultimately had far less impact on forest rural people's finances than on their production practices. The BNCA agent in the Uruapan area reported that he had formed four producers cooperatives in indigenous villages during 1937. He also drew up the contracts that guaranteed a minimum price for the railroad ties they produced, effectively becoming their main client and cutting out the "intermediaries and exploiters," who he said had preyed on the ignorance of villagers. He proudly informed his superiors that one community had started a small savings account and saved enough to buy a pickup truck.[61]

These local experts' authority expanded even more once the president began declaring temporary bans on logging (vedas) in ecologically distressed forests. In 1936, the first year that the forest service was fully operative, Cárdenas banned logging in thirteen regions of nine different states.[62] The decrees usually affected relatively small areas or, at most, the woods in one or two districts (municipios), but Michoacán was different. Quevedo himself traveled through the southern Meseta Purépecha and discovered that most of its woods consisted of young trees under forty centimeters in diameter. He also found instances of peasants who had cleared forest for milpa corn fields, as well as creeping erosion and, above all, overcutting by logging companies in the Uruapan area.[63] Cárdenas responded in late 1937 with a five-year ban on logging in most of the forests in the Meseta, exempting only the malpaís areas of volcanic soil. People throughout the region worried about losing jobs in the timber sector, but the government once again deployed experts to serve as extension agents. Foresters, indigenous affairs officers, and employees of the BNCA fanned out in the sierras to encourage producers cooperatives to adopt the one type of forestry still legally available to them: tapping trees for pine resin. Although the resin industry was already well established in the region, the combined effects of the logging ban, technical assistance from federal experts, and federal loans made it into the region's leading industry for decades to come.

Representatives of the BNCA, many of whom had received advanced technical degrees and held the title of *ingeniero*, took the lead in reorienting peasant production away from logging and toward resin tapping in the Meseta Purépecha. Agents for the bank showed villagers how to cut back the bark using the French "Hughes" system, which did the least damage to the trees, and they provided funds with which villagers could purchase buckets and barrels to capture the pine sap. The bank also extended a 26,000 peso line of credit to fund the construction of a distilling plant that eight communities around Uruapan used to make and sell their own turpentine. The bank's extension agents taught villagers how to run the distilling machinery and alerted foresters about unauthorized logging in their territory. Eventually, they built a few more small-scale distilling plants in the highlands. They even informed the forest service that some of its employees had approved unconscionable contracts between logging companies and cooperatives. In areas unaffected by the logging ban, BNCA agents guaranteed minimum prices for wood products and paid back taxes for communities and ejidos unable to keep up with their obligations after the logging ban cut into their income. It is not clear whether villagers regarded these interventions as beneficial or intrusive, though the indigenous community of Capácuaro held a public meeting to accuse bank agents of reneging on their promise to buy timber. The agents blamed the episode on a division within the community and characterized the malcontents as outsiders who sought unwarranted access to village commons.[64]

The bank extension agents were not the only *técnicos* to arrive in the woods during the waning years of Cardenismo. Beginning around 1939, officials from the Department of Indian Affairs (Departamento de Asuntos Indígenas) organized producers cooperatives of resin tappers in some Meseta Purépecha indigenous communities. The producers organization they founded in Charapan not only coordinated the local tree tappers, but also advocated on behalf of other indigenous communities beset by outsiders who illegally logged their land.[65]

Foresters continued their own efforts to organize cooperatives and regulate peasant practices in the early 1940s. Although they sometimes clashed with the bank agents who had encroached on their area of expertise, they nonetheless helped establish tree-tapping as a viable occupation in the Meseta Purépecha, particularly after the logging ban went into effect. Federal foresters also renewed the campaign to convince villagers to harvest only the trees specifically marked for cutting. They even showed villagers how to cut tejamanil shingles with a minimum of waste after BNCA officials overstepped their authority by granting some communities permission to start a small tejamanil enterprise.[66] These initiatives had their share of problems, not least because officials sometimes neglected to make sure that villagers actually received payments for resin tapping; indeed, a suspicious amount of cash ended up in the pockets of local leaders (or inaccessible bank accounts).[67] The presence of so many federal employees may also help explain the sudden increase, around 1938, in complaints from villagers that every transaction now required appropriate documentation and that foresters used "any and all pretexts" to punish them for improper logging practices. Yet these same functionaries represented a potentially valuable set of allies who had the capacity to help regain control of their woodlands.[68]

The multiplication of forestry experts, extension agents of the BNCA, and other specialists signaled a subtle yet important shift in the Cárdenas political project. The first four years of Cardenismo (1934–1938) represented the apogee of postrevolutionary populism, as officially sanctioned unions and peasant leagues appeared throughout the countryside.[69] The decision to provide technical support for these local institutions was intended to consolidate these organizations and buttress rural people's long-term productive autonomy by teaching them the rudiments of scientific forestry. Cooperatives became the conduit through which villagers might build a bit of wealth and develop new skills, and many villagers eventually received jobs in turpentine distillery plants. Ejidos and native communities in Michoacán were exceptionally well positioned to take advantage of this technification. The state's long history of popular mobilization, beginning with the agrarianism of the 1920s, and its privileged position as Cárdenas's home state, had created local traditions of associational life that primed villagers to accept producers cooperatives. Conditions were quite different in the highlands of Chihuahua, where the absence of a strong agrarian movement and the continuing influence of commercial logging operations made the social terrain less fertile for collective village organizations or the development of local expertise.

COOPERATIVES AND CORPORATIONS IN THE SIERRA TARAHUMARA

Unlike Michoacán, where a significant number of rural people joined cooperatives and, for better or worse, came into contact with the forest bureaucracy and began constructing something that looked like community forestry, Chihuahua was divided between two very different worlds tenuously linked together. On the one hand, large timber companies continued to dominate the commercial sector. The Great Depression and economic nationalism had weakened the largest businesses and pushed some North American owners out, but a new generation of Mexican businessmen rose to take their place, as the northern timber industry retained a central role in the regional economy. On the other hand, some Rarámuri villages formed producers cooperatives (often at the behest of mestizos living within them) and launched modest attempts at locally managed logging. Even in the Sierra Tarahumara, revolutionary forestry made some inroads.

By the mid-1930s, the Department of Agrarian Reform had received petitions for ejidos from scores of mestizo communities and most of the larger indigenous villages in the Sierra Tarahumara. Nevertheless, it appears that few native people knew or particularly cared about the possibility of receiving a land grant. As in Michoacán a decade earlier, schoolteachers often wrote the petitions (with or without residents' knowledge), and they were probably behind the handful of producers cooperatives that appeared in the highlands.[70] The locals' relative apathy kept the land reform bureaucracy and community leaders from following up on most of these requests for land reform, some of which languished for decades, until logging companies (and mestizo immigrants) started to move south of Creel in the 1950s, advancing into the sierras and prompting Rarámuri leaders and mestizo settlers to dust off their old petitions and formally map out ejidos in the high sierras. In the short term, however, most Rarámuri tried to steer clear of mestizo people whenever possible. Many villagers preferred their existing, albeit precarious, strategy of scratching out cornfields and raising tiny herds of cattle and goats. Although they raised enough corn and beans to meet their nutritional needs, one observer wrote that they had "barely enough to subsist on . . . [T]heir food is so scarce that you could practically say they don't eat."[71]

According to one estimate, 33,387 Rarámuri lived in Chihuahua in the 1930s, approximately 1,800 of whom were non-Christian "gentiles," who kept largely to themselves. Few had attended the seven schools scattered about the Sierra Tarahumara because most natives regarded public education as something meant for chabochi (non-Indians). Nevertheless, they continued to regard forests as a bulwark of collective survival.[72] Young men often hunted in the woods, mostly with bow and arrow, and sometimes tracked an animal for days before making a kill. Outsiders judged that the Rarámuri were quite "skilled with hatchets and woodworking generally."[73]

They carved intricate masks and kitchen utensils, but most wood was still used to build houses (some of which also included stone walls) and as cooking fuel. The timber companies agreed about the natives' prowess in the woods and often sent bilingual Rarámuri men into monolingual villagers to hire young men as lumberjacks. Most were paid with *sotol* (a Chihuahuan version of tequila), salt, or bolts of cotton, but remained away for only a few weeks before returning home.[74]

Even the Rarámuri communities that received an ejido continued to face subsistence challenges. The presidential orders approving a land grant in the woodlands included a raft of stipulations, such as the creation of a cooperative and an open line of credit, that had to be fulfilled before land reform beneficiaries could use their forests.[75] Moreover, the delimitation of ejidal plots sparked unexpected conflicts between native communities, many of which had traditionally shared their territories with each other during some parts of the year. Land reform officials made no accommodations for the possibility that ejidal boundaries and forest regulations might undermine these arrangements. For example, certain families in the village of Samachique (in the district of Guachochi) had a long-standing custom of spending the winter months in caves in neighboring Quívaro, whose inhabitants received in exchange the right to cut a modest amount of timber from Samachique's woodlot. The elders of Samachique abrogated this agreement when the forest service built a sawmill in their town in mid-1930s, prompting Quívaro to bar access to the caves.[76] Around the same time, forestry experts began to demand that villagers stop herding goats, because they devoured seed-bearing pinecones and nibbled on saplings and the shoots of young trees, "completely nullifying" the ability of the forest to reproduce. Yet indigenous people needed the animals, which were a key source of protein and family wealth. Most chose to ignore the new regulations.[77]

Some early experiments in community forestry achieved a degree of success. Leaders of the large Rarámuri community of Guachochi were particularly interested in putting their commons into production. Mestizos had arrived in the ranchería around 1900 and claimed some of the villagers' best agricultural lands. Thirty years later, the Rarámuri leader Timoteo Martínez requested an ejido grant that would return those croplands and confirm native people's ownership of the adjacent forests. Seven years passed, but Guachochi eventually received a provisional land grant as well as a small, steam-powered sawmill. The new ejidal leaders gratefully wrote local authorities (presumably with the help of a priest or schoolteacher) to predict that "this indigenous Pueblo [*sic*] will become equal to whites and will finally become useful Citizens to our Country." They also requested permission to organize a cooperative.[78] These advances came at a high price, however. Incensed mestizo settlers killed Martínez that same year, and the request for a cooperative got so mired in red tape that villagers waited for months before they could begin logging.[79]

Notwithstanding the agonizing growth of ejido-based forestry in the sierras, the largest single employer in the forestry sector in the 1920s remained the sawmill in Madera operated by the Canada-based Mexico North Western Railway Company. The original mill had burned to the ground in 1918 and reopened in 1922 with a modern diesel power plant and state-of-the-art debarking machine. The plant also boasted the nation's most advanced box-making shop, which began operation in 1912 and eventually produced around 600,000 fruit crates per year for the Mexican agriculture industry. Despite its technological sophistication, the new mill had a far smaller capacity than the one it replaced and needed a complement of only 680 full-time employees, who worked in two shifts. The plant also generated income for another 640 or so lumberjacks, who worked on ejidal land and the company's own 1.5 million hectare parcel.[80] Trees had already disappeared in the immediate vicinity of Madera by the late 1920s, so native people traveled up to 40 kilometers to sell their logs to the mill. Company lumberjacks also worked stands of timber on either side of the 800-kilometer length of the Mexico North Western Railway line and its dozens of spurs. Logging crews had long since harvested the easiest-to-reach trees there as well, so they made cuts on the mountainside and hired muleteers to drag the wood to the rail lines. Most of the rest of this huge Porfirian-era railroad concession remained largely untouched, however. No fewer than eight species of pine and fir grew in three distinct microclimates, with one-hundred- to three-hundred-year-old trees in abundance and individuals as old as four hundred years not uncommon.[81]

To the Madera Lumber Company's full-time forester, this huge expanse of nearly untouched forest represented not so much an ecosystem to be preserved as a resource to be molded and exploited. Daniel F. Galicia, who later took a job with the forest service and acquired logging rights throughout the sierras, repeated a common refrain in classifying the largest, old growth trees as "decrepit" because they grew more slowly than younger trees. He also intended to "improve" the biological makeup of the forest itself by bringing about the "extinction" of the hardy black pine, which lumberjacks (most of whom worked only with hatchets) hated to cut, because its short, branchy trunk was hard to strip and often got caught in the debarking machines. He recommended a regime of selective logging aimed at thinning the oldest trees and black pines over a fifty-year period in order to encourage "more rapid and uniform growth" of commercially desirable trees, thus maximizing the forest's productivity.[82] Ecologists today often reject this practice (known as "high grading"), but it probably had little effect in this case because, in practice, the loggers made little or no selection of which trees to fell. They continued to cut the most accessible stands of timber, regardless of age or species. And the surging demand for wood during the Second World War soon stubbed out even the minimal pretense of forest management.

The Madera sawmill's status as a prominent employer in the eastern Sierra Tarahumara, combined with its foreign ownership, made it a target for postrevolutionary reformers. Its owners began to feel the effects of economic nationalism in the late 1920s, when Governor Marcelo Caraveo threatened to increase the mill's tax liability. The plant's North American manager shut down operations, putting its employees out of work, in a failed bid to pressure the governor to relent. The mill started working again in 1929, but the higher tax burden made the company's products uncompetitive north of the border, and company owners began to make secret arrangements to evade the tax on foreign corporations by "selling" the sawmill to the Mexican superintendent of the railroad, Gilberto U. Armendáriz, while secretly retaining ownership.[83]

It turned out to be the beginning of a long process in which the mill and its huge landholdings moved into Mexican hands one piece at a time. The next step occurred in 1935, when labor organizers arrived from Mexico City and succeeded in forming a union of mill workers. The corporate owners regarded unionization as the most serious threat to their interests yet. After yet another fire damaged the mill, in 1939, administrators decided to shift production away from the main plant in Madera in favor of smaller (and much more wasteful) steam- or diesel-powered "portable" sawmills that could be disassembled and moved from one logging camp to another in a matter of days. Almost half a century passed before large and efficient sawmills reappeared in Chihuahua. The introduction of logging trucks capable of transporting huge sawlogs made it even more attractive to move smaller mills from one camp to another, though it also meant building roads deeper into the sierras. Even so, the portable mills plants ran at far less than their installed capacity both then and throughout the twentieth century. They hired small contingents of thirty to sixty workers, which

Figure 3.2. Logging in the North Western Railway concession, Chihuahua, 1939. Archivo General de la Nación, SARH/PF, caja 1974, exp. 2/402, leg. 7.

made unionization impractical and put these supposedly separate business ventures below the legal threshold that would have required the company to provide schools, doctors, and other benefits.[84]

Another factor squeezing the mill's profitability was the exhaustion of forests leased from the sprawling ranch known as the Babícora Development Company, owned by the American newspaper magnate William Randolph Hearst. The relationship between the ranch and the sawmill had once seemed mutually beneficial. Logging opened up new pastures, and the mill ferried trainload after trainload out of Babícora at bargain rates. As one forester pointed out, this situation meant that the ranch administrators had no reason to conserve the forests; on the contrary, they hoped to eliminate them altogether. By the mid-1940s, the last stands of trees were on the verge of disappearing. Decades of clear-cutting followed by the introduction of forage grasses and cattle meant the land had permanently changed from a forest ecosystem to pasturage.[85]

The sawmill still had access to the vast North Western Railway concession, which remained largely intact into the late 1930s despite the creation of several ejidos. At least some of these land reform parcels were given to lumberjacks who had once worked as casual laborers for the company.

The mill also continued to buy hand-hewn ties from nearby indigenous communities at twenty-five cents apiece. The continued strong demand for railroad ties was not enough for the once-mighty mill to compete with the multiplicity of "portable" mills in the old railroad concession, however, and the company found it increasingly difficult to compete with small-scale production on ejidos themselves.[86] In 1942 plant managers suspended the night shift, contending that wartime shortages of tires and truck parts left them no alternative. That same year, the owners turned the plant over fully to Armendáriz and an associate, who ran it for another two years, before the expiration of lease agreements with Babícora and other landowners forced them to declare bankruptcy. At that point, a workers' cooperative acquired the mill and hammered out a new and mutually beneficial lease agreement with the ejido in the town of Madera, which held a few thousand hectares of forestlands that formerly belonged to Babícora. The forester assigned to survey the woods arranged for a provisional logging permit but also cautioned that the ejidal woodlots would quickly disappear if they supplied enough wood for the mill to work anywhere close to its capacity. He recommended making quick clear-cuts and held out the vague hope that the forest would eventually recover on its own.[87] In the end, logging out the ejidal lands was a temporary balm, at best. Madera's ejidal woods had virtually disappeared by 1947, forcing the big sawmill to close for good.

Some foreign-owned companies continued to thrive in Chihuahua, though they faced increasingly serious threats from nationalist reformers. For example, the Babícora Development Company survived Cárdenas's attempt to generate an agrarian movement on its lands by sending gunmen to kill the local leader Socorro Rivera. Shielded by "battalions of lawyers and editors," the Hearst family subdivided the property into nine lots, which were titled to relatives and business partners. Each section was small enough to qualify for exemption from the land reform even though William Randolph Hearst maintained effective control of the property and continued to do so (despite the creation of fifteen ejidos on its property between 1915 and 1942) until the federal government finally bought the ranch for 2.5 million U.S. dollars in 1953 and converted it into "agricultural colonies" for the rural poor.[88]

The Cargill Company also retained the quarter-million hectare property along the Papigochic River that it had acquired in 1906 from the most famous of the Porfirian científicos, José Yves Limantour. The company rented the land to the Madera Lumber Company soon afterward, and the federal government expropriated over 7 percent of its territory between 1917 and 1935, to make a total of five ejidos.[89] A more serious threat cropped up in 1922, when President Alvaro Obregón invalidated Limantour's original title. In 1933 the Supreme Court upheld Obregón's decree and ruled that nearly all of the disputed land in fact belonged to the nation. No sooner had the ruling been made than General Antonio A. Guerrero, a former regional military commander who became one of Chihuahua's most notorious landowners when he seized an hacienda during the revolution, convinced sixteen of his friends to solicit their own "individual" concessions of 4,000 hectares on these supposedly vacant federal lands. By this time, the territory was home to Rarámuri and mestizo smallholders, but the group of sixteen cronies nonetheless received their grants and then formed a company known as Maderas de Chihuahua, with General Guerrero as its chairman.[90] President Cárdenas allocated most of the remaining Cargill lands to the 58,030-hectare Papigochic forest reserve in 1939, although his decree did little to protect the northern ecosystem. In the first place, a large number of sawmills surrounded the reserve and sent logging crews over the boundary to cut trees illicitly. Second, Maderas de Chihuahua received permission to begin logging within the forest preserve soon after it was formed and began producing railroad ties for both the domestic and North American markets.[91]

A small proportion of the Cargill lands did end up ejidos, however, the first of which was the 5,493-hectare parcel granted to the town of Bocoyna in 1935. Within a year, eighty-two men in the predominantly mestizo ejido had formed a cooperative and raised a hundred pesos of working capital. The lands they received had once been a logging tract, though only a few stands of timber adjacent to the rail lines had ever been cut. In July the villagers wrote President Cárdenas to say that their meager agricultural lands did not "produce anything because of its extreme sterility and poor quality." They also complained that frequent hail storms ruined whatever crops poked through the ground. They could make a living, they said, if the president gave them funds to buy a small sawmill. They explicitly requested direct access to the money, without the intervention of "outsiders" from the rural development bank (the Banco Nacional de Crédito Ejidal, or BNCE), which had a reputation for excessive bureaucracy and a tendency to meddle in land reform communities' internal affairs. The president agreed to release the funds, but did so via the BNCE just as the cooperative had anticipated.[92]

The cooperative functioned surprisingly well in the following years despite some commonplace setbacks. A question over leadership erupted in 1942, when some members denounced the cooperative's president as an interloper. In fact, this conflict probably arose because some of the young men on the ejido had reached working age but had never been allowed to enroll as members of the cooperative.[93] The land reform beneficiaries also began logging without an approved management plan and initially made slipshod and environmentally damaging clear-cuts wherever it seemed easiest to harvest timber. They selected too many young trees for railroad ties and electrical poles, leaving the older and less productive trees standing in the forest. Yet despite these missteps, a professional forester held out hope that the situation would improve. He determined that the villagers had used their woods "in a more-or-less rational manner, which is to say, in line with certain precepts of a technical nature but without following them completely." He felt confident that if the cooperative would let forest wardens mark the appropriate trees for cutting and monitor its own members' behavior, the ejido's woods should generate a sustained yield of timber for the foreseeable future. Almost as an afterthought, he mentioned that a representative of the Secretariat of Agriculture had visited the ejido and may have disbanded the cooperative. After all, the new forestry code of 1943 did not specifically empower cooperatives to work on ejidal lands, which left their legal status in limbo.[94]

UNFULFILLED PROMISES

Despite what had happened in Bocoyna, some foresters interpreted the 1943 code as prohibiting the creation of *new* producers cooperatives but allowing existing ones to continue working. Nevertheless, it was already clear that Cárdenas's grand experiment in revolutionary forestry would not endure, and the complete prohibition of cooperatives, in 1949, hardly came as a shock.[95] The prospects for village-based logging under the watchful eye of experts had already started to crumble in 1940, when Cárdenas dissolved the Department of Forests, Fish, and Game as an independent entity and placed it back under the authority of the Secretariat of Agriculture. The reorganization forced Quevedo to eliminate his signature programs and ultimately to resign in protest. The Institute of Forest Research closed its doors, ended its work on a national forest inventory, and donated its equipment to the National Museum.[96] Its educational mission eventually came to reside with the National School of Agriculture (now the Autonomous University of Chapingo), though Quevedo continued to maintain, for many years thereafter, that foresters deserved an independent institution of higher education.[97]

Cárdenas cited budget constraints as the reason for his decision to gut the department, but that explanation does not ring true. The department had actually raised more than enough money to fund its own operations, by assessing logging fees. The historian Lane Simonian has suggested that something else lay behind the president's decision. Quevedo's abrasive personality and constant harping about an inadequate budget, not to mention his unrelenting complaint that forests should not be subject to the land reform, had not earned him many friends in the administration or among peasant activists.[98] As early as 1938, a pair of experts had published a thinly veiled attack on Quevedo, calling him a "tree worshiper" (dasólatra) who considered the forests untouchable and comprehended "nothing about campesino misery." Instead of blaming deforestation on rural people and recommending sanctions for unauthorized peasant logging, the writers argued that regulators would do better to clamp down on landowners who clear-cut or torched entire stands of forest rather than turn it over to peasants as ejidos.[99] Regardless of their argument's merit, the writers had succeeded in identifying the primary contradiction in Quevedo's approach to conservation: it focused most attention on campesino behavior, while downplaying the threats posed by logging companies and big landowners. Quevedo's ill-disguised suspicion of rural people and faith in major corporations was simply out of step with the populist spirit of Cardenismo.

Even the forest service's signature initiatives did not live up to expectations. Despite years of work to reforest the southern reaches of the Federal District, for example, land reform beneficiaries continued logging in the area and sometimes cut down the saplings that wardens had just finished planting.[100] Forestry cooperatives also failed to displace contratista middlemen in most instances, nor did they help forestry officials craft a national regime of sustainable logging. More disturbing still, forestry on ejidos never accounted for more than a small fraction of the nation's commercial production.[101] By Quevedo's own assessment, the forest service had made little headway in rationalizing the timber sector. "Despite the best intentions put into practice," he reported in 1939, "the problem [of deforestation] has not been addressed in an integral way; palliative measures that leave much to be desired have failed to get at the root of the problem."[102]

One reason that community forestry did not survive very long after the Cárdenas years was that contratistas quickly adapted to the new regime of cooperative production. Forestry officials recognized in 1939 that speculators and middlemen continued to hold sway in most places. Contratistas encouraged villagers to ignore conservationist regulations and continued to pay them a pittance to cut wood, much as they had before the revolution. In addition, foresters had a hard time convincing rural people to obey their tidy maps and logging plans. Few land reform beneficiaries had access to trucks or even to oxen, so they had to cut the trees closest to roads, paths, and railroad tracks regardless of what the authorities had approved. By 1940, when Cárdenas decided to pare back the authority of forest service, its top officials had all but given up on revolutionary forestry. Better to ban ejidal logging altogether and allow commercial interests into forest preserves, they concluded, than to continue down the uncertain path of locally managed production.[103]

Despite these unfulfilled promises, the policies that Cárdenas and Quevedo put into place constituted the first serious effort to find a more sustainable and equitable use of the nation's forests. For all its scientific chauvinism, the forest service under Quevedo had set as its goal the management of forests on a national scale based in part on the ideal of local management. Foresters began work on a research program to identify and map woods in all of the nation's varied ecosystems. Such a baseline study, had it been completed, would have given insights into the real economic potential of forestry and provided a means to measure overall rates of deforestation over time. Moreover, the Cardenistas hoped that cooperatives would eventually turn rural communities into the primary producers of forest products. Not until the 1980s did Mexican leaders once again make such a serious effort to break villagers' dependence on timber companies and contemplate the possibility of using sustainable, community forestry as a major component of national production. Taken in its broadest context, the eclipse of revolutionary forestry came at a great cost to rural people and the ecosystems on which they depended.

By the early 1940s, the rural populism of Cárdenas gave way to a new, more urban development imperative adopted by his successor, Manuel Ávila Camacho. Mexican leaders from the 1940s to the 1960s tended to regard forests as just one more natural resource that could contribute to the great push for industrialization, particularly in northern cities and the area around the Federal District. Yet cooperatives survived in many places even after they lost their legal standing in the 1940s. Many rural people in Michoacán and Chihuahua continued to describe themselves as members cooperatives when they wrote federal authorities, for example. The

Figure 3.3. Directive Council of the Cusárare ejido and cooperative during construction of a sawmill in the village of Yahuir, ca. 1948. Archivo General de la Nación, SARH/PF, caja 1575, exp. 28, leg. 3.

community of Cusárare in the Sierra Tarahumara even received a special dispensation for its cooperative to continue functioning as a constituent of a new kind of regional development organization known as a Forestry Management Unit, or UOF, and its leaders posed for a photograph in 1948.[104] Some villagers presumably clung to this obsolete institutional form because they never learned that the laws had changed. Yet others recognized the value of a locally controlled institution capable of managing village production and negotiating with outsiders. They seem to have embraced the concept of collective and potentially sustainable forestry, regardless of legal formalisms.

Rather than legal or institutional developments, the effects of the Second World War did the most to put an end to rural people's productive autonomy in the forests, limited though it was. Soon after taking office, Ávila Camacho deepened ties with the United States and agreed to put his country's resources at the service of the war effort. In 1940 he ordered an easing of export restrictions on such primary goods as oil, minerals, and forest products. He consummated Mexico's alliance two years later by declaring war on the Axis powers. The unprecedented demand for wood products undermined the forest service's once scrupulous oversight of logging operations, which all but vanished. North American and Mexican companies raced into the woods, where they built new roads and set up makeshift logging camps at a furious pace. The federal government also hurried the construction of the western branch of the Northeast Railroad (also known as the Chihuahua al Pacífico) by dedicating three labor gangs to the task.[105] Nearly all of the logging for these initiatives was done using "temporary" permits that forestry officials granted without requiring the usual environmental studies or long-term forest-management plans. In many cases, emergency permits did not even specify where to cut, meaning that they generated little or no paperwork for federal officials (or historians) to review.

While some villagers found jobs felling trees and transporting them out of the woods during the war, timber companies rarely hired locals for the highly skilled positions. This was particularly true in indigenous regions such as Michoacán's Meseta Purépecha and Chihuahua's Sierra Tarahumara. Logging companies occasionally ignored ejido boundary lines altogether. They allowed their lumberjacks to make camp wherever they saw fit and to cut the surrounding woods for railroad ties, mining timbers, and construction material for the American military.[106] Something similar occurred in the Papigochic forest reserve, where Maderas de Chihuahua clear-cut woods adjacent to the railroad tracks that kept snaking deeper into the reserve. Once the loggers had exhausted the stands of timber closest to the rail lines, logging crews began to invade Rarámuri lands that abutted the reserve.[107] Even the struggling sawmill in Madera launched an unfettered regime of clear-cutting in the old railroad concession before the disappearance of prime stands of timber turned the ledgers red and convinced the owners to sell.[108]

The scale of logging during the Second World War overwhelmed what remained of the forestry bureaucracy and dealt the coup de grâce to Quevedo's vision of a rational and scientifically regulated regime of forestry. The waning presence of producers cooperatives and the explosion of unregulated markets for forest products closed off the potential for community forestry, while the demands of global warfare favored the rough logic of quick and efficient production. By the time foresters collected themselves after the war, the tide had already turned in favor of industrial logging and scientific planning on a regional scale, neither of which took into account the needs of rural society.

PART II

THE DEVELOPMENT IMPERATIVE

CHAPTER 4

Industrial Forests, 1942–1958

The generation of postpopulist leaders who came to power in the 1940s confronted a domestic and international landscape reshaped by the Second World War. The United States had emerged from the decade-long global conflict as a military and economic superpower locked in competition with the Soviet Union and the specter of international communism. For Mexico, the resurgence of its northern neighbor posed both risks and opportunities. North American investment in industries from automobiles to pharmaceuticals had the potential to underwrite development and prosperity, but unchecked foreign investment had the potential to threaten national sovereignty much the way it had half a century earlier during the Porfiriato. Accordingly, Mexican leaders of the 1940s and 1950s chose a middle ground that embraced the Cárdenas model of state-managed economic development but gave up on the idea that the working poor could bring it to fruition. Postwar political leaders turned instead to a state-managed combination of foreign and domestic investment in Mexican industry.

Presidents Manuel Ávila Camacho (1940–1946), Miguel Alemán Valdés (1946–1952), and Adolfo Ruiz Cortines (1952–1958) tried to walk the line between development and dependency by implementing protectionist policies intended to stimulate industrialization (and its handmaiden, urbanization) without chasing away American investment. Intervention in the economy was both facilitated and, in some ways, necessitated by the official party's increasingly authoritarian command of popular organizations, most notably the National Peasants Confederation (CNC) and the National Confederation of Workers (CTM), that traced their origins to the 1930s and the Cardenista formula of regimented empowerment of the popular classes.[1] The presidents of the 1940s and 1950s succeeded for the most part in capturing these mass organizations and defanging their leaders through a judicious blend of patronage and repression—a practice known as *charrismo*. Land reform slowed to a fraction of its previous pace as the political class shifted its attention from questions of social justice to the creation of a more business-friendly environment in the countryside. From an annual average of 3.1 million hectares turned over to ejidos during the Cárdenas years, the rate fell to slightly over a million hectares per year during Ávila Camacho's tenure and further still, to approximately 570,000 hectares per year during the Alemán years, before rebounding slightly, to 622,000 hectares per year, during the Ruiz Cortines administration.[2] Extension agencies such as the Ejidal Bank (the Banco Nacional de Credito Ejidal, or BNCE) consolidated their foothold in the countryside by using credit to manage crop production and, not coincidentally, to create a patronage network in the ejidal sector. Like most such development programs, the bank functioned as a cog in the increasingly complicated political machine controlled by the long-lived official party founded in 1929 and known since 1946 as the Institutional Revolutionary Party (PRI). The party's growing hegemony coincided with an unprecedented economic boom from the early 1940s to the late 1970s, known as the "Mexican miracle," when gross domestic product grew at an average of 6 percent per year thanks to a favorable combination of economic expansion, demographic growth, and centralized economic planning. The nation also achieved self-sufficiency in the production of food, steel, and many consumer goods.[3] The PRI took advantage of the economic climate to cement its command of mass organizations and strategic sectors of the economy, ensconcing itself in power for the rest of the century.

Forests occupied a strategic niche in the postwar political environment. The thriving national economy revived older industries, such as mining and railroads, while boosting new ones, such as paper production, agro-exports of fruit, and urban construction. All of these sectors demanded forest products ranging from packing boxes and plywood to paper pulp and oleoresins. Timber companies employed tens of thousands of workers at a time when many other sources of income for the rural poor—particularly those who lived on ejidos—fell into a prolonged slide from which they have never recovered.[4] Politicians and forestry experts called for increased production and the application of modern technology in logging and tree-tapping operations. In the rhetoric of the day, this meant "industrializing" the forests—a term that signified both the mechanization of the production process and the modernization of forest landscapes through the proliferation of sawmills, resin distilleries, paper plants, trucks, skidders, and chainsaws.

Economic development of this sort converted woodland ecosystems into the raw materials for a vast machine that promised to manufacture prosperity.[5] Presidents and leading forestry officials repeatedly claimed that industrializing the nation's forests not only underwrote economic progress but represented the most rational and efficient use of natural resources.[6] According to one leading manufacturer, industrialization was "integrally linked" to conservation because modern corporations had both the personnel and the incentive to manage the woods sustainably.[7] Alternatives to the industrial model sometimes made their way into the national political debate—as in September 1958, when a controversy about the possibility of nationalizing all the nation's forests broke out in the pages of *Excelsior*—but most experts insisted that private companies intended to use the woods in the national interest.[8]

Yet the industrial model was as much a product of expediency as of deliberate planning. The demand for forest products had spiked during the Second World War and led to the virtual suspension of logging regulations. Timber companies clambered into the woods, and sawmills whined day and night. Forest boomtowns appeared—such as San Juanito (the mill town near Chihuahua City), dubbed "the Paris of the woods" by its local boosters—nearly all of which degenerated into partially deserted collections of brothels and saloons once the trees disappeared.[9] Forestry experts responded to the uncontrolled extraction of timber with a regime of exclusionary conservation that restricted peasant access to the woods and wrote off small scale-logging operations and other putatively "irrational" forms of extraction in favor of conservationist technologies such as logging bans (vedas) and forest neoconcessions known as Industrial Units for Forest Development (Unidades Industriales de Explotación Forestal, or UIEFs). These institutional mechanisms prioritized large-scale producers capable of managing large territories with the most recent technology.

Some rural people embraced the new order and found ways of benefiting from the industrial paradigm. Already in the1940s, the leader of one indigenous ejido wrote forestry officials requesting a small sawmill to help "industrialize our pueblo's natural resources"—sentiments that village leaders echoed again and again as they concluded that modern technology held the key to local development.[10] Hundreds of ejidos received permission to cut their own wood and deliver it to sawmills or (more commonly) to lease their land to logging companies, though often for a fraction of its true value. In Michoacán and a few other states, villagers earned extra money by tapping pine trees on ejidos or their own property and selling the resin to commercial distilleries. A lucky few found permanent jobs in the timber camps and sawmills that became a fixture in many parts of the nation.

Even so, forestry officials quickly ran up against the limits of their capacity to enforce logging bans in the face of land reform beneficiaries' determined efforts to control their own resources. Forest wardens struggled (and often failed) to ensure that the holders of neoconcessions achieved uncontested access to their woods. Villagers wrote political leaders to denounce what they regarded as injustices. They ignored inconvenient regulations and occasionally threatened officials who ventured into the countryside. If all else failed, they turned to the thriving black market or torched the woods. At some points, nature itself posed a threat to official management plans. Insect plagues, windstorms, and, most spectacularly, the 1943 eruption of the Paricutín volcano destroyed vast stands of timber and obliged foresters once again to throw open some regions to unregulated logging. As a result, the fate of Mexico's forests continued to depend primarily on unequal negotiations between villagers and development experts armed with logging permission forms, backroom deals, and laws issued in Mexico City.

INDUSTRIAL FORESTS

By 1939, Miguel Ángel de Quevedo had effectively declared forest management via producers cooperatives a failure. He concluded that ejidal producers had not stemmed deforestation and recommended that the authorities take a harder stance on conservation by prohibiting pasturage of any sort within areas subject to logging bans. He also endorsed a policy of expanding the size of forest preserves and other protected areas where logging should be prohibited altogether. His final report as head of the Department of Forestry, Game, and Fisheries questioned the viability of community management at the very moment that the Second World War had begun to place new demands on forest resources that ejidal producers could not begin to meet on their own.[11] Cárdenas's successor in the presidency, Manuel Ávila Camacho, declared in 1941 that the "forestry problem had reached grave proportions." He asserted that unqualified officials filled the ranks of a forest service saddled by the "shortsightedness and murkiness" of existing regulations. At the same time, he warned that timber magnates' "limitless quest for lucre" drove logging crews ever more deeply into the woods in an unsustainable quest for virgin stands of trees. The time had come, the new president declared, to formulate a new set of ground rules.[12]

In August of that year, over a hundred forestry experts, peasant representatives, and corporate leaders met in Mexico to hash out a way forward. Most of them clung to the paternalism of an earlier generation of scientists while taking a more critical approach to the political and economic challenges confronting the countryside. One of the convention's featured papers, written by the forester Rigoberto Vázquez, recalled the rhetoric of the 1930s and identified rural people—some of whom he anachronistically identified as "our Indians"—as the primary threat to the woods. Vázquez asserted that "ignorance" had led native people to clear the woods, to burn fields in preparation for planting, and to introduce cattle and crops such as potatoes in wooded areas, all of which compromised the regrowth of trees. Like his predecessors, he found the "vice" of harvesting oyamel trees for roofing boards (tejamanil) particularly objectionable, because indigenous artisans typically drove axes into several trees before settling on one that produced the best shingles.[13] Yet Vázquez also recognized that rural people's undesirable actions were partially conditioned by the forest service's own regulations. He pointed out that campesinos had responded to the prohibition against cutting live trees by deliberately killing them, then waiting a few months before legally harvesting them as dead standing timber. He also observed that if the rural poor found they could not sustain themselves through community forestry projects or small-scale agriculture, they responded by migrating, taking marginal jobs at clandestine logging companies, or illicitly cutting wood wherever they could find it.[14] The convention's summary report recommended strict sanctions for such behavior, but it also suggested that enforcement could not succeed until economic development created a viable alternative to the black market. Delegates had no shortage of ideas on that score. Recommendations included the opening of protected areas to commercial logging, creating economic incentives for timber companies, and implementing other measures to encourage railroads, paper mills, and chicle (chewing-gum base) producers to hire more workers. The convention reached a broad consensus that the injection of credit, technical assistance, and tariff protections would allow private capital to modernize the nation's woodlands in short order and create attractive alternatives to clandestine logging.[15]

These discussions reflected experts' growing dissatisfaction with existing interpretations of peasant behavior. While the younger forestry experts never abandoned their forebears' conviction that rural people's ignorance and cultural backwardness led them to misuse the woods, they nonetheless suspected that poverty was partially to blame. This shift from cultural to sociological explanations for deforestation had profound implications for scientifically informed policy. It suggested that resource managers should place less emphasis on the logistics of local production (i.e., the formation and functioning producers cooperatives) than on ensuring the flow of credit and technical expertise into the countryside. According to this new line of thinking, if rural people could earn more money in the forestry sector, they would also learn to "love" the forests themselves.[16] In essence, experts began to describe campesino stewardship of the woodlands in fiscal terms.

Experts in rural development therefore concluded that the future of forestry lay not with peasant production, ejidos, and local management that generated only moderate income, but with a modern, well-regulated industry that could pay higher wages. By the latter half of the 1950s, experts confidently asserted that the best way to manage forests was by stamping out small-scale producers with their ramshackle sawmills and deficient logging techniques, and turning instead to highly capitalized corporations with both the economic incentive and the technical capacity to manage forests responsibly. Large companies "cannot run the risk of exhausting the resources at their disposal," wrote a quartet of eminent foresters in 1957. The nation had arrived "at the moment when forests and industry constitute[d] two intimately related entities."[17] Economic development, in other words, had become an ecological matter.

In 1942—the same year that Mexico declared war on the Axis powers— legislators passed a new legal code that endorsed many of the propositions that had emerged during the previous year's forestry conference. The new law committed the government to a conservationist agenda, proclaiming that all Mexicans should cooperate with the protection, restoration, and propagation of forests. It defined unoccupied, unclaimed, and federally owned woodlands (*baldíos*) as national forest reserves and authorized the expropriation of any property that landowners logged too intensively or failed to replant with saplings thereafter. Perhaps because some of the nation's top industrialists weighed in on the legislation, these ostensibly conservationist provisions cloaked a loophole that opened public lands to private use on an unprecedented scale. The new law authorized the forest service (now demoted to a subsecretariat of the Department of Agriculture) to grant permission for logging companies to work inside the vastly expanded network of forest reserves. The legislation also made it easier for private enterprises to sign joint venture agreements (*contratos de asociación en participación*) with ejidos, which theoretically obliged timber companies to provide machinery, technical assistance, and in some cases sawmills to ejidos in exchange for a share of profits from local forestry operations.[18] In reality, these agreements usually functioned like the long-term rental contracts between logging companies and rural communities that the Cardenistas had vigorously assailed a few years earlier. (Such agreements also seemed to contradict legal stipulations that prohibited outsiders from working ejidal land.)[19] The 1942 forestry code was superseded by a fundamentally similar law seven years later, which reiterated "conservationist" goals but tellingly pledged that all logging projects needed to follow "a technical plan . . . to obtain the maximum return from the forest."[20] This emphasis on maximum-yield logging contrasted with previous legislation's more modest goal of sustained-yield production. While the new laws did express concerns about hyper-exploitation and deforestation, the 1949 code in particular sought to speed development by reasserting federal sovereignty over woodlands and encouraging private corporations to push ahead with the industrialization of forest products.

To achieve these goals, legislators first needed to address the legacy of Cardenismo, which had placed around a third of the nation's forests into ejidos by that point. The new legal codes displaced forest management from the local to the regional level by progressively dismantling the embryonic regime of community forestry. The 1942 legislation did include a vague injunction that logging on collectively held lands such as ejidos and indigenous commons should "benefit the relevant groups of population," but it made provisions only for the *continued* existence of producers cooperatives.[21] Most foresters interpreted this to mean that existing cooperatives could still operate, but that no new ones should be authorized. As a result, these village organizations slowly disappeared over the course of the decade, as officials rescinded their charters for alleged irregularities, such as ignoring the terms of logging permits, or falling under the control of outsiders, or failing to meet the needs of ejidos and indigenous communities.[22]

The 1949 code omitted its predecessor's rhetorical commitment to local production and further extended the authority of federal officials and private corporations over public, private, and ejidal woods. Whereas the 1942 code allowed the president to grant logging companies permission to operate inside national forest reserves, the 1949 legislation created a National Forestry Council comprising government and business leaders charged with oversight of commercial forestry on a national scale. There is little to indicate that such a body ever convened, meaning that no mechanism existed to manage the nation's woodlands, other than the now-defanged forest service.[23] Moreover, both the 1942 and 1949 laws placed two powerful new tools at the president's disposal: they declared it in the public interest (*de utilidad pública*) to grant timber concessions (UIEFs) to private corporations; and they allowed authorities not only to declare logging bans but also to grant special exceptions to commercial producers wherever necessary.[24] These new institutional forms displaced the primary locus of forest management from the villages that possessed woodlands to a network of official and private-sector decision makers—many of them based in national or state capitals—tasked with industrializing forest landscapes as part of a broader development imperative, rather than as a matter of community welfare or social justice.

LOGGING BANS AND LAND REFORM

There was nothing new about temporarily halting logging to allow distressed forests to recover. Presidents had issued such protective orders as early as 1922, and the Cárdenas administration repeatedly used them to limit deforestation and preserve forests that had an aesthetic value or the potential to attract tourism. These early bans ordered a halt to logging for five or ten years in relatively small areas, such as a particular ejido, a municipal district, or even an individual stand of timber. The Cárdenas administration also began in 1936 to declare so-called total bans, intended to relieve pressure on the most heavily exploited regions of central Mexico. These declarations put a stay on timber extraction within multiple counties or entire states, often for periods of twenty or thirty years. The first two regional logging bans, both declared in 1936, applied to a handful of municipal districts in the president's home state of Michoacán, where boosters hoped to develop tourist destinations. Cárdenas declared new district-level bans three more times before leaving office in 1940, including the one in the Meseta Purépecha that encouraged the development of community tree-tapping projects around Uruapan. By the time that Cárdenas left office, he had issued eleven orders banning commercial logging in Hidalgo, Aguascalientes, and the Federal District, as well as in parts of Michoacán, Jalisco, Guanajuato, and Veracruz. Collectively, they encompassed more than six million hectares.[25]

Troubling signs appeared almost immediately. The logging bans' most egregious failures occurred in the pine-oyamel foothills around the base of the Cofre de Perote, a picturesque volcanic peak in central Veracruz that was designated for a twenty-year logging ban in 1940.[26] In fact, the extraction of timber was supposed to have stopped three years earlier, when the mountain became part of a national park; however, forestry officials decided not to halt logging at that point because the ejido of Jalacingo had just been formed inside the park's proposed borders, and its villagers had no other means of making a living. In the ensuing bureaucratic muddle, a timber company hired villagers to clear the woods and open up new agricultural fields before officials realized what had happened.[27] The 1940 logging ban convinced these land reform beneficiaries to make common cause with poor charcoal manufacturers and clandestine woodcutters, both of whom protested the loss of their livelihood. This eclectic group of rural people soon came under the control of the government-affiliated CTM labor union, which initially directed their complaints to local officials, then quickly escalated to the president himself. A delegation traveled to Mexico City and asked to continue working in the forests "with the understanding that they [were] prepared to satisfy all the pertinent requirements regarding the need to reforest" everywhere they cut.[28] Federal officials stood firm and refused to grant them an exemption, but local forest wardens winked at widespread illegal logging. Nine years later, a surprise inspection discovered illegal sawmills in every municipal district covered by the ban. Forestry officials admitted that their efforts to protect the area had foundered, but blamed the failure on "criminal loggers" and a few "bad seeds [*malos elementos*]" in its own ranks.[29]

Well-publicized fiascos such as the one in El Perote did not dissuade presidents from declaring more logging bans in the decades to come. After a hiatus during the Second World War, President Ávila Camacho and his successor, Miguel Alemán, declared bans on commercial logging in nine entire states as well as in the Federal District. Other edicts put a temporary halt to cutting in the most densely wooded areas of seven other states.[30] The total area affected by bans more than doubled, from 6.8 million hectares to 14.6 million hectares, between 1945 and 1952. Taking into account the half-million hectares already in national parks and protected watersheds, over 60 percent of the nation's forestland enjoyed some form of protection against commercial logging by the early 1950s.[31]

Unlike the targeted logging bans of the 1930s, however, these new regional edicts included exemptions that allowed some groups to continue using the forests. The presidential orders enacting logging bans typically made provisions for indigent people to keep gathering wood for their own domestic use, for example. The forest service created a new category of official, known as a regional superintendent of logging bans (*jefe de zona vedada*), empowered to authorize resin-tapping campaigns, forest clearing to make way for roads and electrical lines, the harvesting of dead trees and downed branches, and the practice known as *cortes culturales*, which involved selectively cutting trees (ideally diseased and decrepit ones) to create openings in the canopy, where young trees could grow.[32] These legally permitted activities added some flexibility to the regulatory structure, but also created powerful incentives for rural people to skirt the law and collude with sawmill owners. Some villagers girdled trees—in other words, they killed them by making deep incisions around the trunk—or set fires capable of damaging but not completely burning the trees, then returned a few months later with official permission to harvest the "dead wood." Others cut live trees for "domestic use," then illegally delivered them to sawmills. Since nearly all bans also allowed rural people to deliver downed branches and other debris to paper mills, some villagers surreptitiously stripped branches from live trees each time they passed them, eventually killing those trees and making them legal to cut. Some experts also observed that since pine tapping did not fall under banned activities, villagers sometimes redoubled production and carved so many faces (the wounds bored into bark to bleed out the pine sap) that they compromised the health of the trees.[33]

The bans provoked a tidal wave of timber poaching that officials typically referred to as clandestinaje (clandestine logging). People ignored the new laws, illegally cut wood, and delivered it to pirate sawmills that specialized in black-market timber. Most of this contraband went to box-making plants, construction companies, and local artisans, although villagers also cut wood for their own houses or to make into charcoal. During the era of logging bans, from the 1950s to the early 1970s, timber poaching accounted for at least half of the nation's wood production and probably caused more damage to the forests than did commercial logging, since rural people and itinerant lumberjacks usually selected relatively young trees, which could be quickly felled and dragged away, whereas commercial loggers preferred mature trees that had more economic value.[34]

The forest service could exempt timber companies and ejidos from the logging bans, provided that they followed a specially approved management plan. It was hard to obtain these variances, however. Forestry officials favored the most highly capitalized (and politically connected) logging companies, which usually became the only businesses legally operating in their respective regions. This situation placed the companies in a strong position to negotiate lease agreements for woods on indigenous communities and ejidos, who now lacked a viable alternative. As a result, the bans aggravated the long-standing problem of rentismo, in which companies

Figure 4.1. A Rarámuri woman carrying *palos* (hand-hewn poles), ca. 1958. Francisco Plancarte, *El problema indígena tarahumara*, vol. 5 of *Memorias del Instituto Nacional Indigenista* (Mexico City: Ediciones del Instituto Nacional Indigenista, 1954), plate after p. 70.

paid a pittance for logging rights, then arrived in the woods with their own logging crews, cut the trees, then moved on.[35]

The logging bans ultimately encouraged a regime of clandestinity and *rentismo* that exposed the forest service's inability to implement a regime of exclusionary conservation in the woodlands. This failure had multiple origins. One problem had to do with incompatible goals. Officials in Mexico City hesitated to enforce policies that impeded industrial development, while forest wardens worried about antagonizing the locals. This put foresters in a bind, because villagers complained vociferously about overreaching regulations that prevented them from using their own woods. If that did not work, some people took a more direct approach: although the nation had only five hundred wardens in 1941, an average of three were killed in the line of duty every year over the following two decades.[36] Business groups also chafed at the bans. Chihuahuan logging firms claimed that the "rash and drastic" declaration of a ban in 1949 choked off development, threw working people out of work, and left valuable forests at the mercy of nature.[37] The largest companies invariably had enough pull with the president or the forest service to win exemptions to the ban and thus continued logging or purchasing wood from villagers (legally, if possible; illegally, if not) as if nothing had happened.[38] Federal authorities opened a broader loophole in 1955, when they declared an emergency plan for the production of railroad ties, which remained in place for four years. It temporarily bypassed the bans and allowed villagers and lumber companies to make cuts without a formal management plan as long as they agreed to produce ties for the Mexican National Railroad. Loggers scurried back into the mountains as forest wardens handed out hundreds of carte-blanche logging permits, and some business interests took advantage of the conjuncture to consolidate their hold on the woodlands. At least one logging company that operated in Veracruz and Oaxaca, for example, managed to cobble together an informal empire comprising forty-two properties that had requested "individual" permits.[39]

THE RETURN OF THE CONCESSION

Logging bans also made explicit exceptions for the "Industrial Units" known as UIEFs, which functioned like the Porfirian-era logging concessions. The term referred to corporations that had received the exclusive right to buy forest products (timber, wood for paper pulp, pine resin) within a defined territory. The idea behind these concessions initially took form in the 1941 forestry congress, when industry delegates argued that timber concessions would jumpstart a domestic paper sector at a time when wartime shortages had choked off Mexico's access to newsprint. The forestry code enacted the following year gave the president authority to grant UIEF concessions to any corporation dedicated to "mining, paper manufacture, construction, the production of war materiel, etc.," but it did not spell out how UIEFs should function in practice.[40] The 1949 code clarified the rules. Companies authorized to form a UIEF received the right to purchase wood products from all private landowners, indigenous communities, and ejidos within a zone demarcated by presidential decree. In exchange, the concessionaires were required to file a comprehensive management plan, replant trees wherever they cut, hire their own foresters, maintain tree nurseries, and pledge not to consume more wood than they needed. From a management perspective, it seemed that UIEFs could simultaneously modernize the woodlands and achieve the sustainable use of natural resources. From a legal perspective, as the supporters of the new legal regime pointed out, the concessions did not really trample property rights, because landowners received remuneration for any wood cut on their land. By the mid-1950s, many experts agreed (over-optimistically) that the neoconcessions were well on their way to industrializing the forestry sector and meeting national demand for wood products.[41]

In addition, UIEFs were touted as a new source of rural employment. Most concession holders pledged to hire people living within their territories as road builders, sawmill operators, and lumberjacks. Yet relatively few jobs materialized in practice. Timber companies preferred to use their existing employees rather than hire locals, who typically had fewer skills and less labor discipline.[42] Nor did most rural people experience UIEFs as a boon to the rural economy. While the law directed concessionaires to pay a "just price" (as well as a stumpage fee known as *derecho de monte*) for the wood harvested on ejidos and other properties within their jurisdiction, it remained silent about how to arrive at such a price. This was a particularly thorny question since the neoconcessions distorted the market by removing other (legal) buyers from the scene and depressing the value of forest products, except in the rare case that an ejidal management plan allowed it to produce more timber (or pine resin or pulpwood) than the concessionaire was able to consume. In many instances, UIEFs aggravated the problem by continuing to pay the same price for forest products from one year to the next, despite the inflation that began to erode rural incomes in the 1950s.

The first three neoconcessions went to paper companies in the central highlands, beginning with the 1945 creation of a UIEF for the Atenquique Paper Company of Jalisco. Two years later, the Loreto y Peña Pobre paper mills in the southern reaches of the Federal District received control of approximately 80,000 hectares. The year after that, the nation's largest paper company, San Rafael y Anexas, was awarded jurisdiction over 117,275 hectares of public land, indigenous commons, and ejidos in Mexico state and in parts of Morelos and Puebla. These early concessions were granted for periods ranging from fifty-five to sixty years, though subsequent presidential decrees reduced them to thirty-five years.[43] The paper companies agreed to plant ten trees for each one they cut, to establish schools and hospitals for workers, and to organize corps of fire fighters and armed forest wardens. Some companies did hire the required personnel, but few if any fulfilled the obligation to finance public works, much less reforest after cutting.

Some UIEF concessions did contribute to regional economic development. Loreto y Peña Pobre opened a new paper mill just before receiving a concession in 1942 and made a major investment in machinery built in Mexico City. Likewise, San Rafael constructed a small company town and installed new water lines for its modernized plant in Mexico state.[44] Most notably, every company that received UIEF concessions employed workers (from several hundred to as many as two thousand) who served as loggers, road builders, truck drivers, sawmill operators, and professional and clerical personnel.

Yet the UIEFs were not universally welcomed by the people who lived inside their territories. One challenge for foresters was that rural people typically wanted a predictable annual income over the longest possible timeframe. That meant leasing to a company that would log a modest number of trees every year on a more-or-less permanent basis. Yet resource managers objected to such arrangements on both logistical and technical grounds. Logistically, companies lacked the capacity to build roads and saw wood on every individual property in their domain simultaneously; it was much easier to build roads, temporary sawmills, and logging camps in one area, work there until the job was finished, then move on to the next place. Rotations of this sort also conformed to best scientific practices, as they were understood at the time. Experts working in Atenquique devised a system, in 1951, known as the "Mexican management method for uneven-age forests" (*método mexicano de ordenación de montes*, or MMOM), which soon became the norm for logging nationwide. (Official policy did not distinguish the use of tropical forests from that of temperate ones until 1963.) The system entailed dividing the landscape into individual stands of trees or properties and selectively cutting 35 percent of the total volume of wood in each of these plots, rotating from one to the next until the earliest-cut woods had recovered and the rotation could start once again.[45] In theory, such a technique assured sustainable harvests; over the long run, however, it favored broadleaf species over the more commercially attractive and heavily harvested conifers.[46] Moreover, it imposed a high cost on landowners and ejidatarios, who might wait two, three, or more years before it was their turn to have their woods cut and they could receive any money from "scientifically" managed UIEFs. Once the lumberjacks had finished cutting, these landowners would have to mark time for another five years or more before the company—and its paymasters—returned to their land.

These structural problems were exacerbated by the UIEFs' inability or unwillingness to fulfill other elements of their social contract. Few if any provided the social services they had promised. For example, Atenquique never established the resin-tapping program it had agreed to, which would have employed hundreds of campesinos. San Rafael dithered for nearly fifteen years before opening schools or medical facilities on its land grant, or even organizing a fire brigade there. The systematic lack of oversight by forest wardens made it easy for corporations with UIEF concessions to ignore the obligations in their charters, making them lightning rods for political opposition and rural discontent. As one of the nation's leading newspapers declared in 1962, it seemed that UIEFs' real mission was merely "to protect private interests."[47]

Disregarding these complaints, presidents approved twenty-one UIEFs—including three in Michoacán and one in Chihuahua—during the developmentalist heyday of the 1940s and 1950s. All told, the neoconcessions gave paper mills and logging companies privileged access to 2.2 million hectares of the nation's most desirable timber reserves.[48]

Unlike the first three grants made to paper companies that had been in business for decades, most subsequent UIEFs went to newly formed timber companies that investors had incorporated for the express purpose of requesting a logging concession. The federal government usually approved these requests, as long as concessionaires agreed to make substantial investments in sawmills, transportation, and social services. True to form, however, nearly all of these UIEFs chronically ignored their contracts. Some observers concluded that concessionaires simply did not want to share the "fabulous wealth" they made in the forests, but it is also true that few if any logging companies profited enough to meet the financial and developmental obligations they had contracted for. Whatever the case, nearly half of the UIEFs managed their territories so poorly—or provoked such vehement opposition from rural people—that forestry officials ended up canceling their concessions before they expired.[49]

Opposition to the UIEFs soon became a regular feature of rural politics. Villagers sometimes complained that they learned that their land fell within the jurisdiction of a concessionaire only when lumberjacks appeared to start cutting, leaving residents scrambling for an explanation. The disappearance of competitive markets meant that they also stood to receive much less from their products, regardless of whether they worked the woods themselves or elected to rent their woodlots to the concessionaries. To make matters worse, company logging crews rarely followed MMOM guidelines; on the contrary, they usually ignored production limits altogether and ravaged village woodlots. It is difficult to quantify the ecological and economic consequences for rural people, but reports of irresponsible clear-cuts and eroded hillsides dogged nearly every major concession. Village leaders complained to the forest service or sympathetic leaders in the CNC peasants' union whenever UIEF managers failed to pay royalties into the bank accounts held in trust by the Ejidal Credit Bank or encroached on communal land. Unsurprisingly, most people desperately tried to make sure that their property was not included in logging concessions. Some refused to let loggers onto their lands or threatened to kill company foresters who scouted stands of timber.[50]

Although the land reform had conveyed around a third of the nation's forestlands to rural people by this point, policy shifts such as logging bans, neoconcessions, and the quashing of producers cooperatives delivered effective control of forests to power-holders with few ties to rural society. This incongruity became a central source of contention between villagers and administrators for decades to come. Yet forest communities still had substantial terrain for political maneuver. Even as new policies stripped away their former prerogatives, the people who lived and worked in the woods found ways to collaborate with the new regime of commercial forestry or to stake claims to local autonomy based on their ownership of the land. Ironically, the same legal and institutional innovations that impinged on rural people's autonomy unleashed countervailing forces they often managed to turn to their advantage.

DEVELOPING CHIHUAHUA

Most of Chihuahua's major forestry companies were founded just after the revolution, as the foreign interests began to abandon northern Mexico. Mexican timbermen extended logging roads southward in the Sierra Tarahumara in search of old-growth forest and hauled timber to the so-called portable sawmills, which could be disassembled and moved from one logging camp to another in a matter of days. About a dozen entrepreneurs entered the Chihuahua timber market during the 1920s, and those that survived the Great Depression prospered in the 1940s. Such was the case of Fernando Alcocer Patiño, who installed a sawmill in the southern reaches of the Sierra Tarahumara in 1920 with the help of a Mormon pioneer and lumberman from Arizona. Alcocer signed his first logging contracts in the Urique district, thereby launching a long and often collaborative relationship with ejidos and indigenous communities in the heartland of Rarámuri society.[51] He eventually sold most of his business to Industrias Río Verde (where he briefly served as executive director), a far larger and much more controversial company owned by the timber magnate Juan González Ugarte, who had similarly entered the business in the 1920s. González Ugarte got his start by leasing logging rights from ejidos and indigenous communities around San Juanito. His big break came when he briefly acquired the lease to the immense Louisiana Timberland concession in Bocoyna a few years before the federal government canceled its charter, in 1930. After that, he brought his sons José and Mario González Múzquiz into what was becoming an increasingly diversified business empire known as Grupo Parral. He also moved the bulk of his operations southward, to the virgin territory of Guachochi and eventually all the way to the state's southernmost district of Guadalupe y Calvo. There, Industrias Río Verde signed lease agreements for hundreds of thousands of hectares of federal and ejidal land. It was the dominant timber company in southern Chihuahua until the 1980s.[52]

In contrast to the family-owned timber companies that grew up piecemeal in the context of postrevolutionary economic reconstruction, the largest and most politically connected of all Chihuahuan forestry interests materialized virtually overnight. In 1946 a consortium of Mexican businessmen headed by Eloy S. Vallina García announced that it had acquired the half-million hectare North Western Railway concession that had once belonged to the Madera Lumber Company. The new corporation, "Bosques de Chihuahua," included some of the nation's most powerful political and economic figures. Vallina himself was the son of Spanish immigrants. His father started out as a bank clerk in Ciudad Juárez and rose through the profession until 1933, when he founded the Banco de Comercio Mexicano. By the late 1940s, it had become the largest bank in Chihuahua and occupied the same building that had once housed the infamous Banco Minero, which had helped to finance the Creel-Terrazas empire during the nineteenth century. Vallina recruited Carlos Trouyet, a prominent Mexico City entrepreneur and close friend of President Alemán, as a joint partner. Other important members of the consortium included José de la Mora, the primary owner of stock in the North Western Railway, as well as President Alemán himself as a silent partner. The consortium raised fifty million pesos and bought the outstanding railroad stock, then announced plans to build a thoroughly modern paper plant outside Chihuahua City. But questions immediately cropped up about the validity and extension of the railroad's land titles. The legal muddle threatened to tie up the woodlands for years to come. Bosques de Chihuahua would probably have been left with virtually no access to the forests had the president himself had not stepped in to cut the Gordian knot. Shortly before he left office in 1952, Alemán granted the company a 315,000 hectare UIEF concession that consisted almost entirely of former North Western Railway holdings—although the company later claimed that the concession gave it the rights to nearly twice that area. Like most UIEF contracts, the concession stipulated that the company would reforest after cutting and would modernize its sawmills by replacing radial saw blades with more efficient band saws. The company also pledged to provide "medical attention, education, recreation opportunities, etc.," and to prohibit the sale of alcoholic beverages within its domains.[53]

Bosques de Chihuahua helped push the logging frontier southward into the Rarámuri heartland. Commercial forestry had complicated effects on native society. Most notably, it made previously inaccessible forests into valuable commodities, as logging companies leased rights deeper and deeper in the forest. By 1951, timber companies had signed twenty leases with indigenous villages, meaning that around 17 percent of all logging in Chihuahua was taking place on communal Rarámuri land.[54] Rather than buying property outright, timber companies preferred to lease logging rights, which ignited a new round of dispossession. The mestizo families that had settled in the Sierra Tarahumara over the previous decades—the outsiders whom the Rarámuri called chabochis—flooded district governments with legal claims known as denunciations (denuncios) requesting legal titles to supposedly "vacant" national forestlands. Most of this territory consisted either of Porfirian-era concessions that had reverted to state ownership or of territory occupied by indigenous people, who frequently lacked a formal title. Even so, local justices-of-the-peace usually approved chabochi land claims with no questions asked. Perhaps they did not know the area well enough to recognize the extent of native lands, but it is more likely that they deliberately ignored the widespread swindling of Rarámuri land.

Scores of fraudulent claims to native land were approved in the 1940s and 1950s, enough to spark a new round of mestizo migration into the sierras. Most often, the settlers built fences around the "vacant" lands they intended to claim and went to court to request ownership of the "former" indigenous commons. Many of these newcomers considered the Rarámuri, and all Indians for that matter, not only as social inferiors but as natural servants whose labor and wealth was essentially free for the taking. Some continued to assume, as their nineteenth-century forebears had done, that native people owed them food, forced loans, sex, and menial work just for the asking.[55]

This new spate of dispossession effectively converted some Rarámuri villagers into landless workers dependent on the emerging class of mestizo landowners. In one instance, an outsider who had lived in the sierras for decades began to recruit cronies to settle nearby so he could add them to the rolls of a village whose 1928 request for an ejido had languished in the bureaucracy for a quarter century. In another—the village of Guachochi—mestizo families arrived in the early 1950s and began to build houses on the village's common lands. Indigenous leaders repeatedly petitioned the president to put an end to the chicanery, but they found it difficult to sustain their drive, because the most aggressive mestizo settlers intimidated or murdered anyone they suspected of disputing their claims. By 1955, the ongoing controversy attracted the attention of the National Indigenist Institute (INI) and other advocates for native people. The INI sent a letter to the newly installed governor, Teófilo Borunda, beseeching him to order judges to reject future denunciations of indigenous lands and send troops into the woods to protect indigenous property.[56] Although no troops appeared, settlers' petitions for land stopped sailing through the courts.

Native people and their allies (schoolteachers, representatives of the Banco Ejidal, the INI, and others) also scrambled to submit their own requests for ejidos or to revive old ones. Communities in the sierras had received nearly half a million hectares of forestland by 1940, but with the exception of Cusárare, Heredia, and Guachochi, most lacked the means to put them into production and therefore fell back on the reliable strategy of signing rental agreements with timber companies.[57] While some mestizo-dominated ejidos earned a reasonable income this way, indigenous people rarely understood the finer points of the documents they signed and had fewer means of enforcing the ones they did comprehend. Companies such as those owned by Alcocer Patiño tried to make the appropriate payments to communities and contributions to the Banco Ejidal, but such scrupulous attention to the law was hardly the rule. When companies did make the proper installments, corrupt ejidal or indigenous leaders sometimes pocketed the money without distributing it to anyone else, and even if communities did collectively agreed to sign a contract, there was no guarantee

Figure 4.2. Ejidatarios from El Vergel building a logging road, March 1951. Archivo General de la Nación, SARH/PF, caja 244, "Memoria relativa a la Unidad Industrial de Explotación Forestal 'Parral.'"

they would receive the payments they were due. The residents of Churo, in the district of Urique, for example, reported that local leaders made an under-the-table deal with timber companies to provide ties for construction, but never paid the ejidatarios for once the ties had been delivered.[58]

The expansion of the logging frontier took place in the virtually unregulated context of wartime timber production and postwar economic boom. By the late 1940s, forestry officials were determined to make at least a token response to the increasing pace of deforestation. Presidential decrees created no fewer than six protected areas in Chihuahua, including modest forest reserves in Tutuaca, established in 1937, and in Papigochic two years later. In 1949 the federal government declared a logging ban on nearly all forestlands in Chihuahua (as well parts as of Sinaloa, Sonora, and Durango), comprising a total of twenty-seven municipal districts.[59] Like all such decrees, this one was deeply unpopular. The timber sector's interest group, known as the Unión de Madereros de Chihuahua, charged that the moratorium did nothing to conserve the forests, but rather "abandoned the woods to the forces of nature" and allowed trees to grow so old and decrepit that they would eventually "fall prey to natural destructive agents such as forest fires, infestations, and hurricanes."[60] The forest's only purpose, from the perspective of the lumbermen's association, was as a source of raw material for commercial production; placing it off limits simply let perfectly good wood go to waste. The organization further claimed that its members were not to blame for the overexploitation of Chihuahua's woods and that the majority of its members were "conscientious Mexicans who do an honest business making the proper use of their lands by strictly following the proper forestry techniques and regulations." The real culprits were campesinos, who felt no such restraints. The union claimed that the forest-service director had made a public statement asserting that most of the damage had been done by ejidatarios, who "cut whatever wood they need[ed] to meet their momentary needs without following any technical direction or scientific study."[61]

The ban brought palpable changes to everyday life in the forestlands. While relatively few Rarámuri people depended solely on logging to make a living, young men often worked informally in the lumber camps.[62] The ban left unemployed many indigenous woodcutters, railroad-tie makers, haulers, and road builders. It also choked off the royalties (derechos de monte) that some communities had come to depend on. In more heavily mestizo areas, local economies withered as small-scale loggers—many of whom had no idea what had happened—lost their jobs overnight.[63] In light of the logging companies' complaints, it is ironic that pressure from rural people was most effective in demanding the ban be lifted. The first step took place in 1954, when the Subsecretariat of Forestry allowed logging to recommence in the district of Creel, after repeated complaints from villagers that the sudden loss of jobs in the timber sector had left them destitute and unemployed.[64]

In practice, the ban did little to slow the pace of deforestation in Chihuahua. While it did create bureaucratic headaches for smaller companies, the larger ones usually received permission to keep cutting timber—often as the sole legal operators in the area. Another administrative pathway opened up in November 1955, when the federal subsecretary of forestry and wildlife, Manuel Hinojosa Ortiz, issued the Emergency Plan for Railroad Tie Production in Chihuahua (and extended it to the rest of the nation the following year). Many of the ties used to rebuild railways after the revolution had not been treated with creosote or other preservatives and had rotted to the point that the rail lines had become impassable. While the declaration of an emergency loosened regulations on railroad-tie production throughout the nation, Chihuahua felt its effects particularly strongly. A few days after the emergency plan came into effect, Secretary Hinojosa and Governor Borunda announced the creation of the "Committee for the Social, Economic, and Environmental [*Forestal*] Recovery of the Tarahumara Region," which was empowered to purchase lumber from ejidos and indigenous communities in the Bocoyna region, notwithstanding the statewide logging ban.[65] The recovery committee circumvented other regulations as well, most notably the requirement that a forester mark trees for felling. On the ejidos of Heredia, Choguita, and several others, the committee issued blanket "emergency permits" that allowed for rapid and often extremely damaging logging. Nearly all of this work was subcontracted to politically connected timber firms.[66]

The region received some benefits from the emergency logging. In the summer of 1957, for example, the recovery committee used a portion of its income to buy several tons of corn, beans, and oats for the district's poorest ejidos.[67] Hundreds of people on predominantly indigenous ejidos such as Heredia, as well as on mestizo ones such as San Rafael, once again hiked into the mountains and began work, and scores of truck drivers in the Bocoyna region also found employment.[68] Perhaps most important, the resumption of (legal) logging restored a trickle of income to the Rarámuri villagers, who worked as unskilled laborers for the timber companies.

Yet the committee's phony *indigenismo* masked its essential character as an instrument to appropriate forest resources. Its agents purchased millions of board feet at prices below market rate from indigenous ejidos such as Panalichi, Arroyo de la Cabeza, Betevachic, and others in the Bocoyna district, and delivered the proceeds directly to the recovery committee itself, which was supposed to spend it on native people's behalf. Instead, it appears to have spent most of the income on boondoggles such as a "zootechnical post" outside the state capital, whose main goal was to breed improved species of livestock destined for mestizo-owned ranches on the fertile lands of central Chihuahua, a day's trip from the sierras.[69] Much of the wood that the villagers produced either went missing or ended up as pulp delivered to the new paper mill outside of Chihuahua City (owned by a subsidiary of Bosques de Chihuahua), rather than being put to its ostensible use as railroad ties.[70] Moreover, the royalties from all this activity took years to materialize. Timber companies deposited the remaining funds into accounts held by the Banco Ejidal, often without a full accounting, leaving villagers at the mercy of bank administrators whenever they needed funds for schools, clinics, and other local needs.[71]

It did not take long for the effects of "emergency" to spark tensions within native communities. Particularly in the Bocoyna district, most people doubted the wisdom of widespread logging in forests already stressed from the previous decade's wartime logging. A vocal minority of native people considered it an opportunity to wring more money out of the commons; and a few tried to enrich themselves at the expense of their neighbors.[72] Most, however, seem to have concluded that the declaration of emergency and the recovery committee represented a thinly disguised scam to deprive them of their woods. Native leaders suspected that the committee's acquisitions chief, the well-known forester Francisco Irigoyen, as well as the contractors with the exclusive right to buy wood, Ignacio and Andrés Chacón, were less interested in "development" than in lucre. Some of their grievances had an explicitly ethnic tenor. The leaders of Betevachic told a newspaper reporter that chabochi outsiders had forced them out of their woodlots. The reporter concluded that the "mestizos who exploit the Tarahumaras have no intention of ranching or farming the land. They are only interested in clear-cutting the forests that the Indians have conserved for many years as their sole patrimony."[73] In a similar vein, the indigenous governor of another community in Bocoyna claimed that representatives of the committee had removed 1.3 million pesos' worth of timber, in exchange for which the villagers received cloth with a value of 30,000 pesos.[74]

The scale of fraud convinced authorities to suspend the committee's operations in the summer of 1958 and to disband it altogether two years later. The forester charged with investigating its fallout concluded that the committee had done little if anything for the social, economic, or environmental recovery of the Sierra Tarahumara. Its main contribution had been to allow ejidatarios to log at a furious pace without official permission, a privilege the forester worried that many people now regarded as their right.[75] Their hundreds of small, individual acts of illegal cutting no doubt degraded the forest, but the woods could grow back as long as the land was not permantly converted to agriculture. The same could not be said for the major commercial interests that had also benefited from the "emergency" logging. The state's largest lumber company, for example, deforested a far larger terrotoriy that would take decades to recover.

THE POLITICAL ECOLOGY OF A NEOCONCESSION

Bosques de Chihuahua began to ramp up logging operations in the late 1940s, even though the remnants of the Madera Lumber Company and several smaller firms continued to extract timber from the former North Western Railway concession for the U.S. market and, increasingly, consumers in northern Mexico. Around 2,000 people still worked in sawmills in this region of the Sierra Tarahumara in the late 1940s. The market remained strong for railroad ties as well as construction material for domestic use and for industries such as the Potosí Mining Company and the Guggenheim family's American Smelting and Refining Company (ASARCO) complex in neighboring Sonora. Another 300 worked in workshops fabricating wooden shipping boxes for the fruit trade. Five hundred made their living hauling logs with mules or trucks, and perhaps twice that number worked on the North Western Railway line, which transported nearly all forest products in the Sierra Tarahumara.[76] The purchase of the railroad properties and official declaration of a UIEF concession in 1949 made Bosques de Chihuahua the sole employer of this farflung workforce. In 1953 it formalized its role as regional employer by signing a collective contract with 2,138 workers who earned anywhere from 7.85 pesos an hour (approximately one U.S. dollar in 2010 terms) for loading logging trucks, to over twice that much for skilled work in the main sawmill.[77]

The logging company could not give jobs to everyone, however. Around 17,500 people lived in the Bosques de Chihuahua concession area, a population that included a few hundred Rarámuri families and a small army of desultory prospectors, known as gambusinos, who worked the played-out silver veins in the canyons. Apart from the Rarámuri, the largest group were mestizos descended from the first generation of timber workers who migrated to the sierras during the logging bonanza of the 1900s. Many of these former loggers settled in ranching towns, including the Mormon colonies of Chuhuichupa and García; others set down roots in logging-camps-turned-townships, such as El Oso and La Avena. When the timber industry roared back in the 1940s, a new wave of workers arrived and founded settlements such as Alto de Dolores and El Largo, the latter of which became the second largest city (after Madera) in the concession zone. The men in these families shuffled in and out of work in the timber sector, while their families took ancillary jobs, planted corn and potatoes, and raised small herds of cattle and goats on land they either rented from the railroad company or had staked out as their own.[78]

These independent villagers and rancheros posed a constant challenge to company foresters who intended to "rationalize" logging operations. In the early years of the Bosques de Chihuahua concession, independent loggers competed directly with the company itself, particularly the indigenous people and settlers who continued to harvest young trees and cut them into railroad ties. The forest service tried to clamp down on this widespread and illegal practice by prohibiting the felling or transport of trees less than fifty centimeters in diameter, which left only trees much too large for independent tie makers to cut with their aging hatchets. That gambit failed when the company realized that very few of the trees in the concession grew that large. The old giants had already succumbed to a previous generation of sawyers, leaving the company with no easy way to halt the cutting of smaller trees.[79]

The company also bickered with settlers over their habit of letting livestock roam the woods. Goats were the main source of friction, since they grazed on saplings and slowed the repopulation of forests. This was a particularly pronounced problem around the settlements founded in the early 1900s, where loggers had made clear-cuts and pastured their animals in the openings. The company's forest wardens—who sometimes made their rounds accompanied by armed guards—ordered people living in the concession zone to keep their animals under control. They slapped small fines on those who disobeyed and in a few instances forcibly removed herds of goats altogether.[80] Rural people complained to officials at all levels about what they saw as the company's high-handed conduct. In 1952, for example, a group of settlers wrote President Ruiz Cortines that the company cared less about conserving the woods than about stripping locals of their property to create a class of landless laborers willing to work for whatever the company cared to pay. Their complaint went unaddressed, and another group of settlers sent a petition the following year, stating that they intended merely "to defend ourselves and appeal for justice, with no wish to impede the industrialization of our Country [sic] nor to impinge the rights of the owners of the enormous tract of land . . . now known as Bosques de Chihuahua." Yet they contested the company's right to operate at all. They included a notarized affidavit showing that Bosques de Chihuahua continued to use radial saws in two of its smaller mills, rather than the band saws required by the concession agreement—a breach that strictly speaking should have led to its outright cancelation. In the end, officials slapped the company with a 20,000 peso fine, and the company backed off from its campaign against grazing.[81]

The company had to engage in similarly tacit negotiations with the locals who flouted its prohibition of hunting without a permit and ignored the hunting clubs that managers tried to organize as a way of ensuring compliance. Rural people continued to catch fish by throwing poison or dynamite into creeks, despite foresters' warnings and signs posted throughout the woods.[82] Rural people often left campfires burning, perhaps intentionally,

Figure 4.3. Poster produced by Bosques de Chihuahua, ca. 1956. The text reads, "Forest Fires and Goats alike burn and destroy Soils, Grasslands, Seeds, Crops, Pastures, Trees. . . . They annihilate and deplete everything and lead communities to ruin. Avoid Them! Banish Them!" Note the smoke from forest fires rising in the distance. Archivo General de la Nación, SARH/PF, caja 249, exp. 54603, leg. 2–3.

which occasionally sparked forest fires, and then refused to volunteer for fire brigades. Foresters muttered about rural people's lack of cooperation, but they reluctantly accepted the limits of their authority. Administrators pleaded with wood-gatherers, most of whom were little more than children, not to leave campfires burning, for example, but they abandoned the idea of meting out fines or some other punishment. Likewise, they reluctantly admitted that rural people would fight forest fires only if they were paid to.[83] Foresters eventually learned to temper their management plans in a bid to improve relations with the populace. For example, one forester agreed to let villagers in Chuhuichupa and La Norteña clear a management plot slated for logging and reforestation so that they could plant corn and oats. "The settlers continually burn the trees and eliminate them in one way or another," he reported, so the company should just issue logging permits and let people clear the land "rather than let the trees go to waste."[84]

The company also learned to accept the land reform after initially responding to villagers who solicited an ejido on Bosques de Chihuahua territory with campaigns of intimidation and bureaucratic chicanery. The pueblo of El Largo was a former logging camp whose residents filed a petition for land in 1950. The company sent thugs to expel the claimants from its domain, but they refused to budge and continued pressing until authorities relented and made a provisional grant, in 1955. Even then, the company refused to give up. The surveyor who mapped the ejido's final boundaries chose a small parcel of dusty, rugged terrain, rather than the rich woods the villagers anticipated. The ejidatarios complained that the company had paid off the surveyor to locate their ejido on miserable land "that in no way meets the needs of campesinos."[85] A pair of inspectors sent to investigate the episode concluded that the company had persuaded agrarian reform authorities not to grant any forestland, despite orders to the contrary. On the other hand, the inspectors ratified the surveyor's judgment that the people of El Largo were not campesinos, but rather truck drivers and other low-level employees of Bosques de Chihuahua who wanted a bit of woodland for themselves.[86] (In the longer term, the ejidatarios prevailed: in 1971 President Luis Echeverría used Bosques de Chihuahua territory to add another 200,000 hectares to El Largo's original grant, making it the largest ejido in the country.)

The failure to derail El Largo's petition convinced the chief administrator of Bosques de Chihuahua, Emilio Flores Calderón, to take a different track. The company dropped overt opposition to the land reform and did nothing to stop the creation of the next two ejidos in El Oso y La Avena (later known as Jesús García), or the expansion of several older ones at the expense of company lands. He sent the new administrators of the ejido a courteous note in 1957, averring that the company was "entirely disposed" to buy any timber it produced.[87] Flores omitted mentioning that Bosques de Chihuahua was the only legal consumer available to them.

He was considerably less circumspect with the chief of the forest service. He reminded the Mexico City official that his corporation followed an approved management plan that made "the most efficient possible use of every tree we cut" and protected the woods against "all manner of enemies," whereas the new ejidatarios used the land "as if they want the forest to disappear." He also complained that the ejidatarios ignored foresters' instructions about which trees to cut and which to spare, that they left debris (slash) on the forest floor, and finally that they refused to cooperate in fire-prevention brigades. In a particularly telling request, he suggested that logging should be prohibited altogether on the ejidos of Madera and La Norteña, which he accused of harvesting trees and chiseling them into railroad ties that they clandestinely sold to the Tarahumara Recovery Committee in charge of the emergency-tie production program.[88] The captains of the emerging industrial forestry regime had learned to make accommodations to social conditions they could not change while refusing to cede their primary sources of profit. Events in Michoacán showed that they were equally adept at turning unforeseen changes in the natural environment to their advantage as well.

DISASTER AND DEVELOPMENT IN MICHOACÁN

On the afternoon of 20 February 1943, a field hand named Demetrio Torral struggled to plow a cornfield near the town of San Juan Parangaricutiro, a predominantly indigenous community of 4,000 tucked in the Itzícuaro valley of northwestern Michoacán. Like everyone else, Torral had felt the earth sway and buck repeatedly over the previous weeks, and the tremors were growing worse. People felt unsettled and seasick, and many of them spent extra time praying to the town's famous icon of Christ.[89] As Torral finished plowing a long, straight furrow, a fissure thirty centimeters wide opened in the field behind him; people later said that Torral had scratched open the earth itself. Ponciano Pulido, the ranchero who owned the farm, scurried over to the crevice and tried filling it in with dirt and stones in a desperate effort to reclose the breach. His wife, Paula, was just cleaning up from lunch, and she looked up in time to see a ghostly dust devil dancing along the opening. Then a small dome of earth that looked to her like "confused cake" slowly pushed upward, collapsed in on itself, and began to vent a thin grey plume of smoke. As Torral and Pulido struggled to unhitch the oxen, a thundering quake threw them both to the ground. They said their prayers and made for town to tell the mayor and parish priest what had happened. Father José Caballero headed directly to the field, by which time the vent had expanded to a width of two meters and hurled incandescent rocks a short way into the air. Returning to his study later that day, the priest consulted a history of Vesuvius and confirmed that he had just witnessed the birth of a volcano.[90]

Figure 4.4. Paricutín Volcano viewed from the northeast (Cerro de Equijuata), March 1944. Photo by A. Brehme. United States Geological Survey. Originally published as plate 39-A in *U.S. Geological Survey Bulletin 965-D*, 1956.

Paricutín was one of only two volcanoes to have appeared in North America within historical memory. (The other was El Jorullo, which erupted in 1759, a mere seventy-five kilometers away.) By the end of its first day, the young volcano had built a cinder cone ten meters high and had started launching globs of magma known as "lava bombs." Actual flows of lava began the following day and continued for another four weeks. In March the volcano was still producing lava, but it entered a cineritic phase, characterized by billowing clouds of ash emitted at an average rate of 1,200 metric tons per minute. By summertime, the cone had grown to a height of 365 meters. Ash continued to fall, as one volcanologist put it, with "a gentle rustle like falling hail," burying crops, stripping the needles from pine trees, and collecting in drifts as far as a hundred miles away. A major new chimney opened at base of the main cone in March 1944 and emitted its own, slow-moving river of magma. The main cone revived again that summer, and on its southwestern flanks appeared new vents that spewed lava and gray or black ash for the next three years. After that, the entire complex grew increasingly quiet until 1952, when the eruptions ended altogether.[91]

The eruption of Paricutín unfolded slowly enough that it caused only two fatalities, both from lightning strikes triggered by the friction of scorching volcanic ash rising into the cool surrounding air. Yet the volcano's unwelcome appearance forced at least 5,200 people to abandon the villages of San Juan Parangaricutiro, Corupo, Zirosto, and Angáhuan, just west of Uruapan. The small Purépecha village Paricutín was the first to succumb. Trucks arrived in June 1943, and aid workers helped residents to disassemble their wooden houses (trojes). The refugees were evacuated to Caltzontzin, a plot of land just outside of Uruapan where they rebuilt their homes and mourned the loss of their ancestral territory and its celebrated pear orchards. People soon began to abandon the larger town of San Juan Parangaricutiro, where half a meter of ash covered the fields by May. Cattle could not dig through the gray dust to get at whatever forage still remained, and respiratory problems began to take a toll as well. Planting corn was a lost cause. The kernels germinated in the ash, but soon withered. The few people (mostly older folk) who intended to wait out the eruption finally gave up when a wall of tar-like lava flowed into the village late that summer, forcing them to follow the rest of their neighbors to an expropriated hacienda named Rancho de los Conejos, not far from Uruapan. By September, lava blanketed the entire village except for the altar and a single spire of the church. Even today, the altar and spire jut out above a dark sea of rock and serve as testimony of the town that once thrived there.[92]

Before the eruption, most villagers in San Juan Parangaricutiro subsisted on milpa agriculture, which they complemented by planting squash and collecting mushrooms in the woods during the cold season. Most families also owned a few cattle or sheep. The community's greatest asset was a forested commons of 21,106 hectares (well over 46,000 acres). Not everyone who lived in the village had the right to use the woods, but those who did (i.e., the comuneros) felled trees to build their houses and to make tejamanil roof shingles for themselves or for sale elsewhere. A small number of people cut oak trees to make charcoal for the market in Uruapan.

The community agreed to rent its commons to a logging company in 1922, and outsiders controlled the woods ever since, despite the formation of a producers cooperative in 1935. It turned out that the cooperative had been created at the behest of timber magnate Paulo Doddoli (himself a former hacienda manager), who had convinced a few residents to sign a new contract giving him access to the woods.[93] His logging operation naturally sparked resentment throughout the area. Not only did the bogus agreement freeze most villagers out of the lucrative timber trade, but loggers soon began cutting wood on land claimed by the neighboring village of Paricutín, miring the two communities in a lengthy court battle over boundary lines. Moreover, the timber operation threatened the livelihoods of villagers who earned money by tapping trees and clandestinely selling the resin to one of five turpentine distilleries that bought from indigenous people with no questions asked. Although only the poorest villagers tried to make a living this way, most families used tree-tapping to supplement their incomes.[94]

A turning point came in 1937, when a forester noticed that the spurious cooperative aligned with Doddoli had never filed documents of incorporation with the federal authorities. He encouraged villagers to found a new cooperative of tree tappers, which promptly received federal approval and signed a contract with the largest distillery in the region (the Resinera Uruapan) on terms far more favorable than those the clandestine distillers had offered. Resinera Uruapan agreed to pay 11 pesos per kilogram for pine resin, and to provide tappers with buckets and knives. It also trained them in proper extraction techniques, since the villagers' existing practice of stripping away large chunks of bark (*cajetes*) weakened the trees and made them susceptible to disease. Outbid by the new contract, the clandestine distillers responded by stirring up resentment against the forester with a letter-writing campaign to federal authorities that eventually led him to be transferred to Nayarit. Nevertheless, the new cooperative made good on its contract with Resinera Uruapan, which generated enough employment that most villagers spent about six days a month collecting sap in the communal woods.[95] That is not to say that the new cooperative functioned perfectly: like its predecessor, it excluded some comuneros, who were left with no alternative but the black market. Yet it did succeed in challenging the influence of the clandestine distillers, including Doddoli himself.[96]

The eruption of Paricutín upended this delicate community ecology. A team of scientists from the United States and Mexico found that the heavy ash-fall of 1943 had defoliated pine, fir, and most oak trees in a fourteen-square-kilometer area around the volcano. Villagers initially found it easy to hunt the deer and rabbits that fled the ash-fall, which provided some relief, but the forests on which they depended clearly confronted a long-term disaster. Saplings could not withstand the weight of ash and doubled over before disappearing altogether beneath the dunes of gray. Pines and firs had apparently died in 1944, although the oaks grew new leaves and seemed healthy. The ash also cauterized the "faces" (i.e., the open incisions) that tappers had made on the outer bark of the pines. Most observers naturally concluded that all the evergreens near the volcano would die, dooming the resin operation to extinction. It later turned out that most mature evergreens had in fact survived. The ash had even eradicated a plague of southern pine beetles in the area.[97] In the immediate aftermath of the eruption, however, the greatest threat came from logging companies that considered the eruption as a windfall.

The federal government had declared a logging ban in the districts of Uruapan and Parangaricutiro in December 1937 in an effort to stanch clandestine logging and illegal timber contracts, but timber companies contended in the wake of the eruption that they should be allowed to salvage whatever they could. The forest service agreed and lifted most restrictions in the immediate vicinity of the volcano. During the short-lived bonanza that followed, politically connected brokers such as Rafael Ortiz and Rafael Vaca Solorio jockeyed to cut prime stands of trees. One company cut 125,000 railroad ties virtually overnight, while another delivered more than 31,000 metric tons of charcoal to Mexico City.[98]

Federal authorities also gave men displaced by the disaster priority for enrolling in the *bracero* guest-worker program, which provided temporary jobs in the United States. The response was overwhelming. According to one estimate, half of the region's men traveled north to find work—so many that some communities had to scale back tree-tapping projects in the late 1940s.[99] In the longer term, many of the displaced villagers found jobs in logging and pine-tapping initiatives organized by the Ejidal Bank and other regional development projects. One of these initiatives took root in the refounded village of Nuevo San Juan Parangaricutiro, which eventually became one of the nation's most successful community-forestry enterprises.

What accounts for this phoenix-like revival of community forestry in Nuevo San Juan? One part of the answer lies with the microclimatic changes wrought by Paricutín itself. While a light coating of nitrogen-rich volcanic ash acted as a fertilizer in many parts of Michoacán and brought forth bumper crops in the mid-1940s, the huge drifts in the volcano's immediate vicinity killed most vegetation. Worse still, the rains that eventually washed the ash away also produced a turgid runoff that scrubbed off the topsoil and eroded the fields. With cattle dying and crops failing, the production of forest products became more important than ever. Community authorities received permission to take direct control of logging operations soon after the eruption, and founded a new village-owned logging enterprise in the wake of the catastrophe.[100] Small-scale private landowners around Paricutín came to depend on tree-tapping and the attendant necessity of carefully managing forests on a scale as small as ten hectares.[101] Another part of the answer is that the former president Cárdenas took a personal interest in the fate of the refugees. He used his honorary position as the chairman (*vocal ejecutivo*) of the Commission on the Tepalcatepec (a regional development initiative) to ensure that men from Nuevo San Juan Parangaricutiro and other communities around Uruapan received jobs in the commercial salvage logging business, and that logging and tapping contracts paid fair wages.[102]

It also seems likely that the seeds of Nuevo San Juan's success had been planted even before the volcano erupted. Villagers had made unusually bold efforts in the 1930s to regain the commons from logging companies. Most of all, the producers cooperative formed in 1937—while still not fully inclusive—provided a means for most villagers to triple their income overnight. The success of these collective actions spilled over to the 1940s and early 1950s, as community leaders retained their commitment to local control of resources and a broadly inclusive use of the commons.

MODERNIZING THE MICHOACÁN FORESTS

Unlike in Chihuahua, Michoacán had few large-scale forest products companies in the early 1940s. The most prominent was the Resinera Uruapan, founded in 1937 by the landowner Manuel F. Moreno and the veteran turpentine maker Ramón Martín del Campo. At its height, the company employed sixty-five rangers (*monteros*) who organized tree-tapping campaigns in slightly more than sixty ejidos and private properties.[103] Most other companies were undercapitalized firms run by families with well-established clienteles in the countryside and good working relations with the region's ubiquitous complement of illegal sawmills. The relative lack of private investment meant that Michoacán depended far more than its northern counterpart on development loans from federal agencies such as the Banco Ejidal, whose Uruapan branch took the lead in financing recovery from the volcanic eruption and dispensed nearly a million pesos to rebuild the local economy. As so frequently occurs after natural catastrophes, however, these relief efforts fostered what Naomi Klein has called "disaster capitalism" that ultimately tightened private corporations' grip on natural resources.[104] In the case of the Paricutín disaster, the Ejidal Bank made loans for roads, water pipes, and other infrastructure projects that left villages indebted, while simultaneously making the woods more available to rescue logging by politically connected timber companies.[105]

In some ways, the disaster capitalism unleashed by Paricutín merely hastened a trend that had begun in the previous decade, in which "development" projects (such as producers cooperatives) and the use of the Banco Ejidal as an extension agency functioned to expand the reach of forestry regulations and inject a new source of competition into the already convoluted architecture of local politics. Producers cooperatives had unintentionally accelerated commercial logging in the Uruapan hinterland and the Meseta Purépecha. The logging frontier had expanded northward, in the early 1940s, to indigenous forests near the town of Zamora (many of which had been cut once before, in the late nineteenth century). The (re)commodification of village commons in that area tended to aggravate long-simmering village rivalries. In the worst cases, logging companies provided arms to village cliques, who hounded their neighbors into opening village woodlots to outsiders.[106] Most conflicts never reached these proportions, but the advent of industrial logging often opened divisions between villagers in a position to seize on the opportunity and lease the woods to timber companies (or cut them on their own), versus those who hesitated because they worried about the loss of woodland or had been frozen out of the race for jobs and income.[107]

The modernization of the timber sector added yet another source of discord. Chainsaws began to appear in the woods due to the BNCE's injection of capital, making both legal and illegal logging more efficient. Skidders replaced burros in some places. Most of all, road construction and easy credit encouraged wealthy villagers, or those with useful political connections, to buy their own flatbed trucks. The men who acquired these expensive vehicles naturally hoped to recuperate their investment as quickly as possible, which often meant creating village clienteles and hauling whatever wood they could, regardless of its provenance. Foresters did little to mitigate the problem. On the contrary, one commission of Purépecha leaders charged that wardens had started a flourishing business by demanding a ten-peso bribe from each truck that passed and then watching idly as 10,000 trees disappeared from one village commons alone.[108] Across the state, near Zitácuaro, the appearance of heavy trucks made it easier for contractors to buy illegally manufactured charcoal and take it to a nearby market or railhead. A 1945 inspection uncovered 190 unregistered charcoal pits in the area, where villagers labored to feed expanding markets in Toluca and Mexico City.[109] Clandestine logging on this almost industrial scale exposed foresters' inability (or self-interested unwillingness) to confront the problem, and it suggested that rural people were committed to make use of their woods however they saw fit.

In 1950 the federal government declared a state-wide logging ban in Michoacán, which barred any ejido or indigenous community from logging their land without special permission from federal officials (unless the community to a forestry union [UOF] or its land fell within a UIEF concession). The ban did not encompass the resin industry, however. Villagers in the Meseta Purépecha and the Sierra de Angangueo, in the eastern part of the state, now had a strong incentive to put away (or at least hide) their axes and pick up resin-collecting buckets. Tree-tapping probably accounted for most forest work, though principally as a supplement to other sources of income, rather than as a primary employment. Around 3,000 heads of household and a total of 15,000 people worked as tappers in Michoacán during the 1950s, suggesting that resin collection was often a family undertaking. Perhaps their demographics mirrored that of one community in west-central Michoacán. Of the sixty-four people who worked in the Purépecha community of Huecorio (just outside Tanaquillo), slightly over half identified themselves as day laborers. Seven were "farmers" (*agricultores*), most of whom owned half a hectare of their own land, though one owned a one-hectare plot and another owned four hectares. Two women identified themselves as unmarried *domésticas*. Only nineteen categorized themselves as full-time tree tappers, three of whom also owned small parcels of land.[110] Tapping was marginal work, but it occasionally generated enough revenue to fund infrastructure projects, such as schools and village medical clinics pushed by federal agencies like the Ejidal Bank.[111]

Rural people found it increasingly difficult to maintain their autonomy and continue to manage these projects on their own. In addition to the webs of patronage that truck owners, clandestine sawmills, and logging companies forged in the 1940s, a series of UIEF neoconcessions appeared in the following decade. Only one UIEF (the Michoacana de Occidente, founded in 1955) came close to matching the regional ambitions of Bosques de Chihuahua, but even so Michoacán soon had more UIEFs than any other state in the republic.[112] Most were granted to marginal companies that hoped to make a quick profit by using antiquated equipment and overcutting whenever they could get away with it, leading among other things to strained relations with communities under their respective jurisdictions. One timber company that received a concession in the Hidalgo, Tuxpan, and Jungapeo districts did not manage to start production at all.[113] Typical of these middling concessions was the fifty-year grant of 49,088 hectares to Montes-Industrias-Minas, a corporation formed to supply mining operations in the Tlalpujahua-Angangueo area of eastern Michoacán, including the nearly-played-out Dos Estrellas gold mine, which had been nationalized and converted into a cooperative in 1937. The mine still employed four thousand workers in the 1950s, however, and required thirty thousand board feet of wood per day for mineshafts, outbuildings, railroad ties, and as fuel for making lime (a key ingredient in the cyanide amalgamation process for gold).[114] Although federal officials directed the company to install new equipment, pay ejidos and native communities a just price for the wood it extracted, and plant twenty-five saplings for every cubic meter of wood it cut, the concession-holders ignored nearly every element of its contract. The timber company continued to use "rudimentary" production techniques, paid villagers far less than market value for their wood, and made only token gestures at reforestation.[115] Most of all, rural people throughout the region complained that corrupt administrators commandeered more wood than they needed and sold the surplus in Mexico City rather than delivering it to the mines. Villagers responded by ignoring the company's elaborate management plan and delivering their wood instead to the black-market sawmills that thrived in the sierras until the timber company finally collapsed, in 1962.[116]

CONCLUSION

President Ruiz Cortines made a series of speeches in the spring of 1957, announcing his administration's commitment to overhaul the nation's use of natural resources. In May newspapers carried his proclamation of a new policy intended to conserve the nation's forests, defend the rights of rural communities, and modernize the timber industry. The president declared that the forest service would mark strict boundaries between commercial forests and protected areas, so that everyone would understand where to log. Henceforth, officials would require producers to "use the wood as efficiently as possible" and require UIEFs to upgrade their equipment and cease selling unfinished products, such as sawlogs or green lumber, on the open market. Finally, wardens would prohibit forestry companies from "exploiting" campesinos, who would find it easier to work their own land rather than to lease logging rights to outsiders. As one newspaper editorialized, the policy added up to "industrial forest management on a national scale."[117]

Like most such proclamations, this one was largely symbolic. In any case, regional authorities lacked the means or political will to bring it to fruition. Nevertheless, public gestures such as this performed a critical function: they articulated a political idiom that linked the goals of forest service to those of rural communities, based on the idea that the rational use of resources could both promote social justice and underwrite economic development. These ideas appeared to have had some traction in the countryside. For example, a handful of Guachochi ejidatarios alluded to the 1957 speech when complaining about municipal officials who mistreated locals and wasted resources. The manager of Montes-Industrias-Minas also referred to the speech in a letter touting the modern efficiencies of his own organization.[118] Appealing to the president's words made good political sense, of course, but the widespread acknowledgment of his ideas suggests that rural people regarded them as something more than empty rhetoric. On the contrary, such ideas helped to consolidate a conceptual common ground used by the various stakeholders in the woods. Although the president's paradigm continued to favor logging companies and UIEFs over local production, it nevertheless reaffirmed the principle that cooperation between forestry experts, timber companies, and villagers would benefit all parties.

This goodwill quickly evaporated, however, when forestry officials attempted to enforce regulations that threatened rural people's livelihoods or contravened local practices. Since forest wardens could inspect only a tiny proportion of the countryside, villagers usually ignored the most inconvenient regulations. They cut trees without permission, lent their logging permits to neighboring communities, forged documents, and covered up their transgressions. Forest wardens understood what was going on and tried to come to an understanding with the locals—an arrangement most often sealed with a modest gratuity. Forestry officials ignored such informal agreements at their own peril. The experiences of one forest warden who tried to fine villagers in central Chihuahua for unauthorized logging was probably typical. Leaders of the ejido started by offering him a bribe. When he demurred, they took him hostage and convened an impromptu community meeting to decide whether to shoot him. They thought better of it, however, and set him free. His report on the incident laconically observed that people in that part of the state "[didn't] welcome the presence of the forest service."[119] If all else failed, villagers unhappy with intrusive wardens or pushy timber companies sometimes exacted revenge by setting fire to the woods: once the trees disappeared, so did the object of contention.

The industrial model of forestry gained a foothold in the 1940s and 1950s despite these sporadic acts of resistance. The new regime of resource management displaced what little authority rural people exercised over their resources and delivered it to administrators whose inability to enforce regulations made logging bans and neoconcessions appear as attractive alternatives. As a result, corporate logging further politicized forest landscapes and made it harder than ever for rural people to contemplate them as living ecosystems. As the failures of exclusionary conservation and industrial logging mounted, experts began to seek alternative means of meeting the nation's demand for forest products, while still integrating local populations more fully into the production cycle. By the mid-1950s, variations on the industrial model began to appear that promised (once again) to benefit the rural people who owned the forests while ensuring the rational and sustainable use of the nation's patrimony.

CHAPTER 5

The Ecology of Development, 1952–1972

As Mexico's leaders turned away from the populist social policies of the Cárdenas years, they embraced a model of modernity and industrialization in which the private sector superficially figured as the protagonist. In reality, policy makers managed the economy on behalf of favored corporations with close ties to the long-ruling Institutional Revolutionary Party (PRI). In the forest sector, the PRI essentially became an environmental kleptocracy. Politicians established a host of new administrative forms, such as UIEF neoconcessions, logging bans, and the increasingly ubiquitous Banco Ejidal, all of which cycled funds back to the political machine but made it difficult for rural communities to maintain their economic independence in the context of such state-led "development." Yet the nation's political class had not completely turned its back on its revolutionary heritage and duty to attend to the neediest citizens. The government provided universal healthcare, better infrastructure, and new opportunities for education and employment. The pace of land reform rebounded somewhat from the late 1950s to the early 1970s, during the presidencies of Adolfo Ruiz Cortines (1952–1958), Adolfo López Mateos (1958–1964), and especially Gustavo Díaz Ordaz (1964–1970). Nevertheless, the PRI effectively jettisoned redistributive pretensions in favor of an economic model called "stabilizing development" (*desarrollo estabilizador*), which promised that greater overall industrialization and national wealth would benefit Mexicans from every walk of life, like John F. Kennedy's proverbial tide that lifts all boats. Something of the Cardenista ghost still lived on in the political machine, however, if only in the guise of increasingly ambitious programs of state-led development.

Stabilizing development was targeted primarily at the burgeoning urban population, which tripled from 5.6 million in 1950 to 16.9 million two decades later.[1] The federal government made huge investments in water and sewerage infrastructure between the 1940s and 1960s, for example, and took several steps to improve urban public health, particularly through the Mexican Institute for Social Security (IMSS), founded in 1943. Public education blossomed in urban areas, as did mass transit, cheap housing, and commerce. Political leaders also penned a series of laws to speed up the industrialization of Mexico City, Monterrey, and other major cities, in part by substituting imported products with ones manufactured in Mexico.[2]

Development of this sort aimed to do far more than create new jobs; it promised to remake society itself. An influential line of reasoning emanating from North American scholars such as Talcott Parsons and Walt Rostow, as well as Latin Americans such as Raul Prebisch, suggested that all societies followed a similar path from "traditional" to "modern" as economic and social structures multiplied and became institutionalized. This was advantageous, according to these scholars, because complex societies tended to embrace democracy and welcome increased prosperity, whereas more "traditional" and "underdeveloped" ones remained economically stagnant and socially rigid. Such conditions, it was thought, might open the door to authoritarian ideologies and communism. Development, in other words, was considered a cultural shift as much as an economic one. Fortunately for "backward" societies such as Mexico, it was considered possible to speed up the process of industrialization and achieve modernity by strategically investing in human capital and technology. Industrialization also promised to break Mexico's political and economic dependency on more developed nations, particularly the United States, and to create more wealth than the export of raw materials ever could.[3]

Development theory also had momentous implications for the countryside. The PRI leadership promoted rural development as a means of keeping as much of the population as possible on ejidos and out of the cities, where uncontrolled migration might overwhelm urban services and municipal infrastructure. The federal government paid particular attention to peripheral areas far from the central plateau. Dams were built to provide hydroelectricity and reservoirs to irrigate previously unused cropland. Forestry was promoted to place products at the disposal of private and public interests.[4] Megaprojects like the extension of rail lines, the establishment of irrigation districts, and the implementation of regional management plans would help rural people to reap the benefits of modernity (and make fortunes for favored corporations). In theory and as a point of law, this process took place through "decentralized" administrative units that operated within each state.[5] In practice, Mexico City remained the seat of true power and political course-setting.[6]

At the center of the PRI's rural policy lay five quasi-autonomous "river basin commissions" launched between 1948 and 1970 and charged with expanding the hydroelectric, agricultural, and social infrastructure in the center-north. This meant building dams, of course, but like the Tennessee Valley Authority in the United States, on which they were explicitly modeled, the Mexican river commissions also had a development mandate. They provided funding for education, healthcare, and road building within their respective jurisdictions. In Michoacán and Oaxaca, they also promoted logging in areas that seemed too remote for traditional timber companies to access.

The National Indigenist Institute (INI) also tried its hand at economic development in native communities. The institution was charged with identifying the chief "problems" (a characteristic term of the era) confronting native peoples and integrating them into the social mainstream. In the early 1950s, the INI opened clinics in several indigenous areas to deliver Western medicine, as well as boarding schools to train native teachers, who were expected to return to their communities and offer instruction not only on reading and writing, but on assimilation to Mexican culture as well. The INI also launched small-scale industries to create an economic base for native communities. In Chihuahua, officials determined that forestry offered the best hope of developing Rarámuri territory. They signed contracts with logging companies on villagers' behalf and in some instances directly assumed management of the woods, then reinvested the proceeds in education and healthcare. In the case of both the INI and the river basin commissions, modernizing experts sought to remake the relationship between rural people and their environment on a scale that had not been contemplated since the heyday of Cardenismo.

ANTHROPOLOGISTS AND RIVER BASINS

The idea that the Mexican state had an obligation to redeem the rural poor—and indigenous people, in particular—from poverty and "backwardness" had a lengthy pedigree. Soon after the revolution, the anthropologist Manuel Gamio called on his countrymen to forsake regional and ethnic differences and forge a "well-defined and coherent nationality" that embraced Mexico's Indian heritage.[7] These ideas became the foundation of postrevolutionary indigenismo, which was a political and intellectual movement suggesting that native culture had an intrinsic value and that the state bore a responsibility to lift Indian communities out of poverty.

Gamio's influence deepened in 1917, when he was named director of Mexico's first Indian affairs bureau (known as the Dirección de Antropología), an organization charged with studying and "redeeming" indigenous communities. The question, of course, was how. Some early anthropologists argued in favor of cultural pluralism, in which native languages and customs would be retained while indigenous people received the training, medical services, and "appropriate" occupations that would bring them into the fold of Mexican society. By the late 1940s, however, most experts agreed that true salvation for Indians could be achieved only through linguistic, economic, and cultural assimilation into mainstream (mestizo) society.[8]

The assimilationist project took a major step forward in 1948, when President Miguel Alemán created the INI. Like the Indian affairs bureaus that had preceded it, the new organization had both a research agenda and a practical mandate to ameliorate the "problems associated with indigenous groups in the nation." Headed for over two decades by the renowned archaeologist Alfonso Caso, the INI became the primary social-service agency for native people throughout the nation. Its portfolio included public-health services, Spanish-language education, and economic development.

The INI worked primarily through regional agencies, known as coordinating centers, that administered education (particularly language instruction in Spanish), healthcare, and agriculture services. These centers nominally answered to a governing council made up of an INI official, a delegate from the state government, and a representative of the communities to be served; in practice, native voices invariably got lost within the bureaucracy and left administrators in virtually unchallenged control of the regional coordinating centers' activities. Building on earlier indigenista initiatives, most centers emphasized the boarding schools that trained young men to become schoolteachers known as "cultural promoters"; these teachers were posted to their hometowns, where they could pass their newly acquired knowledge to the next generation. Most coordinating centers also had medical clinics and agriculture extension stations staffed by representatives of federal agencies.[9] By 1958, the INI had established five such centers (one in Chiapas, one in Chihuahua, three in Oaxaca), which claimed to serve a total of 424,000 people.[10]

The first was founded in 1950, in San Cristóbal de las Casas, Chiapas, and targeted Tzeltal and Tzotzil Maya communities in the highlands. Its signature program was a road-building project intended to connect the indigenous zones with the mestizo world beyond. A boarding school graduated several classes of "cultural promoters" and ran a clinic that attended to the ill and carried out vaccination campaigns.[11] Two years later, the INI chose Chihuahua as the site of its second center, known as the Indigenista Coordinating Center of the Tarahumara (Centro Coordinador Indigenista de la Tarahumara), whose sphere of influence included the districts of Batopilas, Balleza, Guadalupe y Calvo, Morelos, and part of Urique, home to approximately 45,000 Rarámuri and a small number of Tepehuán people.[12]

The river basin projects' intellectual genealogy was less illustrious than the INI's, although they pursued many of the same goals in a more developmentalist mode. In essence they promoted the economic growth and colonization of regions that modernity seemingly had passed by. One of their explicit goals was to promote industry in sparsely populated areas, both to achieve more balanced economic growth and to attract settlers to the coasts.[13] President Ávila Camacho set the tone for the basin projects in a 1943 declaration, stating, "A 'march to the sea' will relieve congestion in our Central Mesa . . . But this march requires, as prerequisites, sanitary measures, communications, reclamation and drainage of swamps, and to make such works possible, the expenditure of vast sums of money."[14] Ávila Camacho did little to realize this vision, but his successors took up the challenge with projects including the creation of ejidos in the rainforests of Quintana Roo to attract colonists from rural parts of central Mexico, the transformation of Acapulco from a forgotten colonial-era seaport into an international tourist destination, and a renewed push to build rail lines from regional capitals to little-used coastal ports. The river basin programs took an even longer-term approach and endured, in some instances, through the beginning of the twenty-first century.

The first river basin project was founded in the Papaloapan watershed and in many ways served as the model for its successors. The pet project of President Miguel Alemán (himself a native of Sayula, Veracruz, which lies alongside a tributary), the Papaloapan Commission sought to bring "integrated development" to over a million people, around a third of whom were identified as indigenous, in a 46,000 square kilometer region that encompassed much of eastern Oaxaca and central Veracruz, as well as southeastern Puebla. One of the commission's central mandates was to manage regional hydrology in the wake of cataclysmic rains that, in 1944, flooded 200,000 hectares and virtually destroyed the town of Tuxtepec, Oaxaca. The commission planned to build roads, schools, urban infrastructure, and public-health clinics. It also took steps to stem deforestation, which threatened to undermine the watershed's hydrological cycle.[15] The commission managed these activities from a headquarters aptly named Ciudad Alemán, an entire town built from scratch on the Veracruz-Oaxaca border. Extension agents provided credit to improve agriculture and laid out plans for a proposed 160,000-hectare irrigation district.

The centerpiece of the initiative was the Miguel Alemán Dam, on the Tonto River, which ranked among Latin America's largest dams when completed, in 1962, albeit at the cost of ethnocidally displacing 22,000 indigenous Manzatec people. It generated over 700,000 megawatts per year, or enough to power a midsized city. It also offered flood control, and the Miguel Alemán reservoir provided a major new supply of water for agriculture and domestic use.[16] Almost as soon as construction drew to a close, however, the commission shifted to less ambitious projects, as its patron's influence waned in Mexico City and its board of directors were accused of corruption and mismanagement. It was disbanded altogether in 1986.[17]

Subsequent river basin projects were soon established: the Tepalcatepec Commission (which was folded into the Balsas Commission in the early 1960s) focused on Michoacán and conjoining states; the Grijalva Commission centered on Tabasco and Chiapas in the south; and the Fuerte Basin Commission focused primarily on Sinaloa. River basin projects also took shape in the north-central Lerma and Pánuco basins, but without the same ambitious mandate for hydroelectrical infrastructure development.[18]

Lázaro Cárdenas personally beseeched Alemán to name him the director of the Tepalcatepec Commission and laid out an ambitious proposal for hydroelectric dams deep in the southeastern tierra caliente of his native state. He hoped that new water sources would irrigate tens of thousands of acres, including those held by ejidos on former agribusiness haciendas, such as Nueva Italia and Lombardia, which might draw new settlers to the state's most remote and least populated regions.[19] For the rest of his life, Cárdenas oversaw the Tepalcatepec and subsequent Balsas Commissions. He made trips at least once a year to observe the progress of roads, canals, and livestock-improvement programs. In the 1950s the commission built three modest dams that concentrated primarily on storing irrigation water. The Balsas Commission erected the much larger Infiernillo Dam, which was completed in 1963 and briefly ranked as the largest hydroelectric project in the country.[20] By most measures, both commissions were a success. They made water available to small farmers and commercial agricultural interests, built new hospitals, schools, and roads, and launched public-health projects that diminished the incidence of malaria and pneumonia.[21] Many people in Tierra Caliente regarded Cárdenas as a champion of regional interests. (For his part, Cárdenas bought a small estate, which he used as a retreat from his ongoing public life.) But his detractors charged that the former president considered the region around Apatzingán his personal domain and that "Tata Lázaro," as he is still sometimes called, continued to personally approve every development project as well as the movement of troops into or out of the area until the late 1960s. In the words of one military commander stationed there, "not a leaf moved" without Cárdenas's approval.[22]

Both the INI coordinating centers and the river basin projects were intended to address the material and social preconditions for development. Both programs sought to shift at least some social service expenses onto rural people themselves and thus to inculcate in them a greater sense of investment in national development. While the rural poor could not build dams or irrigation projects, they could take jobs as woodcutters and sawmill operators in places like Chihuahua and Michoacán, where administrators believed that forestry would give the key economic boost to the respective projects. Cárdenas also envisioned forestry as a keystone of the Tepalcatepec Commission's work, but he worried that unchecked logging threatened the watershed's environment. The trick was to create a regime of restricted extraction on a regional scale that could put thousands of people to work. The former president was known to sermonize that conservation of the forests promised villagers "shade, fruit, and a source of income."[23] Lacking the means to launch its own forestry project, the commission, on the orders of Cárdenas, turned to Michoacana de Occidente, a newly established UIEF, whose directors pledged to employ locals and to use income from logging and tree-tapping to build roads, hospitals, schools, and other infrastructure.

The INI's project in Chihuahua envisioned a similar bootstrapping strategy whereby Rarámuri would fell, transport, and mill their own timber, then use the proceeds to help pay for their own public services. Native people would earn wages and become more fully integrated into the cash economy while learning skills and, eventually, coming to understand how to manage their own land.

Both initiatives, in other words, shared an uncanny conceptual symmetry. Their advocates believed that the mobilization of natural resources for economic progress would provide marginalized peoples with employment and a means of funding their own economic and cultural insertion into the mainstream of mid-twentieth century Mexico. Rural people's encounter with the lands, it was believed, would provide them invaluable lessons about nature, work, and technology, all while producing the commodities (electricity, wood, and crops) required for national progress. Yet the development projects in Michoacán and Chihuahua generated frictions between forest-owning villages and the development specialists meant to help them. In many cases, they opened rifts among these communities themselves. Ultimately, the INI project in Chihuahua and the Michoacana de Occidente squandered the very resources they needed in order to succeed and undermined the forestry enterprises they were intended to nurture.

THE INDIGENISTA COORDINATING CENTER OF THE TARAHUMARA

Two years after its initial program in Chiapas had begun operation, the INI chose Chihuahua as the site of its second center, known as the Indigenista Coordinating Center of the Tarahumara (Centro Coordinador Indigenista de la Tarahumara, or CCIT). The organization targeted the Sierra Tarahumara, an area that suffered from "extreme poverty and rudimentary means of subsistence, deficient nutrition in terms of quantity and quality, exceedingly high rates of infant and general mortality, virtually universal illiteracy, owing to economic and educational deficits."[24] The INI dispatched the cultural anthropologist and Chiapas veteran Gonzalo Aguirre Beltrán to find an appropriate location and to lay the groundwork for construction of the boarding school and clinic. Aguirre selected Guachochi for the headquarters mainly because it was the only village with both good communications and electricity (the latter, thanks to a small hydroelectric plant installed by the forest service). Another point in Guachochi's favor was that its residents already had some experience with indigenista institutions. The town had twice hosted regional meetings of Rarámuri leaders, and a normal school had functioned there during the heyday of Cardenismo that had graduated a single class of indigenous schoolteachers before closing, in 1940. Among other things, the graduates had organized consumers' cooperatives, built an indigenous-language radio station, and published a teaching manual in Rarámuri.[25]

A committed assimilationist and disciple of Gamio, Aguirre believed that indigenous people could retain elements of their cultural heritage, yet he also considered it necessary for natives to overcome generations of marginalization by becoming more integrated into the political and economic structures of the nation.[26] He declared that the CCIT's "cardinal point of action" was to expand the scope of land reform in the Rarámuri area, transforming native people into ejidatarios. He proposed to extend credit and organize new consumers' cooperatives. Demonstration plots and experimental fields would showcase new crops and breeds of livestock. Under Aguirre's guidance, the CCIT built a medical clinic to complement (or, one suspects, to compete with) the Jesuit-run hospital in Sisoguichi, and contemplated making Guachochi into a "model indigenous village" (*comunidad indígena tipo*). Above all, Aguirre proposed to establish village-level forestry enterprises, which would not only earn money but "place in the Tarahumaras' hands a source of wealth that [was] being destroyed by capitalists who [had] no interest in conserving natural resources in the Sierra."[27] New roads would enable indigenous people to sell their timber in nearby towns and replace what he called the "appalling" footpaths in the woods. Electrical plants would provide light and power for machinery. Indigenous "cultural promoters" would catalyze indigenous support for these endeavors, teach basic Spanish literacy to schoolchildren, and bridge mestizo and native societies. Aguirre hoped that the Rarámuri would learn to accept modern healthcare and agricultural techniques, and above all the project of locally managed forestry that would help them "take the first steps on the upward course that is the process of acculturation."[28]

Aguirre selected Francisco Plancarte, a schoolteacher and University of Chicago graduate with decades of experience in the Sierra Tarahumara, as the center's first director. Plancarte had helped plan, in 1939, the first regional congress of Rarámuri leaders, which gave birth to an indigenista association known as the Supreme Council of the Tarahumara that comprised schoolteachers and Rarámuri advocates. Plancarte had held positions in the educational and anthropological bureaucracies of the Sierra Tarahumara ever since. Like most of his peers, his respect for indigenous people was tempered by the conviction that their material and social development hinged on assimilation to the broader Mexican society. As he wrote in 1954,

> The problem consists of including the diverse groups of indigenous people in the forms of national life, preparing them to join in a just and democratic way with other social sectors, so that they can become a pillar of the nation's economic and cultural life in the immediate future. The solution to this problem is to carry out an integrated plan of action that—through indigenous people's work and the use of natural resources in the region—will give them the foundations of a stable economy, accelerate their process of acculturation, and place not only development within their grasp, but social, cultural, and political maturity as well.[29]

Plancarte reported that Rarámuri leaders expressed some interest in community forestry, though in a telling revelation he remarked that they were skeptical about its prospects in light of "so many unfulfilled promises in the past." He also worried that the Rarámuris' dispersed settlement pattern and above all the nomadism of un-Christianized "gentiles" would complicate the center's work. Nevertheless, he predicted that once the land reform began to bear fruit, it would "accomplish not only the settlement of the Tarahumara, but their economic and social development as well."[30]

The INI anthropologists envisioned logging as the CCIT's economic mainspring. In time, they intended to let villagers take over logging operations and the transportation of timber on their own land, and one day to operate their own sawmills as well.[31] There were few other alternatives. The rugged highlands of Chihuahua could not support intensive agriculture or cattle ranching, no matter how much technical expertise the INI might bring to bear.[32] Community forestry, on the other hand, had the potential not only to generate income but to teach indigenous people that they could manage and conserve their own natural resources. "Rational forest use following *management plans that allow for their perpetual exploitation*, by producers cooperatives acting under the guidance by trained experts and principled administrators," Plancarte wrote in 1954, "will become an enduring bulwark for the entire population of the Sierra and will doubtless generate opportunities for all people."[33] He believed that no fewer than thirty indigenous villages would soon begin working their own ejidal woods and commons, generating enough income to lift residents out of poverty and pay for rudimentary public services throughout the sierras.[34] In 1957 President Adolfo Ruiz Cortines ratified this agenda and granted the CCIT authority to implement a plan "to cut out intermediaries and make [residents] the direct beneficiaries" of logging. The president ordered CCIT staff to assume legal responsibility for the "guidance [*orientación*], tutelage, and protection" of the native people under their care and to ensure that logging employed the largest possible number of local inhabitants, ideally in ways that developed indigenous people's technical and professional capacities. Finally, he gave the INI authority to rewrite communities' existing lease agreements with logging companies to ensure that those communities were the primary beneficiaries of employment opportunities and profits from the timber industry.[35]

Plancarte wasted no time in building the infrastructure to realize his ideas. Within two years, the CCIT had opened a clinic and an administrative building, and had admitted the first class of Rarámuri students to its boarding school in Guachochi. Other offices opened in the communities Cusárare and Baquiriachic, each with its own clinic, and plans had been laid for a new road to connect all three townships.[36] The forestry project was slower to get up to speed. Villagers had a checkered experience with outsiders' plans to manage their lands, and the agrarian reform had played havoc with indigenous people's customary land use. It had opened the way for the mestizos who had settled in many parts of the countryside to seize key positions in local administration and to log ejidal land for their own benefit. Timber companies invariably used their own crews to fell trees, and sometimes to transport the sawlogs and to staff sawmills as well. What little employment indigenous people eked out from the timber industry usually came in the form of casual labor hauling timber and building logging roads. Two decades of environmental regulation, combined with the transitory rural development programs of the Cárdenas years, had left only a single community—that of Cusárare—with the capacity to produce timber on its own, but even Cusárare had halted operations between 1957 and 1959, because its management plan languished in the forest-service bureaucracy waiting for reapproval.[37]

The INI lacked the funds and personnel to reproduce Cusárare's experience in other Rarámuri rancherías. Other village settlements lacked the equipment and expertise to build logging roads, fell trees, or transport them out of the mountains, and only Cusárare had its own sawmill. In these circumstances, Plancarte reluctantly agreed to extend the existing rental agreements with lumber companies. In 1955 he suggested that the timber interests should sign collaborative agreements known as "contracts of association" (sometimes called "local production contracts" or *contratos de maquila*) with indigenous communities; these arrangements would oblige the companies to employ villagers and provide them with technical assistance. The companies would also be responsible for building modern roads to transport sawlogs and improve communications throughout the region. Several firms agreed to these terms, and in 1959 Plancarte convened public meetings in a dozen communities, bringing together villagers and company representatives.[38] He served as chief translator and advocate for his charges; during one meeting, he turned to the timbermen and said, "I've just told these Indians that they should not accept the lease agreement you propose. I explained that it amounts to extortion, and they agree with me. I invite you to improve your offer."[39]

Figure 5.1. Francisco Plancarte addressing a Rarámuri community, 1954. Francisco Plancarte, *El problema indígena tarahumara*, vol. 5 of *Memorias del Instituto Nacional Indigenista* (Mexico City: Ediciones del Instituto Nacional Indigenista, 1954), plate after p. 92.

One by one, the companies consented to pay native woodsmen higher wages and to triple the royalties (derecho de monte) that villages received. By the end of the year, Rarámuri ejidos had received permission to cut between 1.6 and 3.8 million board feet of wood for lumber and railroad ties. In some places, women also made broom handles out of branches. Work in the logging operation paid monthly wages ranging from 227 pesos, in Norogachi, to 498 pesos, in Cusárare. This modest income (equivalent to 18 and 40 U.S. dollars a month, in 2010 terms) was substantially higher than what indigenous forest workers had earned just two years before. At a meeting of the Supreme Tarahumara Council the following year, delegates gave their blessing to the INI program and encouraged its continuation.[40] Despite some bureaucratic hitches—like the fact that a single, overworked federal forester had to approve all the paperwork and management plans for the ejidos under the INI's control—community forestry had arrived in the Sierra Tarahumara.[41]

The promise of greater economic autonomy prompted a number of indigenous villages to dust off requests for ejidos that had languished for years in the state and national bureaucracies. For example, in 1960 La Soledad sent a commission to Chihuahua City, requesting that the governor move forward with a request that leaders had filed six years earlier. Residents were moved to take action when they learned that a local mestizo family had instigated the fraudulent tax sale of the village commons with an eye to renting the woods to a timber company. Now eighty-nine families faced expulsion from their own property.[42] Similarly, Guaguachique revived its petition for an ejido. Village leaders had submitted a request in 1928, but they never received a response from the authorities. When the Empresa Maderera Aserraderos González Ugarte began to cut wood in the area in the late 1950s, mestizos settled on ejidal lands and fenced in land that they intended to claim. Village elders reached out to the CCIT, the Consejo Supremo Tarahumara, and President López Mateos himself in a bid to revitalize their petition.[43] In these cases and a few others, some Rarámuri had decided that community forestry represented a viable subsistence strategy as long as they could control their own productive landscape.[44]

By the mid-1960s, CCIT staff had established forestry projects in sixteen indigenous communities located for the most part in the Guachochi district. Around five thousand native families participated in one way or another.[45] Most of these small-scale projects circumvented the despised contratista middlemen and let villagers deliver sawlogs or finished lumber directly to timber companies. The CCIT also hired a second forester to oversee logging and teach villagers to manage their own woods. (In practice, it was hard to keep these positions filled, because private companies kept picking off its underpaid foresters.) The CCIT attempted to keep its operations as transparent as possible. Its staff understood the customary structures of authority and decision-making in Rarámuri communities, and they made a point of discussing the terms of logging operations with ejidal authorities and elders before presenting them to the other residents. Once the logging began, the anthropologists attended open meetings where villagers debated the terms of contracts with timber companies and considered how to spend the resulting income. While the CCIT had to approve any disbursements from local coffers, staff members usually abided by (sometimes inflexibly so) the investment plans hashed out in these public assemblies, a goal that became easier once the CCIT started setting aside half of each community's income in locally accessible accounts. The other half was deposited in the excruciatingly bureaucratic Banco Ejidal.

Most people seemed to accept these arrangements, which typically paid for the construction of schools, sawmills, and clinics, and the purchase of goats, corn, and blankets for the wintertime.[46]

Like most rural development projects of the time, the CCIT's regime of locally managed forestry had originated "from above." Given that it was a plan hatched by Mexico City intellectuals working in concert with local activists, rather than by the Rarámuri themselves, it was sometimes difficult for the CCIT to bridge the gap between administrative objectives and villagers' own expectations. In the first place, assuming responsibility for managing the contracts between communities and timber companies put the staff of the CCIT into the uncomfortable position of both monitoring villagers' use of the woods and distributing the proceeds from logging. The tensions often began at the open meetings where timber companies proposed the "contracts of association." Although the CCIT's staff attended these gatherings, many villagers felt bewildered by the avalanche of new institutions, paperwork, and regulations. Nor did native people assess the costs and benefits of engagement with timber companies according to the same terms as the anthropologists did. Most Rarámuri saw no difference between belonging to the community and membership in the ejido. But not all villagers were formally enrolled as ejidatarios, and this distinction mattered to staffers, who needed to formally enumerate beneficiaries and formalize logging contracts with the signatures (or more commonly, the thumb prints) of ejido members. In any case, few villagers considered the papers they signed with logging companies as agreements they were morally obliged to respect, while the CCIT personnel necessarily dwelled in a world of regulations and procedure made legible by contracts, budgets, and management plans.[47] And while villagers typically distrusted timber companies, INI officials in Chihuahua and Mexico City often treated them as partners in the broader endeavor of assimilating Rarámuri people.[48] It is hardly surprising in these circumstances that some villagers (and not a few later observers) accused the CCIT of promoting modernity at the expense of cultural survival.[49]

Seemingly straightforward directives could unintentionally upset delicate local arrangements. For example, center staffers tried to enforce forest-service prohibitions against using hatchets to cut trees or carve railroad ties, but villagers already owned hatchets and most of them ignored the rules. Nevertheless, the episode raised mutual suspicions that took years to dissipate.[50] In another case, a trio of ejidatarios penned lease agreements with timber companies for parcels they mistakenly considered their own private property; again, CCIT staff had to intervene, to some villagers' disgust.[51] On yet another occasion, staffers instructed villagers in Cabórachi to build fences around their property, but the residents complained that it would prevent them from herding their goats from one part of the commons to the other or arranging for pasturage on each other's land. Perhaps they also knew that fences were often a prelude to dispossession. Whatever the case, CCIT officials quickly backtracked on their proposal.[52]

A second unforeseen problem with the forestry projects was that they exacerbated existing social cleavages in the countryside. In the social context of the sierras, where most information flowed imperfectly through word of mouth, news about development projects and contract agreements with timber companies could raise concern, if not outright panic, about under-the-table deals and graft. Most people lacked the literacy or numeracy skills to review logging contracts or to double-check accounting, so they were left to wonder whether CCIT personnel had collected everything the logging companies owed, or if the logging income had been distributed evenly. The open meetings where staffers discussed investment plans or made cash payments (or distributed seeds, blankets, or food) became potential minefields, particularly in villages where mestizos occupied plumb positions in ejidal administration. The anthropologists tried to avoid direct confrontations with these local strongmen, but village bosses typically felt threatened by the CCIT's promise to democratize the distribution of jobs and income from village forestry projects.[53] One group of disgruntled village leaders from Guachochi, who were also the allies of a local mestizo family, equated the anthropologists with the hated contratistas from timber companies. They penned a letter decrying the INI employees' "complicity" with timber companies and charged that they functioned "as the Agents of the timber barons [taladores] as they pressure ejidatarios to turn their forests over to Francisco M. Plancarte."[54]

Despite these problems, CCIT field personnel succeeded in forging a viable working relationship with most Rarámuri leaders. The anthropologists were in an ideal position to broker the relationship between villagers and federal administrators by helping to file petitions with the land reform bureaucracy. They also met time and again with native people to explain how to follow community forest management plans. Some local leaders sought out staff members they trusted and asked for advice or for help drafting letters to distant federal officials. The indigenistas also built up some goodwill by rushing medicine to the sierras when typhoid broke out in 1961. A few months later, the leaders of Cabórachi and Guachochi contacted the extension agent Roberto González after a hailstorm destroyed their crops to ask for emergency food aid. They authorized him to negotiate a contract with timber companies that would generate enough income and work that the residents could ride out the disaster. A few years later, the CCIT responded to a crop failure in Yoquivo by hiring villagers to cut trees for electric poles and to help build a new line running through the sierras, in exchange for which villagers received food aid in addition to their regular salaries.[55]

Plancarte died in 1959, and the INI tapped the experienced but less pugnacious social anthropologist Agustín Romano to carry on with the CCIT's mission. By that point, the organization ran forty-seven schools staffed by fifty-one indigenous schoolteachers. It had clinics in Cusárare and Guachochi attended by three doctors, one of whom also made regular visits to outlying communities. A third clinic, in Baquiriachic, had closed temporarily when its attending physician resigned to take another job. One agronomist, one supervisor, and three assistants worked in agricultural extension.[56] Despite these advances and the budding conservationist alliance with the Rarámuri, Romano considered that his predecessor had left much undone. Most clinics lacked medicine and equipment, and those in Cusárare and Baquiriachic were poorly located. The agronomists had not done much to improve agricultural practices, because they had to spend most of their time making surveys of ejido boundaries and building meeting houses for the land reform beneficiaries. Administrators and teachers felt stretched thin, and salaries often came weeks or months late.[57] By the time he left the CCIT for another post, in 1962, Romano felt confident the project was on the right track. He asserted that isolated communities, such as Samachique and Rocheáchi, now had their own clinics (the latter staffed by two female doctors who had won the respect of villagers). More schools provided lunch, and some villages had washrooms, apple orchards, electricity, and sawmills, leading Romano to conclude that "the ideals of progress [were] penetrating slowly but steadily."[58] Indeed, many villagers had grown accustomed to the anthropologists' expectations. By the mid-1960s, community meetings routinely included time to discuss reports on forest production and to consider how to handle logging income. Most Rarámuri apparently regarded their timber enterprise as a valued possession.[59] The CCIT's official indigenismo had planted the seeds of a conservationist alliance with sierra communities that lasted well into the next decade.

CUSÁRARE

Nowhere were the aspirations and contradictions of the INI's indigenista ecology clearer than in the village of Cusárare, a Rarámuri ranchería of some 180 families, which emerged as the CCIT's showcase for locally managed forestry. As of the 1930s, most of Cusárare's residents continued to dwell in caves or, less commonly, in wooden huts. As recently as the 1890s, no chabochis lived in town. Half a century later, most people were still monolingual Rarámuri speakers, and few wore mainstream Mexican clothing.[60] A significant proportion of the population lived nomadically and complemented a diet of tortillas and roots by fishing, hunting small game, and collecting pine nuts. Others had largely abandoned nomadism and planted cornfields that brought forth spindly and uncertain crops owing to high altitude, poor soils, and unpredictable but devastating hailstorms. The town's geography conserved the Rarámuri custom of dispersed settlement, but a strong sense of community identity combined with the presence of a radical schoolteacher to make it one of the first indigenous villages in the highlands to receive the grant of an ejido, a parcel of more than 33,000 hectares, uncommonly large for the time, whose transfer was finalized in September 1929. Nearly all of that land had once belonged to the Porfirian-era Martínez timber concession, where some of the men had worked as youths and gained a reputation as skilled woodsmen.[61] Most had also sojourned for weeks or months in the more distant Ciudad Madera, where they had found work as *hacheros* who hewed railroad ties by hand.[62]

In the mid-1940s, the federal forester in charge of the Sierra Tarahumara convinced a controversial local resident named Pablo Zafiro to form a forestry cooperative comprising fifty-five men, or about a third of the village's male population. Like most Rarámuri woodsmen, they made their money felling trees on the commons, which they chiseled into ties delivered directly to the railhead. The cooperative functioned so well that the forester Daniel Galicia arranged to circumvent the 1949 forest code's requirement to suppress cooperatives, by rechristening the organization as a legally recognized Forestry Management Unit (UOF). In theory, these associations were supposed to comprise landowners within a broad management district overseen by the forest service. In Cusárare's case, it appears that the former cooperative was the only active member of the UOF. In other words, the new organization was a legal fiction. Over the next few years, villagers fabricated 30,000 ties, enough for twelve miles of track.[63]

According to the federal experts, all of this work followed the "dictates of forestry science and had produced favorable economic results for the Indians." Cusárare earned enough from logging royalties and the sale of railroad ties to pay for its own medical services, education, and domestic construction materials. It is not clear what residents felt about these services, but they were probably not what the villagers would have chosen on their own. When villagers received a cash payment of 10,000 pesos (over 1,000 U.S. dollars) in 1948, for example, they used it not for public works, but rather to buy sheep for every family in town.[64]

Initially, it seemed that the relationship between the forester Galicia and Pablo Zafiro would be mutually beneficial. Zafiro was one of the few residents of Cusárare who both spoke Spanish and had lived outside the ranchería. He had received a rudimentary education from Catholic missionaries in the 1900s, then left town in 1908 to work in the mines along the eastern foothills. He spent fifteen years away, and by the time he returned, the other villagers no longer considered him Rarámuri, referring to him instead as a chabochi. Nevertheless, he helped collect signatures on Cusárare's petition for an ejido before taking control of the producers cooperative.[65] He and his sons, Juan and José, held positions in the ejidal government for the next two decades and often claimed to speak on behalf of the entire community. Pablo Zafiro took pains to keep on the good side of the village's indigenous "governors" (siríame) by making sure that villagers had enough corn and beans in lean years and that indigenous men who worked as loggers received their wages on time.[66]

The relationship between Zafiro and Galicia began to deteriorate about the time that the UOF was established. In 1949 the village woodcutters accused Galicia of conspiring with timber companies to shortchange them on railroad ties. They refused to honor their existing contract and went behind his back to sell their ties on the black market. They also claimed that the forester had opened a store in Cusárare that charged unreasonably high prices for everyday necessities and that he paid sawmill workers with store credit rather than cash. Galicia shot back that the monolingual Rarámuri leaders behind these complaints were easily influenced by outsiders (presumably a reference to Zafiro) and remained in their offices far beyond their one-year terms. He said that they ignored the contracts they had signed and did not understand anything about scientific management of the forests.[67] Galicia apparently retaliated against villagers by convincing a local timber company to back out of an agreement to hire residents as lumberjacks on Cusárare's common lands. Under these circumstances, the ejidal officers demanded a halt to all logging on their territory because, in their eyes, the forester and timber company did not care about them and "only want[ed] to get richer than they already [were]."[68]

With the logging on hold, some of the village woodcutters once again left for Madera and the promise of steady work. When the INI announced a few years later that it intended to locate the CCIT's main logging operation in town, villagers welcomed the opportunity, but the initiative got off to a shaky start. One problem was that Juan Zafiro and his family advised residents against collaborating with the INI anthropologists.[69] It is not entirely clear why, but perhaps they worried that the appearance of well-connected outsiders might weaken the family's grip on power. Moreover, the forestry operation had to be shuttered in 1950, the village management plan lapsed, and forestry officials were in no hurry to write a new one. Perhaps the forest service resented the INI horning in on its territory, but, for whatever reason, three years passed before a new logging permit was finally issued. Community authorities grew so tired of waiting that they wrote directly to the secretary of agriculture to say that the village should never have tried to log their forests in the first place. "After years of logging and sale of forest products," they wrote, referring to the era when the cooperative had organized local production, "the sawmill has shut down and we find ourselves in circumstances as bad or worse as before, given that we have *never* received our share as owners of the woods and only received work as menial laborers [*peones*]."[70]

Forestry officials finally allowed logging to resume in 1953. By that point, members of the clique formerly aligned with the forester Galicia recognized that they could not reach the same sort of understanding with INI officials; instead, they took the offensive and accused the village's CCIT representative of skimming funds from the sawmill and clinic. They also claimed he looked the other way while the INI forester helped himself to a "loan" of 5,000 pesos from village coffers, while failing to distribute logging income to the residents. An investigative committee of indigenous advocates reported in 1961 that the forester had done nothing illegal but had nonetheless created an appearance of impropriety that ignited "tremendous discontent" in Cusárare. These sorts of missteps were common, as village leaders complained for years to come about the CCIT's lack of transparency.[71] Villagers also told CCIT officials that they wished to learn more about how prices were set for the wood they produced and that they never knew for sure when they would receive their share of the profits from the logging operation.[72] Rather than breaking down the barriers between indigenous and mestizo worlds, it appeared that old frictions over finances would sink the community forestry project before it got off the ground.

In response, CCIT staffers tried to democratize the forestry project and soon began to file sanguine reports about villagers' sense of ownership in the initiative's success. The CCIT director emphasized in 1961, for example, that indigenous woodsmen were working diligently to cut all the wood their permit allowed before the end of the season and that the town's carpentry shop had also begun to deliver student desks to schoolhouses in Cusárare and throughout the sierras.[73] Members of the community (both comuneros and ejidatarios) were especially excited to earn cash from production on their land. It so happened that the peripatetic ethnologist Fernando Benítez was in Cusárare when CCIT officials delivered one of the first dividend payments, which villagers considered "a windfall that fell from the skies in the form of cash." Villagers voted to pool some of their money to build a collective granary and used the rest to empty the shelves of the local store by buying gifts for the children. Afterward, they threw an impromptu celebration in honor of the INI director Alfonso Caso.[74]

The project clearly left a mark on Cusárare. The village earned approximately 2.8 million pesos from the production of railroad ties and lumber between 1961 and 1965, and ejidal authorities agreed in 1964 to deliver branches, dead trees, and other detritus suitable for pulp to a paper mill that had just opened outside of Chihuahua City.[75] Women and children collected wood in the hills after the men had felled trees, then delivered the timber to truckers, who in turn hauled it to the railhead in Creel. The trade in pulp products also benefited the Zafiro family, which had bought some heavy trucks and cornered the timber-hauling business. This arrangement also allowed Pablo Zafiro and his sons to make peace with the CCIT, since the center's staff allowed only them and a few other acculturated Rarámuri to have access to the village's three collectively owned logging trucks.[76]

The logging project gave Rarámuri leaders in Cusárare greater latitude to stand up against the chabochis, who still tended to regard village commerce as their exclusive prerogative. In the early 1960s indigenous villagers displaced many of the mestizos who had monopolized the best jobs in the collectively owned sawmill. They grew skilled at running the machinery, and the CCIT purchased a second, diesel-powered band saw (using funds from the village timber operation), which would minimize the amount of debris lost to the milling process.[77] Tensions between native people and mestizos came to a head in 1966, when Bernardo Pérez—a mestizo who lived in town and cultivated a clientele of Rarámuri who lived near his family settlement—became the primary intermediary with the logging companies and demanded that villagers consent to renew their existing contract. The ejidal executive committee refused to play along, despite Pérez's attempt to bribe its president with a new pickup truck. Instead, they rejected the contracts and demanded that the INI back them up.[78] After that, CCIT personnel slowly isolated the Pérez family and tried to mend relations between his indigenous followers and the wider community.

The forest project in Cusárare not only reconfigured power relations between native people and the chabochis, but also subtly reoriented their attitudes toward nature. Villagers had worked in their own woods and those of more distant locales such as San Juanito long before the anthropologists arrived, and they had some experience with the poorly executed "community" project managed by the forest service and Daniel Galicia. This process of commodification had functioned to weaken villagers' control of their commons and raised questions over the fate of logging income. The CCIT program granted villagers far more economic and productive autonomy, however, and encouraged people to reconsider their economic relationship with the commons. In one anthropologist's opinion, greater local control had enhanced villagers' *cariño* (affection) for the forest.[79] That seems unlikely, but it might suggest that economic valuation of the woods had led at least some Rarámuri to regard forests—among other things—as a community resource whose use could be modulated to meet local needs.

MICHOACANA DE OCCIDENTE

Unlike the CCIT, whose leaders turned to forestry as a development strategy for native people, Michoacana de Occidente (also known as La Michoacana) was a profit-driven corporation first and foremost. Its owners had won the support of Lázaro Cárdenas by portraying the company as a potential engine of regional development, and the former president initially believed that it would complement the Tepalcatepec Commission's broader project of modernization. As it turned out, the development imperative outweighed philanthropic considerations. Although Michoacana de Occidente did generate employment and a certain degree of infrastructure, its rural development strategies fell far short of expectations. The best jobs usually went to people who moved into the tierra caliente from elsewhere, leaving local populations the less attractive work of tapping trees for pine resin. Roads, clinics, and schools did not appear as had been promised. As the years passed, it became clear that the company had failed even in its primary goal of managing the forests for a sustainable yield.

The coastal region's social structure posed the first challenge to La Michoacana's attempts at resource management. Although 95,000 people lived in the Tepalcatepec watershed in 1960, only 15,000 lived in the company's concession zone. Most of this land belonged to 600 predominantly mestizo family farmers (rancheros) who had arrived in the late nineteenth century during a miniature land rush touched off by the redistribution of "vacant" land, nearly all of which actually belonged to indigenous communities. The colonists also acquired property thanks the Lerdo Law, which ordered the allotment-and-privatization (*reparto*) of collectively owned property. The historian Gerardo Sánchez has called the *reparto* in this area an act of "institutionalized dispossession" because most indigenous people—many of whom did not recognize the value of their land—either sold to outsiders or lost their property to foreclosure sales for back taxes.[80] The mestizo families lived in widely scattered settlements and survived primarily by raising livestock. They also grew crops on modest parcels of land with an average size of less than one hundred hectares.[81] The concession also encompassed a handful of ejidos, as well as substantial forestlands claimed by the Nahua communities of Ostula, Coire, and Pómaro, in the coastal district of Aquila. (Nahua-speaking people had arrived as colonists from central Mexico prior to the conquest, and their language became common currency along the Michoacán coast.) The townships had originated as settlements (*congregaciones*) of native people, as ordered by Spanish colonists during an abortive gold rush in the sixteenth century. Over the years, these Nahua speakers had amalgamated with other indigenous groups (Purépecha, for the most part) in the area. In the 1950s, they sought the restitution of several thousand hectares that mestizo municipal authorities had seized during the Porfiriato with the help of powerful outsiders, including foreign timber companies.[82] Although the native residents had demanded the return of their forestlands for decades, they had made little headway by the 1970s. Michoacana de Occidente administrators had no intention of getting involved in the agrarian question and simply ignored it altogether.[83]

Nearly all of the mestizo smallholders, ejidatarios, and Nahua in the concession zone lived in extremely humble conditions and occasionally went hungry. They used the forest as a source of foodstuffs like mushrooms, as well as of cooking fuel, and as a storehouse of more than two hundred species of plants for medicinal use. They let some trees grow because they were (and still are) believed to summon the rains.[84] The rancheros were probably best off, because they ran herds ranging from two or three cows to more than a hundred. All told, more than ten thousand cattle ranged inside the concession's boundaries and represented one of the most important sources of wealth in the region. People used their animals for traction and dairying, and as a source of meat in in the dry season, when the herds needed to be thinned. They occasionally sold an individual cow to the artisanal butchers found in nearly every town, who hung out red flags to signal that fresh meat was available.[85]

Fire had played a fundamental role in this productive landscape. By the time that La Michoacana began operations, in the late 1950s, rancheros in its zone of operations routinely set fire to pastures and sometimes along forest edges to open the way for the saplings and succulent grasses that cattle preferred. Mestizo and indigenous farmers relied on swidden agriculture to grow corn, beans, squash, *chilacayote* (fig-leaf gourd, or *Cucurbita ficifolia*), and other subsistence crops. The productive cycle began when farmers hacked down shrubs and small trees with machetes and hatchets, then set fire to the litter and let it burn intensively until the ground had "boiled," leaving behind a charred top layer of humus—a practice that foresters considered a "stupid custom" and had condemned since the late nineteenth century. By the mid-twentieth century, however, the best land had already been cleared, and slash-and-burn no longer represented a direct threat to the remaining forests, except when an unexpected gust of wind or a farmer's inattention let the flames get too close to the woods. Once the ground had cooled, farmers turned the earth with hoes (plows were uncommon) and planted seeds in anticipation of the first rains. The fields were planted for two growing seasons, then left fallow for five years or more. Since the exposed land was subject to erosion, both pine and broadleaf trees might repopulate areas that had only been burned once, but they rarely reappeared in places fired twice or more.[86]

La Michoacana started operations in 1958, after the forest service had approved the relevant management plans and issued the first logging permits. Its formal concession of 1.25 million hectares (an area somewhat smaller than the U.S. state of Connecticut) had been finalized three years earlier, and the company had a right to use it for twenty-five years. Operations began to ramp up, in 1959, when the company received permission to cut nearly 343,000 cubic meters (145 million board feet) of pine timber per year. It also held permits to cut a modest amount of oak and an initial authorization to produce 1.5 million kilograms of pine resin per year, later increased to over 2 million kilograms annually.[87] Strangely, this management plan—and La Michoacana's subsequent use of the woods—disregarded the unique ecosystem in the Sierra Madre del Sur and the Sierra de Coalcomán mountain range, where most logging took place. Commercially desirable species of pine grew only in scattered stands at the higher elevations of this dry tropical forest. Villagers had used pines for generations to build their houses, and they cut oaks for charcoal, but they scarcely touched the woods otherwise. Mature pine-oak forests covered 15 percent of the land, meaning that they grew far less densely there than in most other parts of Mexico. Not only did the relative scarcity of commercially desirable wood present a significant challenge in purely operational terms, but the soil was uncommonly delicate and prone to erosion unless foresters were assiduous in using minimally damaging, selective cuts.

The company began to hire workers in the mid-1950s and eventually built up a complement of two thousand full-time employees, many of them experienced woodsmen recruited from Uruapan and Zitácuaro. The lumberjacks were sent to camps in one of three management zones, which were located around the towns of Coalcomán, Tumbiscatío, and Arteaga.[88] Local residents missed out on the best employment opportunities, although they did receive the contractually stipulated royalty of between thirty and forty-five pesos per thousand board feet of wood logged on their lands. Many could earn some extra cash by tapping trees on their own properties and selling the resin to La Michoacana. The company also employed a few full-time tree tappers, who lived in primitive camps that shifted from place to place in uninhabited areas. Regardless of whether they worked their own trees or contracted someone else to do the work, property owners received a royalty of fifty-five pesos per metric ton of resin collected on their land. The resin was trucked to one of the company's eleven turpentine distilleries, which collectively employed 504 workers (most of whom, like the loggers, appear to have migrated to the coast from elsewhere in Michoacán). Overseeing all of these operations were seven professional foresters, seventeen forest wardens, and five sawmill inspectors.[89]

Although few coastal inhabitants found permanent employment with La Michoacana, the company did make some strides to develop the Sierra de Coalcomán. It began by building a seven-million-peso road to connect the nearly inaccessible town of Aguililla with the regional hub of Coalcomán—a project supervised by the Comisión del Tepalcatepec and its director, Lázaro Cárdenas. The company opened clinics in each of its

Figure 5.2. Aerial view of Michoacana de Occidente offices, primary sawmill, and workers' housing in Dos Aguas, Michoacán, 1966. Archivo General de la Nación, SARH/PF, caja 972, exp. 54175.

management districts and provided some basic services in logging and pine-tapping camps. The crown jewel was the headquarters complex and primary sawmill, built halfway along the new Aguililla-to-Coalcomán road, at a spot known as Dos Aguas. It had a capacity of 100,000 board feet per day as well as facilities to dry and seal the wood. These installations employed several hundred workers, who received housing equipped with electricity, as well as medical services and access to the town's beloved soccer field and basketball court. In the late 1950s a school staffed by nine teachers was opened. A clinic with six beds could treat basic illnesses and injuries, but more serious emergencies had to travel by truck or airplane to Uruapan.[90] Despite all of these improvements, the township had a provisional and impermanent feel. It lacked paved roads and a sewage system, and effluent flowed into open ditches that ran just outside workers' housing. Moreover, company housing did not meet the needs of a growing population. Ramshackle huts soon ringed the town and placed more demands on its overtaxed infrastructure.[91]

La Michoacana's attention to development and best-practices forestry management initially seemed promising. The company pledged to follow the "Mexican Forestry Method" of selective logging, and its foresters stated that they marked no more than half of the trees for cutting, chosen on the basis of their age and ease of felling. These claims cannot be verified, but no complaints about overexploitation appear in the forestry archives or scientific journals of the early 1960s. Indeed, the company began modest experiments in reforestation in 1959, when it spread one hundred kilograms of pine seed in one section that it had logged out. It also planted saplings in a ten-hectare test plot near the headquarters. Although both of these projects failed, the company's chief forester predicted that a carefully managed forestry regime made reforestation unnecessary, owing to the "abundant" regrowth in areas that had been cut. He reported that the pine trees left standing worked as "veritable *natural tree nurseries*" that repopulated the woods at no cost to the corporation.[92] The scientific management techniques and focus on reforestation earned praise from the state and national experts, who identified Michoacana de Occidente as the state's best-organized timber company and a shining example for other enterprises to emulate.[93]

Yet the definition of "best practices" had changed quite a bit from the early decades of the century, when preservationists like Miguel Ángel de Quevedo had inveighed against any policy that led to the loss of forest ecosystems. In the 1950s and 1960s leading forestry experts considered the conversion of forests to agricultural use acceptable and even desirable in certain cases, although conservation biologists such as Enrique Beltrán continued to insist that soil quality in newly opened land was too poor to justify the ecological cost. The 1960 forest code explicitly authorized the clearing of forests to open new agricultural land as long as the land was relatively flat (less than a 15 percent incline) and forest service approved the project beforehand.[94]

Michoacana de Occidente also learned to make some accommodations to local expectations, beginning with the use of fire. After initially proposing a complete prohibition on the burning of fields, company officials soon relented and allowed rural people to petition for the right to scorch their property in preparation for planting, as long as they promised to protect mature trees. Pines were to be spared at all costs. Requests for burning permits soon flooded the company's offices. In 1962 alone, La Michoacana received 819 petitions, nearly all of which received approval.[95] By the early 1960s, foresters had begun to convene meetings with villagers during the harvest season to explain how to set fires that would not threaten trees (and to admonish the locals not to hunt deer without a permit). They even had some success in organizing fire brigades. A survey in the late

1970s showed that most rural people in the concession zone had received at least minimal training in fighting wildfires. (Interestingly, the same survey showed that around a quarter of forest fires resulted from *venganzas*, intentionally set blazes resulting from personal animosity between smallholders.)[96] The company also had authority to authorize burns aimed at the permanent conversion of forests to agricultural land. As with the field-burning permits, the company approved petitions from landowners to clear-cut woods, burn, and permanently convert the land to agricultural uses whenever it was "appropriate" to do so. In theory at least, forest wardens personally oversaw both clear-cutting and burning, and tried to limit land conversion to second-growth forests rather than the more valuable old growth stands of pine and oak.[97]

La Michoacana's pragmatic approach may have helped to curry favor with the people who lived in the concession area, but it did nothing to promote the integrity of the ecosystem on which it depended. The failure of the company's pilot reforestation efforts should have raised concerns, for example, but foresters ignored the problems and reduced the program to mere window dressing. After five years of work, the company had planted only three thousand saplings in one plot and reseeded pine trees in another twenty-five hectares—all of which were allegedly the result of a six-month campaign.[98] Reforestation on such a tiny scale accounted for no more than 1 or 2 percent of the total area that the corporation logged in any given year. There was virtually no chance that it would redress the damage that commercial logging had caused the delicate dry tropical ecosystem.

THE END OF AN EXPERIMENT

Michoacana de Occidente also ran afoul of the other, arguably more successful development projects in the 1960s, including land reform and colonization initiatives. There were no ejidos in the area that Michoacana de Occidente received as a concession in 1955, but a few years later the Secretariat of Agrarian Reform (DAAC) created two so-called pilot ejidos, intended to encourage colonization along the coast that abutted the Tepalcatepec Valley. Agrarian reform officials promised people from Aguililla and other regional cities that they would receive prime forestland, their own sawmills, housing, and electricity, if they would relocate closer to unpopulated areas. In 1959 the DAAC granted 2,715 hectares to 155 ejidatarios in a new pueblo (township), El Varaloso, located only 10 kilometers south of the company headquarters in Dos Aguas. It granted another 4,215 hectares to 280 beneficiaries in the more remote but less thickly forested ejido of Barranca Seca. The territories of both ejidos were formally detached from the UIEF, freeing them to produce and sell timber to whomever they chose, at least in theory.[99] The ejidos had difficulties from the outset, however. Few of the people who enrolled as members ever actually moved to the new villages and therefore could not be present for community meetings; others settled in the townships after the ejidal roles had been finalized and therefore lacked formal rights as ejidatarios. A few families arrived and began building houses inside ejidal lands without informing local authorities. As a result, only 15 percent of the people who lived within these ejidos had full rights as enrolled ejidatarios by the mid-1970s.[100]

Michoacana de Occidente officials vehemently objected to these new population centers, in part because they siphoned workers away from the company. Administrators were already finding it difficult to staff the sawmill, because so many young people had started to spend several months of every year working as migrant laborers in the United States. Eventually, the company grudgingly bowed to official pressure and installed a sawmill in Varaloso. Both ejidos also inked provisional "contracts of association" that would potentially allow their members to cut trees and sell the wood to La Michoacana. Unfortunately, they could not come to terms on a payment schedule, so no definitive agreement was signed. In 1964 the ejidatarios described the deadlock to President Adolfo López Mateos and asked him to cancel La Michoacana's concession altogether. In response, the company filed a lawsuit (amparo) claiming that the ejidal lands should never have been partitioned from the concession in the first place. Company lawyers claimed that the lack of authority over ejidal forests broke the "basic equilibrium of industrial and economic organization, as well as with the fundamental tenants of the management plan." The court agreed and gave La Michoacana authority to manage the ejidal lands.[101] In exchange, the company agreed to keep its sawmill in El Varaloso, open schools in both ejidos, and create new jobs designated especially for ejidatarios.[102]

In January 1968 the forest service announced an investigation into Michoacana de Occidente's compliance with the terms of its concession. Although it documented a series of failures to meet production benchmarks, the final report concluded that the company's failings did not merit cancelation of the UIEF. The former president Lázaro Cárdenas had a different opinion. Using his position as the executive director of the Balsas Commission (successor to the Tepalcatepec Commission), the seventy-three-year-old Cárdenas took a Jeep tour of the Michoacana de Occidente's territory in the summer of 1968. It was not the first time he had visited the area, and he remarked that the pace of logging had picked up, but that formerly dense forests in the Sierra de Coalcomán had all but vanished. In discussions with ejidatarios at El Varaloso and Barranca Seca, he learned the company had used its own logging crews on ejidal land, instead of hiring the villagers as it had pledged to do, and left behind nothing but some royalty fees and denuded hillsides.[103] Writing in his diary, Cárdenas fumed that the company had founded "neither [pine] plantations nor orchards to make up in part for the deforestation."[104] On his return to Mexico City, he published an open letter to pronounce the UIEF a failure and take the company to task for abandoning its contractual obligation to build a road linking Aguililla with the coast. Moreover, he accused the company of appeasing locals' bitterness about mismanagement and overregulation by blindly approving petitions to burn fields on erosion-prone hillsides. It would have been far better, he said, if La Michoacana had simply met its obligation to "give [campesinos] jobs and a fair share of the profits made in the woods."[105] When he learned the following year that the company had asked to expand its concession territory, the former president suggested that the secretary of agriculture should deny the request. Approval, he feared, would represent "a miscarriage of justice to the owners of the woods and harm the forests and soils of the region." His concerns met with official indifference, and another decade passed before ejidatarios won the right to work their own (now vastly degraded) woods.[106]

Private landowners had complaints of their own. One key problem was that the logging enterprise did little to benefit the smallholders who constituted the majority of people in the concession zone. Few of them had received a job from La Michoacana, and those that did usually worked as day laborers in road-building gangs or logging crews—the least skilled and poorest paying positions. Smallholders did earn money when the company extracted timber from their lands, but this created problems as well. La Michoacana's initial management plan called for a cutting cycle of twenty years, meaning that it would cut trees in one plot, then let the forest regenerate for the following two decades. Foresters realized that they had to assure landowners a regular income, however, and tried to organize a rotating schedule of logging so that crews cut only a portion of the woods on each inholding and could return in successive years. Yet the smallholders complained that logging crews removed some stands of trees entirely, leaving others untouched. This was not the sort of selective cutting they had been promised. They also suggested that the company should compress its cutting cycle by half and cut each stand of woods every ten years regardless of the consequences for the ecosystem.[107] But the single greatest point of contention centered on the royalties paid for timber extraction. The 1955 presidential authorization of the UIEF had set minimum payments for the timber, but the company went over a decade without adjusting its payments to keep up with the inflation that gripped the nation in the 1960s. A testy group of landowners met with administrators in 1969 to press their case, but the company did not begin to pay revised (and only slightly higher) royalties until 1972.[108] Even then, the landowners complained that logging crews left too much potentially usable debris (slash) in the woods or abandoned their properties with the job half-finished. In following years, landowners noticed a more disturbing trend: the company's royalty payments came late or not at all. Indeed, La Michoacana had entered an intractable financial crisis.[109]

Further adding to the company's woes, land reform officials began to investigate requests by the Nahua communities around Pómaro for the restitution and official recognition of their common lands. The village of Coire had been unusually successful in protecting its colonial-era commons, in part because no outsiders had settled within its territory. In 1958 it became the first indigenous group in La Michoacana's concession area to have ownership of these lands officially confirmed, which removed some 54,448 hectares from the company's control.[110] Ostula made its own request in 1952, but another twelve years passed before a presidential resolution validated its claim to 19,032 hectares. The villagers rejected that decree as inadequate, however, resulting in another fifteen years of boundary disputes with nearby indigenous communities and mestizo smallholders. Pómaro also claimed a huge territory, eventually recognized by the federal government, in 1982.[111]

The logging company tried to steer clear of these claims and counterclaims, but it had no intention of leaving native lands untouched. It attempted to enforce regulations against burning and forbade the slash-and-burn cycle that lay at the center of indigenous production, for example. Moreover, the mere existence of so much "unclaimed" land—much of it thinly covered with potentially valuable timber—drew mestizos into the area, and to Pómaro in particular; nearly all of these mestizos hoped to do business with La Michoacana. They began to fell trees to build wooden fences around indigenous land they intended to use as cattle pastures. The remaining wood they sold to La Michoacana, depriving the original inhabitants of both their land and the woods it sustained.[112]

Aside from the increasingly intricate complexion of land tenure in the Sierra de Coalcomán, several other factors contributed to the company's decline in the late 1970s. One had to do with demand for forest products. The price of lumber remained flat for most of the decade, while a global glut of turpentine sent its value spiraling downward; indeed, the company stopped buying pine resin altogether in 1978. The only commodity to increase in value was pulpwood, which initially went to the San Rafael paper company and later to the CEPAMISA paper plant that opened outside Morelia in 1973.[113] At the same time, costs grew rapidly in the second half of the 1970s. Continuing pressure from ejidos and private-property owners (who formed a union in 1973 to bargain with the company) forced La Michoacana to increase its royalty payments to keep up with rising inflation and to expand social services such as education. Between 1971 and 1978, the royalties for first-quality timber for lumber or plywood rose by 832 percent. Second-quality wood destined for paper pulp increased a whopping 3,529 percent. Both drew the highest prices for raw material in Michoacán. Over this same period, the company grew increasingly top-heavy, adding more administrators even as the number of workers (and hence production) remained flat.[114] Another likely cause of decline was the unauthorized and probably illegal sale of Michoacana de Occidente to San Rafael y Anexas, Mexico's largest paper company, in 1971.[115] It seems likely that the new owners steered La Michoacana even further away from its original purpose as an industrial producer of wood products, toward a more modest and relatively low-tech production of wood pulp for paper mills.

As La Michoacana plunged deeper into financial crisis, the local press and its own employees began to turn against it. Workers affiliated with the militant, yet pro-government Revolutionary Confederation of Workers and Campesinos (CROC) complained in 1978 that the company had engineered a labor speed-up by changing the way it measured the amount of wood that passed through the sawmills.[116] Once it was clear, in late 1978, that the company would not survive, around two thousand unionized workers declared a strike and asked the courts to freeze La Michoacana's capital assets, because reports had already begun to circulate that the management was secretly liquidating assets by such means as repainting company trucks with the CEPAMISA logo.[117] Michoacana de Occidente ceased operations in December 1978, and President Miguel de la Madrid formally canceled its concession in February 1979, a mere ten months before it was set to expire. The company's directors did not bother to contest the measure, although most observers believed it was because they hoped to evade responsibil-

Figure 5.3. Cartoon from *Verdad* magazine (Morelia), 1977, showing a timber baron whose *boina* (beret) suggests he is José Antonio Arias, a Spaniard and the primary shareholder of Michoacana de Occidente. He proclaims, "Private initiatives such as ours are creating forestry industries," while the campesino on the right quips, "How little . . . wood," a play on words that readers would recognize as *almost* saying "Qué poca madre" (What a bastard). Archivo General de la Nación, SARH/PF, caja 971, exp. 54175, leg. 61.

ity for indemnifying workers.[118] Within months, the ejidos of Barranca Seca and Varaloso and the indigenous community of Pómaro wrote the authorities asking permission to begin working the woods their own. The smallholders followed suit as well.[119] Community forestry had finally appeared in the coastal mountains, but not in the way that development experts had envisioned.

CONCLUSION

Neither Michoacana de Occidente nor the CCIT succeeded in creating a model for community forestry over the long term, and both eventually fell victim to shifting political priorities in Mexico City. La Michoacana's uncompromising pursuit of revenue alienated most people within its territory. Although it generated some employment and helped build infrastructure, its inflexibility created a political landscape of conflict and resentment. The neoconcession eventually became such a potent symbol of mismanagement and controversy that its own employees and "benefi-ciaries" turned against it. The CCIT, in contrast, shook off its paternalist origins, but in some ways became a victim of its own success. True to its assimilationist goals, the CCIT built clinics, schools, and sawmills, but its most noteworthy success was its capacity to develop human capital. Par-ticularly under Plancarte's leadership, its advocacy of native rights helped to engage native people and encourage their tentative collaboration in locally managed timber production. Yet the CCIT's apparent success in building local capacity helped convince federal officials in 1972 to turn the forestry operation over to a government-affiliated corporation (*paraes-tatal*) that would ostensibly give villagers more latitude in working their own land.

The two experiments in managed development reshaped not only the political environments of the Sierra Tarahumara and the Michoacán tierra caliente, but their respective natural environments as well. La Michoacana's incessant misuse of the woods was a particularly notorious self-inflicted wound. The company had preferred to cut forests nearest its sawmills since its earliest days. By the mid-1970s, the remaining stands of timber were so far from the sawmills at Dos Aguas and Las Playitas that transportation had become a significant expense, one that its managers tried to solve with fraud. The company ended up processing most of its timber at a sawmill at Barranca Seca that was supposed to accept only wood harvested on ejidal lands, for example, and it illicitly chipped first-quality timber and sold it to paper mills as pulpwood, rather than using it for plywood as it was supposed to do.[120] Yet even these fraudulent measures did not allow it to meet production targets. A 1978 review of La Michoacana's operations showed that it had been more than a decade since the company had cut even half of its authorized limit. It is possible that the original authorization was too generous (and hence unsustainable), or that the company underreported its production to avoid taxes. Whatever the case, investigators concluded that Michoacana de Occidente had "subordinated the capacity of the forest to that of its machines," virtually destroying some forests while leaving others untouched.[121]

The CCIT likewise regarded logging as an economic panacea that would fund its ambitious plans for Rarámuri communities; despite rhetoric to the contrary, questions of sustainable management were little more than an afterthought. Ironically, the ecological costs of "development" became most acute in Cusárare itself. The CCIT's forester confidently wrote in 1962 that residents had instituted a "completely rational and sustainable extractive regime to such a degree that, without any doubt the ejido . . . will never exhaust its forest resources."[122] Yet even then it was clear that the forests could not endure the burden of community development. Foresters recognized as early as 1956 that sustainable logging would not produce enough income to support the entire community. Some ejidal forests had been intensively harvested long before the anthropologists arrived, and by then, only the most inaccessible stands of timber remained in pristine condition.[123] In 1963 ejidal administrators learned to their dismay that their new ten-year management plan radically reduced the volume of timber they could cut. They wrote to President Ruiz Cortines explaining that a more conservative pace of logging would force them either to abandon the community forestry enterprise or to rent logging rights to a company that had enough pull with the forest service to have a new management plan written—a step that they said they were "in no way disposed to take."[124] The INI apparently intervened with the forest service, which tossed out the (sustainable) management plan and the following year filed one that authorized production levels six times higher than the original rate. The forester in charge of the operation claimed that the woods would suffer no ill-effects, but he also admitted that economic motives drove his decision and tacitly encouraged villagers to harvest more wood than the new, more generous permit allowed.[125] Over time, this strategy took a toll on village woodlots. A quarter of Cusárare's forests disappeared within a few years, and permits had been issued to cut half of what remained. By 1966, fewer than 4,000 of the community's original 30,000 hectares remained intact as a reserve.[126] Neither the INI nor the federal foresters suggested what might be done once these woods disappeared as well.

Both the CCIT and Michoacana de Occidental depended more on the national state than on local populations for their continued existence. La Michoacana could not remain afloat without its UIEF concession, which guaranteed artificially low prices for forest products and sustained its status as the region's primary employer. Rather than collaborating with local populations as its directors initially promised, the company used its strategic position to slow the process of land reform, keep salaries low, fight CROC unionization, and underpay resin tappers for their products. The CCIT tried harder to meet its constituents' expectations. Staff members emphasized transparency in accounting for income from village forestry projects and in negotiating production agreements with timber companies. But it also functioned within a thoroughly bureaucratic context. Its staffers most frequently dealt not with village elders, but with ejidal officers who had the legal standing to sign rental agreements, forestry documents, and receipts. Nor could the CCIT ensure that villagers received a fair share of the income from community forestry, since half of all earnings were deposited in Banco Ejidal accounts insulated from villagers by layers of bureaucracy. Finally, the CCIT, like the INI itself, was a branch of the federal government that existed at the pleasure of the president. Its employees had to work with four different federal bureaucracies (as well as the Chihuahua state forestry commissions and the National Peasants Confederation), which often had their own plans for the people and resources in the Sierra Tarahumara.[127]

Despite their differences, both the CCIT and Michoacana de Occidente left broadly similar legacies. Both institutions promoted the growth of grassroots organizations, including ejidos disposed to defend their potentially valuable forests. They also spawned local committees of various sorts invested with the authority to make management decisions about communal land. They inadvertently sustained popular organizations, such as CROC or the Consejo Supremo Tarahumara, that represented local constituencies. The political landscape had shifted a bit, as villagers became more accustomed to walking a line between collaboration with sympathetic officials and a defensive posture toward outsiders. While La Michoacana repudiated the sort of empowerment that the CCIT (occasionally) embraced, both organizations were founded on the idea that development projects were *supposed* to benefit local constituencies and sustainably manage forests. Villagers in both Michoacán and Chihuahua soon had a new opportunity to weigh the costs and benefits of such institutional arrangements. In the 1970s the federal government created state-owned logging companies that displaced neoconcessions and most private industry in a bid to organize logging activity on a regional scale and further stimulate local development. Like its predecessors, this grand initiative originated not in the countryside, but from the very top of the political pyramid.

CHAPTER 6

The Romance of State Forestry, 1972–1992

Mexico in the late 1960s and early 1970s faced a crisis of authority unseen since the revolution, as the first signs of a protracted economic downturn spawned rural unrest and bouts of urban protest that the federal government met with violent repression unimaginable a generation earlier. Young people took to the streets in cities like Durango and Morelia to protest the ruling party's repressive and increasingly ubiquitous machine politics, which appeared to have lost any remaining tethers to revolutionary ideals. The boldest movement emerged in Mexico City, where students rallied in the summer of 1968 to demand the release of political prisoners and the expulsion of police from university campuses. The protests continued into the fall. With the Mexico City Olympic Games set to begin and preliminary negotiations with protesting students underway, the Díaz Ordaz administration ordered army units and undercover police to quash an October 2 protest in Tlatelolco Square. Armed forces fired directly into the crowd, leaving perhaps two hundred dead and over a thousand in custody. The massacre dealt a death blow to reformist urban protest movements, but it bankrupted the government's moral authority and spawned scores of smaller and more radical challenges to the ruling Institutional Revolutionary Party (PRI) over the following decade.

The ripples from Tlatelolco spread to the countryside, where small numbers of radicalized urban refugees sought out pockets of peasant discontent. They were not hard to find. The breakneck economic growth of the postwar decades had bypassed most rural people yet forced them to pay its social costs. An increasingly populous peasantry confronted widening economic disparities that set commercial agribusinesses and the timber industry against land reform beneficiaries, indigenous people, and the growing ranks of landless workers. The pre-1970 economic model of "stabilizing development" had spawned dams, irrigation districts, and UIEFs but systematically diverted investment from ejidos. To make matters worse, the agrarian reform was structurally unsuited to end landlessness in the long term. Only the registered heads of households—in other words, adult men—received the so-called agrarian rights necessary to enroll as official members of an ejido. In theory, these beneficiaries could bequeath their rights to only one family member, typically a spouse or eldest son. In the postwar era, declining infant mortality and modestly longer life expectancies placed the land reform sector into a demographic vise. Since land redistribution did not keep up with the expanding population, families had to choose between locking most of their children out of the ejido or illegally subdividing their plot of land and giving everyone a parcel. By 1970, the backlog of campesinos declared eligible for the agrarian reform, but for whom no suitable land was available, reached two million. Observers began to speak of a crisis in the countryside as rural people abandoned their cornfields for the burgeoning cities of Central Mexico or perhaps for the United States.[1] Others elected to take matters into their own hands.

Rural Mexico had never completely demobilized after the revolution. Episodes such as the counterrevolutionary *cristero* movement of the 1920s or the peasant insurgencies led by Rubén Jaramillo in the 1950s and Lucío Cabañas in the early 1970s revealed rural people's willingness to protest machine politics and the shortcomings of agrarian reform. Economic turbulence gave new life to such protests. Local leaders formed independent peasant unions beyond the grip of the PRI-affiliated National Peasants Confederation (CNC) and led their followers in a wave of land invasions. Leading the way was the reinvigorated General Union of Workers and Campesinos (UGOCM), which had pioneered these tactics in the late 1950s and targeted agribusinesses that flaunted constitutionally mandated limits on the size of private landholdings. The majority of land invasions were copycat actions spontaneously organized by rural people tired of waiting for official channels of land redistribution. By one estimate, six hundred land seizures occurred in 1972 and 1973 alone, and most avoided bloodshed. Popular unrest on such a scale threatened to slip beyond official patronage networks, however, and authorities announced in June 1973 that the army would block any new invasions, effectively bringing the episode to a close.[2]

These conditions posed a central challenge to Luis Echeverría, who ascended to the presidency in 1970. He had served as secretary of the interior (*gobernación*) during the previous administration, and many observers held him accountable for the Tlatelolco massacre. To combat this potentially damaging image, Echeverría made a dramatic shift from a stony bureaucrat who had once declared the land reform dead, to a left-leaning populist— although his administration continued its predecessor's covert campaign of repression, torture, and the occasional execution of the regime's most vocal opponents.[3] For those willing to play by the PRI's rules, however, the president offered a program of "shared development" that portended higher wages, more jobs, and a fairer distribution of national income. He anchored this initiative with industrialization and social services in the city and a new round of land reform and credit for the countryside. Echeverría redistributed nearly 13 million hectares to ejidos (compared to almost 19 million by Cárdenas and 24 million by his predecessor, Gustavo Díaz Ordaz). The administration refused to touch the most valuable agribusiness lands, most of which appeared in the registry of deeds as ineligible for redistribution, either because landowners had split them into small parcels titled in the name of friends and family or because they had received "certificates of exemption" (inafectabilidad) supposedly reserved for small family farmers. What Echeverría lacked in redistributive zeal, however, he made up for in bureaucratic intervention. The administration reformed the agrarian code in 1971 to allow women to receive agrarian rights directly, rather than through their husbands. It more than doubled the amount of credit available to ejidos. Three years later, it initiated a massive push to improve productivity, in part through an ill-conceived plan to collectivize labor on ejidos and generate economies of scale.[4] For the forests, however, Echeverría had something different in mind.

STATE FORESTRY

Land invasions and independent peasants' unions spread particularly rapidly into the forestlands, largely because widespread resentment of the forest service and UIEF concessions had fostered clandestine logging in so many communities. Forestry officials tried to gain the upper hand by rewriting management plans and increasing the amount of timber that ejidos could legally extract, but many villagers ignored the documents or illegally sold their logging permissions (guías) to other communities.[5] Campesinos protested the most abusive companies, such as Michoacana de Occidente or Bosques de Chihuahua, with land invasions, occasional acts of arson, and whatever political pressure they could muster. Overlaying these social stresses were material ones. While the overall economy had grown at over 6 percent for the previous decades, the timber sector only managed to eke out a tenth of that pace. Efforts to ratchet up production on forest ejidos by giving them more generous quotas did little to make community forestry more profitable. The decades-long push to make the nation self-sufficient in newsprint had also failed, even though the number of paper mills had more than tripled, from 17 in 1950 to 59 in 1970, and paper companies consumed more wood by 1977 than did the construction and lumber industries combined.[6] The one bright spot was foreign investment. The U.S. company Kimberly-Clark purchased the Aurora paper mill in Naucalpan, just outside the Federal District, in 1959. Four years later, this transnational company expanded into the consumer market by launching its successful line of Scribe notebooks, and it began to manufacture Kleenex and Kotex products (which had been imported since the 1930s) in Mexico a few years later.[7]

Echeverría met the economic and social challenges of the woodlands by instituting a regime of "state forestry": a suite of policies that created highly bureaucratic, publicly owned institutions intended to increase rural people's access to land, equipment, and credit. Echeverría's administration took steps that made it easier for villagers to contract licensed foresters, whose authorization was still required for all (legal) logging operations on ejidal lands. At its most expansive, state forestry shaded into an exercise in environmental populism in which Echeverría fashioned himself as the benevolent leader whose administration would finally make it possible for rural people to make a living in their own woods—provided, of course, that they affirmed their allegiance to his regime and its policies. His successors José López Portillo (1976–1982) and Miguel de la Madrid (1982–1988) jettisoned overt populism in favor of a technocratic leadership style, but they retained most aspects of state forestry until the economic crisis of the 1980s forced a drastic contraction of government services.

State forestry borrowed heavily from urban industrial policies, which emphasized centralized management of the economy exercised primarily though corporations known as paraestatales, which were either owned by the federal government or in which it was the primary shareholder. Over a hundred of these state-affiliated corporations appeared in the 1970s, and they produced everything from subway cars to the artificial hormones used in birth-control pills.[8] In the woodlands, the Echeverría administration put an end to most logging bans and formed paraestatales in Chihuahua, Michoacán, and Durango, which were charged with stabilizing the price of wood products, providing technical expertise to rural people, and making loans available for the purchase of sawmills and other equipment. The government also invested in existing timber companies in Oaxaca, Quintana Roo, and Mexico state. The fund that provided capital to ejidal enterprises (the Fondo Nacional para el Fomento Ejidal, or FONAFE) was likewise converted into a paraestatal that functioned as a development bank to provide capital for community-owned timber companies. In 1972 the minister of agriculture announced that FONAFE would build 160 sawmills and workshops in Chihuahua alone—enough, it was said, to "rescue" rural people, who would finally be able to harvest ejidal timber and sell it on the open market.[9] In the end, this thoroughly bureaucratic entity succeeded in funding 135 ejidal forestry businesses located primarily in Chihuahua, Durango, and Quintana Roo.[10]

Most experts welcomed this turn of events. A forestry professor at the national agronomy university (Chapingo) argued, for example, that paragovernmental corporations would ensure that rural people adopted the best forestry practices while simultaneously contributing to national economic development, thereby fulfilling "the basic function of capitalism, which is to accumulate wealth, but in this instance putting it at the disposal of the federal government."[11] Foresters also supported the administration's proposal to increase production in the remotest parts of the country. Domestic and international experts had argued for years that private logging companies did not make efficient use of natural resources. Now these experts contended that state forestry not only would put rural people to work in unprecedented numbers, but, under the right conditions, could make timber as profitable as petroleum.[12] Others were not so optimistic and cautioned against overtaxing ecosystems that had endured generations of overuse. The loudest voice of restraint belonged to Enrique Beltrán, a distinguished biologist, conservationist, and former director of the forest service. Beltrán had a long record of criticizing overly intrusive conservationist measures like logging bans, which, in his view, did little other than encourage clandestine logging. Now he worried that state forestry would swing too far in the opposite direction. He argued that Echeverría's policies opened the door to "galloping developmentalism," which encouraged rural people to extract wood for short-term profit and irreparably harm forest ecology.[13] His warnings had little appeal in an era of peasant militancy and renewed optimism about locally managed forestry. Young and idealistic professionals flocked to the forest service in record numbers, especially once it added a social-development section, in 1976. They helped over 250 ejidos to found their own timber enterprises and formed twenty-five unions of forestry ejidos nationwide.[14]

State forestry derived from a transactional logic in which natural resources served as bargaining chips to placate rural demands. Yet it gave rise to new institutions that were only marginally more responsive to rural needs than were their predecessors. Instead of empowering forestland communities and placing them in control of their resources, the organs of state forestry reproduced the bureaucratic forms that kept villagers dependent on administrators for access to both resources and markets. While the program did achieve some successes—particularly in temperate northern forests, where it fostered scores of ejidal forestry enterprises that endured for decades—it left a more alarming legacy elsewhere in the country. In the coastal and southern tropics, for example, federal institutions promoted the colonization of "under-utilized" forests well suited, it was believed, to cattle ranching. Almost overnight, sawmills began to appear in some of the nation's most delicate and biodiverse landscapes, where commercial logging would never have made inroads without official support.

COLONIZATION AND THE POLITICS OF DEFORESTATION

With existing agricultural lands off the table for redistribution, the land reform bureaucracy turned to territories once considered too isolated or undesirable for redistribution. One strategy was to reinvigorate colonization initiatives, inherited from the 1960s, that aimed to populate and "develop" tropical jungles in sparsely populated southern states. Officials dangled images of virgin forests and rich pastures before the eyes of landless villagers in central Mexico. They seem to have targeted former braceros from the United States whose exposure to independent labor unions branded them as potential troublemakers. Extension agents arrived in overcrowded ejidos in Michoacán, Jalisco, and other western states, where they convened meetings of people waiting for their own parcels of land (i.e., those with "secure agrarian rights") to elect an executive committee and fill ejidal rolls before the colonists had even seen their new homes in the tropics.[15] Most colonists appear to have relocated to the southeastern territory (now a state) of Quintana Roo, where they received forestlands that often fell inside a UIEF concession held by Maderas Industrializadas de Quintana Roo, a private company that had cut its teeth in the mahogany trade. Many of the agrarian colonists had previous experience working as lumberjacks. They knew how to operate skidders and chainsaws, so they felled timber in their new, tropical ejidos and sold it—typically at below-market prices—to the timber company or to the gray-market brokers that swarmed to the area. Thirty-one new ejidos were formed in the 1970s in coastal Quintana Roo, resulting in the loss of half a million hectares of tropical forest, the near-disappearance of mahogany, and (eventually) an overproduction of cattle that took another decade to balance out.[16]

Policies that explicitly encouraged deforestation had also appeared in the mid-1960s, mostly to facilitate the clearing of new land for cattle ranching. International development agencies—including the Inter-American Development Bank, the World Bank, and the German Technical Cooperation Agency (GTZ)—provided funds and technical assistance for these early colonization projects, while domestic agencies such as the river basin commissions and the Banco Ejidal provided credit to colonists interested in raising cattle or growing cash crops. The land reform bureaucracy mapped out new ejidos in the clearings and either enticed or bullied rural people onto them. Forestry experts remained strangely silent in the face of official deforestation policies. While the 1960 forestry code explicitly authorized clear-cuts (*desmontes*), it also gave the forest service authority to halt any deforestation project that might destroy valuable resources or cause erosion.[17] Foresters may have hesitated to criticize a policy blessed by the international community and supported by the presidency, but perhaps more importantly, few of them cared very much about the particular ecosystems slated for forest removal. In a telling instance, a forest service report from the mid-1970s classified over 90 percent of the species slated for colonization as "low grade" noncommercial wood, a category that apparently encompassed nearly all tropical species.[18] Most professional foresters considered the tropical rainforests as useless wastelands, not true forests. Those who disagreed prudently chose to keep their opinions to themselves.

This relatively unfocused set of forest-clearing policies set the stage for the thoroughly institutionalized regime of deforestation that the Echeverría administration undertook in the southern tropics and along the coasts. The Programa Nacional de Desmontes (National Deforestation Program, or PRONADE), launched in 1972, promised to eradicate "useless" vegetation and reorient peasant agriculture toward the commercial economy, particularly in the realm of beef production for national and international markets. PRONADE funded the destruction of approximately 400,000 hectares of woodland across seventeen states, according to one study. It claimed to have cleared land that was delivered to nearly a quarter million people, before environmental concerns led to the program's quiet suspension, in 1982. The deforestation program had been plagued with unexpected reversals from the outset, however, beginning with the two-year pilot project in the area of San Fernando, Tamaulipas. In the spring of 1970, eight hundred colonists were hired to clear a 30,000-hectare section of forest, after which the ICA engineering corporation used bulldozers to uproot the remaining trees and stumps in preparation for planting. Although colonists wanted to sow corn or allow cattle to forage on native grasses in the clearings, agronomists directed them to plant as fodder a tough and sometimes uncontrollably invasive import from Africa known as buffel grass (*Cenchrus ciliaris*), even though the agronomists knew that most rural people considered it a weed. After some tense negotiations, the colonists agreed to seed most of their land with sorghum instead, but that choice proved equally controversial when local ranchers, fearing competition from ejidatarios, refused to sell them any livestock. Moreover, the ICA's heavy equipment compacted the soil, making it hard for colonists to plow and slowing the filtration of water into the substrate. As a result, the pastures never produced as much fodder as hoped and could only sustain a few cattle. Most colonists eventually abandoned San Fernando, which remained an economically and environmentally distressed area for many years.[19]

Ecological missteps like these, along with tense relations with colonists, plagued PRONADE throughout its existence. Part of the problem was that the organization often assumed responsibility for land-clearing projects initiated under the previous administration, but which had already alienated residents. In Chontalpa, Tabasco, for example, PRONADE took over management of a deforestation-and-colonization project that the Grijalva River Commission had initiated in 1966 with funding from German and American development agencies. It entailed dam construction, as well as the conversion of 50,000 hectares of rainforest into small family farms. The following year, colonists accused administrators of fraud and took a group of surveyors hostage. An army detachment ultimately stepped in to quell the unrest, but no real progress was made until PRONADE used tractors to deforest the land a few years later. Even then, poor earthmoving techniques once again compacted soil and left huge pools of water in areas slated to become cropland. The prospective colonists were already upset about official collectivization initiatives that shunted them into cement housing and demanded a more highly structured (and proletarian) workday than they had been used to as campesinos. Now they refused to plant in the waterlogged clearing because they feared losing a season's worth of work if the rains fell too heavily and the land flooded once more. As the project teetered on breakdown, engineers reluctantly recategorized the cropland land as pasture, and the colonists turned to cattle ranching.[20] These well-publicized fiascos dimmed villagers' enthusiasm for colonization, but not before PRONADE had taken a brutal toll on tropical rainforests and coastal ecosystems. In the temperate forests of central and northern regions, however, state forestry took a dramatically different form.

ENVIRONMENTAL POPULISM IN CHIHUAHUA

On 17 April 1971, Echeverría brought his agrarian populism to Chihuahua in dramatic fashion. The president ducked under the rotors of a helicopter in the town of Madera, stepped up to a podium, and announced the expropriation of a vast territory owned until then by the Bosques de Chihuahua timber company. Industrial logging in Madera dated back to 1909, but most of the forests in the area had fallen to hatchets and chainsaws long before Echeverría's pronouncement. By then, many parts of Chihuahua had become landscapes of chaparral punctuated by lonely stands of second-growth timber. One exception was the El Largo tract, located southwest of the city, which consisted of a quarter-million hectares of forestland that the president turned over to ejidatarios in a sweeping gesture of "social responsibility" meant to punish Bosques de Chihuahua for the "illegitimate hoarding" of the nation's patrimony.[21] The expropriation dealt a stinging blow to the timber company, and it promised a new source of employment for a thousand predominantly mestizo campesinos, who gratefully received the land. But the president was less interested in seeking social justice than in staunching an agrarian movement that had percolated in the sierras for more than a decade. Bosques de Chihuahua was the direct descendent of Porfirian-era timber companies (including the Madera Lumber Company and the North Western Railway), yet it had remained virtually untouchable thanks to the influence of its silent partner, the former president Miguel Alemán. An earlier land grant had caused a small tract of El Largo's forests to 110 families in 1950, but the company had used its influence to modify the execution of the order, and the beneficiaries ended up with nothing more than arid scrubland. The ejidatarios responded by setting forest fires in Bosques de Chihuahua lands for years to come.[22]

Some of these frustrated ejidatarios joined UGOCM, an independent peasant union founded by progressive leaders, which functioned as a counterbalance to the official worker and campesino unions controlled by the PRI. The UGOCM had for years objected that Bosques de Chihuahua and its Spanish-born owner, Eloy Vallina, had grown rich at the expense of people who lived in the sierras. The union targeted the company in the mid-1950s for a series of land invasions that served as an uncomfortable reminder that some great estates had survived the revolution and land reform in Chihuahua. In 1965 a small guerrilla movement headed by the schoolteacher and UGOCM member Arturo Gámiz pressed the issue still farther. On 23 September, Gámiz led twelve companions in an ill-conceived attack on the Madera army barracks that left him and most of his followers dead, along with five soldiers and at least one civilian. The army quickly stamped out the embers of rebellion, but the episode helped spark similar movements elsewhere and forced the rebel group's complaints about Vallina and Bosques de Chihuahua onto the national stage.[23]

Echeverría could not ignore such an obvious blight on his agrarian populism, but he artfully turned the expropriation to his own advantage by putting the government-affiliated peasants confederation (the CNC), rather than the UGOCM, in charge of the redistribution process in El Largo. In one deft move, he succeeded in painting himself as a champion of campesino interests while ensuring that his local supporters in the CNC occupied the key positions in the massive new ejido. He outflanked the more radical and independent peasant organization and generated a powerful new clientele among the new land reform beneficiaries.[24]

Echeverría added 265,111 hectares and 1,215 new families to El Largo, making it the nation's largest ejido and a showcase for the president's campaign of state-led rural development. Federal extension agents arrived within a month and established a community forestry enterprise large enough to employ all of the beneficiaries. Ironically, its administrators secretly penned a cooperative contract (*contrato de asociación en participación*) that leased logging rights back to Bosques de Chihuahua for a twenty-year term. Like most such agreements, the company pledged to put its sawmills at the disposal of ejidatarios and hire the locals for all nonspecialized positions, including transport. But as with most such agreements, much of this contract's language was empty rhetoric that allowed the timber company to use the land more or less as it had always done. Ejidatarios complained about the backroom chicanery, and sawmill workers declared a strike against their own ejidal forestry company, ostensibly seeking better pay and more hours, but actually to protest Bosques de Chihuahua's continuing influence in the area. Residents wrote forestry officials that their ejido's own administrators intended to clear-cut the forest, leaving them with nothing but a vast wasteland.[25]

Only a hastily arranged meeting between ejidatarios and federal foresters averted a full-blown rebellion. The foresters assured the assembly that logging would proceed slowly and methodically. They also pointed out that the contract with Bosques de Chihuahua included some unusually progressive clauses that gave ejidatarios a role in the "planning, organization, and execution of the entire extractive process, from cutting trees until their delivery to sawmill," as well as assurances that the company would log at 70 percent or more of its authorized volume (and hence could not freeze production and put the locals out of work).[26] As it turned out, villagers in El Largo indeed received jobs as loggers, haulers, and millers; some moved into the ranks of management as well. By the late 1970s, the ejidal business held regular public assemblies and hired its own forestry experts. Over a thousand members of the ejido worked most of the year in the collective forest company. The ejidal enterprise eventually purchased a sawmill from the timber company and built a workshop that fabricated furniture and shipping crates. Ejidatarios also cut their own wood for sale, equivalent to about 20 percent of the ejido's total output (with the remaining 80 percent delivered to Bosques de Chihuahua), though the beneficiaries grumbled that they had to travel to the extreme north and south of their territory if they wanted to cut trees, since the logging company still held the logging permissions (guías) for the most readily accessible woods. It seemed that most ejidatarios eventually accepted the arrangement with Bosques de Chihuahua as an unpleasant fact of life. As one ejidatario explained, perhaps a bit wistfully, "Now we own the forests, but the company still owns the logging contracts."[27] And while some observers fretted that the residents were more interested in making money than about caring for the forest's long-term viability, others felt that the ejidatarios had slowly learned to use their land sustainably.[28]

If Echeverría hoped that his dramatic blow against the state's most reviled timber company would tamp down popular discontent, however, he had made a serious miscalculation. Word of the arrangement between Bosques de Chihuahua and the ejido spread quickly, and the members of another large ejido decided they, too, deserved more authority over their woods. This time, the president did not control the script.

The ejido of San Juan Chiantú, in Chihuahua's southernmost district of Guadalupe y Calvo, included 968 mostly Rarámuri beneficiaries, who possessed a vast territory of slightly more than 150,000 hectares in the early 1970s. The land reform community had been formally established in 1948, but it remained largely isolated. Villagers continued to use slash-and-burn agriculture for another two decades, which protected the forests from the far more damaging impacts of commercial exploitation. Even so, timber interests had tried for years to exploit the communal woods. In the mid-1950s, the governor of Chihuahua named a "false campesino" as chairman of the ejidal governing council, much to the disgust of Chiantú's residents.[29] Soon thereafter, the González Múzquiz timber interests built a road linking the village with Parral and signed a lease agreement for the woods. The forest service approved a logging permit, in exchange for which the company promised to build a boarding school (*internado*) for villagers, complete with teachers, school breakfast, medicine, and sports equipment. The timber giant also pledged to fund a local police force and pay for the upkeep of the village church.[30] But none of the promised improvements appeared, and the small-scale logging operation that finally got underway did not provide work for any of the residents. When news arrived in 1972 about Echeverría's immense land grant to El Largo, the Rarámuri ejidatarios of Chiantú expelled the Spanish-speaking (presumably mestizo) ejidal officers, whom they branded "pirates." They denounced the chabochi upstarts as shills for the timber company and accused them of pilfering lease payments meant for the entire community. In a carefully worded statement to the national press, they demanded that authorities approve a collectively owned timber company under the direction of indigenous ejidatarios.[31]

The logging company spokesman shot back that native people had no real desire to work and preferred to "lie around the doorways . . . and do whatever they want. The poor things! They're like little birds."[32] The issue caught the attention of the Supreme Council of the Tarahumara Race (the organization of native and nonnative schoolteachers that represented Chihuahua's indigenous people), which prevailed upon the local agent of the Secretariat of Agriculture to abrogate the lease and, in their words, "rescue" ejidos in Guadalupe y Calvo by building a series of locally managed sawmills.[33] Although villagers celebrated their independence from the logging company, the forest service replayed the strategy followed in El Largo and obliged them to sign a five-year contract with the González Múzquiz corporation. Most locals reluctantly assented to the deal once the company agreed to turn over its sawmills in exchange for exclusive rights to market timber that the villagers cut.[34]

Losing control of events on the ground like this was certainly not what Echeverría or the forest service had in mind for the nation's forests. Neither the president nor the regulators wanted Chiantú to become an example that might inspire other communities to take matters into their own hands. As it turned out, political leaders had another plan in the works that appeared to grant villagers throughtout the nation the means to manage their own lands while ensuring that forestry experts retained the final say over the best woods that still remained in the Sierra Tarahumara.

STATE FORESTRY IN THE SIERRA TARAHUMARA

A few months after the president returned from his sojourn to Madera, representatives from the Supreme Council of the Tarahumara Race held a conference to discuss how indigenous ejidatarios might take advantage of the forest service's newfound emphasis on locally managed forestry. One hurdle was that the Secretariat of Agrarian Reform had never formally executed the documents confirming the rights of many indigenous communities to legally occupy their ejidos, so only a few could legally receive logging permits.[35] More substantively, the delegates agreed to formally request the abrogation of rental agreements with logging companies so that villagers in the Sierra Tarahumara could work their own woods. They praised the CCIT for setting up a dozen community-logging enterprises, but argued that every village deserved such an opportunity. "Rather than wasting our region's forest wealth," the delegates argued, "we can use modern technology to exploit it rationally and guarantee a permanent source of employment . . . to our people who are isolated from the mainstream of civilization."[36] In February, the representatives met with Echeverría in Mexico City and presented their petition in person. He listened attentively to their descriptions of grinding poverty, forest degradation, and the INI's inability to call timber companies to task for misusing village woods. The Rarámuri leaders also worried that agrarian officials had left many people off the official agrarian rolls, effectively locking them out of access to ejidal forests. When they finished speaking, the president praised the courage of those who had traveled so far to meet him and pledged that "all the problems you have brought to me will be addressed." Then he empaneled a group of bureaucrats and local politicians to study the issue further.[37]

The working group predictably concluded that the most direct path for regional development led through the forest. Its recommendations envisioned better roads, newer logging equipment, and more autonomy for campesinos vis-à-vis timber companies. As for the Rarámuri, it recommended "incorporation into the nation via an explicit program that permits above all the development of sedentary [i.e., not transhumant] habits in the use of agricultural and forest resources."[38] Echeverría responded to the report with an executive order, dated 10 August 1972, that created a paragovernmental corporation, PROFORTARH (the Forest Development Agency of the Tarahumara), charged with effectuating the "rational and integral" use of forests in a 3.7 million hectare region of western Chihuahua. Echeverría explicitly ordered the organization to place rural poor at the top of its agenda and invest in new roads, hospitals, schools, and housing.[39] Its administrators understood that logging would continue to represent "the region's primary agent of development" and chief source of income, but they also recognized that forestry could never generate enough revenue to solve all of the region's economic problems. In response, they suggested that resource extraction should be used to build an industrial base that would meet the needs of an impoverished and rapidly growing population. PROFORTARH administrators recognized that similar development projects had fallen short in the past, but they vowed that things would be different this time around. Whereas their predecessors had never managed to square the interests of rural people with the "capital and technical knowledge" of commercial timber companies, the new state-owned organization would deliver to rural people the tools they needed to work their own forests in the foreseeable future. Best of all, from the administrators' standpoint, the commercialization of village logging would finally generate enough employment to acculturate the Rarámuri and fold them into the economic mainstream.[40]

The state-owned company started off on a positive note. It collected annual fees from the rural communities within its territory and used the funds to build hundreds of kilometers of roads that linked far-flung villages with regional population centers. It built a box-manufacturing facility and woodworking workshop in San Juanito, as well as larger, permanent sawmills that were both easier to monitor and more efficient than the itinerant mills favored by logging companies. Perhaps most important, it established collectively owned enterprises in 77 ejidos and Rarámuri communities (out of a total of 120 population centers in its so-called zone of influence), 30 of which joined to form a mestizo-indigenous ejidal union that sent timber to a shared sawmill in Tomochic. These energetic policies increased timber production at an average of 8 percent annually between 1972 and 1976. PROFORTARH also claimed to have founded 27 medical clinics and trained around 200 ejidatarios in various aspects of scientific forestry.

Company administrators also tried to recalibrate the relationship between rural people and timber companies. Before the paraestatal, ejidos and native communities signed "association in participation" contracts that ostensibly devoted half of logging proceeds to village coffers and set aside jobs for residents; in fact, these stipulations were rarely enforced and allowed the less scrupulous timber companies to make a few token payments that many villagers never even knew about. PROFORTARH foresters rewrote these agreements and brokered deals that allowed ejidos and native communities to sell timber directly to sawmills, cutting out the widely reviled contratista middlemen. This procedure limited the chances of fraud and (theoretically) directed payments to the people who had contributed their resources and labor to community enterprises.[41] By the late 1970s, administrators recognized that regional needs still "vastly exceed the Organization's capacity to meet them," but declared that PROFORTARH had nearly put an end to the "irrational use of resources and the exploitation of campesinos . . . and substituted them with new forms of economic organization that guarantee greater productivity and progress toward making social justice a reality."[42] It soon became clear that triumphalism of this sort was a bit premature.

Indigenous people apparently liked the idea of a publicly funded organization that both provided technical support and helped them cut through the tangle of federal regulations. One group of ejidatarios predicted that PROFARTARH would promote the "progress of our Mexico in a way that benefits campesinos" and break their dependency on logging companies.[43] At least some of the company's foresters shared this vision. They fanned into the Sierra Tarahumara beginning in 1972, to rewrite rental agreements and formulate new management plans for ejidos and native commons. They reported that native communities seemed tentatively supportive of their activities. No complaints appear in the archives about the company at this time, despite the fact that villagers had to pay compulsory "contributions" for PROFORTARH's services.

The core forestry ejidos formerly managed by the INI's CCIT did not fall under the paragovernmental corporation's ambit and were grouped instead into a semiautonomous productive unit called the Union of Ejidal Enterprises of the Tarahumara. (The CCIT itself continued to offer education and medical services, but no longer oversaw logging.) In practical terms, however, the union depended on PROFORTARH to provide credit and annual renewals for logging permits. By the early 1980s, the corporation had effectively displaced the Union of Ejidal Enterprises and worked directly with Rarámuri communities throughout the Sierra Tarahumara. Its intervention was particularly valuable around Cusárare and Sisoguichi, where decades of intensive logging had left the area covered with spindly

Figure 6.1. Work at the Sisigochi sawmill managed by Productos Forestales de la Tarahumara, ca. 1974. PROFORTARH, *Memoria 1973–76* (Ciudad Juárez: Imprenta Roa, n.d.), 72.

trees in sparse, secondary-growth forests that demanded careful oversight. The state-owned company arranged for the more progressive timber companies to transfer ownership of sawmills to local authorities, as in the case of the El Pino installation in Guachochi. If necessary, it built new ones, as in Cabórachi.[44] Many native people interpreted these as welcome changes. Local leaders eagerly staffed the mills with people from their communities, while the Union of Ejidal Enterprises explored ways of collaborating with company experts on management plans and contributed ideas for marketing timber products. In a few places, ejidal leaders looked to PROFORTARH for instructions about how to log stands of old-growth forest.[45] Indigenous leaders, it seemed, had decided to take a gamble on cooperation with the new organization.

The paragovernmental forest company was never intended to function as a true partnership, however. Some members of its professional staff clung to conventional ideas about the primacy of expert knowledge in bringing about "the rational and integral utilization of forest resources," and they railed against the supposed tendency of native people to misuse nature.[46] While PROFORTARH foresters realized that native people valued small-scale logging operations and community-owned sawmills, they never attempted to leverage this enthusiasm into grassroots support for PRO-FORTARH's broader development mission. Over time, they increasingly fell back on the same adversarial tactics as their forebears. They punished villagers who allowed goats to browse on saplings and complained that recalcitrant peasants refused to combat forest fires unless their own houses and crops were in peril. They also took measures to end slash-and-burn agriculture, even though they recognized that the poorest people in the Sierra Tarahumara regarded it as a necessary subsistence strategy.[47]

More controversially, PROFORTARH abandoned an important component of its plan for local production when it moved to ban the ubiquitous, so-called portable sawmills equipped with conventional radial blades. These rudimentary machines still processed most timber in the sierras, in part because they were cheap enough for individual communities to purchase and maintain. The foresters pointed out, however, that portable mills were "deficient as a general rule and [could not] produce quality products," and should therefore be replaced with a smaller number of high-capacity mills owned by PROFORTARH and equipped with modern band saws that wasted less wood.[48] Many ejidal leaders objected, particularly when company personnel refused to confer about staffing decisions or negotiate over which community's wood the larger mills would saw first. As the head of the state agrarian league explained, no one opposed the idea of conservation, but villagers simply expected to run their own sawmills. The smaller units cost less to build and ultimately generated more employment at the local level.[49] PROFORTARH eventually relented, but the welter of small mills (which the corporation itself had initially funded), supplemented by a newly built high-capacity installation in Sisoguichi, created a crisis of overcapacity that suppressed the prices that any of the mills could charge for their services. Further aggravating the situation, banks refused after 1980 to extend credit to communities that still wanted to build a sawmill of their own.[50]

A proliferation of red tape and bureaucratic negligence further hampered PROFORTARH's capacity to engage native people. Within a few years, its internal bureaucracy metastasized into a hopelessly complex network of units, subdirectorates, and offices whose organizational chart required a trifold book insert to represent. Villagers had no real point of entry into the top-heavy paraestatal and began to abandon hope that it would ever bestow the guidance and documentation they needed to work the land. Already in the late 1970s, native leaders had lost their enthusiasm and complained that the corporation produced few tangible benefits in the countryside. They also charged that administrators refused to hire native people for management positions. By the early 1980s, some indigenous communities requested permission to withdraw from PROFORTARH, but the forest service denied the petition on the basis that they had already reaped the benefits of the company's technical services.[51] Faced with this officious response, some villagers abandoned the woods or turned once again to the clandestine market. Little by little, the organization lost its footing and lapsed into corruption, inefficiency, and interminable conflicts between management on the one hand, and villagers and sawmill workers on the other. By the mid-1980s, any pretense of local input had evaporated, and the organization had become something of an albatross—a relic of state forestry that had proven ineffectual at best and counterproductive at worst.[52] To the generation of neoliberal politicians coming of age in Mexico City, paragovernmental corporations like PROFORTARH had come to symbolize the failure of state intervention in the economy and to exemplify why state forestry represented a false step down the path of economic development.

A POPULIST PARAESTATAL

In December 1973, the Echeverría administration lifted the logging ban (veda) that had affected the entire state of Michoacán since 1950 and had covered some districts (including those in the Meseta Purépecha) as early as 1937. The ban had not halted logging altogether, of course. UIEF concessionaires including the Michoacana de Occidente and a few other corporations received legal exemptions that allowed them to lease logging rights from ejidos and smallholders and to "cooperatively" log these lands. A number of ejidal unions and regional producers organizations had likewise won permission to use their woods under the scrutiny of forestry officials, but these arrangements were cumbersome and rarely functioned very well. Most people turned instead to tapping pine trees for resin or to the well-developed black market in clandestinely harvested timber.

Most rural people applauded the resumption of legal logging. For the first time in decades, ejidos could request their own management plan from the forest service and—in principle—establish their own, locally managed logging enterprise. The market also cooperated, thanks to Michoacán's expanding paper industry, which grew at a 14.2 percent annual rate between 1970 and 1979, or about three times faster than the national average.[53] With the veda gone, ejidos moved individually or in groups to form small-scale logging enterprises, each with its own low-capacity sawmill. All of these activities required approval from the federal forest service as well as from the state forestry commission. Although officials rushed to approve new lease agreements and draw up village management plans, people in many parts of the state lacked the capacity or perhaps the necessary trust to file formal requests with the forest bureaucracy. The appearance of new sawmills, combined with the perceived difficulty of obtaining logging permits, meant that timber poaching actually increased in some places. One forester also noticed an upsurge of intentionally set forest fires, a well-worn strategy to win official permission to salvage the dead, standing timber. Villagers usually converted the charred land to agriculture, although they also torched the woods to punish neighbors for cutting trees in disputed territory.[54] More typical but less obvious was the process that foresters labeled "ant operations," in which people cut a few trees here and a few trees there, then hauled them, one or two at a time, to some nearby sawmill. The cumulative effect could be ruinous. Around three-quarters of the wood in indigenous ejidos around the Meseta Purépecha was cut this way during the early 1970s.[55]

The spectacular growth of logging and pulp production tarnished the appeal of work as a tree tapper. Bleeding the trees for resin did less damage to forest ecosystems than timber extraction did, but it netted villagers only a modest income even in the best years, and the 1970s were certainly not one of those times. Global overproduction of turpentine and the appearance of synthetic alternatives sent prices for raw pine pitch tumbling. Yet some villagers refused to abandon their trade. A generation had made their living as tree tappers, especially in indigenous communities. Many of them had worked the same stands year after year, protecting "their" trees from fire, timber poachers, and other interlopers. Michoacán's resin industry had received strong support from foresters and development agencies, and many tappers felt proud about having cared for their patch of the woods. The resumption of legal logging meant that chainsaws would inevitably take a place alongside collection buckets, however. As woodsmen set their sights on the trees that tappers needed to make their living, many communities fell into agonizing internecine conflicts that lasted well into the 1980s.[56]

Despite these tensions, the seeds of community forestry were planted in the 1970s. Rejecting federal oversight, the state government of Michoacán created its own paragovernmental corporation to promote locally managed forestry and ensure a reliable flow of wood products to regional consumers. For a brief period, the Promotora Forestal de Michoacán (PROFORMICH) provided significant price supports and technical assistance to ejidos and native communities. Unlike its northern (and federal) counterpart in Chihuahua, it grew in part out of an existing producers organization, which may help to explain its relatively populist character. When the enterprise collapsed a decade later, it meant the last gasp for state forestry in Michoacán and left people in the woodlands with a stark alternative: either turn the woods over to commercial enterprises, such as the state's booming avocado agribusinesses, or find the means to manage their woodlots and market the timber on their own.

PROFORMICH's primary mission was to purchase pine resin and wood products from its member organizations, which included indigenous communities, ejidos, and unions of ejidos, along with a few smallholders. The company provided technical assistance in the form of professional foresters who managed logging and tree-tapping projects, as well as training in sustained-yield forestry techniques. It used some of the wood it bought to build shipping crates and made the rest available to local businesses such as the CEPAMISA paper mill founded just outside Morelia in 1973. It also sold turpentine on the national and international markets. Income from all these transactions covered most operating expenses, with the balance made up by a subsidy from the state government and payments from local producers who benefited from its services. In theory, these member-producers wielded ultimate authority over management decisions. In practice, the top administrators were insulated from local producers by layers of middle management. As in Chihuahua, the idea of creating such an organization garnered support from across the social spectrum. Rural people wanted guaranteed prices and logging permits. Politicians and well-established business interests liked the idea of a locally managed company that generated a steady flow of raw material to paper plants and sawmills, not to mention shipping crates for the nascent avocado industry.

Another group that favored the new corporation was the Acuitzio-Villa Madero Forest Administrative Unit (UAF), a cooperative-like organization that the forest service had organized in the 1960s to manage woods in ejidos, indigenous communities, and a handful of private properties located in the heavily Purépecha region between Morelia and Pátzcuaro. That organization had seen its share of controversy. The timber magnate and Michoacana de Occidente board member Ricardo Sánchez Monroy arranged for his properties to fall within the UAF's ambit so he could sidestep the statewide logging ban, for example. Some observers claimed that the entire organization was nothing more than a shell corporation for Sánchez

Figure 6.2. Cover of a comic book produced in the early 1970s by the forest service to encourage local acceptance of federal foresters. In the story, the light-skinned expert earns villagers' trust when he saves a young girl lost in the woods. Author's collection.

and his cronies.[57] But small-time producers also used the organization as a clearinghouse. They eagerly delivered pine resin to its warehouses, where they received a guaranteed minimum payment, and they maintained generally good relationships with the organization's foresters. Buoyed by these encouraging signs, federal authorities gave the UAF a five million peso grant to build a sawmill and turpentine distillery.[58] By the early 1970s, progressive foresters who worked in the Michoacán state government had come to think of the unit as a "social service agency" working on behalf of the state's poorest people.[59]

PROFORMICH intended to reproduce these successes on a wider scale, and its managers anticipated the day when it would institute a comprehensive management plan statewide. They hoped that it would "remake the forest industry" in Michoacán by integrating small-scale production with the largest and most modern enterprises, all following scientific management practices.[60] Governor Servando Chávez Hernández held a public inauguration ceremony for the paraestatal on 5 January 1974, just two weeks after the federal government lifted the statewide logging ban in Michoacán. The national press paid tribute to the new era in social forestry, which Chávez later claimed would serve "the campesinos who own the forests by establishing an enterprise that seeks . . . greater social justice."[61] Yet some doubts floated behind the fanfare. After all, the corporation was merely the latest organization among many that proposed to "develop" rural areas and integrate peasant producers into the broader timber economy. Most of these schemes had failed, of course. To make matters worse, its first director was none other than Sánchez Monroy, the controversial timber magnate. One veteran forester denounced PROFORMICH as a leviathan unleashed by politically connected businessmen and forestry experts who hoped to line their pockets in the name of community forestry.[62]

In fact, the corporation was more minnow than whale. It began with a relatively modest jurisdiction, which included a million hectares, six sawmills, three plywood factories, and a handful of turpentine distilleries that had all seen better days. Its managers drew up plans to create another six regional management districts (Unidades de Ordenación Forestal) that would complement the existing district in Acuitzio-Villa Madero, each of which would respond to the specific needs and ecological conditions of the state's major geographic divisions. The only new district that actually got off the ground was centered in the Ciudad Hidalgo, and even that district nearly misfired when foresters rushed smallholders and ejidatarios into a producers union and asked them to raise a 100,000-peso bond to ensure that the organization would abide by its management plan and officially determined production levels. Its members eventually agreed to raise the funds, lured by the prospect of legally logging their own woodlands as well as by the corporation's pledge to deliver top prices for their wood. Several communities launched new ejidal enterprises that produced first-quality wood.[63] Officials also began planning for a management district in the Meseta Purépecha and recruited several ejidos and indigenous communities under its jurisdiction. Some native people, such as the twenty-four members of the resin producers cooperative in the Purépecha village of Aranza, found much to like about the new arrangement. They tapped the same trees they always had and delivered resin directly to the regional distillery in the nearby town of Cherán, but now they received double the price for their labor.[64] By the mid-1970s, it appeared that PROFORMICH's two management districts were functioning smoothly, and all that remained was to expand to the rest of the state.

But the organization could not outrun its bureaucratic origins. A series of missteps later in the decade exposed the gap between the increasingly top-heavy bureaucracy and rural producers—a problem that became more visible as the federal forest service displaced their Michoacán state counterparts in the late 1970s and transferred most decision-making authority to Mexico City, in essence federalizing what had been a shoestring operation under the control of the Michoacán state government.[65] The federal authorities refused to update the payment schedule for timber and resin, however, even though inflation reached 30 percent in 1977, before decreasing to just under 20 percent over the next two years. By that point, tree tappers in communities such as Aranza could no longer make a living by selling to PROFORMICH. They abandoned their collection pots and either migrated elsewhere or turned to clandestine logging. Even the Acuitzio-Villa Madero producers union collapsed, as its members desperately sought alternatives to logging. Many took jobs in the Uruapan area, where clandestine loggers were clearing forest to plant avocado.[66] The paragovernmental company's unresponsiveness only added to people's gnawing suspicion that administrators shortchanged them on what little wood and resin they still delivered to company depots. Most of them preferred to deal with the small-time pirate sawmills and distilleries that paid less than PROFORMICH but at least did so in straightforward cash deals rather than in complicated transactions that involved stamps, taxes, and official signatures. Nor did the company make good on its promise to teach villagers new techniques of forest management. Some of the company foresters said that they would take on apprentices, but they were so busy drafting management plans and filling out paperwork that they never quite made the time.[67]

The growing tide of resistance converted the company into yet another failed development project a mere six years after it was founded. As one peasants' union explained, PROFORMICH paid poorly and sporadically, kept villagers from selling their products where they wanted to, and generally suffered from "a lack of defined goals and accomplishments."[68] One community after another gave up on the institution. Some abandoned logging altogether, while others turned to the time-honored contraband trade. With few goods left to sell, the corporation collapsed in late 1980, taking with it any prospect for regional management for years to come. Yet the paragovernmental corporation had succeeded in incubating two critical social groups. In the first place, it had launched the careers of several progressive foresters who understood their role primarily in social rather than technical terms and now intended to work directly with communities outside of a corporatist bureaucracy. In the second, it had convinced some local leaders that professional foresters were willing to step outside their role as functionaries and pay more attention to villagers' own expectations. In other words, the organization had set the stage for a collaboration between experts and villagers, particularly the Meseta Purépecha. It turned out, however, that they soon had to contend with a new threat to the woods in that area.

GREEN GOLD

The revitalization of logging in 1973 also unleashed new ecological pressures in the Meseta Purépecha as planters began to clear the woods for avocado orchards for Michoacán's flourishing new agribusiness. Avocado trees are native to what is now the state of Puebla in south-central Mexico, and many of the nation's most beloved dishes feature the fatty green fruit. People who lived in Uruapan had a long tradition of planting a tree or two in the patios of their houses and flavoring their food with a wide variety of locally grown avocados. The first commercial groves appeared in the area sometime around 1957, but they primarily catered to local consumers and a few regional markets such as Guadalajara. A decade later, a handful of farms planted avocado trees on a modest 13,000 hectares to meet demand from Mexico's growing urban population. International demand also picked up, thanks to the growing popularity of "Mexican food" in the United States. Commercial farms began to scout the warm foothills around Uruapan in the early 1970s, at the very moment when villages were furiously cutting wood in the wake of the logging ban, and small-scale forestry became the primary means of opening land for plantation agriculture. By the mid-1980s, Michoacán had become the world's single largest producer of the sought-after fruit. The acreage dedicated to avocados had grown seven-fold, to approximately 100,000 hectares, enough to supply 40 percent of global demand.[69]

The forest service began to authorize clear-cuts on some ejidos in the late 1970s, allowing villagers to permanently convert their woods into groves of what farmers were already calling "green gold." Even though federal programs like PRONADE actively promoted deforestation by this time, it was still relatively rare for the forest service to explicitly approve the removal of temperate forests for agriculture. But forestry officials understood that they had few alternatives in the avocado zone. Members of the Peribán ejido, twenty kilometers west of Uruapan, told the veteran forester Waldemar Díaz in 1978 that they were tired of earning a pittance tapping their communal forests for pine resin and had decided to clear the land and plant avocado trees, whether he gave them his blessing or not. Díaz gamely granted permission to raze 65 of the ejido's 1,978 hectares. He put the best face on the episode by pointing out that decades of improper tree-tapping had converted most of the ejido's once abundant forests into dying husks, despite the fact that villagers had adopted a less damaging technique of bleeding the trees a few years earlier. In any case, the largest trees in Peribán had already succumbed to clandestine logging, and the remaining forest was too small to meet residents' needs, even if they logged it sustainably.[70]

The forest service soon concluded that most communities around Uruapan would be better off growing avocados than trying to make a living through forestry. After all, the new crop generated far more income than a regime of tree-tapping and low-intensity timber production ever could. Rural people would also receive payments in annual cycles, rather than the more irregular distributions associated with traditional forestry operations. And anyway, forest wardens could not keep villagers and smallholders from opening small clearings to plant avocado trees in areas too remote for officials to police. As the forester Díaz put it, "Everyone who owns or possesses forestlands in these parts has been infected by avocado fever."[71]

The new plantations transformed life on dozens of ejidos and native communities, and the private sector quickly emerged as the major player. Around 80 percent of Uruapan's avocado production took place on private property (rather than ejidos) in the 1980s.[72] The trade was initially dominated by the smallholders known as rancheros, who had a long tradition of planting creole avocado varietals alongside their other crops. They used most of this produce for their own consumption, though some ventured to the open-air markets of Uruapan to test the waters. Like ejidatarios, the rancheros made scores of requests to permanently convert woodlands to avocado orchards in the mid-1970s. Others logged the woods without permission or "accidentally" set fire to inconvenient stands of trees. Officials recognized the pattern and granted virtually every request to convert the forest to agriculture, though they also worried that the homogenization of the ecosystem would impose a heavy environmental and perhaps economic cost in the long run.[73] The rancheros also tended to ignore the precise boundaries that divided their land from that of their neighbors, leading to a spate of complaints from ejidatarios and commonholders about avocado orchards that mysteriously appeared on the margins of their property. A few communities seized on the moment to demand that the authorities adjudicate contested property lines once and for all.[74]

The new plantation economy attracted migrants from the neighboring highlands and as far away as Morelia. Some of the newcomers squatted on attractive parcels owned by desperately impoverished people whose hold on the land was already tenuous. For example, a few indigenous settlements had never titled their property in the district of San Juan Parangaricutiro, and their cornfields soon gave way to rows of bushy, sun-loving trees with waxy leaves as settlers pushed the most vulnerable farmers off of the land. Many of the dispossessed campesinos ended up as field hands on avocado plantations, where they worked long hours while exposed to huge doses of overapplied pesticides.[75]

Although forestry experts had once hoped that avocados would anchor a mixed-use regime of small-scale farming that would in turn provide a degree of agro-ecological diversity, domestic and international markets came to favor the "improved" and easily transported—but nearly tasteless—Hass varietal. Large commercial farms were better positioned to buy and plant Hass saplings en masse, as well as to make use of the agronomists posted at the Universidad Michoacana's new agricultural extension campus in Uruapan. Highly capitalized growers were also the best able to forge long-term contracts with the Mexican, American, and Chilean transnationals that increasingly dominated trade. Soon, even medium-scale rancheros found it difficult to fend off the encroaching plantations. By the end of the twentieth century, most independent farmers had given up and become clients of the larger commercial farms.[76] The homogenization of regional agriculture, it turned out, had foretold an analogous narrowing of land ownership as well.

THE RESURGENCE OF COMMUNITY FORESTRY

In the midst of the advancing avocado plantations lay a small oasis of conifers held by Purépecha communities such as San Juan Nuevo Parangaricutiro, the village forced to relocate after the 1943 eruption of the Paricutín volcano. Residents were given an expropriated hacienda with 18,000 hectares, or 70 square miles, of land blanketed with pines and oaks. These rich common lands could easily sustain San Juan's population, although it appeared for a few decades that conflicts over boundaries would mire the land in endless litigation. Neighboring villages claimed that the relocated village had usurped some of their territory, including a tiny parcel in Angahuan which stood at the center of an ongoing feud between the two communities that eventually cost over a hundred lives. More threatening still, the nonnative Equihua and Anguiano families also claimed the rights to nearly a quarter of San Juan's common lands. Everyone knew that the village had allowed Pedro and Miguel Equihua to use the commons as payment for having represented the village in a 1908 court case that successfully contested the disentailment and privatization of communal land. These men's descendants insisted that the grateful village elders had not only agreed to accept the Equihua family as fellow comuneros, but had given them outright possession of several thousand hectares. In the early 1950s these aspiring landowners secured a legal title to the disputed acreage, prompting many other residents to quickly follow suit. The precise boundaries of the new property that San Juan Nuevo received after the eruption had never been precisely mapped, and by the mid-1950s, a hundred more private titles had been granted to land that most people regarded as part of the village commons. Most of these transactions occurred when villagers bribed a notary public to record their titles, but some people took advantage of the "emergency" railroad-tie production plan of 1955, when county officials were eager to write deeds for anyone willing to harvest timber.[77] Whatever its origins, the ownership controversy lingered until 1991, when President Carlos Salinas annulled most of these transfers and ordered most private claims to be reintegrated into the commons.[78]

Village leaders got along well with the foresters assigned to work in San Juan Nuevo, beginning with Waldemar Díaz, one of the most experienced and diligent foresters in the state. In the 1950s Díaz helped local leaders to organize a community-owned resin-tapping enterprise. The village headmen took the unusual step of dividing the commons into 130 blocks, each controlled by a specific head of household, although the allocation of earnings and deliberations about how intensively to log the forest still took place in the periodic public meetings of comuneros typical of Purépecha communities. In the 1960s the commonholders helped fund the construction of the regional turpentine distillery in the nearby town of Cherán. Most foresters reported that the commonholders embraced the enterprise and did their best to care for "their" block of woods. Townspeople confronted outsiders who invaded communal land and usually refused to tolerate clandestine logging among their own number. They did not mind colluding with each other to collect more resin than their management plan permitted and selling the excess on the black market, however.[79]

Even so, villagers developed a grudging respect for the forest service, or at least enough to ask the federal authorities for help in combatting a plague of sawflies (*Neodiprion vallicola*) that appeared in the late 1960s.[80] The forester billeted to the town arranged for an aerial bombardment of DDT. When that failed to kill the insects, he recommended cutting the infested trees, including some in stands used for resin tapping. He then mediated the inevitable disputes that pitted the villagers who assented to the emergency logging against those who tapped the trees and balked at any form of logging at all. In the end, all but a handful of commonholders consented to remove the infected trees, although some furtively erased the marks that foresters sprayed on blighted trees to signal that they should be cut.[81]

It seems likely that negotiations over the sawfly issue smoothed the way for a broad consensus about the viability of community forestry. The reemergence of legal logging in 1973 caused a great deal of angst in many parts of Michoacán, because tree tappers—who typically numbered among the poorest sectors of rural society—opposed any logging program that threatened the trees that sustained their livelihood. Something similar could have happened in San Juan Nuevo, where around six hundred people, or nearly half of the economically active population, still worked as resin tappers.[82] Once lumberjacks began to cut the fly-infested trees in 1969, however, they used selective logging techniques that did not displace tappers from "their" forest stands. In a further bid to smooth over potential rifts, village leaders included all comuneros—including the tree tappers—as members of the village timber enterprise formed in 1976. This budding sense of solidarity was almost immediately put to the test when the small landholders who claimed land in the village commons signed lease agreements with logging companies later that year. A hastily called meeting to discuss the issue nearly led to bloodshed, but village leaders convinced residents to write a lengthy missive, most likely composed by a resident who had attended school in nearby Uruapan, that laid out their grievances against the private landowners in lawyerly language. It asked the forest service to halt any logging that impugned their "territorial integrity" or that made it possible for "people outside [their] community" to harm their lands and their families. Officials responded by halting logging on disputed lands while still allowing comuneros to cut trees on undisputed areas of the commons.[83]

Much of this wood initially supplied paper mills, but the community established its own sawmill and wood shop in 1981. Although the avocado boom had prompted some of the remaining smallholders to plant trees of their own, it also created an immense demand for packing crates, so the new communal business immediately began to turn a profit.[84] Many of the initial sawmill managers had once worked in the United States as braceros, and their organizational skills helped to get the enterprise up and running. Another factor that helped was the Purépecha tradition of transparency and widespread consultation among stakeholders in collective endeavors. The communal assembly met regularly and had the final word on how to use the woods and where to invest profits. Villagers elected to use some income to buy cattle, machinery, and logging trucks, but they also kept aside some funds to send promising students to study forestry at the federal agriculture school in Chapingo. Most of these young graduates returned home brimming with ideas and technical expertise. By the late 1980s, they had improved the millwork to the point that San Juan Nuevo was producing export-quality products that found buyers among transnational corporations such as Home Depot. Yet the village continued to harvest its woods sustainably, with minimal damage to communal forests.[85] Development experts from the National Autonomous University of Mexico (UNAM) and international funding agencies recognized San Juan Nuevo as one of the nation's most successful experiments in community forestry and strove to translate its lessons in forest ejidos located in Guerrero, Oaxaca, Durango, Quintana Roo, and the Federal District.[86] Yet the community's idiosyncratic experience with the volcano and the selective cutting of fly-infested trees makes it hard to see how easily reproducible the community's experience really is.

NEOLIBERALISM AND COMMUNITY MANAGEMENT

Two trends pulled forest rural society in seemingly opposite directions in the late 1970s. On the one hand, a generation of resistance to blunt and unresponsive development programs such as the UIEFs and paraestatales had opened political space for local forestry enterprises like San Juan Nuevo's. Indeed, many experts suggested that community forestry not only met rural demands for greater economic autonomy, but also plotted a blueprint for conservation on a national scale. Unlike the earliest generation of conservationists, which regarded peasants as backward-looking enemies of nature, the environmentalists of the 1970s suggested that campesinos' own self-interest could be harnessed to the goal of sustained-yield forestry. Since land reform beneficiaries had the most to gain from environmentally responsible logging, why not finally teach them how to do so? This logic had been articulated by a previous generation of ecologists, such as Enrique Beltrán, who had argued a quarter-century earlier that uncompromising conservationism merely promoted illegal and ecologically harmful logging, along with widespread scorn for the woods. Now environmentalists and activist foresters (especially graduates from the national agricultural university at Chapingo) were inclined to agree. An increasingly influential line of reasoning held that rural people, rather than logging companies, held the key to environmentally friendly forestry. In 1980 politicians followed suit and passed a new forestry code that explicitly ordered the Secretariat of Agriculture (SARH) to offer "technical assistance and financing for the production, manufacture, and marketing of forest products" to anyone who owned forestlands, including ejidatarios and comuneros.[87] Six years later, the federal government passed an entirely new forestry code that ordered the eventual elimination of UIEF concessions and paraestatales. It authorized ejidos and indigenous communities to contract with independent foresters for the environmental studies and management plans necessary to log their woods. For the first time since the land reform had begun, rural people achieved a degree of independence from the forest service.[88]

On the other hand, neoliberal restructuring of the national economy put the squeeze on budgets for social services, and soon the funds to implement a coherent national program of community forestry began to disappear. An economic crisis engulfed the nation in 1982, after the federal government announced that it could no longer service its foreign debt and suspended payments to North American banks that had lent the nation billions of dollars at egregious interest rates. Investment disappeared and inflation spiked, leading to a "lost decade" of turmoil, characterized, among other things, by economic restructuring that pinched federal budgets and forced the state to abandon its efforts to manage the national economy. Presidents de la Madrid and Carlos Salinas de Gortari (1988–1994) made a virtue of austerity by embracing a neoliberal doctrine that promised to unleash the power of the free market by shrinking the public sector, deregulating the economy, and opening Mexican markets to international competition.

Neoliberal austerity measures spelled trouble for the bloated and increasingly problematic paragovernmental forestry enterprises. Michoacán's public corporation (PROFORMICH) collapsed in 1980 as a result of a boycott by its own members, but the ones in Durango and Chihuahua lived on. So too did the logging and paper concerns that had received federal subsidies in Oaxaca, Puebla, and Quintana Roo. While some of those semipublic companies turned a profit and became candidates for privatization (which effectively transferred public investment to private hands), nothing could make the largest paraestatales viable. By 1988, they stood as costly reminders of another epoch, and federal authorities finally cut off subsidies altogether. Durango's PROFORMEX collapsed the following year, when members of its own producers union invaded administrative offices in search of management plans and logging permits that would allow them to sell their timber on the open market. The Secretariat of Agriculture capitulated in a matter of days, dooming PROFORMEX to irrelevance. The union continued to press its cause and eventually convinced authorities to turn over the corporation's sawmill and plywood plant as well, making the new communally owned enterprise one of the state's largest producers of finished wood products.[89] Something similar happened in Chihuahua, albeit without a direct confrontation. Between March 1988 and May 1989, PROFORTARH transferred control over the forests to a series of producers unions that comprised the Asociación Rural de Interés Colectivo (ARIC) "General Felipe Angeles," a collective of 21,000 people grouped in 180 ejidos, which took possession of the corporation's production permits, along with its network of increasingly obsolete mills. As it turned out, the new ARIC reproduced the unresponsive bureaucracy of the old paraestatal, and it, too, failed within a year.[90] In 1990 the INI once again took charge of forestry in Rarámuri ejidos of the Sierra Tarahumara.

Although state forestry failed in both Michoacán and Chihuahua, the precise cause of death was different in each case. In Michoacán healthy traditions of local production—above all, in the tree-tapping industry—underpinned the expansion of community forestry projects. Federal officials found themselves on the defensive as expanding avocado groves claimed some of the best forests in the state and created a new class of smallholders. Villagers abandoned PROFORMICH at the same time as commonholders in places like San Juan Nuevo Parangaricutiro chipped away at top-down structures of forest management. Much of this popular resistance was a response to the politicization of forests, which had become spaces subject to laws that rural people could not control, and over which federal officials, timber companies, and (eventually) environmentalists claimed some degree of authority. Yet a renaissance of small-scale production displaced at least some environmental decisions to the local level and opened the potential for a viable alternative to state forestry.

Not so in Chihuahua, where native people never developed the same degree of local expertise or appetite for community forestry. Village landscapes remained divided and politicized over questions of resource use, the ongoing influence of outsiders, and ethnic cleavages. The forest itself almost always lay at the center of these debates. By the early 1980s, smaller Rarámuri ejidos, such as Cusárare, that had the longest history of local production had all but exhausted their relatively small forests, whereas the larger ones, such as Chiantú, were only beginning to work their own land. Yet a long history of work as lumberjacks, road builders, and hewers of railroad ties had not been enough to give most Rarámuri villagers the expertise to manage communal forests. And while a handful of communities continued logging and requested credit for new sawmills, many others continued to chafe under a productive scheme that made them bystanders in the decades-long effort to "develop" the woods on their behalf.

A LAST HURRAH FOR DEVELOPMENTALISM?

Forestry megaprojects had not yet breathed their last in the Sierra Tarahumara, despite the advent of neoliberalism. The collapse of state forestry ironically coincided with the most ambitious project yet envisioned for Mexico's great northern woods. In 1985 the de la Madrid administration approached the World Bank for a loan to rehabilitate the timber industry in Chihuahua and Durango. Three years later, the organization agreed to supplement the federal government's own funds with a $46.6 million line of credit that would bring a total of $91.1 million to the woodlands. The project had an eerily familiar ring, beginning with its primordial goal of "improving productivity and environmental protection by introducing rational forest management practices"—words that easily could have been written by Antonio Sosa half a century earlier.[91] A more recent antecedent was the Inter-American Development Bank's somewhat similar project to inject $51.4 million into the cellulose industry in Guerrero and Oaxaca. Forestry experts had concluded that these states' "underused" resources (including the Chimalapas rainforest) represented ideal candidates for commercial logging and new paper mills; according to one observer, however, the real purpose of these funds was to build logging roads that the military could use to traverse the impoverished and politically restive Costa Grande of Guerrero.[92]

Like its forebears, the World Bank project in the Sierra Madre promised that a reinvigorated timber economy in the northern forests was a win-win scenario that would promote national development and provide jobs for poor rural people. After a century of industrial logging, it was not clear that the forests could withstand another round of intense extraction, however. In many places, timber companies and clandestine logging had either denuded forests or left behind spindly trees that dotted an increasingly eroded landscape. The few old-growth forests that remained were located in the indigenous regions of southern Chihuahua and northern Durango, where few roads existed. Yet some experts continued to envision the woods as a vast untapped source of raw materials and employment opportunities. In 1985 the newspaper *Excelsior* cited a United Nations report that suggested that Mexico could potentially place another 143 million hectares into production—enough to put a substantial dent in rural inequality—if it had the political will to acquire proper technology and teach campesinos to use it.[93] World Bank experts were more circumspect. They recognized that decades of high grading (logging the largest, most easily accessible trees) had compromised ecosystems throughout the sierras. Where logging was still ongoing, ancient trucks rumbled down poorly maintained roads and delivered sawlogs to small and inefficient sawmills. Bank experts estimated that poor forestry techniques limited regrowth to half of its real potential. But they reckoned that this could all be fixed. The World Bank's initial report concluded that capital investment would redress production difficulties and ultimately improve the overall quality of life "by increasing rural and urban employment and family income, especially in the traditionally impoverished Amerindian communities."[94]

The project sparked unease on both sides of the border, however. North American environmentalists worried that commercial logging would continue to degrade forest ecosystems and run roughshod over indigenous rights. While they sympathized with the ideals of sustainable development, most balked at the World Bank project's cost, which would need to be recuperated through profits, and pointed out that it put little real premium on environmental sustainability or on addressing native people's wishes. One watchdog group discovered that environmental and social safeguards were either ignored or poorly implemented. It concluded that the World Bank had violated every one of its own objectives, except for that of increasing timber production.[95] Other observers found it remarkable that so few funds would remain in the countryside, because the terms of the loan made it impossible to extend credit to ejidos that already had debts to repay, meaning that the investments would bypass most rural communities.[96] Some Mexican critics took a harder line and questioned the very concept that capitalist development could benefit the rural masses. The economist and public intellectual Cuauhtémoc González Pacheco, who was also a veteran of the 1968 student movement, wrote that the World Bank project was an excellent model "for extracting more wood . . . but not for social or environmental development, because it was never conceived as a means of strengthening popular organization or enhancing their technical competence."[97] These skeptics drew inspiration from an emerging consensus on the Mexican Left that neoliberal restructuring tended to reward corporate interests at the expense of the environment and of the poorest social groups. On the global level as well, critics charged that World Bank loans for highway projects, dams, and resource extraction facilitated commerce while disregarding the bank's primary goal of alleviating poverty.

Stung by the scale of criticism, the World Bank announced that it would commission the INI to investigate how the logging project would affect native people in the Sierra Tarahumara. The task fell to the Chihuahua City branch of the National School of Anthropology and History (ENAH), which hired cadres of anthropologists and bilingual native schoolteachers (*promotores*) to visit the forests of Chihuahua and northern Durango, beginning in 1989. As the first logging roads began to be built, INI operatives held a series of meetings to gauge native people's thoughts about the project. Most were skeptical. They told the anthropologists that the World Bank-funded outreach project to teach them management techniques was poorly executed and spotty. They worried about losing their woods to contractual obligations they did not understand. Many of them asked the anthropologists to tell them more about legal options to halt the World Bank program, so they could work the woods themselves. In a few instances, activist villagers incorporated community enterprises in a bid to head off commercial loggers. The leaders of Chiantú, for example, decided to structure their local forest company around family units that would extract relatively small amounts of timber close to their homes, rather than follow the traditional logging practice of rotating logging sites from one part of the forest to the other. Further north, villagers in Guachochi and Cusárare insisted that outsiders did not understand the local ecosystem well enough to selectively log the delicate, second- (or third-) growth communal forests. To the INI anthropologists, it seemed clear that most native people were simply not interested in the World Bank's offer of commercial logging.[98]

On 11 November 1992, three thousand Rarámuri gathered in Guachochi to mark the fortieth anniversary of the CCIT. The World Bank project was not their only point of concern: the rise of drug trafficking in the sierras, police repression of indigenous activists, and the reconfiguration of the Supreme Council of the Tarahumara to include more young, bilingual schoolteachers at the expense of elder governors (*siriames*) all came under discussion. But control of the forests generated the most debate, and the governors agreed that the main issue was to ensure that "we, as owners of forest resources, should have in our hands the authority to ensure that their management respects indigenous knowledge about their ecologically balanced use."[99] In this meeting and subsequent interviews with the INI anthropologists, one Rarámuri leader after another explained the basic inconsistency between the World Bank's goals and their own. Whereas the best practices of commercial forestry envisioned maximum-sustained-yield logging that would guarantee as much income as possible, most of the Rarámuri felt it was better to cut as little as they needed in order to sustain themselves and their rancherías. For them, logging complemented herding and agriculture and allowed for collective survival. It was a means to an end rather than an end in itself.

Faced with the evident lack of local enthusiasm and an increasingly combative stance by the INI anthropologists, the World Bank quietly shelved the project in early 1993. The national forestry plan published two years later still referred to possible reinvestment in the Sierra Tarahumara, but it no longer described it as a massive venture to develop the woods. Instead, the Secretariat of Agriculture demoted it to a mechanism of bringing "alternative" forestry practices to the woodlands.[100] Two years later, the project was formally canceled. Fifteen years after a broad-based campaign of passive resistance had undermined PROFORMICH in Michoacán, a coalition of native people and anthropologists had accomplished something similar on a much grander scale in Chihuahua as well.

CONCLUSION

Slivers of Hope in the Neoliberal Forest

—————————

At the break of dawn on 15 April 2011, several women fired a volley of fireworks at three logging trucks loaded with timber illegally cut from the village commons of Cherán, Michoacán. The clap of "rockets" is nothing unusual in Purépecha villages like Cherán. People shoot them off to mark saints' day celebrations and announce festivals, but they are also used to raise the alarm in an emergency. A crowd quickly assembled around the women and began to pelt the trucks with rocks and more fireworks. A few of the drivers were briefly detained, and soon enough the vehicles beat a retreat out of town. The villagers knew the timber poachers would not stay away. The loggers had ties to narcotraffickers and had pillaged timber from neighboring villages for several years. Three elders from Cherán had already been killed, when they hiked into the woods and asked the narco-loggers to leave, or at least to spare a treasured stand of ancient trees.

The villagers soon learned that they could expect nothing more than rhetorical support from the authorities. The state police ignored the murders even though local leaders had pressed their case with the governor himself. The army also refused to get involved. So the residents built barricades to keep the trucks away and imposed a curfew on anyone from out of town. They issued press releases and posted messages on the Internet until bloggers and the international press took an interest in their story. Finally, they invoked their constitutional right to impose customary law (*usos y costumbres*) in a bid to defend themselves and maintain a degree of political autonomy. Residents formed a militia (manned in part by migrants who had returned from the United States) and stood vigil in the roads and hillsides, despite warnings from the police that so-called *ronda* militias were illegal, and despite the reprisal of narco-loggers, who murdered villagers as they replanted saplings in the communal woodlot. Some internal divisions also appeared, as it became clear that a few families had cut deals with the interlopers. For the most part, however, the villagers insisted on their right to protect their natural patrimony and collective security.[1]

The uprising echoed events that had taken place in Cherán a century earlier, when the American timberman Santiago Slade sent logging crews into the village commons. Slade's lumberjacks appeared in Cherán sometime around 1902, brandishing cross-cut saws and rental agreements allegedly signed by village leaders. They clambered into the woodlots and returned with timber destined for train cars and eventually for the company sawmill in Uruapan. The residents understood that it would be futile to bring a lawsuit. The Porfirian-era legal system almost invariably sided with the wealthy, and company lawyers could always produce spurious contracts in court. So they decided to bide their time. Their opportunity for retribution came during the 1910 revolution, which broke the back of the Porfirian state and threw the countryside into turmoil. In 1913 villagers from Cherán fell in beside the troops of Eliseo Elizondo, a revolutionary general who intended to force Slade and his pro-government militia out of the hillsides and back to the city. The timber baron barely escaped with his life, but returned a few years later to restore his logging consortium. The mobilization in the Meseta Purépecha had galvanized the villagers, however, some of whom joined Michoacán's powerful agrarian movement and helped bring Lázaro Cárdenas to the governorship a few years later. The young governor and future president abrogated rental agreements such as Slade's and opened the way for what in Cherán became a long tradition of local autonomy in the woodlands.[2]

Over a century separated Santiago Slade's assault on the village commons from the narco-loggers' incursion of 2011, but the two events shared some remarkable similarities. Both occurred at moments of government "weakness," when authorities had few means at their disposal to enforce the law, even if they had wanted to, leaving villagers isolated as they confronted threats to their property and their welfare. The (neo)liberal policies that guided political life in each of these eras promoted free markets and placed minimal constraints on "entrepreneurs" or the use of natural resources. Like its Porfirian predecessors, the regime of the Institutional Revolutionary and National Action parties in the 1990s and 2000s put so much emphasis on creating a favorable climate for investment that it undercut environmental and social conditions. Finally, while the residents of Cherán eventually succeeded in expelling the outsiders in both cases, their capacity to stave off outsiders over the long term remained very much an open question.

Cherán was not the only place where the Porfirian tradition of impunity and land dispossession had reappeared. In one particularly well-documented case, villagers in the Sierra Petatlán, Guerrero, mounted a successful protest in 1998 against the Boise Cascade timber company. They accused the transnational corporation of colluding with the federal army to log their land without permission. The episode garnered enough bad press that Boise abandoned Guerrero altogether. Four years later, federal authorities falsely accused the protest movement's leader, Rodolfo Montiel, of drug trafficking, then sentenced him and an associate to seven years in prison. President Vicente Fox pardoned them a few years later, but not before Montiel had been tortured and his attorney, the human-rights advocate Digna Ochoa, had been assassinated.[3] Another protest movement in the Rarámuri ejido of Pino Gordo, in the far south of the Sierra Tarahumara, also attracted international attention when villagers denounced illegal logging operations that had encroached on their territory. Stunned by the unwanted attention from the international press, federal authorities put the brakes on commercial logging and pledged to address the problem.[4] Neither of these movements represented unqualified successes, however. Years later, Pino Gordo's case remained unresolved, and villagers accused their neighbors of invading their ejido at the behest of logging companies. The situation in Guerrero was more dire still, as a dozen or more peasant leaders lost their lives in confrontations with pirate loggers protected by the authorities, or narcotraffickers, or both. Their followers had to choose between organizing self-defense corps like those in Cherán or ceding their patrimony to timber poachers. Many chose the latter course and relocated in the cities or deeper into the forest, adding their number to Mexico's growing ranks of environmental refugees.[5]

These episodes reflect a heritage of rural resistance to forest dispossession that stretches back to the Porfiriato, but they occurred at a peculiarly unsettled moment in Mexican history, thanks to the paradoxical effects of neoliberalism. The disappearance of muscular development programs and unwieldy regulatory structures unquestionably opened a space for villagers to stake stronger claims to the woods. Progressive expert foresters and local activists leapt at the opportunity to establish ejidal timber enterprises in Michoacán, Guerrero, Oaxaca, and elsewhere. In a few instances, such as in Quintana Roo, forest ejidos banded together in independent producers unions. David Bray, a longtime observer of the woodlands, has suggested that the 2010s may well represent the "optimal moment" for villagers and their allies to forge ahead with local experiments in locally managed, sustainable forestry.[6] Nevertheless, neoliberal deregulation has made it hard for rural people to take advantage of this historical conjuncture. Neolib-

eralism relies on markets to allocate capital, which has effectively privatized management planning, formerly the sole domain of federal experts.
Cutbacks and restructuring have forced the forest service to discontinue
its free technical assistance, meaning that villagers need to fund their own
management studies and seek capital from philanthropies and from the
shrinking pool of rural credit. Timber companies that had once managed
to secure logging permits by negotiating with the forest service have
turned to other means. Some have taken advantage of business-friendly
legislation that has once again opened federal land to foreign companies.
Others have reached covert "understandings" with local powerbrokers
such as military commanders, municipal presidents, and narcotraffickers.
In many parts of the country (Michoacán, Chihuahua, and Guerrero in
particular), organized criminal syndicates have lent support to illegal loggers. Apart from earning easy money, narcotraffickers use timber theft to
intimidate rural people into capitulating to their authority and perhaps
paying protection money as well. Neoliberalism has thus placed many rural
communities on the precarious boundary between self-determination and
abandonment.

The similarities between the early 1900s and early 2000s should not
obscure the substantial changes in forest landscapes, however. Over a
quarter of the nation's woods disappeared in that span of time. In the far
north, commercial logging pushed the forest frontier southward, while
colonization projects along the coasts and in the south helped to convert
tropical forests into pastures and cornfields. Nearly all of the nation's
woodlands experienced some degree of degradation, usually as a result of
fire, pasturing cattle in the forest understory, or small-scale logging for
domestic uses. By 2006, a mere 10 percent of the nation's woods could
be considered primary (old growth) forest.[7] Conditions changed in social
terms as well. Unlike in the nineteenth century, rural people owned most
of the nation's woodlands—60.3 percent by the most careful estimate—in
the early 2000s.[8]

The nature of scientific forestry also changed dramatically over the
course of the twentieth century. The first generation of conservationists,
epitomized by Miguel Ángel de Quevedo, worried that peasant backwardness made them fundamentally unfit to possess the nation's woodlands,
much less manage it on their own account. While these early twentieth-
century intellectuals cautiously hoped that education and didactic rituals
like Arbor Day might one day change rural people's attitudes and convince
them to "love the trees," experts in the era of revolutionary forestry

continued to place much of their faith in robust regulations and mechanisms, like producers cooperatives, that facilitated a paternalist regime of environmental surveillance intended at its core to transform peasants' environmental consciousness. By the 1950s, scientists in the mold of Enrique Beltrán took a step away from this viewpoint to suggest that rural poverty—rather than peasant attitudes—drove land reform beneficiaries and indigenous people to overuse the woods. The midcentury generation of conservationist thinkers continued to believe in regulation and the inherent superiority of modern forms of extraction, such as carefully managed commercial logging, but they had become less certain that campesinos posed an inherent threat to nature. The foresters who came of age in the 1980s grew increasingly convinced that rural communities represented a potential solution to the problem of deforestation. Many of them believed that local knowledge and collective resource management could become the foundations of a scientifically informed regime of community forestry.[9]

Rural people's relationship to the woods had also shifted over time. Comuneros, land reform beneficiaries, and smallholders never stopped advocating for their rights to the land, but their use of resources and relationships to outsiders evolved dramatically. Whereas rural people dedicated most of their efforts to staving off outsiders' attempts to acquire their land during the Porfirian and revolutionary eras, the middle decades brought new opportunities and disappointments. Most communities received legal possession of the forests without earning corresponding authority over the landscape. Rather than dispossession, the main threat to local autonomy now derived from forestry regulations, logging contracts, and development projects. In addition to submitting petitions to political leaders to protest fraud and unclear boundary lines, some rural people began to request logging permits, tools, and technical assistance so they could make a living in their woods, but do so without harming their ecological integrity. By the beginning of the twenty-first century, many villagers' understanding of forests had begun to converge—on some points—with that of the forestry experts.

THE REVOLUTION AND THE COMMONS

Cherán's century-long bid to preserve its patrimony underscores the links between local histories of activism and the ecological integrity of forests over the long term. Villagers in Cherán (and elsewhere) employed a variety of practices to defend their territory. They petitioned the authorities and selectively ignored problematic regulations. They forged alliances with neighboring villages, if possible, and with accommodating officials. If necessary, they took up arms against loggers and pushy neighbors, and sometimes against each other as well. Villagers not only developed what Charles Tilly has called a "repertoire of contention" to confront threats to their subsistence, but also learned when to use a particular strategy and which tactics to avoid altogether.[10] In tight-knit native communities like Cherán, oral traditions constituted the most useful archive of such knowledge. Elders and local intellectuals preserved the memory of past trials and made it available at moments of crisis. These collective memories also functioned as a symbolic link among residents and in this sense helped define community identity. Popular ballads, such as the pirekua of Santiago Slade that many Purépecha schoolchildren still sing in Cherán today, for example, have become part of an imagined collective experience that (regardless of its factual basis) posits a strong symbolic bond between the villagers and their woodlands.[11]

The links between community and landscape were especially pronounced in indigenous townships, most of which had occupied the same territory over the course of several centuries. Generations of the same families had worked the land and, in some cases, assembled a nuanced understanding of the local ecosystem. By the twentieth century, most of Mexico's remaining "self-governing peoples" inhabited remote regions like the forested uplands, far from commercial centers and the inquisitive gaze of government authorities.[12] These same landscapes began to acquire unprecedented commercial value around 1900, when the Porfirian boom in mining, transport, and export agriculture accentuated the demand for wood products. Indigenous land had come under intense pressure in most places by the time the revolution broke out, in 1910. Agrarian demands did not detonate the uprising, but the promise of land reform did inspire some peasant groups to join the fray—with the notable exception of native people, most of whom tried to avoid the conflict altogether. And yet the revolutionary process represented a turning point in many native regions. It gave rise to a land reform that encompassed the forests and set the stage for an indigenista movement intended to "redeem" native people and improve their material and social conditions.

The Cárdenas administration stepped up the pace of land reform and rescinded the long-term contracts that allowed logging companies virtually unrestricted access to village commons. It enforced regulations that made producers cooperatives the only entities legally permitted to log

Figure C.1. Lumber carts on the highway near Pátzcuaro, 1907. Photograph by
Sumner W. Matteson. Milwaukee Public Museum.

ejidos and common lands. The success or failure of the Cardenistas' plan for the woodlands hinged on authorities' ability to direct rural people's desire for greater productive autonomy toward the institutional goal of encouraging ejidos and cooperatives to collaborate with the forest service. The cases of Chihuahua and Michoacán suggest that this initiative met with mixed results at best. Foresters found it difficult to overcome rural people's distaste for management policies that vitiated their autonomy, while the cooperatives themselves almost invariably fell under the sway of local bosses (caciques) or agents of the timber companies. Nevertheless, the establishment of more than 850 producers cooperatives in the 1930s made it clear that rural populations, including indigenous people, could accommodate to official management policies, particularly if they retained some means of using their land.

That does not mean that native people reflexively sought to conserve "nature." The Rarámuri and Purépecha rarely articulated a desire to return the land to some former pristine state, much less to cease using it altogether. They had no shortage of uses for their woods, which they employed for everything from tejamanil shingle-making and artisanal charcoal manufacture to ambitious regional projects of sustainable forestry or resin production. Rarely did they intend to leave their forestland completely untouched. Native people often deployed liberal concepts of property rights leavened with some revolutionary concepts of social justice, to explain that they had both the right and the capacity to care for their property. They tended to petition the authorities under one of two circumstances: either when they believed that some entity (a logging company, a greedy neighbor, or someone within their own village) was exploiting their property without permission, or at least without paying appropriate compensation; or when power-holders (foresters, timber barons, or government authorities) refused them access to their own woods. In other words, native people, like rural folk generally, were most troubled by the pilfering of their timber and the bureaucratic roadblocks to cutting the wood themselves.

The ecologist Garrett Hardin contended in an influential 1968 essay that collective ownership of natural resources invariably leads to a "tragedy of the commons" or, in other words, to the depletion of a collectively held resource by those who use more than their fair share. Hardin argued that individuals not only had no motive to conserve common pool resources, but that they had strong incentives to take as much as possible before someone else did it first. It was only a matter of time before self-interest induced people to graze too many sheep on village pastures, to draw too much water from the village well, or to cut down too many trees from the collectively owned woodlot. It only takes one bad individual taking more than his due to destabilize the collective, because it creates an incentive for everyone else to escalate their own consumption before the resource is exhausted.[13] Deforestation in Mexican ejidal forests might seem at first blush like fodder for Hardin's theorem. The local histories of Michoacán, Chihuahua, and other locations in Mexico disclose many instances of villagers who clear-cut the forest to turn a quick profit, or perhaps to make sure that they made a bit of cash before someone else finished off the woods first. On some occasions (such as the cases of intentional arson in the contested stands of timber), ejidatarios and rancheros destroyed the woods rather than let them fall into their neighbors' hands. In the tropics, colonists hacked down rainforest and fenced the land for cattle ranching before someone else could stake their own claim to the newly opened land.[14]

Yet relatively few of Mexico's forest commons resembled the unregulated free-for-all that Hardin described. On the contrary, rural people often went to great lengths to protect their forests, either by agreeing on mutually acceptable uses of the land (as in many mestizo ejidos) or by adapting existing practices to the new realities of local commercial forestry (as often occurred in indigenous commons).[15] Mestizo ejidos like El Largo in Chihuahua were hardly alone in establishing successful ejidal businesses that promised jobs in the mountainsides and sawmills to ejidatarios.[16] Nor were indigenous communities like San Juan Nuevo or Cherán unique in developing viable, transparent local production processes. Native people in several states likewise succeeded in leveraging a heritage of collective decision making (and decades of work as resin tappers) to create successful community enterprises.[17]

A closer look at the history of forest-management policy in twentieth-century Mexico suggests that the destruction of forests stemmed less from rural people's anarchic misuse of the commons than from punitive regulations, official corruption, and poorly conceived development models that transformed forests into political landscapes. Rural people understood that they were in a precarious position, with little capacity to determine how their resources would be used. Forestry experts, Mexico City bureaucrats, and well-connected timber companies had much more influence with the federal government and hence more authority in the woodlands. While a heritage of collective action helped villagers to resist some of the most blatant efforts to wrest away their forests, they almost invariably needed to forge some sort of alliance with outside power-holders. In many instances, they turned to federal foresters posted in the countryside and tasked with overseeing ejidal production. Some of these professionals favored the more "rational" timber companies over community production; these experts had no intention of easing peasant access to the woods. Yet others had been reared on the promises of social justice that marked the Cárdenas years or on the more economistic logic of midcentury conservation practices. For these experts, as for so many rural people, the promises of the revolution might be in abeyance, but they had not disappeared altogether.

THE LEGACIES OF REVOLUTIONARY FORESTRY

The ideology of social justice that emerged from the revolution and inspired the constitution of 1917 opened a middle ground where expert foresters and rural people could arrive at a tentative working arrangement—a sort of ecological praxis—that allowed for both local use and expert oversight of the woods. Such an arrangement was all but inescapable insofar as poor rural people possessed an ever-increasing proportion of the nation's forests, even though the state directly or indirectly controlled their use. Postrevolutionary ideology cast doubt on Porfirian "development" policies, which was reimagined as an ill-considered strategy that granted foreign corporations unimpeded access to natural resources in ways that did little to appreciably improve the domestic economy. Postrevolutionary populism made it both feasible and expedient to enact the variety of populist development I have called "revolutionary forestry," that is, small-scale ejidal production, supervised by professional foresters, that provided rural people a source of income while making available the products necessary to rebuild Mexico's economy.

The experiment with producers cooperatives in the 1930s inaugurated one of the first global experiments in what has become known as "social" or "community" forestry. The cooperatives were predicated on some degree of collaboration between experts and rural people who, in theory, would be incentivized to protect and maintain their own woods to ensure their own economic survival. It is impossible to know whether the cooperatives would have lapsed into corruption and patronage like so many other ejidal organizations of the mid-twentieth century or whether they might have fostered a sense of environmental stewardship among rural people, as in the case of Cusárare, where the cooperative became embedded within existing traditions of community and collective labor. Given that so many village leaders continued to beseech for the right to manage their own woods, it seems clear that at least some people would have consented to a system that combined expert management with local production. Yet the postrevolutionary flirtation with community forestry never came of age. The Second World War and the ensuing developmentalist regime intensified the demand for wood products and opened the door to industrial logging on a scale that doomed the nascent system of ejidal production. Policymakers opened the way for private concerns by suppressing cooperatives in favor of UIEF neoconcessions, logging bans that exempted favored corporations, and the legalization of rental agreements that gave timber interests easy access to ejidal lands.

Peasant timber production and local management ceased to be national priorities, but they did not disappear altogether. Foresters using creative interpretations of logging regulations rechristened cooperatives such as Cusárare's as Forest Management Units (Unidades de Ordenación Forestal, or UOFs), effectively allowing them to endure the adverse regulatory conditions of the 1940s. Within a decade, other UOFs appeared, too. Organizations such as the UOF "Morelos" in northeastern Michoacán comprised multiple ejidos (as well as small private properties and indigenous commons), which they managed on a regional scale, all while injecting the countryside with new sources of income and employment. Federal foresters penned elaborate management plans intended to guarantee sustained-yield logging based on the "Mexican method" of selective extraction. Some UOFs essentially functioned, in other words, like the 1930s-era cooperatives, but on a wider scale. With the advent of paragovernmental enterprises (paraestatales), progressive foresters began to dream of a statewide productive landscape managed by experts and worked by a synergistic combination of village enterprises and timber companies.

Diluted variants of revolutionary forestry persisted in other pockets as well, both on the local level and within the federal bureaucracy. Regional initiatives such as the Coordinating Center of the Tarahumara in Chihuahua (CCIT) or the pine-resin industry promoted by the former president Cárdenas and the Banco Ejidal in the Meseta Purépecha of Michoacán kept the ideal of local production alive. Like the cooperatives, these ventures bonded expert oversight of resource extraction to bootstrapping models of community production. Foresters taught people in both these sites how to cut trees (or make incisions in them), while locally managed sawmills and resin-refining plants provided jobs and training in an industrial setting. Institutional and ecological factors kept many of these projects from scaling up to the national level, but they nonetheless became important platforms for subsequent experiments in community production. Even initiatives such as the UIEF forest concessions of the 1950s and 1960s and the paragovernmental organizations of the 1970s used the rhetoric of social justice and local autonomy to justify their procedures, despite the fact that industrial extraction converted most villagers into passive spectators to the destruction of their forests. Rural people repeatedly expressed disillusionment with these organizations' mismanagement of resources and stingy remuneration; many of them tried to undermine the UIEFs and paraestatales by selling their wood on the black market or abandoning the forests altogether. Yet villagers' exposure to forestry projects, even the mismanaged ones, helped lay the groundwork for the turn to community forestry in the late 1970s and 1980s, by giving them practical knowledge about resource management, industrial practices, and the federal bureaucracy.

These experiences turned out to be more valuable in Michoacán than in Chihuahua. Ejidatarios and indigenous people in the far north had to adapt more frequently to ventures designed for them by outsiders and put into effect with minimal consultation. The CCIT, for example, was the brainchild of the National Indigenist Institute, rather than a local invention. Sympathetic officials such as Francisco Plancarte and the schoolteachers in the Supreme Council of the Tarahumara managed to bend the CCIT's programs more closely to local expectations, but with considerably less success after Plancarte's death, in 1959. Moreover, the immense extension and hence commercial value of forests in the Sierra Tarahumara attracted well-funded logging firms, including those associated with powerful figures like President Miguel Alemán. In this sense, forest wealth constituted a sort of regional "resource curse" that distorted politics and development in Chihuahua.[18] The Rarámuris' historical success in maintaining their distance from mainstream (chabochi) society began to work against them in the twentieth century, because they had few political allies willing or able to take up their struggle.

Land reform beneficiaries in Michoacán, and Purépecha people in particular, confronted some of the same hierarchies as their northern counterparts, but they had several key advantages. In the first place, the history of agrarian militancy and alliance-making with political outsiders paid dividends in the mid-twentieth century. Lázaro Cárdenas and his enduring political dynasty in Michoacán cultivated clienteles in the countryside and paid particular attention to the forestlands. More to the point, the former president helped to build the nation's most dynamic pine-resin industry in his home state and also helped to secure a concession for Michoacana de Occidente. The paraestatal corporation followed the well-trodden path of incompetence and corruption that characterized UIEF concessions, but its resin-buying program generated supplemental income for thousands of poor people, particularly after the 1950 logging ban made tree-tapping the only legal way for most villagers to use their land. Tensions between people who tapped their trees and villagers who wanted to log them became a staple of village politics in the following years (especially after the resumption of statewide logging in 1973), but San Juan Nuevo and a few other villages around Uruapan sidestepped some of these conflicts because they had recognized the potential for selective cutting in the wake of the Paricutín volcano and the sawfly remediation project.

Revolutionary forestry withered in the 1940s, along with many of the other Cardenista initiatives. Wartime demand and postwar industrialism favored commercial production over rural development and sapped the postrevolutionary state's commitment to social-justice initiatives. But revolutionary forestry did leave two key legacies that facilitated the reemergence of community forestry in the final decades of the twentieth century. In the first place, it survived institutionally, as the CCIT, the Banco Ejidal, and some elements of the forest service continued to support village-level production. In the second, it modeled what local control of forestry might look like. Experiments with producers cooperatives, UOFs, unions of ejidos, and other such institutional forms rarely achieved their full potential, but they gestured toward the possibility of community forestry. Unsurprisingly, villages that had positive experiences with midcentury populist initiatives in forestry were home to some of the most successful small-scale enterprises in the 1980s and 1990s.

THE UNSTEADY STATE

It is hard not to interpret Mexico's history of state forestry for most of the twentieth century as a succession of missed opportunities. The single greatest failure of Mexican management policy was that it subordinated the material needs and social aspirations of rural people to a model of development that treated economic growth as an end unto itself and privileged the nation's most influential commercial and political interests. Timber companies, paragovernmental enterprises, and forest-service personnel mouthed platitudes about social justice and shared development throughout the postrevolutionary era and into the 1980s, but most of these institutions treated land reform and the legacies of revolutionary forestry as problems to overcome, rather than as potential assets to mobilize. The legal environment placed significant limits on local production in favor of large-scale, supposedly more rational institutions. In short, Mexican policy for most of the twentieth century disempowered rural people and politicized forest landscapes.

The debacle of twentieth-century forestry was not solely a product of bad politics, however. The institutional structures of land reform also created deep challenges for resource management. As the central institution of agrarian policy, ejidos were not mere plots of land. They organized the most privileged members of rural communities into an officially recognized collectivity that occupied a symbolically and economically significant territory. Ejidos also represented the main administrative bridge between rural people and state institutions such as the forest service. Ejidal leadership committees managed local production, executed contracts with timber companies, supervised sawmills, kept the books, and ensured that villagers (or company lumberjacks) followed forestry-management plans. As development projects grew increasingly complicated, it fell to the ejido and its leadership to ensure that villagers obeyed federal regulations and respected the mandates of project directors. Organizations that operated on a smaller scale than the ejido, such as the producers cooperatives of the 1930s or certain village pine-tapping organizations, often became lightning rods of local controversy because they excluded some ejidatarios, opening themselves to accusations of favoritism and corruption. On the other hand, it was difficult to manage forests on a regional level because entities such as UIEFs and paraestatales routinely discounted villagers' expectations and nourished a sense of resentment and powerlessness. Regional unions of ejidos and management districts fared somewhat better, but they typically lacked the technical capacity or moral authority to implement logging plans. That left the ejido as the primary unit of land management. In many parts of Mexico, forests became a patchwork of individually managed ejidal forests, each with its own leaders, productive routines, and sawmills.

A second structural challenge originated with overambitious proposals to place forests at the center of rural economic development in some of the most desperately poor regions of the country. Experts and land reform beneficiaries routinely overestimated the capacity of forests to generate jobs and revenue, and they allowed these unrealistic expectations to guide their ambitions. Political leaders hoped that small-scale logging projects would inject cash into the countryside and develop the rural economy, while at the same time providing raw materials to timber companies, railroads, and paper mills. Anthropologists such as the ones in the CCIT hoped that employment in the forests and sawmills would coax native people into the nation's cultural and economic mainstream. Most experts understood forests as renewable resources that could be sustainably harvested, whether by local residents or timber companies. And national leaders like Cárdenas and Echeverría portrayed forests as renewable engines of social justice and rural development on a vast scale. Yet the nation's woodlands, extensive though they were, could never meet the crosscutting demands placed on them. Already in the 1970s, some foresters recognized that ejidal forests—including the ones that were "properly managed, milled, and marketed"—could never provide a livelihood for everyone in the burgeoning rural population, much less function as the fulcrums of cultural change or national development.[19] At best, a few mega-ejidos had access to enough timber to keep most or all of their members employed. In most cases, however, more modest projects were the most sustainable, such as the sawmill that provided jobs to a relative handful of people, the logging project that operated seasonally, or the resin-tapping enterprises that supplemented but in most instances did not replace villagers' other sources of income.

One of the greatest shortcomings of state forest policy had less to do with its substantive content than with its inconsistent application and nearly continual revision. The model of management shifted from the revolutionary forestry of the 1930s to the muscular developmentalism of the 1950s and 1960s, to the state forestry model of the 1970s, and finally to the neoliberalism and community forestry of the 1990s and beyond. The unstable regulatory terrain made it difficult for rural leaders to find their footing. It took time for rural people to learn the rules and establish the requisite ejidal institutions and practices associated with each system. Each new change depleted this organizational capital a little bit more and sapped rural people's willingness to comply with the next big plan for the forestlands, no matter how well intentioned. For most of the twentieth century, development-minded politicians and expert foresters tended to interpret rural people's resistance to change as evidence of peasant backwardness and reticence. It may, in fact, have represented an informed response to their precarious legal and institutional circumstances and a prudent strategy for inhabiting a political landscape they could not manage.

Many factors contribute to deforestation. The construction of railroads and highways makes it cheaper and easier to transport sawlogs from woodlands once considered too remote for commercial use. Settlement and colonization typically place new stress on forest ecosystems, especially if the newcomers elect to clear land for agriculture. Wildfires—whether set intentionally or inadvertently—can take a toll, as can shortsighted development policies that encourage unsustainable logging or fail to stem the collateral damage associated with the extraction of oil and minerals. Official incompetence, ambiguous or impotent land-tenure rights, and official incapacity or unwillingness to enforce regulations can undermine forest ecosystems. Measures intended to protect the woods can also backfire and encourage deforestation if they create incentives for landholders to remove certain species or entire stands of trees in a bid to avoid scrutiny from the authorities.[20]

All these factors have contributed to yet another historical phenomenon in twentieth-century Mexico: the transformation of forests into political landscapes, which I understand as spaces where conflicts over the use of forests both provoke and are provoked by state intervention that historical actors regard as illegitimate. The first hints of this process appeared during the Porfiriato, when authorities made woodlands available to foreign corporations at the expense of local populations The revolution accentuated the political character of forests. The state began to hand woodlands over to ejidos and indigenous communities beginning in 1917 and continued to do so until 1992. At the same time, it severely restricted rural people's ecological and productive autonomy. Lázaro Cárdenas and Miguel Ángel de Quevedo initially finessed this disjuncture in the 1930s, by instituting revolutionary forestry, but the development imperative of the postwar years vitiated many social-justice initiatives, promoted large-scale industry, and further politicized the forest landscape. By the final decades of the twentieth century, an incredible tangle of regulations and institutional forms—many of them blatantly ignored by people who lived and worked in the woods—had converted forests into deeply political spaces whose fate depended on negotiations between stakeholders and the state. In part for this reason, Mexico in the early 1990s was losing a larger annual proportion of its forests than was any other major country in the Americas, and it had the fifth highest absolute rate of deforestation in the world.[21]

Yet this trend reversed soon thereafter. By most estimates, Mexico's overall rate of deforestation fell from around 1 percent per annum in the mid-1990s, to 0.5 percent between 1997 and 2002, and then to just over 0.2 percent over the next five years.[22] The dramatic turnabout cannot be attributed to a single factor, but migration from some parts of the country side may have relieved population pressures, while a tenuous economic rebound created alternatives to clandestine logging. Moreover, the expansion of community forestry on a national scale and its increasingly visible success in states such as Oaxaca, Michoacán, Quintana Roo, and Durango helped slow the destruction of temperate forests. For the first time since the 1930s, rural people were in a position to manage (and profit from) their own property using sustained-yield logging techniques. International funding agencies provided working capital and expertise to many of these projects, and communities such as San Juan Nuevo Parangaricutiro have succeeded in training their own cadres of homegrown experts. Some rural people tentatively accepted those tenets of scientific conservation that made sense in their own lives—a process that the anthropologist Andrew Matthews calls "the uneven, halting, and hesitant journey of forestry science into indigenous forest communities."[23] The community-forestry approach cannot work everywhere and has trouble gaining traction in ecosystems like mangroves and dry tropical forests, where woody species regenerate slowly and have little economic value. But it has thrived in regions with commercially viable temperate pine-oak forests, which are precisely where deforestation has slowed the most.[24]

Another factor has been at work as well. As the state has withdrawn from the countryside, forest landscapes have become less politicized. Neoliberalism has limited the forest service's administrative presence and diminished the government's coercive power in the woodlands. Deregulation has not merely opened a space for community forestry, but has reshaped the orientation of rural people, environmental activists, and other stakeholders toward the woods. As access to forests has grown less contingent on seemingly ad hoc regulations and bureaucratic decisions coming from Mexico City or unresponsive rural institutions such as paraestatales, it has become possible to imagine Mexican forests as natural landscapes, albeit ones that remain threatened by many of the same problems as before, including illegal logging, clearing for agriculture, and, in some instances, unclear ownership. The state has continued to set the rules governing resource management, but it has ceded its role as the sole (and

Figure C.2. A forest guard in the Cherán community militia, 2011. Getty/AFP.

oftentimes partisan) arbiter of who has access to the woodlands. For better or worse, rural people have learned to rely not only on regulations and bureaucrats to protect their commons, but also on self-help and appeals to sympathetic outsiders such as NGOs, environmentalists, and the media. Nor is it a coincidence that new environmental movements appeared just as forest landscapes grew less politicized, in the late 1990s and early 2000s. For the first time, rural people and urbanites have been able to join forces to imagine forest ecosystems whose fate they can influence.

Mexican forests are no longer the highly political landscapes they once were, but that does not mean that deforestation no longer represents a threat. Impoverished rural people must still sustain themselves, and many continue to clear the woods or overtax their commons. Conflicts between neighboring villages still provoke acts of arson and clear-cutting in contested territories. Powerful outsiders like timber companies and narco-loggers exploit resources with impunity in many places. Community forestry projects have provided a partial bulwark against these problems, but they cannot function in a vacuum. In many ways, such projects were better off during the era of revolutionary forestry, in the 1930s, when a robust state enforced policies explicitly meant to empower rural people and promote social justice. Indeed, the experience of Cardenismo suggests that the mere application of state authority is not what politicizes forest landscapes; rather, it is the misuse and uneven application of that authority that does so. This may help to explain why many rural people today wish the state would become *more* involved in sustainable-development initiatives. They still need technical assistance, security, and legal protections for their property. Forest management on a regional scale is still required to keep the landscape from becoming a patchwork of ejidal and communal forests.

The people who live in the forestlands and depend on them for material and cultural survival in the early twenty-first century face some of the same challenges as their forebears did in the late nineteenth century. In both historical moments, laissez faire governments turned to private corporations as a means to "develop" the countryside. Both moments were times of personal and collective insecurity made all the more grievous by a mode of economic development that left the rural poor out of the equation. Yet much has changed during the intervening century. Rural people in contemporary Mexico can draw on their own histories of shielding their forest patrimony from the threats posed by outsiders. They can also evoke the best legacies of revolutionary forestry and scientific management. In many places, rural people can draw on practical knowledge built through generations of work in the woodlands, negotiations within their communities, and interaction with professional foresters. This history has made many campesinos skeptical about development projects and "win-win" scenarios that promise to bolster regional economies while changing their own lives for the better. But it has also created a valuable storehouse of knowledge that can help them to balance their needs with the not-so-political landscape they inhabit.

APPENDIX 1

Federal Forestry Codes, 1926–2008

Year	Observations
1926	Establishes conservationist principles; requires producers cooperatives
1942	Allows exclusionary management structures such as UIEFs and logging bans (*vedas*)
1948	Elaboration and clarification of 1942 code; explicitly suppresses cooperatives
1960	"Decentralizes" some management to state forestry councils; allows for paragovernmental corporations
1986	Suppresses UIEFs; restricts rental agreements between communities and timber companies; promotes community forestry enterprises (1)
1992	Deregulation of forestry by breaking Forest Service monopoly on management; diminished support for conservation; contemplates privatization of ejidal forests (2)
2003	Builds on 1992 code; requires long-term planning mechanisms (e.g., forest districts)
2008	Promotes community forestry within broad management districts

(1) Complemented by the 1988 Ley General del Equilibrio Ecológico y la Protección al Ambiente (General Law of Ecological Equilibrium and Environmental Protection), which provided additional encouragement for local production under federal foresters' oversight.
(2) Reformed in 1997 to encourage development of tree plantations.

UIEFs, 1945–1986

Date	UIEF Holder	Location	Duration	Rescinded?
27 March 1945	Cia. Industrial Atenquique	Jalisco, Colima	55 Years	
19 May 1947	Fábricas de Papel Loreto y Pena Pobre	DF, México, Morelos	60 Years	
11 February 1948	Fábricas de Papel de San Rafael y Anexas	México, Puebla, Morelos	60 Years	1992
16 December 1948	Industrial Tlacatepec (Fiszel Sommer)	Guerrero	60 Years	1953
28 July 1949	Maderera del Trópico, Maderas de Yucatán, and Maderas Laminadas	Yucatán	30 Years	1971
15 October 1949	Mario Lopez Llera y Cía & Maderas Impregnadas	Nuevo León	50 Years	1964
25 June 1950	Cia Industrial Maderera San José	Michoacán	60 Years	1954
12 February 1951	La Providencia (Alberto Romo Ortiz)	Durango	30 Years	1953
15 August 1952	Bosques de Chihuahua	Chihuahua	30 Years	1971
21 October 1952	Maderas de Papanoa	Guerrero	50 Years	
6 December 1952	Maderas Campechanas	Campeche	20 Years	
9 December 1952	Telefonia, S. de R. L.	Puebla, Hidalgo	25 Years	1956
12 December 1952	Triplay y Maderas de Durango	Durango	10 Years, Renewable	
18 December 1952	Montes Industrias Minas	México, Michoacán	50 Years	

continued

Date	UIEF Holder	Location	Duration	Rescinded?
4 August 1954	Maderas Industrializadas de Quintana Roo	Quintana Roo	29 Years	
12 January 1955	Michoacana de Occidente	Michoacán	25 Years	1979
29 June 1956	Silvicultura Industrial	Guerrero	25 Years	1976
14 November 1956	Fábricas de Papel Tuxtepec	Oaxaca	25 Years	
12 April 1957	Triplay de Mexico	Oaxaca	25 Years	1960, 1962
28 April 1958	Chapas y Triplay, S.A.	Guerrero	25 Years	
15 October 1958	Compañía Forestal de Oaxaca	Oaxaca	25 Years	
15 January 1964	Bosques de México	Durango	25 Years	
11 May 1964	Federación de Cooperativas de Felipe Carillo Puerto	Quintana Roo	25 Years	1967
8 December 1969	Industrial Forestal del Poniente	Guerrero		
20 March 1972	Productora Forestal Acuitzio y Villa Madero	Michoacán	25 Years	

Sources: José Luis Calva Téllez, ed., *Economía política de la explotación forestal en México: Bibliografía comentada, 1930–1984* (Texcoco: Universidad Autónoma de Chapingo, 1989), 421–439; Secretaría de Agricultura y Ganado, "Indice de disposiciones legislativas sobre agricultura, ganadería y recursos forestales y de caza," unpublished typescript, 1962; Roque Oscar Aguilar Espinoza, "Organización forestal en México," Seminario de Titulación, Universidad Autónoma de Chapingo, 1990; AGN, SARH/PF, caja 902, exp. 37555; *Diario Oficial*.

NOTES

Escuela Nacional de Antropologia e Historia, Sede Chihauhua – ENAH
 Documentos del Centro Coordinador Indigenista de la Tarahumara – CCIT
 expediente (exp.); legajo (leg.)
John Hamilton McNeely Papers, University of Texas at El Paso Library – JHM
 legajo (leg.)
Registro Agrario Nacional – RAN

INTRODUCTION

1. Population figures are based on Basauri, *Monografía de los tarahumaras*, 13; Antonio H. Sosa, "Exploración forestal en la Alta Sierra Tarahaumara del Estado de Chihuahua," *Boletín del Departamento Forestal de Caza y Pesca* 3.9 (December 1937–Februrary 1938), 197.

2. Sosa, "Exploración forestal en la Alta Sierra Tarahaumara del Estado de Chihuahua," 222.

3. Foresters often displace their existing knowledge onto new and unfamiliar landscapes, at least until they learn more about it. See Langston, *Forest Dreams, Forest Nightmares*, 20–41.

4. Antonio H. Sosa, "A través de la Tarahumara," *México Forestal* 29.4 (July–May 1965): 1–4, continued in 29.5 (September–October 1965): 1–4, p. 4:1.

5. Sosa, "A través de la Tarahumara," 4:1.

6. Sosa, "A través de la Tarahumara," 4:3.

7. Acta de infracción, 2 November 1955, AGN, SARH/PF, caja 192, exp. 23855, leg. 1.

8. Nicolás Villalobos to Enrique Beltrán, 22 March 1961, AGN, SARH/PF, caja 152, exp. 3. The full quotation reads (textually, with errors and all): "Nosotros les preguntamos a todos y a cada uno de Uds. ¿no creen que los que nacimos en este suelo; Aunque ese terreno no sea nuestro, nosotros somos de él? Somos hijos de esa Tierra, y como hijos creémos tener mas derecho que un Influllente que por tener dinero se lleve todas las riquezas de esos Bosques, sin recibir nosotros ni siquiera consideraciones.

"Estos Bosques Dios los Crió para todos sus hijos; nosotros hemos cresido juntos con ellos, los hemos defendidi de los incendios; pero los que se nos llevan, nunca se han charrascado un dedo por defenderlos."

9. Consejo Supremo Tarahumara to Presidencia de la República, 10 June 1960, ENAH, CCIT 15/25/9, doc. 6. For an early example of complaints about bureaucracy, see Benjamín González et al. to Lázaro Cárdenas, 13 July 1936, AGN, SARH/PF, caja 192, exp. 23855, leg. 1; Roberto Barrios to Secretaría de Agricultura, 21 September 1948, AGN, SARH/PF, caja 197, exp. 29952, leg. 1.

10. See Matthews, *Instituting Nature*.

11. For overviews, see Challenger, *Utilización y conservación de los ecosistemas terrestres de México*, 75–93; and Redowski, *Vegetación de México*, 91–96.

12. For the big picture, see Williams, *Deforesting the Earth*.

13. Aguirre Beltrán, *Regiones de refugio*.

14. Tsing, *Friction*, 16. See also Scott, *Seeing Like a State*, 11–52. For an ecologist's critique of simplification, see Maser, *The Redesigned Forest*.

15. Guha, *The Unquiet Woods*, 48–61, 69–72; Peluso, *Rich Forests, Poor People*, 50–72. Both of these authors regard scientific forestry as a form of social control. For a case study in 1820s France, see Sahlins, *Forest Rites*; and in the United States, Kosek, *Understories*, 65–102.

16. Matthews, "Suppressing Fire and Memory."

17. Agrawal, *Environmentality*, 164–65, 167–81.

18. This ironic turn of phrase headlines a 1972 book denouncing technocratic rule and the endemic shortage of credit in the land reform sector. See Warman, *Los campesinos, hijos predilectos del regimen*.

19. For a discussion of landscape and territoriality, see Radding, *Landscapes of Power and Identity*, esp. 5–8.

20. Boyer, *Becoming Campesinos*.

21. I am not the first to recognize the relationship between politics and environmental degradation. Several studies have attributed deforestation to insecure property rights, for example, or to the incapacity to enforce environmental regulations. See the pathbreaking work of Deacon, "Deforestation and the Rule of Law in a Cross-Section of Countries"; and Mendelsohn, "Property Rights and Tropical Deforestation."

22. For definitions of *commons* and *ejidos*, see the preface.

23. Here, I follow the definition of a commodity offered by Arjun Appadurai, who interprets commodities as "economically valuable objects that nevertheless have their own biography, their own commonly-agreed-upon history, social meaning, and social value." See Appadurai, "Introduction," 32.

24. Compare with "Autoridades indígenas buscan fortalecer la política Rarámuri," *La Jornada*, 13 June 2000.

25. Matthews, "Unlikely Alliances."

26. On "legibility," see Scott, *Seeing Like a State*.

27. Today, the archive is located in the National Archives (AGN). On nomenclature for the forest service, see the preface.

28. Torres-Rojo and Flores-Xolocotzi, "Deforestation and Land Use Change in Mexico."

29. Scholars have done relatively little to investigate the relationship between environmental change and migration in Mexico. For a view from Africa, see White, *Climate Change and Migration*.

30. Migration alone is not enough to protect forests, although it can offer a partial respite. See Klooster, "Forest Transitions in Mexico."

31. For an overview, see Bray, Merino-Pérez, and Barry, "Community Managed in the Strong Sense of the Term."

32. Barsimantov and Kendall, "Community Forestry, Common Property, and Deforestation in Eight Mexican States."

33. Among the numerous examples, see Challenger, *Utilización y conservación de los ecosistemas terrestres de México*, 201–65; Klooster, "Campesinos and Mexican Forest Policy during the Twentieth Century"; Merino Pérez, *Conservación o deterioro*, 175–234; and Weaver, "Neoliberalism and the Social Relations of Forestry Production in the Sierra Tarahumara."

34. "Exposición de motivos que funda el proyecto de la ley forestal y de Arboledas," *México Forestal* 1.1 (January 1923): 10–17, 12.

35. See Wakild, *Revolutionary Parks*.

36. Villaseñor, "Los Bosques de México," 9.

1. THE COMMODIFICATION OF NATURE, 1880–1910

1. For an overview, see Hart, *Empire and Revolution*, 173–267.

2. Hale, *Transformation of Liberalism in Late Nineteenth-Century Mexico*, 219–31; Weiner, *Race, Nation, and Market*, 33–42.

3. Holden, *Mexico and the Survey of Public Lands*, 16–22.

4. Holden, *Mexico and the Survey of Public Lands*, 159–66.

5. On growing inequality within villages, see Knight, *The Mexican Revolution*, 2:112–15. On popular-class attraction to private ownership, see Kourí, *A Pueblo Divided*, 157–86.

6. Santiago, *The Ecology of Oil*, 61.

7. On Michoacán, see Friedrich, *Agrarian Revolt in a Mexican Village*, 41–56. On Morelos, see Tortolero Villaseñor, "Water and Revolution in Morelos."

8. Salvia Spratte, *Los Laberintos de Loreto y Peña Pobre*, 30–37; Haber, *Industry and Underdevelopment*, 46–47, 96–99.

9. Coatsworth, *Growth against Development*.

10. On Oaxaca and Puebla, see H. S. Beattie to Secretario de Fomento, 8 November 1910, AGN, SB, caja 8, exp. 25.

11. Vos, *Oro verde*; Evans, "King Henequen."

12. On Chihuahua, see below. For Cuanajo, see AHPEM, Hijuelas, libro 11, Pátzcuaro, foja 112–12v, Cuanajo, 24 January 1878. Thanks to Juan Manuel Mendoza for bringing this document to my attention.

13. Population statistics derive from the 1900 census, which underestimated the native population at 41,035.

14. Lumholtz, *Unknown Mexico*, 2:363.

15. Ruiz, *Michoacán*, 199–202, 65–71.

16. Lumholtz, *Unknown Mexico*, 2:366.

17. See the historical analysis in Unidad Industrial de Explotación Forestal Michoacana del Occidente, "Proyecto General de Ordenación Forestal," typescript, Uruapan, December 1959, 77–78, COMFORMICH.

18. Beltrán, *Los recursos naturales de México*, 6; Vázquez, "Los actos depredatorios del hombre en la conservación forestal," 60, 64.

19. Romero, *Noticias para formar la historia y la estadística del obispado de Michoacán*, 86; Anonymous report to Francisco Múgica, 1916, AHCERM, FJM, DS, 6/1218; Report of Adolfo Espino Arpio, 3 December 1915, AHCERM, FJM, DS, 5/1064a.

20. Hinojosa, *Memoria*, 22, 23.

21. Waldemar Díaz, "Plan de Explotación," 15 December 1958, AGN, SARH/PF, caja 880, exp. 32298, leg. 1; see also the case of the Anguiano family in Parangaricutiro in AGN, SARH/PF, caja 746, exp. 1839.

22. See, for instance, the case of Los Alzati (Zitácuaro district), AGN, SARH/PF, caja 3–2, exp. 275, leg. 1.

23. See, e.g., Juárez Flores, "Alumbrado público."

24. Hinojosa, *Memoria*, 24.

25. Report of Luis Varela Ponce de León, 13 June 1963, AGN, SARH/PF, caja 917, exp. 40678, leg. 1.

26. Guzmán Ávila, *Michoacán y la inversión extranjera*, 39–67.

27. *Diario Oficial*, 26 August 1893.

28. Díaz, "Plan de Explotación," 15 December 1958, AGN, SARH/PF, caja 880, exp. 32298, leg. 1.

29. Francisco Carvajal Ch., "Informe de revisión de gabinete . . . San Lorenzo," 30 April 1965, AGN, SARH/PF, caja 753, exp. 2333, leg. 2.

30. "Proyecto general de ordenación . . . ," by Ing. Régulo García M. and David Bello M., 30 September 1964, AGN, SARH/PF, caja 768, exp. 2393, vol. 1.

31. López Maya, *Ciudad Hidalgo*, 168–69.

32. These were Tingambato, Cirucat, San Angel, and Comachuén. See Guzmán Ávila, *Michoacán y la inversión extranjera*, 109–11.

33. Guzmán Ávila, *Michoacán y la inversión extranjera*, 115.

34. Vázquez, *Diagnóstico estatal*, 8.

35. Guzmán Ávila, *Michoacán y la inversión extranjera*, 125–28; Sánchez Díaz, "Reparto y resistencia en las comunidades nahuas de la costa de Michoacán."

36. Guzmán Ávila, *Michoacán y la inversión extranjera*, 129.

37. Anonymous report to Francisco Múgica, 1916, AHCERM, FJM, DS, 6/1218; Purnell, "With All Due Respect."

38. Vidal Aguilar Soto and Felipe Ruiz Anguianoto to Comisión Mixta Agraria, 18 April 1977, AGN, SARH/PF, caja 746, exp. 1839, vol. 5.

39. Ramírez, *La verdad sobre la Revolución Mexicana*, 1:139–42.

40. Some of the crooked village representatives that Governor Mercado named on behalf of Slade's company included Lic. Ignacio Hernández for Paricutín, Nabor Flores for Capácuaro, and Vicente Gómez for Parangaricutiro. Anonymous report to Francisco Múgica, 1916, AHCERM, FJM, DS, 6/1218; Report of Adolfo Espino Arpio, 3 December 1915, AHCERM, FJM, DS, 5/1064a.

41. For an overview, see Aboites, *Breve historia de Chihuahua*, 118–25.

42. Hart, *Silver of the Sierra Madre*, 105–21.

43. Complaint of Luis Musy et al., 15 October 1901, CIDECH, RB, P&T, SA, caja 34, exp. 7.

44. Hart, *Silver of the Sierra Madre*, 62–63. On the history of cyanide, see Edward Beatty, "'*El más sutil proceso de química*': Cyanide and the Transformation of Mining in Mexico," forthcoming.

45. Hart, *Silver of the Sierra Madre*, 25.

46. W. S. Kirby Buurt to Departamento de Agricultura, 1 August 1910, AGN, FO, SB, caja 8, exp. 17.

47. The Rio Grande, Sierra Madre and Pacific Railway, inaugurated in 1896, connected Ciudad Juárez with Casas Grandes; its subsidiary, the Sierra Madre and Pacific, pushed further south. Most of the third railroad, the Chihuahua and Pacific, was built between 1899 and 1900, although it was not formally completed until 1905. It ran westward from the main line of the National Railway, which crossed through Chihuahua City into the heart of the Sierra Madre, through Madera and Pearson (now Mata Ortiz). For histories, see unsigned, undated "History" (ca. 1904), JHM, box 8, fol. 8; and French, "Business as Usual," 221–38.

48. Unsigned, undated "History," JHM, box 8, fol. 8.

49. Spude, "Frank Morrill Murphy."

50. Report entitled "Sierra Madre Country," n.d. (ca. 1904), JHM, box 8, fol. 11.

51. Report entitled "Sierra Madre Country," n.d. (ca. 1904), JHM, box 8, fol. 11; unsigned report dated at Prescott, Arizona, 24 June 1903, JHM, box 8, fol. 11.

52. Almada and Martínez, "El Norte," 157–58; Padilla Sánchez, "Estudio forestal del Estado de Chihuahua," 34; Report of Alberto García Balda, 4 August 1944, AGN, SARH/PF, caja 1576 (antes Chihuahua 2–1), exp. 2/402, leg. 13.

53. Emilio Flores Calderón, "Proyecto de Ordenación por Reserva Forestal Nacional Papigochic," 28 February 1945, AGN, SARH/PF, caja 202, exp. 34270, leg. 4, "Reserva de Papigochic"; Antonio H. Sosa, "Exploración forestal en la Alta Sierra Tarahumara del Estado de Chihuahua," *Boletín del Departamento de Caza y Pesca* 3.9 (December 1937–February 1938), 187–235, p. 200; Hart, *Empire and Revolution*, 174–77.

54. JHM, box 10, fol. 1, file S-10.

55. G. B. Schley to H. C. Ferris, 6 January 1908, JHM, box 8, correspondence book entitled "Confidential."

56. Report of Alberto García Balda, 4 August 1944, AGN, SARH/PF, caja 1576 (antes Chihuahua 2–1), exp. 2/402, leg. 13.

57. Ignacio Ruiz Martínez, "Expediente relativo a la inspección practicada al Ferrocarril Noroeste de México," 18 December 1924, AGN, SARH/PF, caja 1577 (antes Chihuahua 2–3), exp. 2/402, leg. 1. See also "Manufacturing and Sales Estimate for Six months ending 12/31/10," JHM, box 10, fol. 1, file S-9.

58. "Estimates of Cash Requirements Account New Capital," 1910, JHM, box 10, fol. 1, file S-1; Padilla Sánchez, "Estudio forestal del Estado de Chihuahua," 41.

59. "La industria forestal en el Estado de Chihuahua," *El Correo de Chihuahua*, 11 November 1910.

60. Walter M. Brodie to Jefe Político de Batopilas, 5 October 1887, and depositions later that month, in CIDECH, RB, P&T, SJ, caja 3, exp. 39.

61. Testimony of Refugio Hernández, Juan Gutiérrez, and José María Meza, 5 October [*sic*.; should be September] 1887, CIDECH, RB, P&T, SJ, caja 3, exp. 39.

62. Hart, *Silver of the Sierra Madre*, 186–88.

63. "Averiguación," 12 August 1909, CIDECH, RB, P&T, SJ, caja 3, exp. 8; Francisco Salazar, 29 August 1927, AGN, SARH/PF, Chihuahua, caja 152–53.

64. Deeds, *Defiance and Deference*, 67–80, 108–24.

65. Gonzalo Aguirre Beltrán to Alfonso Caso, 18 June 1952, ENAH, CCIT 47.3.5, doc. 1.

66. Lumholtz, *Unknown Mexico*, 1:139–43; Zingg, *Behind the Mexican Mountains*, 67–73; Kennedy, "Tesguino Complex."

67. Lumholtz estimated 25,000, according to *Unknown Mexico*, 1:119. The Comisión Nacional Agraria made a detailed census in 1926–1927 that enumerated 28,000; however, the lead surveyor estimated that the actual population was closer to 40,000. Bennett and Zingg, *The Tarahumara*, vii. The 1900 general census enumerated 19,778 "Tarahumara" speakers in Chihuahua, which is likely an undercount.

68. Speech by Roberto Gonzalez to Club Rotario de Monterrey, 1962, ENA/C, ENAH, CCIT, caja 7, exp. 13, fol. 6a; Plancarte, *El problema indígena tarahumara*, 33.

69. Bennett and Zingg, *The Tarahumara*, 42–44, 48–77. See also Schwatka, *In the Land of the Cave and Cliff Dwellers*, 230–33.

70. Plancarte, *El problema indígena tarahumara*, 65.

71. Lumholtz, *Unknown Mexico*, 1:127.

72. Reports of Hilario Espinoza, 5 February 1895, and Martín Ramos, 8 January 1895, CIDECH, RB, P&T, SJ, caja 1, exp. 4.

73. Letter from Trinidad Martínez et al., 18 May 1898, CIDECH, RB, P&T, SJ, caja 1, exp. 4. See also Vanderwood, *The Power of Guns against the Guns of Government*, 135–38.

74. The 1812 Cádiz constitution specifically charged ayuntamientos with administration of the woods (*montes*), a provision that appears to have remained in effect until it was reaffirmed by Antonio López de Santa Anna in 1855. See Dublán and Lozano, *Legislación Mexicana*, vol. 1, doc. 96 and vol. 7, doc. 4401.

75. For a narrative of this progression in the case of water, see Aboites, *El agua de la nación*, 81–89.

76. Dublán and Lozano, "Reglamento expedido por el Ministerio de Fomento á que deben los cortadores de árboles en terrenos nacionales," *Legislación Mexicana*, vol. 9 (18 April 1861), doc. 5315.

77. See Vos, *Oro verde*, 75–100; Konrad, "Tropical Forest Policy and Practice during the Mexican Porfiriato."

78. García Martínez, "Legislación forestal," 236–37.

79. The total value of wood production was approximately 10 million pesos in 1890 and 31 million pesos a decade later. Data from Dirección General de Estadística, *Estadístico de la Republica Mexicana*, 1893 and 1900.

80. "Reglamento para la explotación de los bosque y terrenos baldíos y nacionales" [Law of 1 October 1894], in Villamar, *Leyes federales*, 52–79.

81. On desiccation theory, see Grove, *Green Imperialism*, 156–57, 168–263.

82. Humboldt and Bonpland, *Personal Narrative of Travels to the Equinoctial Regions of the New Continent*, 4:143. See 4:134–60 for a full elaboration. Humboldt and Bonpland's narrative was translated and published in Spanish in 1826.

83. Humboldt, *Political Essay on the Kingdom of New Spain*, 60. Humboldt's essay appeared in Spanish in 1822.

84. Rómulo Escobar, "Las lluvias en México," 7, 55–56.

85. Desiccation theory was too widespread to trace exhaustively here; an early case was made in Hinojosa, *Memoria*, 1, and repeated in Bárcena, *Selvicultura*, 3–5. Desiccation theory became a part of the national curriculum for forest wardens (compare with *Cartilla Forestal*, vol. 2). It was still widely believed by the educated classes at least through the 1950s. See the three-part series by Hans Lenz in *Excelsior*, 23–26 December 1957.

86. Bárcena, *Selvicultura*, 54.

87. The theory of hygienic forests and their effects on miasmas was likewise extremely widespread. Notable discussions include Hinojosa, *Memoria*, 10–11; and Guzmán, "Climatología de la República Mexicana," 181–85.

88. Rómulo Escobar, "Las lluvias en México," 7.

89. Simonian, *Defending the Land of the Jaguar*, 57–58.

90. Rómulo Escobar, "Las lluvias en México." On the use of river water for irrigation, see Tortolero Villaseñor, "Water and Revolution in Morelos"; and Aboites, *El agua de la nación*.

91. Edicto No. 50, reproduced in Pérez Gil, *Primer inventario de los bosques y montes de Michoacán*, viii–ix.

92. See a list of concessions in Secretaría de Agricultura y Fomento, *Memoria de la Primera Convención Nacional Forestal*, 123–38; on the lawsuit, see *Dictamen del Lic. Andrés Horcasitas*, 3–15.

93. Quevedo, *Relato de mi vida*, 9–37. On torrentialism in French thought, see Whited, *Forests and Peasant Politics in Modern France*, 56–74.

94. Miguel Ángel de Quevedo, "Las Resoluciones . . . ," *México Forestal* 18.3–4 (March–April 1940): 20–24.

95. Report of Gilberto Crespo Martínez, April 1896, and other documents in AGN, FO, SB, caja 3, exp. 1; Quevedo, *Relato de mi vida*, 37–46.

96. See the discussion of the conference in Konrad, "Tropical Forestry Policy and Practice during the Mexican Porfirato," 133–35.

97. Report of Junta Central de Bosques, 1910–1911, AGN, FO, SB, caja 68, exp. 9. See also *Revista Forestal Mexicana* 1 (1909), 16–17.

98. Kalaora and Savoye, *La forêt pacifiée*, 15–46. The French contingent included George Lapie, Edmond Bournet, Lucien Gainet, Henry Burces, and Eugène Beaux. See Vásquez de la Parra, "Reminiscencia histórica."

99. *México Forestal* 14.9–10 (September–October 1936), 76.

100. Presupuesto Dirección de Bosques, 1912–1913, AGN, FO, SB, caja 30, exp. 4; *México Forestal* 14.9–10 (September–October 1936), 76 and 16.10–12 (October–December 1938), 61–62. In the Federal District, trees were planted in Desierto de los Leones, Acopilco, Santa Fe, Villa de Guadalupe, and Texcoco.

101. Vitz, "La ciudad y sus bosques," 138.

102. Vitz, "La ciudad y sus bosques," 138; *Cartilla Forestal*, no. 3: *Reforestación* (Mexico City: Secretaría de Fomento, 1911), 55–57; Bárcena, *Selvicultura*, 50–52.

103. Federico Reyes to Jefe del Departamento de Bosques, 10 August 1910, AGN, FO, SB, caja 68, exp. 12.

104. Hart, *Empire and Revolution*, 122.

2. REVOLUTION AND REGULATION, 1910–1928

1. McCaa, "Missing Millions."

2. Notable exceptions include Aboites, *El agua de la nación*; Cotter, *Troubled Harvest*; and Santiago, *The Ecology of Oil*.

3. Miguel Ángel de Quevedo, "Exposición de motivos que funda el Proyecto de la Ley Forestal de Arboleadas," *México Forestal* 1.1 (January 1923): 10–17, p. 10.

4. On Quevedo's concerns, see chapter 1 in this volume. For a complementary view by one of his followers, see Salvador Hernández Barrón, "La influencia de los desmontes en la disminución de las aguas corrientes," *México Forestal* 7.1 (January 1929): 1–7.

5. Miguel Ángel de Quevedo, "Alocución," reprinted in *México Forestal* 1.2 (February 1923): 18–20, p. 19.

6. Guha, *The Unquiet Woods*, 59.

7. For case studies of the mismanagement of the early land reform, see Craig, *The First Agraristas*; Fallaw, *Cárdenas Compromised*; Gledhill, *Casi Nada*; Nugent, *Spent Cartridges of Revolution*; and Warman, *Y veninos a contradecir*.

8. On the agrarian elements of the revolution, see Gilly, *La revolución interrumpida*; Katz, *The Life and Times of Pancho Villa*; Knight, *The Mexican Revolution*. For a discussion of communities that at least partially accommodated to market society, see Kourí, *A Pueblo Divided*.

9. For workers and the revolution, see Guerra, *México*; and Lear, *Workers, Neighbors, and Citizens*.

10. For interpretations that emphasize nationalism, see Gilly, *La revolución interrumpida*, and Hart, *Revolutionary Mexico*.

11. For treatments of Zapatismo, see Brunk, *Emiliano Zapata*; and Womack, *Zapata and the Mexican Revolution*. On the Plan de Ayala, see appendix 1 in Womack, *Zapata and the Mexican Revolution*.

12. Falcón, "San Luis Potosí," 149.

13. Vos, *Oro verde*, 229.

14. Vos, *Oro verde*, 228–39.

15. Miguel Ángel de Quevedo, "La necesaria acción conjunta en pro de la higiene y del aprovechamiento de los recursos naturales en México," *México Forestal* 6.9 (September 1928): 167–72.

16. Miguel Ángel de Quevedo, "Feliz coincidencia climáctica que produce grandes bienes a nuestra Nación," *México Forestal* 16.10–12 (October–December 1938): 61–62.

17. Katz, *The Life and Times of Pancho Villa*, 291–92.

18. Ruiz Martínez, "Discurso," 56.

19. M. Sánchez (Xochimilco) to Jefe del Departamento de Bosques, 10 November 1914, AGN, FO, SB, caja 71, exp. 46.

20. Miguel Ángel de Quevedo, "La Riqueza Forestal de México," paper presented at the 1918 meeting of the Sociedad de Geografía y Estadística, reprinted (with annotations) in *México Forestal* 1.3 (March 1923): 1–13. The specific areas where timber companies ceased operations included Milpa Alta, Xochimilco, Cumbres de Maltrata, and the eastern slopes of the Pico de Orizaba range. Chihuahua is discussed below.

21. H. S. Beattie to Secretario de Fomento, 8 November 1910; "Informe" of Dirección de Bosques, 23 November 1910, AGN, FO, SB, caja 8, exp. 25.

22. Marcos V. Méndez to Gobernación, 30 July 1911, quoted in Knight, *The Mexican Revolution*, 1:107.

23. The major exception was the area around Zitácuaro, where Joaquín Amaro and his lieutenants did recruit among peasant villages. See *El Baluarte* (Zitácuaro), 14 February 1926.

24. Oikión Solano, *El constitucionalismo en Michoacán*, 337–40.

25. These events are mentioned in Knight, *The Mexican Revolution*, 1:220 and 1:350. On the Mirabeau-Rothschild properties, see Guzmán Avila, "Michoacán en vísperas."

26. Oikión Solano, *El constitucionalismo en Michoacán*, 333–35.

27. Quevedo, "Riqueza." The specific areas where timber companies ceased operations included Milpa Alta, Xochimilco, Cumbres de Maltrata, and the eastern slopes of the Pico de Orizaba.

28. Report of Miguel Silva, 26 July 1911, AHPEM, Bosques, caja 2, exp. 5.

29. The expansion of commerce was hardly uncommon during the revolution. In addition to the case of the Madera Company discussed below, see Womack, "The Mexican Economy during the Revolution."

30. Report of Adolfo Espino Arpio, 3 December 1915, AHCERM, FJM, DS, 5/1064a; Calderón, "*Caciquismo* and *Cardenismo* in the Sierra Purépecha, Michoacán," 136.

31. Zacarías Gómez Urquiza to Secretaría de Gobernación, 20 June 1921, AGN, DGG, B.2.71–107, caja 4, exp. 2.

32. H. I. Miller to P. C. Theade, 11 March 1912, JHM, box 10, fol. 2, unnumbered file.

33. Anon. report to F. S. Pearson, 7 February 1914, JHM, box 10, fol. 1, file S-1.

34. On capital investments, see "Estimates of Cash Requirements Account New Capital," 1 March 1910–1 January 1911, JHM, box 10, fol. 1, file S-1; and M. A. Leach to H. C. Smith, 29 August 1911, JHM, box 10, fol. 1, file S-2.

35. Unsigned telegram (Pearson?) to Pearmiler, 27 February 1912, JHM, box 10, fol. 2, file S-8.

36. French, "Business as Usual," 226–27.

37. Madera Company to Sr. General Don Victoriano Huerta, 27 September 1912, JHM, box 10, fol. 1, file S-1; on the United States, see H. I. Miller to Thomas P. Littlepage, 26 April 1912, JHM, box 10, fol. 2, file S-8; and on Villa, see H. I. Mille to Luis Riba, 13 January 1914, JHM, box 11-A, fol. 1.

38. Unsigned letter (J. O. Crockett?) to Hiram C. Smith, 18 March 1911, JHM, box 10, fol. 1, file S-15. On slingshots, see J. M. Peek to P. C. Thede, 6 September 1913, JHM, box 11, fol. 5.

39. Parra Orozco, *Madera*, 61–62.

40. Beezley, "State Reform during the Provisional Presidency," 531.

41. J. M. Peek to P. C. Thede, 6 September 1913, JHM, box 11, fol. 5; unsigned letter (E. H. Clark?) to the American Council in Chihuahua City, 23 August 1913, JHM, box 10, fol. 1, file S-15; *El Paso Times-Democrat*, 25 August 1913.

42. Translation of coded telegram (no writer or recipient named), February 1912, JHM, box 10, fol. 2, file S-8.

43. Report of Alberto García Balda, 4 August 1944, AGN, SARH/PF, caja 1576

(a.k.a. Chihuahua 2–1), exp. 2/402, leg. 13, 1944. On Orozqista sympathies, see below and J. M. Peek to P. C. Thede, 6 September 1913, JHM, box 11, fol. 5.

44. F. L. Kinsman to A. M. Trueb, 23 August 1913, JHM, box 10, fol. 1, file S-15.

45. J. O. Crockett H. I. Miller, 23 August 1913, JHM, box 10, fol. 1, file S-15.

46. Ruiz Martínez, "Discurso."

47. Ruiz Martínez, "Discurso," 21–23, 39.

48. For an overview, see López, *Crafting Mexico*, esp. 65–94, 127–35.

49. Quevedo, *Relato de mi vida*, 40.

50. The language giving the nation the right to regulate the use of natural resources did not appear in the original version of Article 27, drafted by Pastor Rouaix and his collaborators. It was inserted by the review committee (the Primera Comisión de Constitución), headed by Francisco J. Múgica and Enrique Colunga. See Rouaix, *Génesis de los artículos 27 y 123 de la Constitución Política de 1917*, 175, 184–86.

51. For an overview, see Tobler, "Peasants and the Shaping of the Revolutionary State."

52. Córdova, *La ideología de la revolución mexicana*, 177–87.

53. Nugent, *Spent Cartridges of Revolution*, 91. On the desire by Chihuahua communities to receive restitution rather than grants, see 88–92.

54. Hall, "Alvaro Obregón and the Politics of Mexican Land Reform," esp. 213–15.

55. See, for example, "Informe del Consejo Directivo o de Gerentes ante la Asamblea General de Accionistas Propietarios, acerca de los trabajos llevados a cabo durante el año Social dd 1922 a 1923," by Miguel Ángel de Quevedo (pres) and Ángel Roldán (srio), 27 February 1923, *México Forestal* 1.4 (April 1923): 21–23.

56. Miguel Ángel de Quevedo, "Alocución," reprinted in *México Forestal* 1.2 (February 1923): 18–20, p. 19.

57. Roque Martínez, "Cooperativas ejidales: Determinación de zonas forestales y agrícolas: Reglamentación del pastoreo," *México Forestal* 8.4 (April 1930): 67–69, p. 68.

58. Report of Salvador Guerrero, 23 September 1922, AGN, SARH/PF, caja 1577 (antes Chihuahua 2–3), exp. 2/402, leg. 1.

59. "La necesidad de una política de protección forestal de parte de nuestras empresas Ferrocarrileras," *México Forestal* 2.5–6 (May–June 1924): 43–45, p. 43.

60. Ángel Roldán, "Las delegaciones municipales y la cuestión forestal," *México Forestal* 7.8 (August 1929): 165–68, p. 167.

61. "Explotaciones Colectivas," by Ing. Forestal Sergio Barojas A., presented at the Congreso Forestal Mexicano, 3a mesa, reproduced in *México Forestal* 8.5 (May 1930): 90–92, p. 90.

62. Compare with "Sección Administrativa," in *México Forestal* 1.4 (April 1923): 21–23 and in *México Forestal* 3.5 (May 1925): 43–46.

63. Miguel Ángel de Quevedo, "Exposición de Motivos que funda el Proyecto de la Ley Forestal de Arboleadas," *México Forestal* 1.1 (January 1923): 10–17, pp. 10, 11. For a history of *México Forestal*, see Cortez Noyola, "*México Forestal.*"

64. "La necesidad de una política de protección doestal de parte de nuestras empresas Ferrocarrileras," *México Forestal* 2.5–6 (May–June 1924), 7–9.

65. Undated "Circular" of Ramón P. de Negri, circa May 1922; and "Decreto" of Alvaro Obregón, 4 October 1923, both in AGN, PR, SOC, 121-A-B-3.

66. Secretaría de Agricultura y Fomento, *Ley forestal y su reglamento*, 6.

67. Sebastian Bautista Madrigal to Lázaro Cárdenas, Uruapan, 16 November 1938, AHCERM, LC, caja 32. See also Miguel Angel de Quevedo, "Informe sobre los principales trabajos desarrollados por el Departamento Forestal y de Caza y Pesca durante el año de 1936," *Boletín del Departamento Forestal y de Caza y Pesca* 2.6 (March 1937): 1–12, p. 4.

68. See the enacting legislation (*reglamento*) of the 1926 forest code in Secretaría de Agricultura y Fomento, *Ley forestal [de 1926] y su reglamento*, especially chapters 6 (on communal, ejidal, and municipal land) and 7 (on private land).

69. *Ley Forestal [de 1926]*, 51–57.

70. *Ley Forestal [de 1926]*, chap. 1, article 33, p. 12.

71. "Informe sobre la necesaria aplicación de medidas tendientes a corregir las malas prácticas en la Explotación de los Bosques de México," *México Forestal* 7.11 (November 1929): 228–32; Presidente Municipal de San José Allende to Gerardo González, 21 August 1907, AHPEM, Bosques, caja 1, exp. 16.

72. Boyer, "Revolución y paternalismo ecológico." Other interpretations include Hinojosa Ortiz, *Los bosques de México*, 25–28; Klooster, "Conflict in the Commons," 122–29; and Simonian, *Defending the Land of the Jaguar*, 82–84.

73. Domínguez Rascón, *La política de la reforma agraria en Chihuahua*, 79–95; Wasserman, *Persistent Oligarchs*, 34–37.

74. Domínguez Rascón, *La política de la reforma agraria en Chihuahua*, 44–48.

75. Alonso, *Thread of Blood*; Nugent, *Spent Cartridges of Revolution*.

76. Daniel F. Galicia, "Plan de Explotación del Predio denominado Chihuahua Lumber, Bocoyna," October 1928, AGN, SARH/PF, caja 152, exp. 1227. On the use of wood as fuel, see Proyecto General de Ordenación Forestal, Unidad de Ordenación Forestal "Industrial Río Verde," August 1968, AGN, SARH/PF, caja 158.

77. L. R. Hoard, undated memorandum [ca. 25 February 1921], JHM, box 11-B, fol. 2, file S-4.

78. Vatant, "Un ejido forestal de la alta Tarahumara," 45.

79. Data from Domínguez Rascón, *La política de la reforma agraria en Chihuahua*, "Anexo," 159–62.

80. Decreto presidencial, 9 June 1937, AGN, SARH/PF, caja 261, exp. 18064, leg. 1.

81. Rodolfo Rodríguez Caballero, "Proyecto General de Ordenación Forestal,

Unidad de Ordenación Forestal "Industrial Río Verde," August 1968, AGN, SARH/ PF, caja 158.

82. "Acta," by Inspector General A. Martínez, San Juanito, Bocoyna, 4 December 1927, AGN, SARH/PF, 152–53; Sociedad de Padres y Maestros de la Escuela de Bahuinocachi (Bocoyna) to Adolfo López Mateos, 8 June 1961, AGN, SARH/PF, caja 153, exp. "Protección Forestal." See also Molinari Medina, "Protestantismo y explotación forestal," 26–28.

83. Daniel F. Galicia, "Plan de Explotación," October 1928, AGN, SARH/PF, caja 152–53. See transcription of Esteban L. Almeida to Agencia General, 21 November 1930, AGN, SARH/PF, caja 152, exp. 1227.

84. Report of Daniel F. Galicia, 30 April 1928, AGN, SARH/PF, caja 152–53.

85. Alcocer Patiño, *Un siglo en el bosque*, 112–13.

86. "Únicamente pequeños bosquetes vírgenes," according to Armando Fuentes Flores (n.d. in 1961), AGN, SARH/PF, caja 152–53. See also report of Armando Fuentes Flores, 23 August 1960, AGN, SARH/PF, caja 1575 (antes Chihuahua 1–2), exp. 2/28, leg. 5; and report of Martín López Astudillo, 6 April 1961, AGN, SARH/ PF, caja 152–53.

87. Agente General de la Secretaría de Agricultura y Fomento (Chihuahua) to Director Forestal y de Caza y Pesca, 23 June 1927, AGN, SARH/PF, caja 152, exp. 844. See also the memo from Director Interino DFCP Celistino Coq, 29 June 1927, in the same folder.

88. "Es de lamentar que nuestras autoridades Forestales autorizen ó apoyen á personas de origen extrangero como al citado Señor Broks para que maten neustra riqueza Forestal cinninguna consideración racional humana, menos patriotica" [multiple spelling errors in the original]. C. B. Silva (Urique) to Secretaría de Agricultura y Fomento (Chihuahua), 24 July 1927, AGN, SARH/PF, caja 152–53.

89. Report of Compañía Industrial Mercantíl, n.d. [ca. March 1939], AGN, SARH/PF, caja 152–53.

90. On Galicia, see Report of Roberto Barrios, 23 January 1948, AGN, SARH/ PF, caja 1575 (antes Chihuahua 1–2), exp. 2/28, leg. 3. On González Ugarte, see Rodolfo Rodríguez Caballero, "Proyecto General de Ordenación Forestal, Unidad de Ordenación Forestal 'Industrial Río Verde,'" August 1968, AGN, SARH/PF, caja 158.

91. On agrarian leaders in Michoacán, see Boyer, *Becoming Campesinos*; Friedrich, *Agrarian Revolt in a Mexican Village*; and Guerra Manzo, *Caciquismo y orden público en Michoacán*.

92. ASARCO to Enrique Ramírez, 23 July 1925; and Secretaría de Gobernación (Michoacán) to Secretaría de Gobernación (D.F.), 2 September 1925, AGN, DGG, E.2.71–135.

93. Examples include the petitions filed by the barrio of San Francisco (Uruapan), as discussed in the amparo of José Encarnación Jiménez, 17 December

1928, AHPEM, Amparos, caja 266, exp. 9; and the amparo on behalf of Tingambato brought by Manuel Tercero on 15 March 1922, AHPEM, Amparos, caja 212, exp. 27.

94. See, for example, the armed conflict on the hacienda Atecuario, per the transcript of meeting in the *presidencia municipal*, 29 October 1931, AMZ, Justicia, 1931, exp. 3.

95. Representante Agraria de Atécuaro to Procuraduría de Pueblos, 16 December 1924, AHMM, caja 75, exp. 9.

96. Ejidatarios rancho Coro Grande to Secretaría de Gobernación, 6 February 1929, AHMM, caja 99, exp. 19.

97. Report of Vicente Cedillo, 17 April 1925, AHPEM, Amparos, caja 238, exp. 3.

98. For a discussion, see Ginzberg, *Lázaro Cárdenas*, 206–14.

99. *El Gráfico* (Mexico City), 19 February 1938. See also Cenobio E. Blanco, "La Ley Forestal," *México Forestal* 7.2 (February 1929): 25–27; and *El Universal*, 2 January 1936. On the species favored for charcoal making, see comments by the president of the Unión de Productores, Introductores, Detallistas y Despachadores de Carbón Vegetal de la República, in *El Universal*, 7 November 1951.

100. Report of Pedro Roa V., 18 September 1925, AGN, DT, caja 841, exp. 3.

101. Joaquín Iranzo to Secretaría de Agricultura y Fomento, 7 June 1927; and Pomposo Solís to Secretaría de Agricultura y Fomento, 9 July 1926, both in AGN, SARH/PF, Michoacán caja 4–2, exp. 364, leg. 1.

102. Alfonso Escudero to Gobernador, 8 October 1926, and Salvador Guerrero to Jefe del Distrito Forestal en Michoacán, 29 June 1926, AGN, SARH/PF, Michoacán caja 1–1, exp. 107, leg. 1.

103. Vecinos of Aputzio to Presidente de la República, 28 September 1927, AGN, DGG, 2.321 (13)-1 (caja 2). On social conditions, see the report of Cuca García, 28 August 1922, AHSEP, caja 747, exp. 49.

104. Report of Secretaría del Estado, 7 November 1927, and the report of José J. Parres, 2 January 1928, in AGN, DGG, 2.321 (13)-1 (caja 2).

3. REVOLUTIONARY FORESTRY, 1928–1942

1. Report of Andrés Orozco, 26 December 1929, AGN, SARH/PF, caja 719, exp. 8600.

2. In this sense, villagers had the capacity to behave very much like a "closed corporate community," in Eric Wolf's terms. However (as Wolf also foresaw), some members of these same communities might welcome outsiders or fragment in such a way that one or more factions *sought out* allies from outside the village—for example, allies within the forest bureaucracy—once they no longer faced a common threat. For the original discussion of the closed corporate community, see Wolf, "Closed Corporate Peasant Communities in Mesoamerica and Central Java."

3. Report of Andrés Orozco, 28 February 1930, AGN, SARH/PF, caja 719, exp. 8600.

4. This discussion is inspired in part by Arun Agrawal's reflections on the making of environmental subjects in *Environmentality*.

5. In 1930, for example, President Pascual Ortiz Rubio suggested that forest products might ultimately prove more valuable to the nation than petroleum, insofar as forests were a renewable resource. "Unificar las labores," *El Nacional,* 10 September 1930.

6. For an overview of popular responses to postrevolutionary social projects, see Knight, "Revolutionary Project, Recalcitrant People." See also the pivotal discussions in Joseph and Nugent, *Everyday Forms of State Formation.*

7. McCook, *States of Nature,* 47–76.

8. Eduardo García Díaz, "La conservación de las maderas industriales," *México Forestal* 4.5–6 (May–June 1926): 50–53; "La conveniente reserva forestal de propiedad de la nación," *México Forestal* 3.8–9 (August–September 1925): 107–10. At a later point, Díaz also suggested that Mexican requirements for the production of railroad ties were *more* stringent than in Europe, meaning that some otherwise useful stands of timber were never put into production. See his "Algunas consideraciones . . . ," *México Forestal* 6.1 (January 1928): 4–6.

9. Miguel Ángel de Quevedo, "Discurso de inauguración del Primer Congreso Forestal Mexicano," *México Forestal* 8.3 (March 1930): 31–35, p. 31.

10. Miguel Ángel de Quevedo, "La quema de pastos es la causa principal del incendio de nuestros bosques," *México Forestal* 6.12 (December 1928): 233–37, p. 235.

11. Roberto Gayol, "La Repoblación como Problema Nacional," *México Forestal* 8.11–12 (November–December 1930): 269–76, p. 273.

12. See for example "La Unión Nacional de Resineros," *México Forestal* 7.7 (July 1929): 145–46; and Ricardo Lezama y Michel, "La Resinación en el Estado de Durango," *México Forestal* 8.6 (June 1929): 124–25.

13. "Exposición de motivos que funda el proyecto de la ley forestal y de Arboledas," *México Forestal* 1.1 (January 1923): 10–17, p. 13.

14. Ignacio E. Zepeda, "La Repoblación Forestal," *México Forestal* 8.5 (May 1930): 93–94, p. 93.

15. In addition to the discussion in chapter 1, see Montes Eduardo García Díaz, "Conferencia dedicada a la Fiesta del Arbol," *México Forestal* 3.2 (February 1925): 26–29, p. 29.

16. Quevedo, "Alocución," *México Forestal* 1.2 (February 1923): 19–20, p. 19. On Michoacán, see circular 12 of the Dirección General de Educación Pública, 15 February 1920, AMZ, Instrucción Pública, 1920, exp. 12.

17. "La Fiesta del Árbol en San Angel, D.F.," *México Forestal* 2.3–4 (March–April 1924): 34–35.

18. See, for example, the "Conferencia dedicada a la Fiesta del Árbol" given by forest warden Eduardo García Díaz in the Colonia Acera of Compañía Fundidora de Fierro y Acero de Monterrey, 8 February 1925, printed in *México Forestal* 3.2 (February 1925): 26–29.

19. See, for example, the photographs of schoolchildren and community leaders planting trees in Mexico City, Michoacán, and Yucatán during the 1938 Arbor Day celebrations, in *México Forestal* 16.1 (January–March 1938): 8–9.

20. "Acta," Cofradía (Túxpan), 18 February 1927, AHSEP, caja 7221, exp. 8.

21. "Discurso pronunciado en la Fiesta del Árbol, organizada por la Secretaría de Agricultura en el Bosque de Chapultepec, por el Sr. General Francisco J. Mújica [*sic*]," *México Forestal* 12.2 (February 1934): 39–40, p. 39.

22. "Las Fiestas del Día del Árbol en el año de 1938," *México Forestal* 16.1 (January 1938): 6–7, p. 7.

23. "Las 'Fiestas del Árbol' en el Presente Año," *México Forestal* 17.1 (January–March 1939): 27–28, p. 28.

24. *Boletín del Departamento Forestal y de Caza y Pesca* 1.4 (August 1936): 52–54, pp. 52–53.

25. *Boletín del Departamento Forestal y de Caza y Pesca* 2.7 (April–August 1937): 8–12, p. 10.

26. "La Palpitante Cuestión Forestal," *El Gráfico*, 17 August 1929.

27. Fabián G. Sánchea et al. to Departamento Forestal, 17 March 1933, AGN, SARH/PF, Serie Michoacán caja 3–2, exp. 275, leg. 1.

28. Jefe del Departamento de Bosques Salvador Guerrero to Jefe del Distrito Forestal de Michoacán, 29 June 1926, AGN, SARH/PF, Serie Michoacán, caja 1–1, exp. 107, leg. 1.

29. On national parks, see Wakild, *Revolutionary Parks*. On the parks and reserves, see Secretario de Agricultura y Ganadería, "Indice general de disposiciones legislativas sobre agricultura, ganadería y recursos forestales y de caza," unpublished manuscript, 1962, available in the library of the Comisión Forestal Estatal de Michoacán in Morelia. On the progress of reforestation, see the "Informes" published in the *Boletín del Departamento Forestal y de Caza y Pesca* between 1936 and 1939. On the bans, see chapter 4 of this book, as well as Calva Téllez et al., *Economía política de la explotación forestal en México*, app. 4. The best overview of conservation during the Cárdenas presidency remains Simonian, *Defending the Land of the Jaguar*, 85–110.

30. Cárdenas decreed the establishment of the Departamento Autonomo Forestal y de Caza y Pesca on 29 December 1934. The description of personnel is based on an organizational chart printed on the inside of each issue of *Boletín del Departamento Forestal y de Caza y Pesca*, published 1935 to 1940, and on Julio Riquelme Inda, "Tres años de campaña forestal," in the *Boletín del Departamento Forestal y de Caza y Pesca* 4.12 (September–November 1938), 119–27.

31. "Programa de trabajos . . . ," *Boletín del Departamento Forestal y de Caza y Pesca* 1.4 (August 1936): 217–27.

32. "Existencias . . . ," *Boletín del Departamento Forestal y de Caza y Pesca* 4.12 (September–November 1938): 266–30, p. 266.

33. Agrawal makes a similar point with regard to the (far earlier) consolidation of scientific knowledge of forests in India (see *Environmentality*, 39, and 32–39 more generally). On the relationship between expertise and resource governance, see Mitchell, *The Rule of Experts.*

34. Quevedo, *Relato de mi vida*, 63–64.

35. Boyer, *Becoming Campesinos*, 226–29. On the massive push to organize the popular classes, see Córdova, *La política de masas del Cardenismo.*

36. These were San Nicolás Totolapan, Magdalena Contreras, San Bartolo Ameyalco, San Mateo Tlaltenango, Acopilco, and San Salvador Cuatenco. See Francisco Salazar, José Gutiérrez, and Felipe Santibáñez, "Criterio de la Comisión N. Agraria respeto a la Organización Económica que debe darse al Sistema de Explotación Forestal en Terrenos Comunales y Ejidales," *México Forestal* 8.4 (April 1930): 78–81; "Las Cooperativas Forestales," *Boletín del Departamento Forestal y de Caza y Pesca* 2.7 (April–August 1937): 98–110, pp. 100 and 108.

37. In addition, there were twenty-seven cooperatives comprising smallholders, renters, and people working in national forests. See "Informe mensual," *Boletín del Departamento Forestal y de Caza y Pesca* 4.12 (September–November 1938): 1–10, p. 5; Departamento Agrario, *Memoria del Departamento Agrario, 1941–1942*, 232.

38. Sergio Barojas A., "Explotaciones colectivas," *México Forestal* 8.5 (May 1930): 90–92. Another presenter at the conference arrived at essentially the same conclusion; see Roque Martínez, "Cooperativas ejidales," *México Forestal* 8.4 (April 1930): 67–69, p. 68.

39. "Cooperativas para explotación de bosques," *El Nacional*, 7 May 1934; Armando Mancilla Chávez and Manuel Caballero Olguín, "Los Estados," *Agricultura*, (July–August 1938): 1–6.

40. Salvador Guerrero, "Conveniencia de que el Estado Controle Técnica y Económicamente la Producción Forestal," *Boletín del Departamento Forestal y de Caza y Pesca* 2.7 (April–August 1937): 121–33.

41. On the discounts, see "Resumen," *México Forestal* 16.1–3 (January–March 1938): 1–3, p. 2. On charcoal makers, see *El Nacional*, 20 January 1938.

42. "Cooperativas para explotación de bosques," *El Nacional*, 7 May 1934.

43. See, for example, Salvador Guerrero, "Conveniencia de que el estado controle técnica y económicamente la producción forestal," *Boletín del Departamento Forestal y de Caza y Pesca* 2.7 (April–August 1937): 123–24.

44. "Informe . . . ," *Boletín del Departamento Forestal y de Caza y Pesca* 2.6 (January–March 1937): 1–12, p. 4.

45. "Informe . . . ," *Boletín del Departamento Forestal y de Caza y Pesca* 4.12 (September–November 1938): 1–12, p. 5.

46. Michoacán's 91 cooperatives thus accounted for slightly more than 10 percent of the 866 cooperatives in the nation, second only to the State of Mexico's 216 cooperatives. An unknown number of informal cooperatives also existed whose leaders had never filled out the proper paperwork. See Departamento Agrario, *Memoria 1941–1942*, 155, 161, 232.

47. Juan Contreras and Srio Féliz Joaquín to Jefe Delegación Forestal, 31 July 1936, AGN, SARH/PF, caja 896, exp. 36119, leg. 1.

48. The emergence of resin tapping and the role of the Banco Nacional de Crédito Agricola in providing subsidies are discussed below. For Cárdenas's decree exempting cooperatives from 50 percent of the fees and taxes for logging, see the *Periódico Oficial*, 8 November 1936.

49. Report of Graciano Sánchez, 3 February 1938, AGN, SARH/PF, caja 880, exp. 32298, leg. 1.

50. Acta de investiagación, Charapan, 23 October 1938, and report of David Riquelme, 7 July 1939, AGN, SARH/PF, caja 880, exp. 32298, leg. 1.

51. "Acta y Bases . . . ," 26 March 1937, AGN, SARH/PF, caja 719, exp. 14027.

52. Acta, 15 December 1937, AGN, SARH/PF, caja 719, exp. 14027.

53. Report of Luis Sánchez Sandoval, 19 July 1940, AGN, SARH/PF, caja 822, exp. 19937, leg. 1.

54. Reynaldo Torres to Agente de la Secretaría de Agricultura en Uruapan, 19 February 1941, AGN, SARH/PF, caja 822, exp. 19937, leg. 1.

55. Reynaldo Torres to Agente de la Secretaría de Agricultura en Uruapan, 19 February 1941, AGN, SARH/PF, caja 822, exp. 19937, leg. 1.

56. Reynaldo Torres to Agente de la Secretaría de Agricultura en Uruapan, 7 June 1941, AGN, SARH/PF, caja 822, exp. 19937, leg. 1.

57. The verbatim quote is: "Anda gente del Pueblo soloquehesdefuera i tumbando madera sin marquear es parte que hasta hen Beda" [spelling errors in original]. "Algunos Siudadanos del Pueblo de Cheran" to Departamento Forestal, 12 February 1940, AGN, SARH/PF, caja 896, exp. 36119, leg. 1.

58. Report of Estidígrafo Agustín Calderón Rodríguez, 12 November 1940, AGN, SARH/PF, caja 896, exp. 36119, leg. 1.

59. Vecinos de Cherán, n.d. (ca. January 1941), AGN, SARH/PF, caja 896, exp. 36119, leg. 1.

60. On the organization that Cárdenas created as governor, see Hernández, *La Confederación Revolucionaria Michoacana del Trabajo*; and Boyer, *Becoming Campesinos*, 190–95.

61. Sebastian Bautista Madrigal to Lázaro Cárdenas, 16 November 1938, AHCERM, LC, caja 32. He had established cooperatives in Capacuaro (Uruapan),

Pomocuarán (Paracho), San Felipe de los Herreros (Charapan), and Ahuíran (Paracho).

62. See copies of the presidential declarations in *Boletín del Departamento Forestal y de Caza y Pesca* 3–4 (1936–1937). Also during 1936, Cárdenas established nine national parks, but these were principally intended as nature reserves to attract tourists, not as instruments to protect over-exploited forests. See Simonian, *Defending the Land of the Jaguar*, 94–100; and Wakild, *Revolutionary Parks*. The bans are discussed in greater detail in chapter 4.

63. See Miguel Ángel de Quevedo, "Recorrido," *Boletín del Departamento Forestal y de Caza y Pesca* 2.5 (September–December 1936): 137–42.

64. "Acta" in Capácuaro, 1 September 1941, AGN, SARH/PF, Michoacán, caja 2–3, exp. 212, leg. 2; BNCA to Lázaro Cárdenas, 12 December 1938, AHERMLC, LC, caja 32. See also Gaspar González (BNCA) to Representante Forestal Uruapan, 4 October 1941, and BNCA to Director Dirección General Forestal, 22 September 1943, both in AGN, SARH/PF, Michoacán, caja 2–3, exp. 212, leg. 2.

65. See for example Graciano Sánchez to Dirección Forestal y de la Caza y Pesca, 3 February 1938, and other correspondence in AGN, SARH/PF, caja 822, exp. 19937, leg. 1.

66. Report of Jesús Ceja Banajas, 8 October 1941, AGN, SARH/PF, Michoacán, caja 2–3, exp. 212, leg. 2; report of David Riquelme, 7 July 1939, AGN, SARH/PF, caja 880, exp. 32298, leg. 1.

67. González de la Cadena, "Sugestiones para una mejor organización de los núcleos campesinos," 165.

68. For example, Vecinos Paracho to Presidente de la República, 27 February 1939, AGN, SARH/PF, caja 848, exp. 23528, leg. 1.

69. Boyer and Wakild, "Social Landscaping in the Forests of Mexico." See also González y González, *Los artífices del Cardenismo*.

70. "Decreto Presidencial" regarding Rochéachi, 9 June 1937, AGN, SARH/PF, caja 261, exp. 18064, leg. 1.

71. Julián Guerra et al. to Secretaría de Agricultura y Ganadería, 24 December 1933, AGN, SARH/PF, caja 261, exp. 18064, leg. 1. See also Basauri, *Monografía de los tarahumaras*, 33–34.

72. Basauri, *Monografía de los tarahumaras*, 13–15, 42–43.

73. Schwatka, *In the Land of the Cave and Cliff Dwellers*, 242–45.

74. Basauri, *Monografía de los tarahumaras*, 64–65.

75. A typical example can be found in the Decreto Presidencial for El Nogal y Anexos, 16 April 1940, AGN, SARH/PF, caja 152, exp. 543.

76. Molinari Medina, "Protestantismo y explotación forestal en la Tarahumara," 38–40.

77. Antonio H. Sosa, "Exploración forestal en la Alta Sierra Tarahumara del Estado de Chihuahua," *Boletín del Departamento de Caza y Pesca* 3.9 (December

1937–February 1938): 185–235, p. 234. Foresters were still complaining about goats three decades later: see Luis Espejel D., "Plan Provisional de Explotación" (Bocoyna), 20 April 1967, AGN, SARH/PF, caja 192, exp. 23855, leg. 2.

78. "En fin deseamos darle ser a este Pueblo que los indígenas se nivelen con los blancos y sean al fin buenos Ciudadanos y útiles a su Patria." Transcription of Comisariado Ejidal de Guachochi to Producador Comunidades Indígenas, n.d. (ca. June 1937), AGN, SARH/PF, caja 190, exp. 23605, leg. 1. Indigenous community leaders also expressed interest in forestry projects a few years later, during the 1939 Primer Congreso de la Raza Tarahumara: see report of Prof. Rafael Castro, 7 June 1939, AGN, SARH/PF, caja 190, exp. 23605, leg. 1.

79. Benítez, *Los indios de México*, 107–9; Juan F. Treviño to Departamento Forestal, 8 September 1937, and Juan F. Treviño to Jefe de la Guardia Forestal en San Juanito, 29 November 1939, AGN, SARH/PF, caja 190, exp. 23605, leg. 1.

80. The original mill had a capacity of 500,000 board feet per day, whereas the new one had a capacity of 150,000. Padilla Sánchez, "Estudio forestal del Estado de Chihuahua," 49–50, 73. The company owned 1,141,641 hectares outright and leased another 300,000 from the San José Babícora hacienda; half a million hectares were classified as forest. See Daniel F. Galicia, "Plan de Explotación," 24 September 1928, AGN, SARH/PF, caja 1573 (antes Chihuahua 2–4), exp. 2/402, leg. 2.

81. The microclimate depended on altitude: 1,500–2,000 meters had oak, Mexican piñon pine (*Pinus cembroides*), sugar pine (pinabete or *P. lambertiana*); 2,000–2,250 meters had ponderosa pine (*P. ponderosa*) and Jeffrey pine (pino negro or *P. jeffreyi*); 2,250–2,500 meters had Chihuahua pine (*P. leiophylla* var. *chihuahuana*), bristlecone pine (*P. aristada*), southwestern white pine (*P. strobiformis*); 2,500–3,000 meters had Chihuahua pine, Douglas firs (*Pseudotsuga*), and others. Daniel F. Galicia, "Plan de Explotación," 24 September 1928, AGN, SARH/PF, caja 1573 (antes Chihuahua 2–4), exp. 2/402, leg. 2.

82. Daniel F. Galicia, "Plan de Explotación," 24 September 1928, AGN, SARH/PF, caja 1573 (antes Chihuahua 2–4), exp. 2/402, leg. 2. On the taxes, see Daniel F. Galicia and Adolfo E. Galicia, "Proyecto de Ordenación," July, AGN, SARH/PF, caja 1573 (antes Chihuahua 2–4), exp. 2/402, leg. 2.

83. Memorandum, 18 July 1928, JHM, box 8, fol. 2.

84. Padilla Sánchez, "Estudio forestal del Estado de Chihuahua," 74–75; Parra Orozco, *Madera*, 62.

85. Padilla Sánchez, "Estudio forestal del Estado de Chihuahua," 40.

86. Transcription of Departamento de Bosques to Compañía Maderera y Manufacturera, S.A., 7 July 1932, AGN, SARH/PF, caja 1573 (antes Chihuahua 2–4), exp. 2/402, leg. 3; transcription of Procuraduría de Comunidades Indígenas to Departamento de Asuntos Indígenas, 13 December 1939, caja 1574 (antes Chihuahua 2), exp. 2/402, leg. 7, 1939.

87. Raul Vargas, "Proyecto de Explotación," June 1944, AGN, SARH/PF, caja 195, exp. 29942.

88. "End of an Empire," *Time*, 7 September 1953. On Socorro Rivera and Babícora, see Palomares Peña, *Propietarios norteamericanos y reforma agraria en Chihuahua*, 124–29.

89. The ejidos of Pichachí, Arisiachi, Tomachi, Guadalupe, and Bocoyna received a paltry 12,295 hectares. Palomares Peña, *Propietarios norteamericanos y reforma agraria en Chihuahua*, 26–27.

90. In addition to Antonio Guerrero, the members of the group that became Maderas de Chihuahua, S.A., included Alvaro Guerrero García, José Amézquita de los Pinales, Eduardo Guerrero Peralta, Simón Ventura Neri, Adolfo Trespalacios, Greagorio Castañeda V., Jacobo L. Castro, Eugenio Caballero, J. J. Gil Sandoval, Fidel Toledo Gómez, Felipe Naveda Rosario, Mario Velazquez V., Gregorio Ponce, and Carlos Alvarez Q. See Emilio Flores Calderón, "Proyecto de Ordenación for Reserva Forestal Nacional Papigochic," 28 February 1945, AGN, SARH/PF, caja 202, exp. 34270, leg. 4. On Guerrero's seizure of the Ojo Caliente hacienda, see Wasserman, *Persistent Oligarchs*, 114. On his purchase of the box-making plant, see Parra Orozco, *Madera*, 62. As we shall see in chapter 4, Antonio Guerrero sold his company in the mid-1950s to Eloy S. Vallina Jr. and Carlos Trouyet, the founders of Grupo Chihuahua, the parent company of the huge forestry concern Bosques de Chihuahua, S.A., which became one of northern Mexico's largest corporations.

91. See Flores Calderón, "Proyecto . . . ," 23 March 1944, AGN, SARH/PF, caja 202, exp. 34270, leg. 4; and Agencia General Forestal de Chihuahua to Compañía Maderas de Chihuahua, 20 September 1950, AGN, SARH/PF, caja 202, exp. 34270, leg. 5.

92. Benjamín González et al. to Lázaro Cárdenas, 13 July 1936, AGN, SARH/PF, caja 192, exp. 23855, leg. 1. See also the BNCE's memorandum of 17 August 1936 memorandum, in the same file.

93. Abraham González and Ignacio Carrasco to Director de Organización Ejidal, 27 October 1943; and Luis Espejel D., "Plan Provisional de Explotación," 12 November 1943, AGN, SARH/PF, caja 192, exp. 23855, leg. 1.

94. Abraham González and Ignacio Carrasco to Director de Organización Ejidal, 27 October 1943; and Luis Espejel D., "Plan Provisional de Explotación," 12 November 1943, AGN, SARH/PF, caja 192, exp. 23855, leg. 1.

95. On "grandfathering" existing producers cooperatives, see Waldemar Díaz, "Plan de explotación," 3 October 1947, AGN, SARH/PF, caja 896, exp. 36119, leg. 2. On the 1949 forestry code, see chapter 4 in this volume.

96. Instituto Nacional de Investigación Forestal en México, *50 años de investigación forestal en México*, 9–10.

97. Miguel Ángel de Quevedo (D.F.) to Manuel Ávila Camacho, 19 April 1944, AGN, PR, MAC, 501.1/79.

98. Simonian, *Defending the Land of the Jaguar*, 107–8.

99. *El Nacional*, 18 January 1938.

100. "Informe," *Boletín del Departamento Forestal y de Caza y Pesca* 3.7 (April–August 1937): 90–91.

101. According to one estimate, ejidos produced a mere 2 percent of the nation's commercial output in 1936, the only year for which such data are available. On the other hand, it is likely that this figure does not include the railroad ties, electrical poles, and other productions fashioned by rural communities and then sold to sawmills and lumber company. See *Excelsior*, 25 December 1936.

102. Miguel Ángel de Quevedo, "Anteproyecto del plan sexenal para el periodo 1941–1946 . . . ," *Boletín del Departamento Forestal y de Caza y Pesca* 4.14 (March–May 1939): 1–18, p. 1.

103. "Informe mensual," *Boletín del Departamento Forestal y de Caza y Pesca* 4.13 (December 1938–February 1939): 1–12, p. 2. For an example of a contratista who had never managed to control his largely indigenous workforce, see Antonio Alarcón, "Informe de paso de anualidad," 12 August 1947, AGN, SARH/PF, caja 192, exp. 23855, leg. 1.

104. The only other community in the highlands with such an arrangement was in Heredia, but that one never got off the ground. See Roberto Barrios to Dirección General Forestal y de Caza, 23 January 1948, AGN, SARH/PF, caja 1575, exp. 2/28, leg. 3.

105. Alcocer Patiño, *Un siglo en el bosque*, 78.

106. Emilio Flores Calderón, "Plan Provisional de explotación," 23 March 1944, and Guillermo Pischansky Miguel to Agente General de la Secretaría de Agricultura, 8 December 1944, AGN, SARH/PF, caja 196, exp. 29882, leg. 1.

107. Transcription of letter from Confederación Nacional Campesina to Dirección General Forestal y de la Caza, 4 June 1947, AGN, SARH/PF, caja 202, exp. 34270, leg. 4.

108. Padilla Sánchez, "Estudio forestal de Estado de Chihuahua," 40.

4. INDUSTRIAL FORESTS, 1942–1958

1. I explore the concept of regimented empowerment in *Becoming Campesinos*, 226–29.

2. Data from Walsh Sanderson, *Land Reform in Mexico*, app. E, 164–65.

3. For an overview, see Babb, *Managing Mexico*, 75–87.

4. For an overview, see Hewitt de Alcántara, *La modernización de la agricultura mexicana*.

5. This is the evocative formulation of Tsing, *Friction*, 21.

6. Examples include Alemán Valdés, *Un México mejor*, 3:180–85; and Adolfo Ruiz Cortines, "Se proyecta la planificación de la industria forestal del país," *El Popular*, 3 May 1957.

7. Víctor M. Arreola to Secretaría de Agricultura y Ganadería, 9 May 1955, AGN, SARH/PF, caja 245, exp. 54603, leg. 1, part I.

8. See the series of articles in *Excelsior* instigated by the journalist Rodrigo del Llano's call for nationalization on 6 September 1958. Del Llano was responding in part to a series of articles that the former forestry secretary Enrique Beltran had published beginning on 1 September 1958 in *El Universal*, the first of which said it all with the title "El desastre forestal."

9. Benítez, *Los indios de México*, 80.

10. Felipe Cuara Echeverría to Departamento Forestal, 2 September 1947, AGN, SARH/PF, caja 745, exp. 1938, leg. 2. The idea continued to have purchase among rural people, at least in some instances, until well into the 1970s. See Ejido Sorobuena (Chihuahua) to Cuauhtémoc Cárdenas, 31 May 1978, AGN, SARH/PF, caja 161, exp. 2958, leg. 11.

11. Miguel Ángel de Quevedo, "Anteproyecto del plan sexenal para el periodo 1941–1946 . . . ," *Boletín del Departamento Forestal y de Caza y Pesca* 4:14 (March–May 1939): 1–18, pp. 4–9.

12. Ávila Camacho, "Convocatoria," 3–4.

13. Vázquez, "Los actos depredatorios del hombre en la conservación forestal," 60, 64.

14. Vázquez, "Los actos depredatorios del hombre en la conservación forestal," 67.

15. Fifty-one of the convention's 179 global recommendations dealt with questions of commercial development. See *Memoria de la Primera Convención Nacional Forestal*, 29–32.

16. González de la Cadena, "Sugestiones para una mejor organización de los núcleos campesinos," 164.

17. See Dictamen Pericial by Ings. Juan Manuel González, Ricardo Tecanhuey M., Miguel Esquivias O., and Emilio Flores Calderón, 15 April 1957, AGN, SARH/PF, caja 246, exp. 54603, leg. 3.

18. Mexico, *Nueva ley forestal y reglamento* (1942), 5–6. On industrialists' involvement in writing the new law, see Salvia Spratte, *Los laberintos de Loreto y Peña Pobre*, 72.

19. Hinojosa Ortiz, *Los bosques de México*, 91–97.

20. Mexico, *Nueva ley forestal y reglamento* (1951), 7.

21. Mexico, *Nueva ley forestal y reglamento* (1942), 3.

22. *Novedades*, 9 August 1950; *El Universal*, 16 June 1951. A list of presidential

orders quashing the cooperatives can be found in Calva Téllez, *Economía política de la explotación forestal en México*, 418–35.

23. Mexico, *Nueva ley forestal y reglamento* (1942), 3, 6.

24. Mexico, *Nueva ley forestal y reglamento* (1942), 2, 8; Mexico, *Nueva ley forestal y reglamento* (1951), 11–12, 59–60.

25. In addition, there were nineteen smaller vedas established by the forest service itself, including eleven in Mexico state alone. See Secretaría de Economía, *Anuario estadístico . . . 1957*, 815, tables 212 and 213; and Barrena, "Zonas Forestales Vedadas."

26. *El Universal*, 5 December 1939. The ban had actually been declared in 1937, but the forest service did not try to enforce it until three years later.

27. Nicolás J. Banda to Manuel Ávila Camacho, Mexico City, 5 November 1944, AGN, PR, MAC, 501.1/5; see also Gerez Fernández, "¿Qué pasa en el Cofre de Perote?" 152.

28. *El Universal*, 13 March 1940. See also *El Nacional*, 12 March 1940. González was Secretario de Acción Campesina de la Federación de Trabajadores del Estado de Veracruz.

29. *Excelsior*, 25 April 1959; Benito Coquet to Director General de Información, Mexico, 15 July 1946, AGN, PR, MAC, 545.22/573.

30. "Indice general de disposiciones legislativas sobre agricultura, ganadería y recursos forestales y de caza," unpublished manuscript (1962), available in the library of the Universidad Autónoma de Chapingo. Statewide bans were declared in Aguascalientes (1940); Mexico State, Puebla, and the Federal District (1947); Jalisco (1949); Michoacán and Querétaro (1950); Colima and Guanajuato (1951); and Veracruz (1952). Partial moratoria were declared for most forested districts of Tlaxcala (1940); Hidalgo (1947); Chihuahua, Durango, Sinaloa, Sonora, and Tamaulipas (1949); and Nayarit (1951).

31. Ferreyra Soriano, "Las vedas forestales en México y sus consecuencias," 52.

32. For an analysis of the 1930s-era moratoria, see Barrena, "Zonas Forestales Vedadas."

33. For careful analyses, see Report of Guarda Forestal Sexta Luis Sánchez Sandoval, 19 July 1940, AGN, SARH/PF, caja 822, exp. 19937, leg. 1; and Report of Jesús Zárate Hernández, 5 September 1977, AGN, SARH/PF, caja 799, exp. 2–6625.

34. Nacional Financiera, S.A., "Proyecto Celulosa de Michoacán," unpublished typescript (1958), AGN, SARH/PF, caja 806; Merino Pérez, *Conservación o deterioro*, 45–46.

35. In addition to the discussions below, see Klooster, "Conflict in the Commons," 129–35.

36. *Excelsior*, 30 October 1957; *Memoria de la Primera Convención Nacional Forestal*, 146.

37. *Boletín Forestal*, "Visita del Sr. Subsecretario . . . ," 15 May 1951, 15.

38. *Excelsior*, 16 June 1946. For specific examples of companies' efforts to win exemptions, see Salvia Spratte, *Los laberintos de Loreto y Peña Pobre*, 71–75, on Loreto y Peña Pobre; and on the Dos Estrellas Mine, see the voluminous correspondence between managers and the forest service during the 1940s, in AGN, SARH/PF, caja 902, exp. 37555, leg, 1, discussed in greater detail below.

39. Alcocer Patiño, *Un siglo en el bosque*, 21; *Excelsior*, 11 May 1957.

40. Mexico, *Nueva ley forestal y reglamento* (1942), 3; Roberto Barrena, "Unidades de Ordenación Forestal," *México Forestal* 35.4 (June–August 1961): 11–15, p. 12.

41. Dictamen Pericial, 15 April 1957, AGN, SARH/PF, caja 246, exp. 54603, leg. 3; Alberto Terrones Benítez, in *El Universal*, 19 June 1951.

42. Mexico, *Ley forestal y su reglamento* (1942), 12, 19–20.

43. In addition to appendix 2 of this volume, see also Felipe Birgos Martínez, "Proyecto General de Ordenación Forestal: Unidad Industrial de Explotación Forestal de las Fábricas de Papel San Rafael y Anexas, S.A.," unpublished typescript (1965), 3, COMFORMICH; Chambille, *Atenquique*, 35–39.

44. Salvia Spratte, *Los laberintos de Loreto y Peña Pobre*, 69–70; Rodríguez Caballero et al., *Algunas prácticas de ordenación de montes*, 13; Raufflet, "Institutional Change and Forest Management," 6–7.

45. On Atenquique's role in the MMOM, see Rodríguez Caballero et al., *Algunas prácticas de ordenación de montes*; and Ing. Tirso Gutiérrez Jarquín, "Proyecto General de Ordenación Forestal, Unidad Ejidal de Ordenación Forestal "'Melchor Ocampo,'" typescript (Ocampo, Michoacán: n.p., 1969), 243–45, COMFORMICH.

46. Broadleaf species tend to reproduce more rapidly after logging in Mexico, and loggers usually cut more pines than oaks to begin with. In either case, this led to high grading. This was not usually a serious problem, however, since so few loggers actually followed the guidelines. See Bray and Merino-Pérez, *La experiencia de las comunidades forestales en México*, 157, 222–23; Snook and Negreros, "Effects of Mexico's Selective Cutting System"; and *El Nacional*, 27 February 1963.

47. *El Universal*, 31 January 1962. See also Union Nacional de Resineros to Dámaso Cárdenas, 25 July 1951, AGN, SARH/PF, caja 6, exp. 3.

48. On the establishment of UIEFs, see appendix 2 of this volume. See also Aguilar Espinoza, "Organización forestal en México," 36.

49. *Excelsior*, 11 June 1956 and 9 February 1957.

50. Salvia Spratte, *Los laberintos de Loreto y Peña Pobre*, 114–16; *Excelsior*, 3 November 1962.

51. Alcocer's Arizona partner was Warren M. Tenney. For more on Alcocer, see chapter 5 of this volume, as well as his autobiography, *Un siglo en el bosque*, esp. 101.

52. Ing. Rodolfo Rodríguez Caballero, "Proyecto General de Ordenación Forestal, Unidad de Ordenación Forestal 'Industrial Río Verde,'" 9 August 1968, AGN,

SARH/PF, caja 158; Enríquez Hernández, "Análisis geoeconómico del sistema regional de la Sierra Tarahumara," 173–78. The Grupo Parral companies included Duraplay de Parral S.A., Industrial Río Verde S.A. de R.L., Industrial González Ugarte S.A. (IGUSA), and Empaques Ugarte S.A.

53. Enríquez Hernández, "Análisis geoeconómico del sistema regional de la Sierra Tarahumara," 57–60, 135, 169–71; Carlos Trouyet to Secretaría de Agricultura y Ganadería, 18 April 1952, AGN, SARH/PF, caja 245, exp. 54603, leg. 1, part I; and "Decreto Presidencial," *Diario Oficial*, 14 August 1952. On Vallina, see Wasserman, *Persistent Oligarchs*, 111–12. For allegations of Alemán's pecuniary involvement, see Antonio P. Rodríguez to Lic. Noel Alrich Solano, 20 July 1953, AGN, SARH/PF, caja 245, exp. 54603, leg. 1, part I.

54. Untitled list of logging operations in Chihuahua, 1948–51, ENAH, CCIT, 37.56.6.

55. Gómez González, *Rarámuri*, 113–18.

56. Memorandum of Francisco M. Plancarte et al. to Governor of Chihuahua, 22 October 1955, ENAH, CCIT, 37.57.21, doc. 1. See also Gonzalo Aguirre Beltrán to Alfonso Caso, 18 June 1952, ENAH, CCIT, 47.3.5, doc. 1.

57. Meza Flores, *San José Baqueachi*, 32.

58. Acta, 24 June 1960, ENAH, CCIT, 15.25.9, doc. 8.

59. The other protected zones were protective forest zones created on the San Elías hacienda in Bocoyna in 1933, around Chihuahua City in 1936, and around the city of Aldama in 1940, as well as a small reserve made in Campo Verde, Madero. See Ferreyra Soliano, "Las vedas forestales en México y sus consecuencias," 28–29.

60. "Editorial," *Boletín Forestal* (Organo de la Unión de Madereros de Chihuahua) 1.2 (November 1948): 1–2, p. 2.

61. *Boletín Forestal* 3.31 (May 1951): 14–17, pp. 15, 14. The union itself had been formed in 1942; among its founding members were Antonio Guerrero Peralta, Mario González Múzquiz, Eduardo Ortiz, Ing. Raúl Chávez, and Fernando Alcocer Patiño (who erroneously states it was founded in 1946). See Alcocer Patiño, *Un siglo en el bosque*, 17.

62. Plancarte, *El problema indígena tarahumara*, 68.

63. See for example the report of Francisco M. Plancarte, n.d. (ca. September 1955), ENAH, CCIT, 37.57.21, doc. 3.

64. *Novedades*, 19 August 1954; and Jordán, *Crónica de un país bárbaro*, 407–13.

65. Benítez, *Los indios de México*, 1:138; *El Popular*, 29 January 1958; and Madereras de Chihuahua to Enrique Beltrán, 3 July 1964, APEB, caja 18, exp. 31.

66. Dictámen of Vicente H. Cedillo, 7 May 1962, AGN, SARH/PF, caja 1578 (formerly Chihuahua 1–3), exp. 2/28, leg. 7; Dictámen of Luis Espejel D., 28 March 1964, AGN, SARH/PF, caja 1583 (formerly Chihuahua 4–1), exp. 2/988, leg. 8.

67. *El Nacional*, June 9, 1957.

68. The other communities were Panalachi, Pichachi, and Maguayachi. See Domingo R. Vázquez to León García, 19 January 1961, AGN, SARH/PF, caja 152, exp. 3.

69. Benítez, *Los indios de México*, 1:138; *El Popular* (Mexico City), 29 January 1958, 125.

70. Domingo R. Vázquez to León García, 19 January 1961, AGN, SARH/PF, caja 152, exp. 3.

71. Benítez, *Los indios de México*, 1:124–38.

72. This was the case in San Rafael. See Agente General to Director General de Supervisión y Vigilancia, 2 February 1959, AGN, SARH/PF, caja 153, exp. "Protección Forestal" no. 1.

73. *El Popular*, 29 January 1958.

74. *Excelsior*, 30 November 1959.

75. Agente General to Eduardo Uribe, 16 August 1961, AGN, SARH/PF, caja 153, exp. "Protección Forestal" no. 1.

76. "Proyecto de Ordenación para la UIEF B.C.: Serie de Explotación El Largo," December 1954, and "1949 Anexo," AGN, SARH/PF, caja 255.

77. Report of V. M. Arreola, 28 July 1953, and collective contract, 1953, AGN, SARH/PF, caja 245, exp. 54603, leg. 1, part I.

78. "Proyecto de Ordenación para la UIEF B.C.: Serie de Explotación El Largo," December 1954, and "1949 Anexo," AGN, SARH/PF, caja 255.

79. Report of Carlos Treviño Saldaña, 15 December 1952, AGN, SARH/PF, caja 245, exp. 54603, leg. 1, part I.

80. Report of Emilio Flores Calderón, 15 July 1956, AGN, SARH/PF, caja 246, exp. 54603, leg. 2; Herminio Aceves Ruiz, "Acta de Inspección," 8 July 1959, AGN, SARH/PF, caja 247, exp. 54603, leg. 6.

81. Sindicato de Trabajadores Madereros de Chihuahua to Pres Ruiz Cortínez [*sic*], 28 July 1952, AGN, SARH/PF, caja 245, exp. 54603, leg. 1, part I.

82. "Informe Bimestral," 18 June 1956, AGN, SARH/PF, caja 246, exp. 54603, leg. 2; and "Informe Bimestral," 2 February 1958, AGN, SARH/PF, caja 246, exp. 54603, leg. 4.

83. "Informes bimestrales," 15 January 1956 and 15 March 1957, AGN, SARH/PF, caja 246, exp. 54603, leg. 3.

84. Report of Tito Herca de la O., 2 April 1957, AGN, SARH/PF, caja 246, exp. 54603, leg. 3.

85. Cayetano Zamarrón et al. to Adolfo Ruiz Cortines, 19 December 1956, AGN, SARH/PF, caja 246, exp. 54603, leg. 3.

86. Informe of Agustín Galindo Alfonseca and Víctor V. Lara Pelayo, 23 March 1957, AGN, SARH/PF, caja 246, exp. 54603, leg. 3.

87. Emilio Flores Calderón to Comisariado, 22 July 1957, AGN, SARH/PF, caja 246, exp. 54603, leg. 4.

88. Emilio Flores Calderón to Director Forestal y de la Caza, 23 January 1958, AGN, SARH/PF, caja 246, exp. 54603, leg. 4.

89. See the eyewitness accounts in Lázaro Jiménez, *Paricutín a cincuenta años de su nacimiento*, 20–22.

90. Foshag and González, "Birth and Development of Paricutín Volcano," 375–85.

91. Foshag and González, "Birth and Development of Paricutín Volcano," 396.

92. Scarth, *Vulcan's Fury*, 203–7; Rees, "Effects of Parícutin [*sic*] Volcano on Landforms, Vegetation, and Human Occupancy," 277–79.

93. Report of Manuel Fernández Anaya, 27 April 1936, AGN, SARH/PF, caja 745, exp. 1839, leg. 1; AHPEM, Hijuelas, libro 20, pp. 1–119. These were Rafael Ortiz, José María Méndez Orozco, Luis Méndez Orozco, Heliodoro Méndez, and Reynaldo Vargas, the first three of whom had also formed an alliance with the regional agent of the Banco Nacional de Crédito Agrícola, Rafael Hinojosa, who had some family in San Juan Parangaricutiro.

94. See Report of Luis Espejel, 1 June 1937, AGN, SARH/PF, caja 745, exp. 1839, leg. 1.

95. Report of Alfredo Ortiz Barragán, 28 October 1937; Report of C. Martínez, March 1937; dasonometric study by Waldemar Díaz M., 10 May 1937, all in AGN, SARH/PF, caja 745, exp. 1839, leg. 1.

96. Rafael Echeverría and Vicente Aguilar to Presidente de la República, 19 October 1939, AGN, SARH/PF, caja 745, exp. 1839, leg. 1.

97. Rees, "Effects," 257–58; Lázaro Jiménez, *Paricutín a cincuenta años de su nacimiento*, 52–53; Report of Francisco Valdés Benítez, 18 March 1967, AGN, SARH/PF, caja 746, exp. 1839, leg. 4; Report of José García Martínez, 10 January 1944, AGN, SARH/PF, caja 717, exp. 1545.

98. Ortiz was one of the community's leading residents. He presided over a network of tree tappers and had developed a close relation with the BNCE agent in Uruapan. Vaca was a well-known Michoacán politician with close ties to the Cárdenas family. See the "recibos oficiles" in AHPEM, Bosques, caja 4, exp. 6; and *El Universal*, 21 August 1945.

99. Dasonometric study [of Cherán] by Waldemar Díaz, 8 January 1948, AGN, SARH/PF, caja 880, exp. 32298, leg. 3; Arias Portillo, "La región devastada por el volcán de Paricutín."

100. See, for example, Miguel Antolino Anguiano to Carlos Navarro, 13 August 1948, AGN, SARH/PF, caja 880, exp. 32298, leg. 3.

101. Management Plan by Waldemar Díaz, 26 October 1956, AGN, SARH/PF, caja 760, exp. 2558.

102. Contract between Parangaricutiro and Eufemio Ortiz Chávez, 10 November 1952, AGN, SARH/PF, caja 745, exp. 1839, leg. 3; and Contract between San Lázaro Uruapan and Luis Méndez Orozco, 29 May 1952, caja 753, exp. 2333, leg. 1.

103. These projects employed around 1,500 people, though as I suggest in

chapter 5, most of these people used tapping as part of a broader subsistence strategy. The Resinera Uruapan also ended up hiring the most experienced federal forester in the Uruapan area, Waldemar Díaz, sometime in the 1950s; it also appears that the timber magnate Paulo Doddoli may have been a silent partner. See the files marked "Relativa Resinera Uruapan," AGN, SARH/PF, caja 939, exp. 48891, legs. 1 and 2. The primary family companies were owned by Pomposo Solís and his heirs in the region around Ciudad Hidalgo, Rafael Vaca Solorio in the Parangaricutiro area, and, in Uruapan, the eponymous Lluch y Llanderal company and Industrial Uruapan, owned by Rafael Ortiz.

104. Klein, *The Shock Doctrine*, esp. 390–407.

105. *El Universal*, 21 August 1945.

106. Vecinos of Cherán to Secretaría de Agricultura, n.d. [ca. January 1941]; María Estefanía García de Chávez, María Juventina Muñoz, et al., 11 March 1942; and José García Márquez, "Revisión," 14 June 1948, all in AGN, SARH/PF, caja 896, exp. 36119, leg. 1; Report of Alfredo Ortiz Barragán, 22 September 1949, AGN, SARH/PF, caja 896, exp. 36119, leg. 2.

107. Examples are too numerous to list, but a representative case is Charapan, discussed in Pablo Velásquez Gallardo to Director General Forestal, 14 November 1946, AGN, SARH/PF, caja 880, exp. 32298, leg. 1. Another case is the multiyear conflict between Tanaquillo and its dependent community of Rancho Huecito, as described in Waldemar Díaz, "Plan de Explotación," 10 June 1958, AGN, SARH/PF, caja 823, exp. 19937, leg. 2.

108. Vecinos of Acachuén to Secretaría de Agricultura, 23 January 1942, and Porfirio Vallejo et al. to Director General Forestal y de Caza, 15 July 1946, AGN, SARH/PF, caja 916, exp. 40678, leg. 1.

109. Report of Delegado of Secretaría de Agricultura, 8 August 1944, and Waldemar Díaz, "Plan de Explotación," 25 June 1955, AGN, SARH/PF, caja 921, exp. 41636, leg. 1.

110. Bello Méndez and Carreón Reyes, "La industria resinera en el Estado de Michoacán," 68; Severino Herrera Bazán, "Informe de inspección," 28 August 1954, AGN, SARH/PF, caja 823, exp. 19937, leg. 2.

111. See the cases of Charapan, Tanaquillo, and Capácuaro, in Waldemar Díaz, "Plan de Explotación," 15 December 1958, AGN, SARH/PF, caja 880, exp. 32298, leg. 2; Waldemar Díaz, "Informe," 29 August 1946, AGN, SARH/PF, caja 823, exp. 19937, leg. 2; Report of Fernando Romero Quintana, 22 April 1941, AGN, SARH/PF, caja Michoacán 2–3, exp. 212, leg. 2; Gaspar González and Angel Aceves Paredo to Jesús Ceja Banajas, 4 October 1941, AGN, SARH/PF, caja Michoacán 2–3, exp. 212, leg. 2; and Humberto Ortega C, 27 November 1941, AGN, SARH/PF, caja Michoacán 2–3, exp. 212, leg. 2.

112. For a complete listing of UIEFs, see appendix 1 of this volume.

113. On San José, see Régulo García M. and David Bello, "Proyecto general de ordenación," tomo I, 1964, AGN, SARH/PF, caja 768, exp. 2393.

114. Datos que rinde la Cooperativa Minera, 1946, AGN, SARH/PF, caja 902, exp. 37555, leg. 1.

115. "Decreto Presidencial," *Diario Oficial*, 18 December 1952; Report of Antonio Martínez Báez, 31 May 1952, AGN, SARH/PF, caja 902, exp. 37555, leg. 1.

116. Luis D. Galindo, "Estudio Técnico Forestal," 12 December 1953, and complaints among others by Asociación de Mineros en Pequeño, 9 October 1953, AGN, SARH/PF, caja 902, exp. 37555, leg. 2.

117. The most comprehensive coverage of this announcement is in *El Popular*, 3 May 1957.

118. Ismael Arteaga et al. to CNC, 23 July 1957, AGN, SARH/PF, caja 190, exp. 23605, leg. 1; León Soto Campa et al. to Adolfo Ruiz Cortines, 16 May 1957, AGN, SARH/PF, caja 903, exp. 37555, leg. 5.

119. Acta de Infracción by Erasmo Gutiérrez Ricaño, 2 May 1954, AGN, SARH/PF, caja 153, exp. "Protección Forestal No. 1."

5. THE ECOLOGY OF DEVELOPMENT, 1952–1972

1. Data based on Garza, *La urbanización de México en el siglo 20*, tables A1, A2, and A3.

2. For an overview of public health, see Moreno Cueto, *Sociología histórica de las instituciones de salud en México*. On water and parks, see, respectively, Aboites Aguilar, "The Illusion of National Power"; and Wakild, "Parables of Chapultepec."

3. González Casanova, *La democracia en México y la banca internacional*.

4. Barkin and King, *Regional Economic Development*, 1–4.

5. For example, the 1960 forestry law gave state-level "forest commissions" the final word on how resources would be used. See chapter 1 of "Ley Forestal," *Diario Oficial* 238.13 (16 January 1960): 7–17.

6. I am not the first to note the utopian quality of development paradigms, particularly in the context of finite natural resources. Consider, for example, David Blackbourn's discussion of hydroelectricity in *The Conquest of Nature*, 217–28, or James C. Scott's discussion of utopian social engineering in *Seeing Like a State*, chap. 1.

7. Gamio, *Forjando patria*, 183.

8. On Gamio and the development of official indigenismo between 1916 and 1940, see Dawson, *Indian and Nation*, 6–15. The Departamento de Asuntos Indígenas briefly considered using pine trees to produce turpentine in 1944, though nothing came of that project. Report of Isidro Candia, 20 January 1944, AGN, SARH/PF, caja 233, exp. 43807.

9. Olivé Negrete, *Antropología mexicana*, 224–27.

10. Olivé Negrete, *Antropología mexicana*, 227.

11. Lewis, "Mexico's National Indigenist Institute and the Negotiation of Applied Anthropology in Highland Chiapas."

12. Cited in Olivé Negrete, *Antropología Mexicana*, 226; Gonzalo Aguirre Beltrán to Alfonso Caso, 18 June 1952, ENAH, CCIT, 47.3.5, doc. 1.

13. Barkin and King, *Regional Economic Development*, 91–92.

14. Cited in Poleman, *The Papaloapan Project*, 28.

15. Tamayo et al., *Recursos naturales de la cuenca del Papaloapan*, 46–51; Poleman, *The Papaloapan Project*, 46–54.

16. Poleman, *The Papaloapan Project*, 115.

17. The commission is the subject of a doctoral dissertation in progress by Diana Schwartz, at the University of Chicago.

18. Barkin and King, *Regional Economic Development*, 102–19.

19. Cárdenas, *Apuntes*, 2:238; Barrett, *La cuenca del Tepalcatepec*, 2:93–94. The three smaller dams were the Piedras Blancas, the Jicalan, and the Cajones.

20. For example, see Cárdenas, *Apuntes*, 2:338, 571.

21. Barrett, *La cuenca del Tepalcatepec*, 2:83–143; Baker, "Salud Colectiva," 56–91.

22. For local memories of Cárdenas, see interviews in Ramírez Heredia, *Lázaro Cárdenas en la Tierra Caliente*. For the alternative view, see Veladíaz, *El general sin memoria*, 146.

23. Calderón, "Lázaro Cárdenas del Río en la cuenca Tepalcatepec-Balsas"; interviews with José Chávez Ruiz and Roberto Salgado Terán, in Ramírez Heredia, *Lázaro Cárdenas en la Tierra Caliente*, 24 and 58, respectively.

24. Cited in Olivé Negrete, *Antropología Mexicana*, 226; Gonzalo Aguirre Beltrán to Alfonso Caso, 18 June 1952, ENAH, CCIT, 47.3.5, doc. 1.

25. Plancarte, *El problema indígena tarahumara*, 29–30; Cummings O'Hara, "Transforming the Sierra Tarahumara," 195–200.

26. Romero Contreras and Castaños Montes, "Gonzalo Aguirre Beltrán."

27. Gonzalo Aguirre Beltrán to Alfonso Caso, 18 June 1952, ENAH, CCIT, 47.3.5, doc. 1

28. Gonzalo Aguirre Beltran, untitled manuscript, ca. 1955, ENAH, CCIT, 36.55.7, doc. 1. This assessment echoes observations that Eric R. Wolf began to make around the same time, about the pivotal role of cultural brokers in so-called traditional communities. See Wolf, "Aspects of Group Relations in a Complex Society."

29. Plancarte, *El problema indígena tarahumara*, 12.

30. Plancarte, *El problema indígena tarahumara*, 8.

31. Sariego, *El indigenismo en la Tarahumara*, 174.

32. Sariego, *El indigenismo en la Tarahumara*, 182–84.

33. Plancarte, *El problema indígena tarahumara*, 67. Emphasis in original.

34. Francisco M. Plancarte, n.d. (ca. September 1955), ENAH, CCIT, 37.57.21, doc. 3

35. *Diario Oficial*, 25 July 1957.

36. Map insert after p. 8 in Plancarte, *El problema indígena tarahumara*.

37. Agustín Romano D. to Arnaldo Gutiérrez Hernández, 10 July 1959, ENAH, CCIT, 40.65.3, doc. 10.

38. Francisco M. Plancarte, n.d. (ca. September 1955), ENAH, CCIT, 37.57.21, doc. 3.

39. Benítez, *Los indios de México*, 95.

40. Contracts of association were signed by Basíguare, Cabórachi, Choguita, Guaguachique, Norogachi, and Samachique. In addition, the CCIT had helped negotiate traditional lease agreements (in which timber companies paid a royalty for wood, but used their own crews to fell the timber and transport) with two other communities—Rocheáchi and Papajichi. The CCIT also oversaw the community-forestry program in Cusárare. Report of Agustín Romano, 10 July 1959, ENAH, CCIT, 40.65.3, doc 10. By 1960, Yoquivo had signed a contract of association as well. See Report of Armando Fuentes Flores, 26 November 1959, AGN, SARH/PF, caja 233, exp. 43807. On the Supreme Council's response, see VI Congreso Tarahumara, "Resoluciones," November 1960, ENAH, CCIT, 15.1.14.1.

41. "Síntesis Justificativa," n.d. (ca. 1962), ENAH, CCIT, 33.52.21a, doc. 1.

42. Leopoldo Yáñez et al. to Gov. Teófilo Borunda, 17 February 1960, ENAH, CCIT, 15.25.9, doc. 1.

43. Santiago Recalache et al. to Oficina de Quejas de la Presidencia de la República, 10 July 1960, ENAH, CCIT, 15.25.9, doc. 6.

44. Transcription of Compañía Maderera Río Septentrión to Departamento de Asuntos Agrarios y Colonización, 27 April 1960, ENAH, CCIT, 15.25.9, doc. 7.

45. These were Basíhuare, Caborachi, Choguita, Cusárare, Guachochi, Guaguachique, Nararichi, Norogachi, Pahuichique, Papajichi, Rocheáchi, Samachique, Tecorichi, Tehuerichi, Tonachi, and Yoquivo. Aboréachi, Sehuérachi, and Tatahuichi also began production in 1968–1969, while Rocheáchi completed its project. Untitled reports, 18 November 1968, ENAH, CCIT, 5.9.12; and untitled reports, November 1969, ENAH, CCIT, 26.41.10, doc. 2.

46. Memorandum by Horacio Lira Esquivel, n.d. (ca. August 1967), ENAH, CCIT, 5.10.27b.

47. Confidential memo, 17 May 1960, ENAH, CCIT, 40.65.9a, doc. 5.

48. See, for example, Fernando Alcocer Patiño to Alfonso Caso, 28 July 1960, ENAH, CCIT, 15.25.9, doc. 4; or Horacio Lira Esquivel to Juan de Dios Pérez, 30 October 1967, ENAH, CCIT, 12.21.11.

49. Sariego, *El indigenismo en la Tarahumara*, 184.

50. Report of Maurilio Muñoz Basilio, 30 April 1966, ENAH, CCIT, 11.20.16, doc. 1.

51. Report of Gildardo González Ramos, 16 April 1964, ENAH, CCIT, 15.26.19, doc. 5.

52. Report of Maurilio Muñoz Basilio, 2 November 1959, ENAH, CCIT, 40.65.3, doc. 5; Report of Maurilio Muñoz Basilio, 9 February 1960, ENAH, CCIT, 40.65.9b, doc. 1.

53. See, for example, Ramón Valenzuela et al. to Adolfo Ruiz Cortines, 4 August 1958, AGN, SARH/PF, caja 261, exp. 18064, leg. 1.

54. Ismael Arteaga, Antonio García, and Librado P. Ronquillo to Confederación Nacional Campesina, 23 July 1957, AGN, SARH/PF, caja 190, exp. 23605, leg. 1. It is not clear what prompted this letter, but it may have reflected an effort to discredit Plancarte after the INI had sided with indigenous people in a land dispute in Guachochi.

55. See, for example, Reports of Roberto González, April and August 1962, ENAH, CCIT, 7.12.1, docs. 5 and 6; and Report of Horacio Lino Esquivel, 7 July 1969, ENAH, CCIT, 5.10.27b.

56. Agustín Romano to Alfonso Caso, 27 February 1959, ENAH, CCIT, 40.65.3, doc. 1.

57. Agustín Romano to Alfonso Caso, 27 February 1959, ENAH, CCIT, 40.65.3, doc. 1.

58. Romano, "El Centro Coordinador Indigenista de la Tarahumara," 80. On the Rocheáchi clinic where the doctors Mejía and Rodríguez worked, see Francisco Javier Alvarez to Alfonso Caso, 2 July 1961, ENAH, CCIT, 38.59.15, doc. 1.

59. Report of Roberto González, September 1961, ENAH, CCIT, 7.12.1, doc. 1.

60. Lumholtz, *Unknown Mexico*, 1:136.

61. Oscar Flores Loza, Estudio Dasonómico, April 1956, AGN, SARH/PF, caja 1575, exp. 2/28, leg. 4.

62. Oscar Flores Loza, Estudio Dasonómico, April 1956, AGN, SARH/PF, caja 1575, exp. 2/28, leg. 4; Vatant, "Un ejido forestal de la alta Tarahumara," 39–40.

63. Technically, the cooperative was refounded in 1945 as a Sociedad Local de Crédito Ejidal, though foresters continued to refer to it as a "cooperative" until well into the 1950s. See Memorandum by Miguel Esquivas, 11 August 1953, and Report of Roberto Barrios, 23 January 1948, AGN, SARH/PF, caja 1575, exp. 2/28, leg. 3.

64. Report of Silvestre Aguila, 10 March 1948, and Daniel Galicia, Telegram, 18 March 1948, AGN, SARH/PF, caja 1575, exp. 2/28, leg. 3.

65. Vatant, "Un ejido forestal de la alta Tarahumara," 35–37.

66. Francisco Javier Alvarez to Roberto González, 29 April 1961, ENAH, CCIT, 36.55.8, doc. 1.

67. Report of Daniel F. Galicia, 20 February 1948, AGN, SARH/PF, caja 1575, exp. 2/28, leg. 3.

68. Heredia Alfredo Rascón et al. to Nazario Ortiz Garza, 8 September 1948,

AGN, SARH/PF, caja 1575, exp. 2/28, leg. 3. On taxes, see Alfredo Navarro Cortina to Dirección General Forestal y de Caza, 6 June 1949, AGN, SARH/PF, caja 1575, exp. 2/28, leg. 3.

69. Roberto González Loya to Agustín Romano, 21 December 1961, ENAH, CCIT, 7.12.1, doc. 2. See also Roberto Barrios to Departamento Forestal y de la Caza, 9 March 1949, AGN, SARH/PF, caja 1575, exp. 2/28, leg. 3.

70. Comisariado Ejidal Cusárare to Alberto Flores Muñoz, 15 July 1953, AGN, SARH/PF, caja 1575, exp. 2/28, leg. 3. Emphasis in the original.

71. Eleuterio Rodríguez to Agustín Romano, 19 December 1961, ENAH, CCIT, 27.44.13, doc. 1; Consejo de Vigilancia (Cusárare) to Presidente de la República, 3 March 1966, ENAH, CCIT, 5.8.10.

72. See, for example, Prof. Roberto González Loya, "Informe de labores," December 1961 and January 1962, ENAH, CCIT, 7.12.1, docs. 3 and 4.

73. Prof. Roberto González Loya, "Informe de labores," September 1961, ENAH, CCIT, 7.12.1, doc. 1.

74. Benítez, *Los indios de México*, 1:113–14.

75. "Análisis de la cuenta," 15 January 1966, ENAH, CCIT, 17.28.13.

76. Vatant, "Un ejido forestal," 60–63. See also Contract between Fernando Alcocer Patiño and Cusárare, 15 January 1964, ENAH, CCIT, 17.29.26, doc. 9; Report of Virgilio Bustillos Orpinel, 30 April 1965, ENAH, CCIT, 10.17.2, doc. 2.

77. Roberto González Loya, "Informe de labores," December 1961 and January 1962, ENAH, CCIT, 7.12.1, docs. 3 and 4; and Industrializadora de Desperdicios Forestales to Agustín Romanos, 22 March 1962, ENAH, CCIT, 12.22.18.

78. Comisariado Ejidal to Maurilio Muñoz, 23 December 1966, ENAH, CCIT, 17.29.26, doc. 1.

79. "Síntesis Justificativa," n.d. (ca. 1962), ENAH, CCIT, 33.52.21a, doc. 1.

80. Sánchez Díaz, *El suroeste de Michoacán*, 82. For a detailed analysis of this process, see Gledhill, *Cultura y desafío en Ostula*, 228–70. Population figures from Barrett, *La Cuenca de Tepalcatepec*, 2:12.

81. María de Lourdes Canul, "Aspectos socioeconómicos del area de influencia de la U.I.E.F. Michoacana de Occidente S. de R. L.," unpublished typescript (1972), AGN, SARH/PF, caja 971, exp. 54175, leg. 61, pp. 18, 20–24.

82. Gledhill, *Cultura y desafío en Ostula*, 166–69; Marín Guardado, "Etnicidad, territorio y cultura en la costa nahua de Michoacán."

83. Marco Buenrostro to León J. Castaños Martínez, 23 November 1979, AGN, SARH/PF, caja 971, exp. 54175, leg. 63.

84. Alarcón Cháires, *Flora, fauna y apropiación de la naturaleza en la región nahua de Michoacán*, 20–21.

85. Aguirre Beltrán, *Problemas de la población indígena de la Cuenca de Tepalcatepec*, 178–82.

86. Unidad Industrial de Explotación Forestal Michoacana del Occidente, S. de

R. L., "Proyecto General de Ordenación Forestal," December 1959, COMFORMICH. For authorities' nineteenth-century complaints, see AHPEM, Hijuelas, libro 2, fojas 23–24V, 1892, reproduced in Gledhill, *Cultura y desafío en Ostula*, 243.

87. "Estudio Dasonómico," 1951, AGN, SARH/PF, caja 973, exp. 54175; Roberto Mendoza Medina, "Memorandum," 23 February 1962, AGN, SARH/PF, caja 956, exp. 54175, leg. 12.

88. Informe paso de anualidad from SAG Agencia Forestal Morelia, 20 August 1973, AGN, SARH/PF, caja 964, exp. 54175, leg. 45; Cochet, Léonard, and de Sirgy, *Paisajes agrarios de Michoacán*, 267.

89. Michoacana de Occidente, "Presupuesto," 1963, AGN, SARH/PF, caja 958, exp. 54175, leg. 17; Informe of Lic Francisco Xavier Ovando H., 6 September 1978, AGN, SARH/PF, caja 971, exp. 54175, leg. 61.

90. "Informe de la Inspección," 1966, AGN, SARH/PF, caja 972, exp. 54175.

91. Informe of Lic Francisco Xavier Ovando H., 6 September 1978, AGN, SARH/PF, caja 971, exp. 54175, leg. 61.

92. Roberto Mendoza Medina, "Programa de Reforestación 1962," AGN, SARH/PF, caja 956, exp. 54175, leg. 12. Emphasis in original.

93. Report by Enrique Beltrán, n.d. (ca. 1961), APEB, caja 22, exp. 28.

94. "Ley Forestal," *Diario Oficial de la Federación* 13 (16 January 1960): arts. 44–48; Beltrán, *La batalla forestal*, 95–101.

95. "Informe de labores," February 1963, AGN, SARH/PF, caja 958, exp. 54175, leg. 15; for an example of the burning permits, see AGN, SARH/PF, caja 962, exp. 54175, leg. 30.

96. María de Lourdes Canul, "Aspectos socioeconómicos del area de influence de U.I.E.F. Michoacana de Occidente S. de R. L.," AGN, SARH/PF, caja 971, exp. 54175, leg. 61, pp. 66–68; Report of Guillermo Herrera Hernández, 3 October 1964, and Report of Artemio Heredia Ochoa, 4 October 1964, AGN, SARH/PF, caja 959, exp. 54175, leg. 19.

97. "Informe de labores," March to April 1963, AGN, SARH/PF, caja 958, exp. 54175, leg. 16.

98. Roberto Mendoza Medina, "Informe de labores," 10 December 1968, AGN, SARH/PF, caja 962, exp. 54175, leg. 30.

99. José M. Cárdenas to Presidente de la República, 27 October 1964, AGN, SARH/PF, caja 959, exp. 54175, leg. 19; *Diario Oficial*, 18 April 1959; Cochet, Léonard, and de Sirgy, *Paisajes agrarios de Michoacán*, 264.

100. Acta Notarial of José Navarrete Guizar, 13 November 1969, AGN, SARH/PF, caja 964, exp. 54175, leg. 34; "Acta" El Varaloso, 25 September 1964, AGN, SARH/PF, caja 959, exp. 54175, leg. 21. According to one study in the late 1970s, 56 percent of all men and 64 percent of ejidatarios between the ages of 18 and 30 temporarily migrated out of the area each year; most went to the United States. See María de Lourdes Canul, "Aspectos socioeconómicos del área de influencia de

U.I.E.F. Michoacana de Occidente S. de R. L.," AGN, SARH/PF, caja 971, exp. 54175, leg. 61, pp. 24–26, 88.

101. José M. Cárdenas to Presidente de la República, 27 October 1964, AGN, SARH/PF, caja 959, exp. 54175, leg. 19; *Amparo* of Michoacana de Occidente, 18 March 1964, AGN, SARH/PF, caja 959, exp. 54175, leg. 19.

102. Informe of Lic Francisco Xavier Ovando H., 6 September 1978, AGN, SARH/PF, caja 971, exp. 54175, leg. 61.

103. Lázaro Cárdenas to José Antonio Arias, 15 June 1968, in Cárdenas, *Epistolario de Lázaro Cárdenas*, 266–67.

104. Cárdenas, *Apuntes*, 4:83.

105. Cárdenas, "Declaraciones del vocal ejecutivo . . . ," 8 May 1968, in Cárdenas, *Palabras y documentos públicos de Lázaro Cárdenas*, 3:247–49.

106. Lázaro Cárdenas to Juan Gil Preciado, 12 April 1969, in Cárdenas, *Epistolario de Lázaro Cárdenas*, 271. Cárdenas continued to condemn La Michoacana even in the final days of his life. See *Apuntes*, 4:230–32.

107. Unidad Industrial de Explotación Forestal Michoacana del Occidente, S. de R. L., "Proyecto General de Ordenación Forestal," December 1959, COMFORMICH; María de Lourdes Canul, "Aspectos socioeconómicos del área de influencia de U.I.E.F. Michoacana de Occidente S. de R. L.," AGN, SARH/PF, caja 971, exp. 54175, leg. 61, p. 6.

108. Informe de Investigación of Cecilio Romero Romero, 19 November 1968, AGN, SARH/PF, caja 962, exp. 54175, leg. 30; Informe paso de anualidad, 20 August 1973, AGN, SARH/PF, caja 964, exp. 54175, leg. 45.

109. Unión de Pequeños Propietarios de Montes y Ganado to Secretaría de Agricultura, 11 September 1973, AGN, SARH/PF, caja 964, exp. 54175, leg. 45; and Unión de Pequeños Propietarios to Secretaría de Agricultura, 11 February 1975, AGN, SARH/PF, caja 966, exp. 54175, leg. 50.

110. Gledhill, *Cultura y desafío en Ostula*, 282–87.

111. Gledhill, *Cultura y desafío en Ostula*, 294–371; *La Jornada*, 20 September 2007.

112. Report of Marco Buenrostro, 23 November 1979, AGN, SARH/PF, caja 971, exp. 54175, leg. 63; Cochet, Léonard, and de Sirgy, *Paisajes agrarios de Michoacán*, 285–302.

113. In 1978, for example, the company's net sales totaled more than 124 million pesos, but it still ran a deficit of 26.1 million pesos. Grupo San Rafael, "Presentación a la Subsecretaría Forestal y de la Fauna," 4 August 1978, AGN, SARH/PF, caja 971, exp. 54175, leg. 61; Gerente de CEPAMISA to Subsecretaría Forestal y de la Fauna, 11 April 1972, AGN, SARH/PF, caja 796, exp. 2–6011. On resin, see the report of Federico Carrillo Aguilera, 7 December 1987, AGN, SARH/PF, caja 971, exp. 54175, leg. 62.

114. Grupo San Rafael, "Presentación a la Subsecretaría Forestal y de la

Fauna," 4 August 1978, AGN, SARH/PF, caja 971, exp. 54175, leg. 61; María de Lourdes Canul, "Aspectos socioeconómicos del área de influencia de U.I.E.F. Michoacana de Occidente S. de R. L.," AGN, SARH/PF, caja 971, exp. 54175, leg. 61, pp. 10–11.

115. On the terms of the sale, see Informe of Lic Francisco Xavier Ovando H., 6 September 1978, AGN, SARH/PF, caja 971, exp. 54175, leg. 61.

116. Letter from Sindicato General de Trabajadores "Gral. Rafael Sánchez Tapia" to Cuauhtémoc Cárdenas, 5 April 1978, AGN, SARH/PF, caja 971, exp. 54175, leg. 61.

117. *La Voz de Michoacán*, 20 and 25 October 1978.

118. *Diario Oficial* (Mexico City), 13 February 1979; *Verdad* (Morelia) no. 251 (15 October 1978).

119. Cipriano González Barajas et al. to Subsecretaría de Recursos Forestales y de Caza, 21 September 1978, AGN, SARH/PF, caja 971, exp. 54175, leg. 62.

120. "Acta de inspección," 8 November 1978, AGN, SARH/PF, caja 971, exp. 54175, leg. 63.

121. Informe of Lic Francisco Xavier Ovando H., 6 September 1978, AGN, SARH/PF, caja 971, exp. 54175, leg. 61.

122. "Síntesis Justificativa," n.d. (ca. 1962), ENAH, CCIT, 33.52.21a, doc. 1.

123. Oscar Flores Loza, Estudio Dasonómico, April 1956, AGN, SARH/PF, caja 1575, exp. 2/28, leg. 4.

124. Comisariado Ejido de Cusárare to Adolfo Ruiz Cortines, 10 March 1957, AGN, SARH/PF, caja 1575, exp. 2/28, leg. 4; "Estudio dasonómico," by José M. Aguilar, November 1958, AGN, SARH/PF, caja 1575, exp. 2/28, leg. 5.

125. Roberto González Loya to Francisco Javier Alvarez, 5 March 1960, ENAH, CCIT, 36.44.8, doc. 6; Francisco Javier Alvarez to SAG, 26 January 1960, ENAH, CCIT, 37.57.17, doc. 1.

126. The 1966 management plan stated that 30,777 hectares were classified as forests in Cusárare: 14,863 were in production, 7,890 had already been logged, and 4,042 were inappropriate for logging (i.e., *inexplotable*), leaving a reserve of 3,982. Report of José Aguilar Uranga, 6 December 1966, AGN, SARH/PF, caja 1572, exp. 2/28, leg. 10.

127. The federal entities included the Agriculture Department (Secretaría de Agricultura y Ganadería, via its dependency, the Subsecretaría de Recursos Forestales y de Caza), the Agrarian Reform Department (Departamento de Asuntos Agrarios y Colonización, via its dependency the Derección General de Fomento Ejidal), the Rural Development Organization (Comité Técnico de Inversión de Fondos), and the Institute of Indian Affairs (Instituto Nacional Indigenista).

1. Morett Sánchez, *Reforma agraria*, 102–8.

2. For a contemporary viewpoint, see Montes de Oca Luján, "La cuestión agraria y el movimiento campesino," 62–64.

3. For an overview, see Herrera Calderón and Cedillo, "Introduction."

4. Walsh Sanderson, *Land Reform in Mexico*, 117–20.

5. Jesús Vázquez Soto, *La política forestal de México*, 32.

6. Vázquez León, *Antropología política de la comunidad indígena en Michoacán*, 56, 71; and Mexico, *Manual de estadísticas básicas*, 779–92.

7. Kimberly-Clark de México, www.kimberly-clark.com.mx/Empresa/KCM _historia.asp, accessed 12 December 2011.

8. On birth-control pills, see Soto Laveaga, *Jungle Laboratories*.

9. *Excelsior*, 15 October 1972.

10. Bray and Merino-Pérez, *La experiencia de las comunidades forestales en México*, 56–60.

11. Jesús Veruette Fuentes, "Una alternativa para el desarrollo de la actividad forestal," *Revista del México Agrario* 9.2 (March–April 1976): 30–34, p. 31.

12. See, for example, *Excelsior*, 10 October 1964; *El Universal*, 11 October 1964.

13. Beltrán, "La conservación como instrumento de desarrollo," 190.

14. Klooster, "Conflict in the Commons," 145–55.

15. See, for example, the 1976 documents relating to the creation of the ejido Lázaro Cárdenas, in Quintana Roo, with colonists from Cuanajo, in RAN, "Cuanajo," exp. 443. My thanks to Juan Manuel Mendoza for passing this along.

16. Merino Pérez, *Conservación o deterioro*, 95–96.

17. Mexico, "Ley Forestal," *Diario Oficial* 238.13 (16 January 1960): chap. 2.

18. Subsecretaría Forestal y de la Fauna, *Silvicultura* 77: 119–22, p. 121. This chart divided forest species as "pine," "oak," "oyamel," and, of course, "*corrientes*." Further evidence that deforestation projects expressly bypassed commercial forests can be seen by their exemption from the National Deforestation Program, discussed below.

19. Moreno Unda, "Environmental Effects of the National Tree Clearing Program, Mexico," 32–33; Andrade Limas, del Carmen, Ramírez, and Serrato, *La región agrícola del norte de Tamaulipas (México)*, 35–36.

20. Moreno Unda, "Environmental Effects of the National Tree Clearing Program, Mexico," 42–60; Bartra, "¿Colectivización o proletarización?"

21. Parra Orozco, *Madera*, 143.

22. Cayetano Zamarrón, Tiburcio Domínguez, and F. Chávez O to Ruiz Cortines, 19 December 1956, and undated report of forest wardens, ca. 1959, AGN, SARH/PF, caja 246, exp. 54603, legs. 3 and 4, respectively.

23. For analyses of the Gámiz uprising, see Henson, "Madera 1965"; and the carefully researched fictional account in Montemayor, *Las armas del alba*.

24. Juan Rodríguez González and Gerardo Martínez Uriarte to Echeverría, 30 October 1975, AGN, SARH/PF, caja 254, exp. 54603, leg. 33.

25. Report of Manuel de los Santos, 25 January 1972, AGN, SARH/PF, caja 251, exp. 54603, leg. 27; Rafael Quiñones V to Echeverría, 26 May 1972, AGN, SARH/PF, caja 251, exp. 54603, leg. 27; Acta of 21 April 1975, AGN, SARH/PF, caja 254, exp. 54603, leg. 32.

26. Contrato de asociación en participación, 2 August 1971, AGN, SARH/PF, caja 250, exp. 54603, leg. 25.

27. Enríquez Hernández, "Análisis geoeconómico del sistema regional de la Sierra Tarahumara," 155–56.

28. Abraham Escarpita Herrera, "Ajuste al proyecto general de ordenación," April 1976, AGN, SARH/PF, caja 156; Gingrich, "The Political Ecology of Deforestation in the Sierra Madre Occidental of Chihuahua," 20.

29. Emetrio Ponce to Adolfo López Mateos, 10 March 1959, AGN, SARH/PF, "Chihuahua" 152–53.

30. Manuel Corona G., "Estudio Dasonómico," December 1963, AGN, SARH/PF, caja 159.

31. *Excelsior*, 1 February 1972.

32. *Excelsior*, 1 February 1972.

33. *Excelsior*, 15 October 1972.

34. Enríquez Hernández, "Análisis geoeconómico del sistema regional de la Sierra Tarahumara," 156–58.

35. It also turned out that the vast majority of native people in the Sierra Tarahumara actually had a legal standing to do so but the Secretariat of Agrarian Reform had never formally certified their status (that is, it had never granted certificates of agrarian rights to 90 percent of native ejidatarios). Acta of VII Congreso de los Pueblos Tarahumaras, 27 January 1972, ENAH, CCIT, 9/17/22.

36. Acta of VII Congreso de los Pueblos Tarahumaras, 27 January 1972, ENAH, CCIT, 9/17/22. The communities with their own logging enterprises included Tatahuichi, Cabórachi, Tacorichi, Guahuachique, Aporéachi, Yoquivo, Pahuichique, Tónachi, Sehuérachi, and Guachochi. Samachique and Narárachi would also soon have their own logging enterprises.

37. "Palabras prunciadas por el Lic. Luis Echeverría Álvarez," reproduced in López Velasco, *Y surgió la unión*, 162. See also Augusto Gómez Villanueva, "Informe," in López Velasco, *Y surgió la unión*, 149–58.

38. PROFORTARH, *Memoria*, 21.

39. PROFORTARH, *Memoria*, 27. The entire presidential decree can be found on pp. 26–32.

40. PROFORTARH, *Memoria*, 9–11, 102, 107.

41. PROFORTARH, *Memoria*, 60–67, 74–88, 93–95.

42. PROFORTARH, *Memoria*, 98.

43. José Rodríguez C. to Luis Echeverría, n.d. (ca. 10 January 1974), AGN, SARH/PF, caja 1581 (antes Chihuahua 3–2), exp. 2/402, leg. 29.

44. José Gascón Mercado to Jesús Vásquez Soto, 30 November 1972; Report of Juvenal Ramos Aguirre, 29 January 1974, AGN, SARH/PF, caja 153, exp. "Aserraderos," leg. 2; notes from meeting of José Rodríguez Vallejo, Lázaro Ramos Esquer, and Manuel Luna Verduzco, 8 December 1981, AGN, SARH/PF, caja 179, exp. 2/6093, Cuaderno "Informe de Labores"; Mexico, "Silvicultura '77," 151.

45. See, for example, Enrique Estrada Chávez to Subsecretaría, 26 January 1977, AGN, SARH/PF, caja 242, exp. 30092, leg. 5 "Aboreachic."

46. Abraham Escárpita H., "Estudio Dasonómico," 27 October 1977, AGN, SARH/PF, caja 179, exp. 2/6093.

47. Abraham Escárpita H., "Estudio Dasonómico," 27 October 1977, AGN, SARH/PF, caja 179, exp. 2/6093; Report of José Ramírez Maldonado, 3 August 1973, AGN, SARH/PF, caja 242, exp. 30092, leg. 5 "Aboreachic."

48. Report of Unidad de Ordenación Forestal Tutuaca, n.d. (ca. January 1978), AGN, SARH/PF, caja 153, exp. "Aserraderos," leg. 3.

49. Manuel Jaques Olivas to Francisco Merino Rábago, 14 February 1978, AGN, SARH/PF, caja 153, exp. "Aserraderos," leg. 3; Report of Janitzio Múgica Rodríguez Cabo, 16 February 1978, AGN, SARH/PF, caja 1581 (antes Chihuahua 3–2), exp. 2/402, leg. 31.

50. Ejido Madera to Abraham Escarpita Herrera, n.d. (ca. June 1980), AGN, SARH/PF, caja 153, exp. "Aserraderos," leg. 3.

51. "Discurso," by Paulino López Velsco, 19 April 1977, reproduced in López Velasco, *Y surgió la union*, 297; Report of Jorge Sánchez Aldana, 9 March 1981, AGN, SARH/PF, caja 242, exp. 30092, leg. 5 "Aboreachic."

52. Instituto Nacional Indigenista, "Programa de desarrollo integral para la Sierra Tarahumara," unpublished typescript (1 August 1990), 60, ENAH, CCIT.

53. Vázquez León, *Antropología política de la comunidad indígena en Michoacán*, 56, 71.

54. Report of Ing. Zárate H., May 1975, AGN, SARH/PF, caja 800, exp. 2–6875.

55. Sánchez Herrera et al., "Explotación del bosque en la Meseta Purépecha y su impacto en la población," 1:38–42.

56. Vázquez León, *Antropología política de la comunidad indígena en Michoacán*, 76–79.

57. Anonymous letter to SAG, April 1971, annexed in Severino Herrera Bazán, "Algunos antecendentes relativos a la politica forestal en Michoacán," unpublished typescript (July 1971), COMFORMICH.

58. Severino Herrera Bazán, "Algunos antecedentes relativos a la política forestal en Michoacán," unpublished typescript (July 1971), COMFORMICH.

59. Comisión Forestal del Estado de Michoacán, "Actividades de la Comisión Forestal del Estado de Michoacán 1970," 9.

60. Comisión Forestal del Estado de Michoacán, "Michoacán forestal," 43.

61. *El Día*, 19 December 1974. See also *El Nacional*, 7 January 1974.

62. Antonio Várgas Macdonald [*sic*], "PROFORMICH prepara la ruina de Michoacán," *México Forestal* 48 (November 1974): 26–28. See also *La Voz de Michoacán*, 6 November 1978.

63. Report of Juan Figueroa Torres, Director Gen Proformich, 6 August 1976, AGN, SARH/PF, caja 796, exp. 2–5953.

64. Estudio Dasonómico de Aranza by Silverio Hernández Gutiérrez, 2 May 1975, AGN, SARH/PF, caja 722/18483, leg. 2, pp. 544–54.

65. Vázquez León, *Antropología política de la comunidad indígena en Michoacán*, 76–77.

66. Informe Técnico de Aranza by Agustín Sánchez Espinoza, August 1979, AGN, SARH/PF, caja 722/18483, leg. 3, pp. 1–8; see also Merino Pérez, *Conservación o deterioro*, 46.

67. "Acta," 17 December 1977, AGN, SARH/PF, caja 796, exp. 2–5953.

68. "Acta," 17 December 1977, AGN, SARH/PF, caja 796, exp. 2–5953.

69. Barsimantov and Antezana, "Forest Cover Change and Land Tenure Change in Mexico's Avocado Region"; Bárcenas Ortega and Aguirre Paleo, *Pasado, presente y futuro del aguacate en Michoacán, México*, 51.

70. Waldemar Díaz Martínez, "Estudio Forestal," 15 March 1978, AGN, SARH/PF, caja 750, exp. 2/2160, leg. 5.

71. Waldemar Díaz Martínez, "Estudio Forestal," 15 March 1978, AGN, SARH/PF, caja 750, exp. 2/2160, leg. 5. See also Francisco Opengo Salvador, "Revisión de Campo y de Gabinete," 15 December 1978, AGN, SARH/PF, caja 750, exp. 2/2160, leg. 5.

72. Sánchez Herrera et al., "Explotación del bosque en la Meseta Purépecha y su impacto en la población," 1:42–43, 109–14.

73. Ing. Agustín Sánchez Espinosa, "Informe técnico justificativo . . . ," August 1980, AGN, SARH/PF, caja 805, wherein many smallholder requests for desmonte and land conversion may also be found.

74. Report of Luis Hernández, September 1971, AGN, SARH/PF, Serie Michoacán, caja 3–2, exp. 275, leg. 2; Vidal Aguilar Soto and Felipe Ruiz Anguiano to Comisión Mixta Agraria, 18 April 1977, AGN, SARH/PF, caja 746, exp. 1839, leg. 5; Bárcenas Ortega and Aguirre Paleo, *Pasado, presente y futuro del aguacate en Michoacán, México*, 25–27.

75. Sánchez Herrera et al., "Explotación del bosque en la Meseta Purépecha y su impacto en la población."

76. Bárcenas and Aguirre, *Pasado, presente y futuro del aguacate en Michoacán, México*, 24.

77. Vidal Aguilar Soto and Felipe Ruiz Anguiano to Comisión Mixta Agraria, 18 April 1977, and administrative settlement 207.92, 15 July 1977, AGN, SARH/PF, caja 746, exp. 1839, leg. 5.

78. *Diario Oficial*, 25 November 1991.

79. Reports of Waldemar Díaz, 30 July 1958, and Director General de Supervisión Técnica y Vigilancia, 17 October 1962, AGN, SARH/PF, caja 745, exp. 1839, leg. 3.

80. Comunidad Indígena de Nuevo Parangaricutiro to Sub-Secretaría Forestal y de Caza, 4 February 1967, AGN, SARH/PF, caja 745, exp. 1839, leg. 4.

81. Memorandum of Alfonso Loera Borja, 20 May 1969, Acta de conformidad, 23 February 1970, and Report of Lázaro Mejía Fernández, 15 December 1972, AGN, SARH/PF, caja 745, exp. 1839, leg. 4.

82. Report of Agustín Sánchez Espinosa, 10 July 1978, AGN, SARH/PF, caja 745, exp. 1839, leg. 4.

83. Meeting minutes, 27 April 1977, and Felipe Aguilar Soto and Felipe Ruiz Anguiano to Comisión Mixta, 18 April 1977, AGN, SARH/PF, caja 746, exp. 1839.

84. SARH, Logging Permission of 16 January 1978, AGN, SARH/PF, caja 746, exp. 1839, leg. 5.

85. Torres, Bocco, and Velázquez, "Antecedentes históricos"; Álvarez Icaza, "Forestry as a Social Enterprise"; Sánchez Pego, "The Forestry Enterprise of the Indigenous Community of Nuevo San Juan Parangaricutiro, Michoacán, Mexico," 148–52.

86. Specifically, UNAM researchers sought to transmit San Juan's lessons to the Organización de Ejidos Forestales "Hermenegildo Galeana," in Guerrero; to indigenous communities in the region of Ixtlan de Juárez, Oaxaca; to mestizo ejidos in Durango; to the Organización de Ejidos Productores Forestales de la Zona Maya "Felipe Carrillo Puerto," in Quintana Roo; and to the Ejido de San Nicolás Totolapan, on the Ajusco volcano of the Distrito Federal. Bray and Merino-Pérez, *La experiencia de las comunidades forestales en México*, 80–82.

87. Mexico, "Ley Forestal," *Diario Oficial* 396.19 (30 May 1986): art. 67.

88. For an analysis, see Bray and Merino-Pérez, *La experiencia de las comunidades forestales en México*, 62–64.

89. Taylor, "Community Forestry as Embedded Process," 63–65.

90. Instituto Nacional de Investigación Forestal en México, "Programa de desarrollo integral para la Sierra Tarahumara," unpublished typescript (1 August 1990), 60–61, ENAH, CCIT.

91. World Bank, "Staff Appraisal Report," 1.

92. González Pacheco, *Bosques de México*, 81–93.

93. *Excelsior*, June 30, 1985.

94. World Bank, "Staff Appraisal Report," 13.

95. Lowerre, "Evaluation of the Forestry Development Project of the World Bank," 7.

96. Gingrich, "The Political Ecology of Deforestation in the Sierra Madre Occidental of Chihuahua," 37–41.

97. González Pacheco, *Los bosques de México y la banca internacional*, 71.

98. Instituto Nacional Indigenista, Delegación Chihuahua, "Programa de desarrollo forestal Chihuahua-Durango: Pueblos indígenas y microdesarrollo en la Tarahumara," typescript (1993), 73, ENAH, CCIT.

99. Instituto Nacional Indigenista, Delegación Chihuahua, "Programa de desarrollo forestal Chihuahua-Durango: Pueblos indígenas y microdesarrollo en la Tarahumara," typescript (1993), 52, ENAH, CCIT.

100. Secretaría de Medio Ambiente, Recursos Naturales y Pesca, *Programa forestal y de suelo, 1995–2000*, 51, 62.

CONCLUSION

1. There are many online sources that address this event. Two of the best are El Enemigo Común, elenemigocomun.net (see especially x carolina, "Autonomous Paths Converge in Cherán," 3 June 2012, http://elenemigocomun.net/2012/06 /autonomous-paths-converge-cheran/) and NACLA: North American Congress on Latin America, nacla.org (especially Clayton Conn, "Cherán: Community Self-defense in Mexico's Drug War [Photo Essay]," 3 July 2011, http://nacla.org/news /cherán-community-self-defense-mexico's-drug-war-photo-essay).

2. These events are described in chapter 2 in this volume.

3. See, for example, "Mexican Human Rights Lawyer Is Killed," *New York Times*, 22 October 2001, 12. See also Diebel, *Betrayed*, 202–32.

4. See, for example, "Ejido Pino Gordo Journal; All Across Mexico, a Chainsaw Massacre of Trees," *New York Times*, 28 April 1999.

5. For news on Pino Gordo, see *La Jornada*, 8 March 2005. In Guerrero several local leaders have been killed as of the time of this writing (September 2013). Most notably, Juventina Villa Mojica—herself the widow of a murdered community leader—was ambushed and killed in 2012, prompting her followers to flee from the well-armed loggers presumably responsible for her death. See, for example, "Environmental Activist and Her Son Slain in Mexico," *Los Angeles Times*, 29 November 2012; and "Sin destino, campesinos ecologistas de Guerrero," *La Jornada*, 7 December 2012.

6. Bray, "Community Forestry in Mexico," 348.

7. Secretaría del Medio Ambiente y Recursos Naturales, *Informe de la situación del medio ambiente en México*, 71–80.

8. Madrid, Núñez, Quiroz, and Rodríguez, "La propiedad social forestal en México," 196, table 3.

9. Matthews, *Instituting Nature*, 160–202.

10. Tilly, *The Contentious French*.

11. The pirekua can be found in the epigraph of this book.

12. For an extended discussion of the link between mountains and sociopolitical autonomy, see Scott, *The Art of Not Being Governed*, 31.

13. Hardin, "The Tragedy of the Commons."

14. Secretaría del Medio Ambiente y Recursos Naturales, *Informe de la situación del medio ambiente en México*, 71, 79–82.

15. For discussions of how a community can develop a moral economy that favors the conservation of the commons, see Ostrom, *Governing the Commons*. For the case of Mexico, see Basurto, "Biological and Ecological Mechanisms Supporting Marine Self-Governance"; and Basurto and Ostrom, "The Core Challenges of Moving beyond Garrett Hardin."

16. El Largo is discussed in chapter 6. For Durango, see Taylor, "Reorganization or Division"; and Taylor, "New Organizational Strategies in Community Forestry in Durango, Mexico."

17. See an overview in Bray, Merino-Pérez, and Barry, "Community Managed in the Strong Sense of the Term."

18. For an overview and definition of resource curse literature, see Ross, "The Political Economy of the Resource Curse."

19. Agustín Sánchez Espinosa, "Proyecto de integración y funcionamiento de los servicios técnicos forestales de la Unidad de Administración Forestal No. 6 'Meseta Tarasca,'" 20 July 1978, AGN, SARH/PF, caja 805.

20. For an overview, see Neumann, *Making Political Ecology*, 80–114. For a historical example, see Miller, *Fruitless Trees*.

21. Food and Agriculture Organization of the United Nations, *Global Forest Resources Assessment 2000*, 391–94, table 4.

22. Secretaría del Medio Ambiente y Recursos Naturales, *Visión de México sobre REDD+*, 13, table 2.

23. Matthews, *Instituting Nature*, 239.

24. For an overview, see Bray, Merino-Pérez, and Barry, *The Community Forests of Mexico*.

BIBLIOGRAPHY

ARCHIVES

Archivo de la Comisión Forestal del Estado de Michoacán (Morelia, Michoacán) – COMFORMICH

Archivo General de la Nación (Mexico City) – AGN

    Departamento del Trabajo – DT

    Dirección General de Gobierno – DGG

    Fomento – FO

        Sección Bosques – SB

    Presidentes – PR

        Manuel Ávila Camacho – MAC

        Sección Obregón y Calles – SOC

    Secretaría de Agricultura y Recursos Hidráulicos / Política Forestal – SARH/PF

Archivo Histórico del Centro de Estudios de la Revolución Mexicana "Lázaro Cárdenas," A.C. (Jiquilpan, Michoacán) – AHCERM

    Fondo Papeles de Francisco J. Múgica – FJM

        Sección de Documentación Suelta – DS

    Fondo Papeles de Lázaro Cárdenas del Río – LC

Archivo Histórico de la Secretaría de Educación Pública (Mexico City) – AHSEP

Archivo Histórico del Poder Ejecutivo de Michoacán – AHPEM

Archivo Histórico Municipal de Morelia (Michoacán) – AHMM

Archivo Municipal de Zamora (Michoacán) – AMZ

Archivo Personal de Enrique Beltrán (originally in Mexico City, now at the Universidad de Guadalajara) – APEB

Centro de Investigaciones de Chihuahua (Chihuahua City) – CIDECH

    Ramo Batopilas – RB

        Fondo Porfiriato y Terracismo – P&T

            Sección Administración – SA

            Sección Justicia – SJ

Escuela Nacional de Antropologia e Historia, Sede Chihauhua (Chihuahua City) – ENAH

    Documentos del Centro Coordinador Indigenista de la Tarahumara – CCIT

John Hamilton McNeely Papers, University of Texas at El Paso Library – JHM
Registro Agrario Nacional (Morelia, Michoacán) – RAN

NEWSPAPERS AND PERIODICALS

Boletín del Departamento Forestal de Caza y Pesca (Mexico City)
Agricultura (Mexico City)
Boletín Forestal (Chihuahua City)
Cartilla Forestal (Mexico City)
Diario Oficial (Mexico City)
El Baluarte (Zitácuaro, Michoacán)
El Correo de Chihuahua (Chihuahua City)
El Día (Mexico City)
El Gráfico (Mexico City)
El Nacional (Mexico City)
El Paso Times-Democrat (El Paso, Texas)
El Popular (Mexico City)
El Universal (Mexico City)
Excelsior (Mexico City)
La Jornada (Mexico City)
La Voz de Michoacán (Morelia)
Los Angeles Times
México Forestal (Mexico City)
New York Times
Novedades (Mexico City)
Revista Forestal Mexicana (Mexico City)
Revista del México Agrario (Mexico City)
Silvicultura (Mexico City)
Time (New York City)
Verdad (Morelia)

PUBLISHED PRIMARY SOURCES

Alcocer Patiño, Fernando. *Un siglo en el bosque (1887, 1987)*. Chihuahua: Unión de
  Productores e Industrias Forestales, 1987.
Alemán Valdés, Miguel. *Un México mejor: Discursos e informes*. 3 vols. Mexico City:
  Editorial Ruta, 1953.
Ávila Camacho, Manuel. "Convocatoria." *Memoria de la Primera Convención,
  Nacional Forestal, agosto de 1941*, by Secretaría de Agricultura y Fomento, 2–8.
  Mexico City: Secretaría de Agricultura y Fomento, 1942.

Bárcena, Mariano. *Selvicultura: Breves consideraciones sobre explotación y formación de los bosques*. Mexico City: Oficina Tipográfica de la Secretaría de Fomento, 1892.

Barrena, Roberto. "Zonas Forestales Vedadas." *Memoria de la Primera Convención, Nacional Forestal, agosto de 1941*, by Secretaría de Agricultura y Fomento, 69–77. Mexico City: Secretaría de Agricultura y Fomento, 1942.

Calva Téllez, José Luis, et al. *Economía política de la explotación forestal en México: Bibliografía comentada, 1930–1984*. Mexico City: Universidad Autónoma Chapingo / Universidad Nacional Autónoma de México, 1989.

Cárdenas, Lázaro. *Apuntes*. 4 vols. Mexico City: Universidad Nacional Autónoma de México, 1972.

———. *Epistolario de Lázaro Cárdenas, 1895–1970*. Mexico City: Siglo Veintiuno Editores, 1974.

———. *Palabras y documentos públicos de Lázaro Cárdenas, 1928–1970*. 3 vols. Mexico City: Siglo Veintiuno Editores, 1979.

Comisión Forestal del Estado de Michoacán. "Actividades de la Comisión Forestal del Estado de Michoacán 1970." 2.2 (October 1971): n.p.

———. "Michoacán forestal: Datos y cifras." Morelia: Comisión Forestal del Estado de Michoacán, 1979.

Departamento Agrario. *Memoria del Departamento Agrario, 1941–1942*. Mexico City: Talleres Gráficos de la Nación, 1942.

Dictamen del Lic. Andrés Horcasitas sobre la responsibilidad que se contrae por el corte de árboles en bosques nacionales sin la competente autorización. Mexico City: Ministerio de Fomento, 1889.

Dirección General de Estadística. *Estadístico de la República Mexicana*. Mexico City: Dirección General de Estadística, 1893, 1900.

Dublán, Manuel, and José María Lozano. *Legislación Mexicana*. 42 vols. Mexico City: Imprenta del Comercio, 1876–1912.

Food and Agriculture Organization of the United Nations. *Global Forest Resources Assessment 2000*. Rome: Food and Agriculture Organization, 2001.

Gómez González, Filiberto. *Rarámuri: Mi diario tarahumara*. Mexico City: Tipográficos de Excelsior, 1948.

González de la Cadena, Edgardo. "Sugestiones para una mejor organización de los núcleos campesinos." *Memoria de la Primera Convención, Nacional Forestal, agosto de 1941*, by Secretaría de Agricultura y Fomento, 163–69. Mexico City: Secretaría de Agricultura y Fomento, 1942.

Guzmán, José. "Climatología de la República Mexicana desde el punto de vista higiénico." *Memorias de la Sociedad Científica "Antonio Alzate"* no. 20 (1903): 181–289.

Hinojosa, Gabriel. *Memoria sobre la utilidad de los bosques y perjuicios causados por su destrucción dedicada al Gobierno del Estado de Michoacán*. Morelia: Imprenta de la Viuda é Hijos de O. Ortiz, 1873.

Humboldt, Alexander von, and Aimé Bonpland. *Personal Narrative of Travels to the Equinoctial Regions of the New Continent during the Years 1799–1804*. 6 vols. Translated by Helen María Williams. London: Longman, Hurst, 1819.

Instituto Nacional de Investigación Forestal en México. *50 años de investigación forestal en México*. Mexico City: Instituto Nacional de Investigación Forestal en México, 1982.

Lázaro Jiménez, Simón. *Paricutín a cincuenta años de su nacimiento*. Guadalajara: Editorial Agata, 1993.

López Velasco, Vicente Paulino. *Y surgió la unión . . . Génesis y desarrollo del Consejo Nacional de Pueblos Indígenas*. Mexico City: Centro de Estudios Históricos del Agrarismo en México, 1989.

Lumholtz, Carl. *Unknown Mexico*. 2 vols. New York: Scribner, 1902.

Mexico. *Ley forestal y su reglamento*, annotated by Enrique González Flores. Mexico City: Ediciones Botas, 1951.

———. *Manual de estadísticas básicas: Sector agropecuario y forestal*. Mexico City: Secretaría de Agricultura y Recursos Hidráulicos, 1978.

———. *Nueva ley forestal y reglamento* [1942]. Mexico City: Información Aduanera de México, 1943.

———. "Silvicultura '77." Mexico City: Subsecretaría Forestal y de la Fauna, 1977.

Montemayor, Carlos. *Las armas del alba*. Mexico City: Joaquín Moritz, 2003.

Pérez Gil, Francisco. *Primer inventario de los bosques y montes de Michoacán*. Reprint edn. Morelia: Gobierno del Estado de Michoacán de Ocampo / Universidad Michoacana de San Nicolás de Hidalgo, 2002.

PROFORTARH. *Memoria, 1973–1976*. Ciudad Juárez: Imprenta Roa, 1977.

Quevedo, Miguel Ángel de. *Relato de mi vida*. Mexico City: n.p., 1942.

Ramírez, Felix C. *La verdad sobre la Revolución Mexicana*. 2 vols. Mexico City: Casa Ramírez Editores, 1960.

Ramírez Heredia, Rafael, ed. *Lázaro Cárdenas en la Tierra Caliente*. Mexico City: Instituto Politécnico Nacional, 1997.

Rodríguez Caballero, Rodolfo, et al. *Algunas prácticas de ordenación de montes*. Morelia: Comisión Forestal del Estado de Michoacán, 1960.

Romano, Agustín. "El Centro Coordinador Indigenista de la Tarahumara." *Los Centros Coordinadores Indigenistas*, 61–92. Mexico City: Instituto Nacional Indigenista, 1962.

Romero, José Guadalupe. *Noticias para formar la historia y la estadística del obispado de Michoacán*. Mexico City: Imprenta de Vicente García Torres, 1862.

Rouaix, Pastor. *Génesis de los artículos 27 y 123 de la Constitución Política de 1917*. 2d edn. Mexico City: Instituto Nacional de Estudios Históricos de la Revolución Mexicana, 1959.

Ruiz, Eduardo. *Michoacán: Paisajes, tradiciones y leyendas*. Mexico City: Secretaría de Fomento, 1891.

Schwatka, Frederick. *In the Land of the Cave and Cliff Dwellers*. New York: Cassell, 1893.

Secretaría de Agricultura y Fomento. *Memoria de la Primera Convención Nacional Forestal, agosto de 1941*, by Secretaría de Agricultura y Fomento. Mexico City: Secretaría de Agricultura y Fomento, 1942.

Secretaría de Agricultura y Fomento, Dirección Forestal y de Caza y Pesca. *Ley forestal [de 1926] y su reglamento*. Mexico City: Talleres Gráficos de la Secretaría de Agricultura y Fomento, 1930.

Secretaría de Economía, Dirección General de Estadística. *Anuario estadístico de los Estados Unidos Mexicanos 1957*. Mexico City: Tallares Gráficos de la Nación, 1958.

Secretaría del Medio Ambiente, Recursos Naturales y Pesca. *Programa forestal y de suelo, 1995–2000*. Mexico City: Secretaría de Medio Ambiente, Recursos Naturales y Pesca, 1994.

Secretaría del Medio Ambiente y Recursos Naturales. *Informe de la situación del medio ambiente en México*. Mexico City: Secretaría del Medio Ambiente y Recursos Naturales, 2006.

———. *Visión de México sobre REDD+*. Zapopan, Jalisco: Comisión Nacional Forestal, 2010.

Vázquez, Luis, coordinator. *Diagnóstico estatal: Michoacán*. Oaxaca City: Centro de Investigaciones y Estudios Superiores en Antropología Social, Pacífico Sur, n.d.

Vázquez Soto, Jesús. *La política forestal de México y el aprovechamiento de sus bosques*. Mexico City: Sociedad Mexicana de Historia Natural, 1971.

Veladíaz, Juan. *El general sin memoria: Una crónica de los silencios de Ejército Mexicano*. Mexico City: Random House Mondadori, 2010.

Villamar, Aniceto. *Leyes federales vigentes sobre tierras, bosques, aguas, ejidos, colonización, y gran registro de la propiedad*. Mexico City: Herrero Hermanos Editores, 1904.

World Bank. "Staff Appraisal Report: Mexico Forestry Project." Report no. 7432-ME. 2 August 1989.

Zingg, Robert. *Behind the Mexican Mountains*. Edited by Howard Campbell, John Peterson, and David Carmichael. Introduction by Howard Campbell. Austin: University of Texas Press, 2001.

SECONDARY SOURCES

Aboites Aguilar, Luis. *El agua de la nación: Una historia política de México (1888–1946)*. Mexico City: Centro de Investigaciones y Estudios Superiores en Antropología Social, 1998.

———. *Breve historia de Chihuahua*. Mexico City: Colegio de México / Fondo de Cultura Económica, 1994.

———. "The Illusion of National Power: Water Infrastructure in Mexican Cities, 1930–1990." *A Land between Waters: Environmental Histories of Modern Mexico*, ed. Christopher R. Boyer, 218–44. Tucson: University of Arizona Press, 2012.

Agrawal, Arun. *Environmentality: Technologies of Government and the Making of Subjects*. Durham, NC: Duke University Press, 2005.

Aguilar Espinoza, Roque Oscar. "Organización forestal en México." Seminario de Titulación, Universidad Autónoma de Chapingo, 1990.

Aguirre Beltrán, Gonzalo. *Problemas de la población indígena de la Cuenca de Tepalcatepec*. Mexico City: Ediciones del Instituto Nacional Indigenista, 1952.

———. *Regiones de refugio: El desarrollo de la comunidad y el proceso dominical en mestizo América*. Mexico City: Instituto Indigenista Interamericano, 1967.

Alarcón Cháires, Pablo. *Flora, fauna y apropiación de la naturaleza en la región nahua de Michoacán*. Mexico City: Centro de Investigaciones en Ecosistemas, Universidad Nacional Autónoma de México / Conservación Comunitaria de la Biodiversidad, 2005.

Almada, Francisco R., and Oscar J. Martínez. "El Norte: Chihuahua." *Visión heróica de la frontera norte de México*, vol. 4: *De la nueva frontera al porfiriato*, 2d edn., 153–215. Mexicali: Universidad Autónoma de Baja California, 1994.

Alonso, Ana María. *Thread of Blood: Colonialism, Revolution, and Gender on Mexico's Northern Frontier*. Tucson: University of Arizona Press, 1995.

Álvarez Icaza, Pedro. "Forestry as a Social Enterprise." *Cultural Survival* 17.1 (1993): 45–47.

Andrade Limas, Elizabeth del Carmen, Martín Espinosa Ramírez, and Francisco Belmonte Serrato. *La región agrícola del norte de Tamaulipas (México): Recursos naturales, agricultura y procesos de erosión*. Murcia, Spain: Universidad de Murcia, 2011.

Appadurai, Arjun. "Introduction: Commodities and the Politics of Value." *The Social Life of Things: Commodities in Cultural Perspective*, ed. Arjun Appadurai, 3–63. Cambridge: Cambridge University Press, 1988.

Arias Portillo, Pedro. "La región devastada por el volcán de Paricutín." Tesis de Agronomía, Escuela Nacional de Antropología (Chapingo), 1945.

Babb, Sara. *Managing Mexico: Economists from Nationalism to Neoliberalism*. Princeton: Princeton University Press, 2001.

Baker, Stephanie L. "Salud Colectiva: The Role of Public Health Campaigns in

Building a Modern Mexican Nation, 1940s–1960s." PhD diss., Department of History, University of Illinois at Chicago, 2012.

Bárcenas Ortega, Ana Elizabeth, and Salvador Aguirre Paleo. *Pasado, presente y futuro del aguacate en Michoacán, México*. Uruapan: Universidad Michoacana de San Nicolás de Hidalgo, Facultad de Agrobiología "Presidente Juárez," 2005.

Barkin, David, and Timothy King. *Regional Economic Development: The River Basin Approach in Mexico*. Cambridge: Cambridge University Press, 1970.

Barrett, Elinore M. *La cuenca del Tepalcatepec*. 2 vols. Mexico City: SepSetentas, 1975.

Barsimantov, James, and Jaime Navia Antezana. "Forest Cover Change and Land Tenure Change in Mexico's Avocado Region: Is Community Forestry Related to Reduced Deforestation for High Value Crops?" *Applied Geography* 32.22 (March 2012): 844–53.

Barsimantov, James, and Jake Kendall. "Community Forestry, Common Property, and Deforestation in Eight Mexican States." *Journal of Environment and Development* 21.4 (October 2012): 414–37.

Bartra, Armando. "¿Colectivización o proletarización?: El caso del Plan Chontalpa." *Cuadernos Agrarios* 1.4 (October–December 1976): 56–110.

Basauri, Carlos. *Monografía de los tarahumaras*. Mexico City: Talleres Gráficos de la Nación, 1929.

Basurto, Xavier. "Biological and Ecological Mechanisms Supporting Marine Self-Governance: The Seri Callo de Hacha Fishery in Mexico." *Ecology and Society* 13.2 (2008): art. 20.

Basurto, Xavier, and Elinor Ostrom. "The Core Challenges of Moving beyond Garrett Hardin." *Journal of Natural Resources Policy Research* 1.3 (July 2009): 255–59.

Beezley, William H. "State Reform during the Provisional Presidency: Chihuahua, 1911." *Hispanic American Historical Review* 50.3 (August 1970): 524–37.

Bello Méndez, David, and Francisco Carreón Reyes. "La industria resinera en el Estado de Michoacán." *Monografía forestal del Estado de Michoacán*, 59–69. Morelia: Comisión Forestal del Estado, 1958.

Beltrán, Enrique. *La batalla forestal: Lo hecho, lo no hecho, lo por hacer*. Mexico City: Editorial Cultura, 1964.

———. *La conservación como instrumento de desarrollo*. Mexico City: Ediciones Instituto Mexicano de Recursos Naturales Renovables, 1974.

———. *Los recursos naturales de México: Estado actual de las investigaciones forestales*. Mexico City: Instituto Mexicano de Recursos Naturales Renovables, 1955.

Benítez, Fernando. *Los indios de México*. Vol. 1. Mexico City: Era, 1967.

Bennett, Wendell C., and Robert M. Zingg. *The Tarahumara: An Indian Tribe of Northern Mexico*. Chicago: University of Chicago Press, 1935.

Blackbourn, David. *The Conquest of Nature: Water, Landscape, and the Making of Modern Germany*. New York: W. W. Norton, 2006.

Boyer, Christopher R. *Becoming Campesinos: Politics, Identity, and Agrarian Struggle in Postrevolutionary Michoacán*. Stanford: Stanford University Press, 2003.

———, ed. *A Land between Waters: Environmental Histories of Modern Mexico*. Tucson: University of Arizona Press, 2012.

———. "Revolución y paternalismo ecológico: Miguel Ángel de Quevedo y la política forestal, 1926–1940." *Historia Mexicana* 57.1 (July–September 2007): 91–138.

Boyer, Christopher R., and Emily Wakild. "Social Landscaping in the Forests of Mexico: An Environmental Interpretation of Cardenismo, 1934–1940." *Hispanic American Historical Review* 92.1 (February 2012): 73–106.

Bray, David Barton. "Community Forestry in Mexico: Twenty Lessons Learned and Four Pathways." *The Community Forests of Mexico: Managing for Sustainable Landscapes*, ed. David Barton Bray, Leticia Merino-Pérez, and Deborah Barry, 335–49. Austin: University of Texas Press, 2005.

Bray, David Barton, and Leticia Merino-Pérez. *La experiencia de las comunidades forestales en México: Veinticinco años silvicultura y construcción de empresas forestales comunitarias*. Mexico City: Secretaría del Medio Ambiente y Recursos Naturales / Instituto Nacional de Ecología / Ford Foundation, 2004.

Bray, David Barton, Leticia Merino-Pérez, and Deborah Barry, eds. *The Community Forests of Mexico: Managing for Sustainable Landscapes*. Austin: University of Texas Press, 2005.

———. "Community Managed in the Strong Sense of the Term: The Community Forest Enterprises of Mexico." *The Community Forests of Mexico: Managing for Sustainable Landscapes*, ed. David Barton Bray, Leticia Merino-Pérez, and Deborah Barry, 3–26. Austin: University of Texas Press, 2005.

Brunk, Samuel. *Emiliano Zapata: Revolution and Betrayal in Mexico*. Albuquerque: University of New Mexico Press, 1995.

Calderón, Marco Antonio. "*Caciquismo* and *Cardenismo* in the Sierra P'urépecha, Michoacán." *Caciquismo in Twentieth-Century Mexico*, ed. Alan Knight and Wil Pansters, 131–50. London: Institute for the Americas, 2005.

———. "Lázaro Cárdenas del Río en la cuenca Tepalcatepec-Balsas." *La Tierra Caliente de Michoacán*, ed. José Eduardo Zárate Hernández, 243–46. Zamora, Michoacán: El Colegio de Michoacán / Gobierno del Estado de Michoacán.

Challenger, Antony. *Utilización y conservación de los ecosistemas terrestres de México: Pasado, presente y futuro*. Mexico City: Comisión Nacional para el Conocimiento y Uso de la Biodiversidad, 1998.

Chambille, Karel. *Atenquique: Los bosques del sur de Jalisco*. Mexico City: Universidad Nacional Autónoma de México, Instituto de Investigaciones Economicas, 1983.

Coatsworth, John H. *Growth against Development: The Economic Impact of Railroads in Porfirian Mexico.* DeKalb: Northern Illinois University Press, 1981.

Cochet, Hubert, Eric Léonard, and Jean Damien de Sirgy. *Paisajes agrarios de Michoacán.* Zamora: El Colegio de Michoacán, 1988.

Córdova, Arnadlo. *La ideología de la revolución mexicana.* Mexico City: Era, 1992.

———. *La política de masas del Cardenismo.* Mexico City: Era, 1974.

Cortez Noyola, Martín. *"Mexico Forestal: Una historia."* Licenciatura thesis, Departamento de Historia, Universidad Michoacana de San Nicolás de Hidalgo, 2009.

Cotter, Joseph. *Troubled Harvest: Agronomy and Revolution in Mexico, 1880–2002.* Westport, CT: Praeger, 2003.

Craig, Ann L. *The First Agraristas: An Oral History of a Mexican Agrarian Reform Movement.* Berkeley: University of California Press, 1983.

Cummings O'Hara, Julia. "Transforming the Sierra Tarahumara: Indians, Missionaries, and the State in Chihuahua, Mexico, 1890–1960." PhD diss., Department of History, Indiana University, 2004.

Dawson, Alexander S. *Indian and Nation in Revolutionary Mexico.* Tucson: University of Arizona Press, 2004.

Deacon, Robert T. "Deforestation and the Rule of Law in a Cross-Section of Countries." *Land Economics* 70.4 (November 1994): 414–30.

Deeds, Susan M. *Defiance and Deference in Mexico's Colonial North: Indians under Spanish Rule in Nueva Vizcaya.* Austin: University of Texas Press, 2003.

Diebel, Linda. *Betrayed: The Assassination of Digna Ochoa.* New York: Carroll and Graf, 2005.

Domínguez Rascón, Alonso. *La política de la reforma agraria en Chihuahua, 1920–1924.* Mexico City: Instituto Nacional de Antropología e Historia / Plaza y Valdés, 2003.

Enríquez Hernández, Jorge. "Análisis geoeconómico del sistema regional de la Sierra Tarahumara." Master's thesis, Colegio de Geografía, Universidad Nacional Autónoma de México, 1988.

Escobar, Arturo. *Encountering Development.* Princeton: Princeton University Press, 1995.

Escobar, Rómulo. "Las lluvias en México." *Memorias de la Sociedad Científica "Antonio Alzate"* no. 20 (1903): 5–57.

Evans, Sterling. "King Henequen: Order, Progress, and Ecological Change in Yucatán, 1850–1950." *A Land between Waters: Environmental Histories of Modern Mexico*, ed. Christopher R. Boyer, 150–72. Tucson: University of Arizona Press, 2012.

Falcón, Romana. "San Luis Potosí: Confiscated Estates—Revolutionary Conquest or Spoils?" *Provinces of the Revolution: Essays on Regional Mexican History, 1910–1929*, ed. Thomas Benjamin and Mark Wasserman, 133–62. Albuquerque: University of New Mexico Press, 1990.

Fallaw, Ben. *Cárdenas Compromised: The Failure of Reform in Postrevolutionary Yucatán*. Durham, NC: Duke University Press, 2001.

Foshag, William F., and Jenaro González R. "Birth and Development of Paricutín Volcano, Mexico." *Geological Survey Bulletin* 965-D369. Washington: Department of the Interior, 1956.

Ferreyra Soriano, Francisco. "Las vedas forestales en México y sus consecuencias." Ingenería thesis, Escuela Nacional de Agricultura (Chapingo), 1958.

French, William E. "Business as Usual: Mexico North Western Railway Managers Confront the Mexican Revolution." *Mexican Studies/Estudios Mexicanos* 5.2 (summer 1989): 221–38.

Friedrich, Paul. *Agrarian Revolt in a Mexican Village*. Chicago: University of Chicago Press, 1977.

Gamio, Manuel. *Forjando patria (pro nacionalismo)*. 2d edn. Mexico City: Porrúa, 1960.

García Martínez, José. "Legislación forestal como base de una mejor administración de los recursos forestales naturales de los bosques de nuestro país." *Memoria de la Primera Convención Nacional Forestal, agosto de 1941*, by Secretaría de Agricultura y Fomento, 233–42. Mexico City: Secretaría de Agricultura y Fomento, 1942.

Garza, Gustavo. *La urbanización de México en el siglo 20*. Mexico City: El Colegio de México, 2005.

Gerez Fernández, Patricia. "¿Qué pasa en el Cofre de Perote?" *Desarrollo y Medio Ambiente en Veracruz*, ed. Eckart Boege and Hopólito Rodríguez, 2–5. Mexico City: Centro de Investigaciones y Estudios Superiores en Antropología Social / Fundación Friedrich Ebert, 1992.

Gilly, Adolfo. *La revolución interrumpida: México, 1910–1920: Una guerra campesina por la tierra y el poder*. Mexico City: Ediciones El Caballito, 1971.

Gingrich, Randall. "The Political Ecology of Deforestation in the Sierra Madre Occidental of Chihuahua." Master's thesis, University of Arizona, 1993.

Ginzberg, Eitan. *Lázaro Cárdenas: Gobernador de Michoacán (1928–1932)*. Morelia: Colegio de Michoacán / Universidad Michoacana de San Nicolás de Hidalgo, 1999.

Gledhill, John. *Casi Nada: A Study of Agrarian Reform in the Homeland of Cardenismo*. Albany, NY: Institute for Mesoamerican Studies, 1991.

———. *Cultura y desafío en Ostula*. Zamora: El Colegio de Michoacán, 2004.

González Casanova, Pablo. *La democracia en México*. Mexico City: Era, 1965.

González Pacheco, Cuautémoc. *Los bosques de México y la banca internacional*. Mexico City: Instituto de Investigaciones Económicas, Universidad Nacional Autónoma de México, 1995.

González y González, Luis. *Los artífices del Cardenismo*. Vol. 14 of *Historia de la Revolución Mexicana*. Mexico City: El Colegio de México, 1979.

Grove, Richard. *Green Imperialism: Colonial Expansion, Tropical Island Edens, and the Origins of Environmentalism, 1600–1960*. Cambridge: Cambridge University Press, 1995.

Guerra, François-Xavier. *México: Del antiguo régimen a la revolución*. 2 vols. Mexico City: Fondo de Cultura Económica 1988.

Guerra Manzo, Enrique. *Caciquismo y orden público en Michoacán, 1920–1940*. Mexico City: El Colegio de México, 2002.

Guha, Ramachandra. *The Unquiet Woods: Ecological Change and Peasant Resistance in the Himalaya*. Expanded edn. Berkeley: University of California Press, 2000.

Guzmán Ávila, José Napoleón. "Michoacán en vísperas de la revolución." *La Revolución en Michoacán 1900–1926*, 3–15. Morelia: Departamento de Historia, Universidad Michoacana San Nicolás de Hidalgo, 1987.

———. *Michoacán y la inversión extranjera, 1880–1900*. Morelia: Universidad Michoacana de San Nicolás de Hidalgo, 1982.

Haber, Stephen H. *Industry and Underdevelopment: The Industrialization of Mexico 1890–1940*. Stanford: Stanford University Press, 1995.

Hale, Charles. *Transformation of Liberalism in Late Nineteenth-Century Mexico*. Princeton: Princeton University Press, 1989.

Hall, Linda B. "Alvaro Obregón and the Politics of Mexican Land Reform, 1920–1924." *Hispanic American Historical Review* 60.2 (May 1980): 213–38.

Hardin, Garrett. "The Tragedy of the Commons." *Science* 162 (1968): 1243–48.

Hart, John Mason. *Empire and Revolution: The Americans in Mexico since the Civil War*. Berkeley: University of California Press, 2002.

———. *Revolutionary Mexico: The Coming and Process of the Mexican Revolution*. Berkeley: University of California Press, 1987.

———. *Silver of the Sierra Madre: John Robinson, Boss Shepherd, and the People of the Canyons*. Tucson: University of Arizona Press, 2008.

Henson, Elizabeth. "Madera 1965: Primeros Vientos." *Challenging Authoritarianism in Mexico: Revolutionary Struggles and the Dirty War, 1964–1982*, ed. Fernando Herrera Calderón and Edela Cedillo, 19–39. New York: Routledge, 2012.

Hernández, Manuel Diego. *La Confederación Revolucionaria Michoacana del Trabajo*. Jiquilpan, Michoacán: Centro de Estudios de la Revolución Mexicana "Lázaro Cárdenas," 1982.

Herrera Calderón, Fernando, and Adela Cedillo. "Introduction: The Unknown Mexican Dirty War." *Challenging Authoritarianism in Mexico: Revolutionary Struggles and the Dirty War, 1964–1982*, ed. Fernando Herrera Calderón and Adela Cedillo, 1–18. New York: Routledge, 2012.

Hewitt de Alcántara, Cynthia. *La modernización de la agricultura mexicana, 1940–1970*. Mexico City: Siglo 21 Editores, 1978.

Hinojosa Ortiz, Manuel. *Los bosques de México: Relato de un despilfarro y una injusticia*. Mexico City: Instituto Mexicano de Investigaciones Económicas, 1958.

Holden, Robert. *Mexico and the Survey of Public Lands: The Management of Modernization, 1876–1911*. DeKalb: Northern Illinois University Press, 1994.

Humboldt, Alexander von. *Political Essay on the Kingdom of New Spain*. Translated by John Black. New York: I. Riley, 1811.

Jordán, Fernando. *Crónica de un país bárbaro*. Chihuahua: Centro Librero La Prensa, 1981 [1956].

Joseph, Gilbert M., and Daniel Nugent, eds. *Everyday Forms of State Formation: Revolution and the Negotiation of Rule in Modern Mexico*. Durham, NC: Duke University Press, 1994.

Juárez Flores, José Juan. "Alumbrado público en Puebla y Tlaxcala y deterioro ambiental en los bosques de La Malintzi, 1820–1870." *Historia Crítica* 30 (2005): 13–38.

Kalaora, Bernard, and Antoine Savoye. *La forêt pacifiée: Les forestiers de l'Ecole de le Play, experts des sociétés pastorales*. Paris: Editions L'Harmattan, 1986.

Katz, Friedrich. *The Life and Times of Pancho Villa*. Stanford: Stanford University Press, 1998.

Kennedy, John G. "Tesguino Complex: The Role of Beer in Tarahumara Culture." *American Anthropologist* 65.3 (June 1963): 620–40.

Klein, Naomi. *The Shock Doctrine: The Rise of Disaster Capitalism*. New York: Picador, 2008.

Klooster, Daniel James. "Campesinos and Mexican Forest Policy during the Twentieth Century." *Latin American Research Review* 38.2 (June 2003): 94–126.

———. "Conflict in the Commons: Commercial Forestry and Conservation in Mexican Indigenous Communities." PhD diss., Department of Geography, University of California, Los Angeles, 1997.

———. "Forest Transitions in Mexico: Institutions and Forests in a Globalized Countryside." *Professional Geographer* 55.2 (2003): 227–37.

Knight, Alan. *The Mexican Revolution*. 2 vols. Lincoln: University of Nebraska Press, 1990.

———. "Revolutionary Project, Recalcitrant People: Mexico, 1910–1940." *The Revolutionary Process in Mexico*, ed. Jaime E. Rodríguez O., 227–64. Los Angeles: University of California, Los Angeles, Latin American Center Publications, 1990.

Konrad, Herman W. "Tropical Forest Policy and Practice during the Mexican Porfiriato, 1876–1910." *Changing Tropical Forests: Historical Perspectives on Today's Challenges in Central and South America*, ed. Harold K. Steen and Richard P. Tucker, 123–43. Durham, NC: Forest History Society, 1992.

Kosek, Jake. *Understories: The Political Life of Forests in Northern New Mexico*. Durham, NC: Duke University Press, 2006.

Kourí, Emilio. *A Pueblo Divided: Business, Property, and Community in Papantla, Mexico*. Stanford: Stanford University Press, 2004.

Langston, Nancy. *Forest Dreams, Forest Nightmares: The Paradox of Old Growth in the Inland West*. Seattle: University of Washington Press, 1995.

Lear, John. *Workers, Neighbors, and Citizens: The Revolution in Mexico City*. Lincoln: University of Nebraska Press, 2001.

Lewis, Stephen E. "Mexico's National Indigenist Institute and the Negotiation of Applied Anthropology in Highland Chiapas, 1951–1954." *Ethnohistory* 55.4 (fall 2008): 609–32.

López, Rick A. *Crafting Mexico: Intellectuals, Artisans, and the State after the Revolution*. Durham, NC: Duke University Press, 2010.

López Maya, Roberto. *Ciudad Hidalgo*. Morelia: Gobierno del Estado de Michoacán, 1980.

Lowerre, Richard. "Evaluation of the Forestry Development Project of the World Bank in the Sierra Madre Occidental in Chihuahua and Durango Mexico." Working Paper, Texas Center for Policy Studies, Austin, November 1990.

Madrid, Lucía, Juan Manuel Núñez, Gabriela Quiroz, and Yosu Rodríguez. "La propiedad social forestal en México." *Investigación Ambiental* 1.2 (2009): 179–96.

Marín Guardado, Gustavo. "Etnicidad, territorio y cultura en la costa nahua de Michoacán." *El fin de toda la tierra: Historia, ecología y cultura en la costa de Michoacán*, ed. Gustavo Marín Guardado, 243–73. Mexico City: El Colegio de México, 2004.

Maser, Chris. *The Redesigned Forest*. San Pedro, CA: R. and E. Miles, 1988.

Matthews, Andrew S. *Instituting Nature: Authority, Expertise, and Power in Mexican Forests*. Cambridge: Massachusetts Institute of Technology Press, 2011.

———. "Suppressing Fire and Memory: Environmental Degradation and Political Restoration in the Sierra Juárez of Oaxaca, 1887–2001." *Environmental History* 8.1 (January 2003): 77–108.

———. "Unlikely Alliances: Encounters between State Science, Nature Spirits, and Indigenous Industrial Forestry in Mexico, 1926–2008." *Current Anthropology* 50.1 (February 2009): 75–89.

McCaa, Robert. "Missing Millions: The Demographic Costs of the Mexican Revolution." *Mexican Studies/Estudios Mexicanos* 19.1 (summer 2003): 367–400.

McCook, Stuart. *States of Nature: Science, Agriculture, and Environment in the Spanish Caribbean, 1760–1940*. Austin: University of Texas Press, 2002.

Memoria de la Primera Convención Nacional Forestal, agosto de 1941. Mexico City: Secretaría de Agricultura y Fomento, 1942.

Mendelsohn, Robert. "Property Rights and Tropical Deforestation." *Oxford Economic Papers* 46 (October 1994): 750–56.

Merchant, Carolyn. *Ecological Revolutions: Nature, Gender, and Science in New England*. 2d edn. Chapel Hill: University of North Carolina Press, 2010.

Merino Pérez, Leticia. *Conservación o deterioro: El impacto de las políticas públicas en las institucionas comunitarias y en los usos de los bosques en México.* Mexico City: Secretaría de Medio Ambiente y Recursos Naturales / Instituto Nacional de Ecología / Consejo Civil Mexicano para la Silvicultura Sostenible, A.C., 2004.

Meza Flores, Mayra Mónica. *San José Baqueachi: Historia de un ejido tarahumara que se resiste al despojo de sus tierras.* Chihuahua: Instituto Chihuahuense de Cultura, 2001.

Miller, Shawn William. *Fruitless Trees: Portuguese Conservation and Brazil's Colonial Timber.* Stanford: Stanford University Press, 2000.

Mitchell, Timothy. *Rule of Experts: Egypt, Techno-Politics, Modernity.* Berkeley: University of California Press, 2002.

Molinari Medina, Claudia. "Protestantismo y explotación forestal en la Tarahumara." Licenciatura thesis, Antropología Social, Escuela Nacional de Antropología e Historia, Mexico, D.F., 1993.

Montes de Oca Luján, Rosa Elena. "La cuestión agraria y el movimiento campesino: 1970–1976." *Cuadernos Políticos* 14 (October–December 1977): 57–71.

Moreno Cueto, Enrique, ed. *Sociología histórica de las instituciones de salud en México.* Mexico City: Instituto Mexicano del Seguro Social, 1982.

Moreno Unda, Arcelia Amaranta. "Environmental Effects of the National Tree Clearing Program, Mexico, 1972–1982." Master's thesis, Universidad Autónoma de San Luis Potosí / Cologne University of Applied Sciences, 2011.

Morett Sánchez, Jesús Carlos. *Reforma agraria: Del latifundio al neoliberalismo.* Mexico City: Plaza y Valdés, 2003.

Neumann, Roderick P. *Making Political Ecology.* London: Routledge, 2005.

Nugent, Daniel. *Spent Cartridges of Revolution: An Anthropological History of Namiquipa, Chihuahua.* Chicago: University of Chicago Press, 1993.

Oikión Solano, Verónica. *El constitucionalismo en Michoacán: El periodo de los gobiernos militares (1914–1917).* Mexico City: Consejo Nacional para la Cultura y las Artes, 1992.

Olivé Negrete, Julio César. *Antropología Mexicana.* 2d edn. Mexico City: Instituto Nacional de Antropología e Historia / Plaza y Valdés, 2000.

Ostrom, Elinor. *Governing the Commons: The Evolution of Institutions for Collective Action.* Cambridge: Cambridge University Press, 1990.

Padilla Sánchez, Ramón. "Estudio forestal del Estado de Chihuahua." Master's thesis, Escuela Nacional de Agricultura, 1944.

Palomares Peña, Noé G. *Propietarios norteamericanos y reforma agraria en Chihuahua, 1917–1942.* Ciudad Juárez: Univarsidad Autónoma de Ciudad Juárez, 1991.

Parra Orozco, Miguel Ángel. *Madera: Vida de una región chihuahuense.* 3d edn. Chihuahua: n.p., 1979.

Peluso, Nancy Lee. *Rich Forests, Poor People: Resource Control and Resistance in Java.* Berkeley: University of California Press, 1992.

Plancarte, Francisco M. *El problema indígena tarahumara*. Vol. 5 of *Memorias del Instituto Nacional Indigenista*. Mexico City: Ediciones del Instituto Nacional Indigenista, 1954.

Poleman, Thomas T. *The Papaloapan Project: Agricultural Development in the Mexican Tropics*. Stanford: Stanford University Press, 1964.

Purnell, Jennie. "With All Due Respect: Popular Resistance to the Privatization of Communal Lands in Nineteenth-Century Michoacán." *Latin American Research Review* 34.1 (1999): 85–121.

Radding, Cynthia. *Landscapes of Power and Identity: Comparative Histories in the Sonoran Desert and the Forests of Amazonia from Colony to Republic*. Durham, NC: Duke University Press, 2005.

Raufflet, Emmanuel. "Institutional Change and Forest Management: The Case of Tlalmanalco, Mexico." PhD diss., McGill University Faculty of Management, 2002.

Redowski, Jerzy. *Vegetación de México*. Mexico City: Editorial Lumusa, 1978.

Rees, John D. "Effects of Parícutin [*sic*] Volcano on Landforms, Vegetation, and Human Occupancy." *Volcanic Activity and Human Ecology*, ed. Payson D. Sheets and Donald K. Grayson, 249–92. New York: Academic Press, 1979.

Romero Contreras, Tonatiuh, and Carlos Castaños Montes. "Gonzálo Aguirre Beltrán: Su aporte a la antropología mexicana." *Historia de la ciencia en México: La antropología*, ed. Tonatiuh Romero Contreras, 83–91. Toluca: Universidad Autónoma del Estado de México, 2001.

Ross, Michael L. "The Political Economy of the Resource Curse." *World Politics* 51.2 (January 1999): 297–322.

Ruiz Martínez, Ignacio. "Discurso." *Memoria de la celebración del quincuagésimo aniversario de la enseñanza forestal en México*, ed. Sociedad Forestal Mexicana, 56–62. Mexico City: n.p., 1960.

Sahlins, Peter. *Forest Rites: The War of the Demoiselles in Nineteenth-Century France*. Cambridge: Harvard University Press, 1994.

Salvia Spratte, Héctor Agustín. *Los laberintos de Loreto y Peña Pobre*. Mexico City: Ediciones El Caballito, 1989.

Sánchez Díaz, Gerardo. "Reparto y resistencia en las comunidades nahuas de la costa de Michoacán 1869–1908." *Boletín de Centro de Estudios de la Revolución Mexicana Lazaro Cardenas AC*, 3–18. Jiquilpan, Michoacán: Centro de Estudios de la Revolución Mexicana "Lázaro Cárdenas," 1982.

———. *El suroeste de Michoacán: economía y sociedad, 1852–1910*. Universidad Michoacana de San Nicolás de Hidalgo, Instituto de Investigaciones Históricas, 1988.

Sánchez Herrera, Sergio, et al. "Explotación del bosque en la Meseta Purépecha y su impacto en la población (1950–1987)." 2 vols. Tesis colectiva de Ingenría, Universidad Autónoma Chapingo, 1988.

Sánchez Pego, María Angélica. "The Forestry Enterprise of the Indigenous Community of Nuevo San Juan Parangaricutiro, Michoacán, Mexico." *Case Studies of Community-Based Forestry Enterprises in the Americas*, ed. Nancy Forster, 137–60. Madison: University of Wisconsin Land Tenure Center, 1995.

Santiago, Myrna I. *The Ecology of Oil: Environment, Labor, and the Mexican Revolution, 1900–1938*. Cambridge: Cambridge University Press, 2006.

Sariego, Juan Luis. *El indigenismo en la Tarahumara: Identidad, comunidad, relaciones interétnicas y desarrollo en la Sierra de Chihuahua*. Mexico City: Instituto Nacional Indigenista / Instituto Nacional de Antropología e Historia, 2002.

Scarth, Alwyn. *Vulcan's Fury: Man Against the Volcano*. New Haven: Yale University Press, 2001.

Scott, James C. *The Art of Not Being Governed: An Anarchist History of Upland Southeast Asia*. New Haven: Yale University Press, 2009.

———. *Seeing Like a State: How Certain Schemes to Improve the Human Condition Have Failed*. New Haven: Yale University Press, 1999.

Simonian, Lane. *Defending the Land of the Jaguar: A History of Conservation in Mexico*. Austin: University of Texas Press, 1995.

Snook, Laura C., and Patricia C. Negreros. "Effects of Mexico's Selective Cutting System on Pine Regeneration and Growth in a Mixed Pine-Oak (*Pinus-Quercus*) Forest." *USDA Forest Service General Technical Report SE-48*. Asheville, NC: The Station, 1986.

Soto Laveaga, Gabriela. *Jungle Laboratories: Mexican Peasants, National Projects, and the Making of the Pill*. Durham, NC: Duke University Press, 2009.

Spude, Robert L. "Frank Morrill Murphy, 1854–1917: Mining and Railroad Mogul and Developer of the American Southwest." *Mining Tycoons in the Age of Empire, 1870–1945: Entrepreneurship, High Finance, Politics and Territorial Expansion*, ed. Raymond E. Durmett, 151–69. London: Ashgate, 2008.

Tamayo, Jorge L., et al. *Recursos naturales de la cuenca del Papaloapan*. Vol. 1. Mexico City: Secretaría de Agricultura y Recursos Hidráulicos / Comisión del Papaloapan / Instituto Nacional de Estudios Históricos de la Revolución Mexicana, 1977.

Taylor, Peter Leigh. "Community Forestry as Embedded Process: Two Cases from Durango and Quintana Roo, Mexico." *International Journal of Sociology of Agriculture and Food* 9.1 (winter 2001): 59–81.

———. "New Organizational Strategies in Community Forestry in Durango, Mexico." *The Community Forests of Mexico: Managing for Sustainable Landscapes*, ed. David Barton Bray, Leticia Merino-Pérez, and Deborah Barry, 125–49. Austin: University of Texas Press, 2005.

———. "Reorganization or Division: New Strategies of Community Forestry in Durango, Mexico." *Society and Natural Resources* 16.7 (2003): 141–56.

Tilly, Charles. *The Contentious French: Four Centuries of Popular Struggle.* Cambridge: Belknap, 1989.

Tobler, Hans Werner. "Peasants and the Shaping of the Revolutionary State." *Riot, Rebellion, and Revolution: Rural Social Conflict in Mexico*, ed. Friedrich Katz, 487–518. Princeton: Princeton University Press, 1988.

Torres, Alejandro, Gerardo Bocco, and Alejandro Velázquez. "Antecedentes históricos." *Las enseñanzas de San Juan: Investigación participativa para el manejo integral de recursos naturales*, ed. Alejandro Torres, Alejandro Velázquez, and Gerardo Bocco, 51–56. Mexico City: Secretaría de Medio Ambiente y Recursos Naturales, 2003.

Torres-Rojo, Juan Manuel, and Ramiro Flores-Xolocotzi. "Deforestation and Land Use Change in Mexico." *Climate Change and Forest Management in the Western Hemisphere*, ed. Mohammed H. I. Dore, 171–92. Binghamton, NY: Food Products Press, 2001.

Tortolero Villaseñor, Alejandro. "Water and Revolution in Morelos, 1850–1915." *A Land between Waters: Environmental Histories of Modern Mexico*, ed. Christopher R. Boyer, 124–49. Tucson: University of Arizona Press, 2012.

Tsing, Anna Lowenhaupt. *Friction: An Ethnography of Global Connection.* Princeton: Princeton University Press, 2005.

Vanderwood, Paul J. *The Power of Guns against the Guns of Government: Religious Upheaval in Mexico at the Turn of the Nineteenth Century.* Stanford: Stanford University Press, 1998.

Vásquez de la Parra, Rigoberto. "Reminiscencia histórica." *Memoria de la celebración del quincuagésimo aniversario de la enseñanza forestal en México*, by Sociedad Forestal Mexicana, 9–13. Mexico City: Sociedad Forestal Mexicana, 1959.

Vatant, Françoise. "Un ejido forestal de la alta Tarahumara: Cusárare." Master's thesis, Ciencias Antropológicas, Universidad Nacional Autónoma de México, 1979.

Vázquez, Roberto H. "Los actos depredatorios del hombre en la conservación forestal, su concepto y problemas para México." *Memoria de la Primera Convención Nacional Forestal, agosto de 1941*, by Secretaría de Agricultura y Fomento, 57–68. Mexico City: Secretaría de Agricultura y Fomento, 1942.

Vázquez León, Luis. *Antropología política de la comunidad indígena en Michoacán.* Morelia: Secretaría de Educación en el Estado de Michoacán, 1986.

Villaseñor, Roberto. "Los bosques de México." *Mesas redondas sobre problemas forestales de México*, by Instituto Mexicano de Recursos Renovables, 3–44. Mexico City: Ediciones del Instituto Mexicano de Recursos Naturales Renovables, A. C., 1956.

Vitz, Matthew. "La ciudad y sus bosques: La conservación forestal y los campesinos en el valle de México, 1900–1950." *Estudios de Historia Moderna y Conemporánea de México* 43 (January–June 2012): 135–72.

Vos, Jan de. *Oro verde: La conquista de la Selva Lacandona por los madereros ta-basqueños, 1822–1949*. Mexico City: Fondo de Cultura Económica, 1988.

Wakild, Emily. "Parables of Chapultepec: Urban Parks, National Landscapes, and Contradictory Conservation in Modern Mexico." *A Land between Waters: Environmental Histories of Modern Mexico*, ed. Christopher R. Boyer, 212–17. Tucson: University of Arizona Press, 2012.

———. *Revolutionary Parks: Conservation, Social Justice, and Mexico's National Parks, 1910–1940*. Tucson: University of Arizona Press, 2011.

Walsh Sanderson, Susan R. *Land Reform in Mexico: 1910–1980*. New York: Academic Press, 1984.

Warman, Arturo. *Los campesinos, hijos predilectos del régimen*. Mexico City: Editorial Nuestro Tiempo, 1972.

———. *Y veninos a contradecir: Los campesinos de Morelos y el estado nacional*. Mexico City: Ediciones de la Casa Chata, 1978.

Wasserman, Mark. *Persistent Oligarchs: Elites and Politics in Chihuahua, Mexico, 1910–1940*. Durham, NC: Duke University Press, 1993.

Weaver, Thomas. "Neoliberalism and the Social Relations of Forestry Production in the Sierra Tarahumara." *Neoliberalism and Commodity Production in Mexico*, ed. Thomas Weaver, James B. Alexander, and William L. Partial, 187–207. Boulder: University of Colorado Press, 2012.

Weiner, Richard. *Race, Nation, and Market: Economic Culture in Porfirian Mexico*. Tucson: University of Arizona Press, 2004.

White, Gregory. *Climate Change and Migration: Security and Borders in a Warming World*. New York: Oxford University Press, 2011.

Whited, Tamara. *Forests and Peasant Politics in Modern France*. New Haven: Yale University Press, 2000.

Williams, Michael. *Deforesting the Earth: From Prehistory to Global Crisis*. Abridged edn. Chicago: University of Chicago Press, 2006.

Wolf, Eric R. "Aspects of Group Relations in a Complex Society: Mexico." *American Anthropologist* 58.6 (December 1956): 1065–76.

———. "Closed Corporate Peasant Communities in Mesoamerica and Central Java." *Southwestern Journal of Anthropology* 13.1 (spring 1957): 1–18.

Womack, John, Jr. "The Mexican Economy during the Revolution, 1910–1920: Historiography and Analysis." *Marxist Perspectives* 1.1 (winter 1978): 80–123.

———. *Zapata and the Mexican Revolution*. New York: Knopf, 1968.

INDEX

Note: page numbers in italics refer to illustrations; those followed by "n" indicate endnotes.

Echeverría, Luis, 17, 155, 204–7, 211–16
ecosystem impacts: Humboldtian desiccation thesis, 53–54, 270n85; Michoacana de Occidente and, 190; overview, 16–17, 242; of silver mining, 41–42. *See also* deforestation
educational campaigns: Arbor Day celebrations, 98–101, 99; transnational comparison and, 96
ejidos: CCIT and, 179–80; commercial output of, 285n101; debts of, 110–11; defined, xvi; *dotación* process, 76–77; joint venture agreements with, 134–35; number of, by presidential administration, 130. *See also* cooperatives; land reform; *specific places*
Elizondo, Eliseo, 240
El Jorullo volcano, 157
El Largo, Chihuahua, 152, 155, 211, 212–13
El Oso y La Avena (later Jesús García), Chihuahua, 152, 155
El Rosario, Michoacán, 87–88
El Varaloso, Michoacán, 193–94, 195
El Vergel, Chihuahua, *148*
Emergency Plan for Railroad Tie Production, 140, 149–51, 229
Enríquez, Ignacio C., 81–82
Equihua family, 229
Escobar, Rómulo, 54

federalization, in Porfiriato, 51
fire: campfires and, 153–54; Michoacana de Occidente and, 189, 192–93; railroads and, 43–44; *venganzas*, 193
Flores Calderón, Emilio, 155
Fondo Nacional para el Fomento Ejidal (FONAFE), 206–7
Forest Development Agency of the Tarahumara (PROFORTARH), 216–20, 233
Forest Management Units (Unidades de Ordenación Forestal; UOFs), 124, 163, 183–84, 249
forest reserves, national: 1942 Forestry Code and, 134; 1949 Forestry Code and, 135; establishment of, 79, 102, 148;

federalization and, 56; Papigochic, 120, 125; U.S. as role model for, 96
Forestry Code of 1926, 11–12, 79–81, 91, 259
Forestry Code of 1942, 134–35, 140, 259
Forestry Code of 1949, 135–36, 140, 259
Forestry Code of 1960, 259
Forestry Code of 1986, 259
Forestry Code of 1992, 259
Forestry Code of 2003, 259
Forestry Code of 2008, 259
forestry conference (1941), 132–34
Forestry Management Units (UOFs), 124, 183
Forestry Society, 98, 100
forest service, national: administrative status changes, xv–xvi, 121–22; cooperatives and, 104, 122; elevation to cabinet level, 95, 279n30; names of, xv–xvi; Quevedo and, 55–58, 132; reputation of, 101; research studies, 103; revolution and, 65. *See also* Quevedo, Miguel Ángel de
Fox, Vicente, 241
fraudulent contracts, 39–40
French National School of Forestry, 56
Fuerte Basin Commission, 172

Galicia, Daniel, 86–87, 116–17, 183–85, 187
Gamio, Manuel, 74–75, 169–70
Gámiz, Arturo, 212
García, Chihuahua, 152
Gayol y Soto, Roberto, 97
General Felipe Angeles collective, 233
General Union of Workers and Campesinos (UGOCM), 204, 211–12
Geronimo, 40
goat herding, 115, 153
goat-maize subsistence ecology, 49
González, Roberto, 182
González Múzquiz, José and Mario, 145, 214
González Pacheco, Cuahtémoc, 236
González Ugarte, Juan, 83, 86, 145
Greene, William C., 43, 58